PHILIP EA... ...nist, and
for several ... ...legraph.
His first book, *Sylvia, Queen of the Headhunters*, was published in
2007 to widespread acclaim. He lives in London.

From the reviews of *Young Prince Philip*:

'Sympathetic and tartly funny'   *Sunday Times*, Books of the Year

'An amazing story of an incredible life. I learned a lot from reading it
and literally couldn't put it down'   VICTORIA HISLOP, *Easy Living*

'Sure-footed and sparkling ... I finished [this biography] with an
admiration I had not expected for this brave, brusque, imaginative
oddball'   FERDINAND MOUNT, *Wall Street Journal*

'Given what a rackety childhood Prince Philip had, it's astonishing
that he hasn't spent half his life in therapy. By concentrating on the
extreme oddity of his childhood, [Eade] makes the prince's character
more explicable and therefore more sympathetic. The narrative is as
suspenseful as any thriller. Truly, an excellent read'
    LYNN BARBER, *Sunday Times*

'Under Mr Eade's pen, the story races along'
    CLIVE ASLET, *Country Life*

'A remarkable new biography ... does for the royal consort what
Helen Mirren did for his wife in the 2006 movie *The Queen*, breathing
life into a figure who had seemed stiff and remote'   *New York Times*

'Fascinating ... carefully researched, warm-hearted and unjudge-
mental'   ANDREW BARROW, *Evening Standard*

'*Young Prince Philip* is not a forelock-tugging royal biography ... Philip Eade casts a clear eye over his subject's first thirty years, fleshing out with intelligence and sympathy the man whose gaffes have entertained the nation'   FRANCES WILSON, *Times Literary Supplement*

'As Philip Eade demonstrates in this highly readable biography of Prince Philip's first 30 years, this extraordinary man endured a childhood of such turmoil that nowadays the social services would have placed him in care. ... This balanced, sympathetic, engaging book deserves to take its place among the first rank of modern royal biographies'   CHRISTOPHER HUDSON, *Daily Mail*

'Prince Philip has learnt to play a convincing version of himself: quizzical, tetchy, no-nonsense, shipshape. Yet his was the least shipshape of all backgrounds. Ninety years ago, he was born into a family so nutty that they could have eaten ten fruitcakes each for breakfast, and still had room for more at lunch ... [it] was like something from a film by David Lynch'   CRAIG BROWN, *Mail on Sunday*, Book of the Week

'Brilliant'   *Irish Independent*

'This excellent study ... will be deemed too critical by royalists and too sympathetic by republicans. As this suggests, it is finely balanced. It is also lucidly written and based on solid research'

PIERS BRENDON, *Oldie*

'A great read'   *Huffington Post*

———————————————————

By the same author
Sylvia, Queen of the Headhunters

PHILIP EADE

Young Prince Philip

His Turbulent Early Life

Harper
Press

Harper*Press*
An imprint of HarperCollins*Publishers*
77–85 Fulham Palace Road
Hammersmith, London W6 8JB
www.harpercollins.co.uk

This Harper*Press* paperback edition published 2012

1

First published in Great Britain by Harper*Press* in 2011

A catalogue record for this book
is available from the British Library

ISBN 978-0-00-730539-1

Typeset in Minion by G&M Designs Limited,
Raunds, Northamptonshire
Printed and bound in Great Britain by
Clays Ltd, St Ives plc

MIX
Paper from
responsible sources
FSC C007454

FSC™ is a non-profit international organisation established to promote
the responsible management of the world's forests. Products carrying the
FSC label are independently certified to assure customers that they come
from forests that are managed to meet the social, economic and
ecological needs of present and future generations,
and other controlled sources.

Find out more about HarperCollins and the environment at
www.harpercollins.co.uk/green

To my sisters Fiona, Belinda and Jo

The House of Greece

Christian IX *m.* Louise of Hesse-Cassel
King of (1817–98)
Denmark
(1818–1906)

Frederick VIII *m.* Louise of Sweden   William *m.* Olga of Russia   Marie *m.* Alexander III
King of   (1851–1926)   George I   (1851–1926)   Feodorovna   Tsar of Russia
Denmark   King of   (1847–1928)   (1845–94)
(1843–1912)   Greece
                                            (1845–1913)

Constantine I *m.* Sophie   'Big' George *m.* Marie   Alexandra *m.* Paul of Russia
King of   of Prussia   (1869–1957)   Bonaparte   (1870–91)   (1860–1919)
Greece   (1870–1922)   (1882–1962)
(1868–1923)

                    Peter   *m.* Irene Outchinikova   Eugenie
                    (1908–80)   (1904–90)   (1910–89)

George II   *m.* Elisabeth   Alexander *m.* Aspasia Manos   Helen *m.* Carol II
King of Greece   of Romania   King of Greece (1896–1972)   (1896–1982)   King of
(1890–1947)   (1894–1956)   (1893–1920)   Romania
                                                                                               (1893–1953)

                                           Alexandra *m.* Peter   Michael I
                                           (1921–93)   King of   King of Romania
                                                          Yugoslavia   (b. 1921)
                                                          (1923–70)

Waldemar   *m.*   Marie d'Orleans
(1858–1939)   (1865–1909)

Alexandra   *m.*   Edward VII
(1844–1925)   (1841–1910)

Margrethe   *m.*   Rene of
'Meg'   Boubon-
(1895–1992)   Parma
            (1894–78)

George V
(1865–1936)

George VI
(1895–1952)

Jacques
(1922–1964)

Anne   *m.*   Michael I
(b. 1923)   King of Romania
         (b. 1921)

Nicholas   *m.*   Ellen of Russia
(1872–1938)   (1882–1957)

Olga
(b. and d. 1880)

Christopher   *m.*   (1) Nancy Leeds
(1888–1940)   (1873–1923)

               (2) Francoise
               of France
               (1902–53)

Maria   *m.*   George
(1876–1940)   of Russia
         (1863–1919)

Andrea   *m.*   Alice of
(1882–1944)   Battenberg
         (1885–1969)

— Margarita
   (1905–81)
— Theodora
   (1906–69)
— Cecile
   (1911–37)
— Sophie
   (1914–2001)

Michael
(b. 1939)

Olga   *m.*   Paul
(1903–97)   of Yugoslavia
         (1893–1976)

Elisabeth
(1904–55)

Marina   *m.*   George
(1906–68)   Duke of Kent
         (1863–1919)

— **Philip**   *m.*   Elizabeth II
  (b. 1921)   (b. 1926)

Paul   *m.*   Frederika
King of Greece   of Hanover
(1901–64)   (1917–81)

Irene   *m.*   Duke of Aosta
(1904–74)   (1900–48)

Katherine   *m.*   Richard
(1913–2007)   Brandram
         (1911–94)

Constantine II
King of Greece
(b. 1940)

Sofia
Queen of Spain
(b. 1940)

Irene
(b. 1942)

The Houses of Windsor, Hesse and Battenberg

Grand Duke Louis II of Hesse
(1777–1848)

Louis III
(1806–77)

Alexander _m._ Julie von Hauke
(1823–88)   (1825–95)

Marie   _m._ Alexander II
(1824–80)   Tsar of Russia
              (1818–81)

Charles   _m._ Elisabeth
(1809–77)   of Prussia
              (1815–85)

Louis IV   _m._ Alice of
of Hesse   Great Britain
(1837–92)   (1843–78)

Louis of   _m._ Victoria
Battenberg,   (1863–1950)
1st Marquess
of Milford
Haven
(1854–1921)

Irene   _m._ Henry of
(1866–1953)   Prussia
               (1862–1929)

Alix   _m._ Nicholas II
(1872–1918)   Tsar of Russia
               (1868–1918)

Elisabeth _m._ Serge of
'Ella'   Russia
(1864–1918)   (1857–1905)

Ernst Ludwig _m._ (2) Eleonore
'Ernie'   of Lich
(1868–1937)   'Onor'
                      (1871–1937)

George   _m._ Nadejda 'Nada'
2nd Marquess   Countess de Torby
of Milford   (1896–1963)
Haven
(1892–1938)

Louis   _m._ Edwina
'Dickie'   Ashley
Mountbatten   (1901–60)
(1900–79)

Ludwig   _m._ Margaret
'Lu'   Geddes
(1908–68)   (1913–97)

Louise   _m._ Gustav VI
(1889–1965)   Adolf of
                Sweden
                (1882–1973)

George   _m._ Cecile of
Donatus   Greece
'Don'   (1911–37)
(1906–37)

Tatiana
(1917–88)

David
3rd Marquess of
Milford Haven
(1919–70)

Patricia
Countess
Mountbatten
(b 1924)

Lady Pamela
Hicks
(b 1929)

Ludwig
(1931–37)

Alexander
(1933–37)

Johanna
(1936–39)

CONTENTS

LIST OF ILLUSTRATIONS

King George I of Greece. *(The Art Archive/Alamy)*

Queen Olga of Greece. *(Topfoto)*

Prince Louis and Princess Victoria of Battenberg, with their children Louise, Georgie, Dickie and Alice. *(Broadlands Archives)*

Prince Andrew (Andrea) of Greece and Princess Alice of Battenberg, at the time of their marriage in 1903. *(Topfoto)*

Mon Repos, the villa on Corfu where Philip was born.

Alice with three-month-old Philip on a visit to England in September 1921. *(Broadlands Archives)*

Philip's family, happy at Mon Repos, Corfu, Easter 1922. *(Broadlands Archives)*

Five-year-old Philip with his uncle Dickie Mountbatten, Adsdean, July 1926. *(Broadlands Archives)*

Aged seven in Paris, winning a biscuit-eating competition. (Topfoto)

In Greek national costume. *(AP/Press Association Images)*

Philip's aunt and uncle, Princess Marie Bonaparte and Prince George of Greece. *(Getty Images)*

Philip's sister Sophie on her marriage in 1930 to Prince Christoph of Hesse. *(Charlotte Zeepvat/ILN/Mary Evans Picture Library)*

As a schoolboy at Salem in Germany in 1934, aged 12, with his elder sister Theodora and her daughter Margarita in the pram being inspected by another Salem pupil. *(Private Collection)*

Salem pupils picnicking beside Lake Constance. *(Private Collection)*

Philip's uncles and aunts on his mother's side, in 1928. *(Broadlands Archives)*

Nada Milford Haven with her son David and daughter Tatiana at Lynden Manor. *(Getty Images)*

Philip's sister Cecile with her husband George Donatus, 'Don', of Hesse and their three children, shortly before the Steene air disaster in 1937. (*Image supplied by Mirrorpix*)

Their funeral procession at Darmstadt. (*Broadlands Archives*)

Philip as a schoolboy at Gordonstoun, honing his sailing skills on the Moray Firth. (*Topfoto*)

In the harbour at Hopeman. (*Private Collection*)

Cobina Wright. (*Time & Life Pictures/Getty Images*)

Osla Benning at the Whaddon Chase point-to-point in 1939, with Babette Talbot Baines. (*Getty Images*)

Philip acting as best man at the wedding of his close friend Hélène Foufounis (later Cordet) to William Kirby in 1938. (*Topfoto*)

The first significant meeting, at Dartmouth Naval College in July 1939, between the cadet Philip and Princess Elizabeth. (*Topfoto*)

A bearded Philip during the war. (*ILN, Camera Press London*)

Philip and Elizabeth at the wedding of Patricia Mountbatten and John Brabourne in 1946. (*Topfoto*)

Philip walks alongside the compact family unit on the way to the Brabourne wedding in 1946. (*Broadlands Archives*)

Philip and Elizabeth on their wedding day, 20 November 1947, in the Throne Room at Buckingham Palace. (*Bettmann/Corbis*)

In Malta in 1949. (*Broadlands Archives*)

Philip waterskiing while in command of the frigate *Magpie* in the Mediterranean, 1951. (*Camera Press, London*)

Philip's best man, David Milford Haven, with his girlfriend Robin Dalton, on holiday in France in 1946. (*Private Collection*)

The showgirl Pat Kirkwood. (*Getty Images*)

The Thursday Club cricket team. (*Private Collection*)

Philip's mother Alice leads the procession of his relations out of Westminster Abbey after the coronation in 1953. (*Topfoto*)

AUTHOR'S NOTE

The idea for this biography came a little unexpectedly from a book I briefly toyed with writing about prominent ufologists in the period just after the Second World War. In the course of cobbling together a proposal to try and persuade my sceptical agent, I was struck by the revelation in Francis Wheen's book *How Mumbo Conquered the World* that Prince Philip's equerry once went off at the prince's bidding to meet an extraterrestrial humanoid at a house in Ealing. The equerry in question, Sir Peter Horsley, had been on the prince's staff from 1952 until 1955, before climbing to great heights in the RAF. 'Oh God,' sighed an official at the Ministry of Defence when Horsley's memoirs came out in 1997, 'how unfortunate that the public will learn that the man who had his finger on the button of Strike Command was seeing little green men.'

For better or worse, the public also learned that, for several years in the early 1950s, Prince Philip had enthusiastically swapped UFO stories with his uncle Louis 'Dickie' Mountbatten, a fellow subscriber to the *Flying Saucer Review*, and kept himself abreast of developments in the field. According to Horsley, 'Prince Philip was open to the immense possibilities leading to space exploration, while at the same time not discounting that, just as we were on the fringe of breaking into space, so older civilizations in the universe might already have done so'. Horsley also recalled that the prince 'agreed that I could investigate the more credible reports provided that I kept it all in perspective and did not involve his office in any kind of publicity or sponsorship'. A number of witnesses were invited to Buckingham Palace to discuss their experiences, partly, as Horsley later explained, to 'put them on the spot' and to test their honesty 'in the presence of royalty, a method as effective as any truth serum'.

This was all intriguing news to me, yet the more I read about Prince Philip, the more it became apparent that his interest in flying saucers was very far from being the most intriguing thing about him. He is, after all, famously revered as a living god by the islanders of Vanuatu in the South Pacific. More than anything, though, I was drawn to the remarkable story of his early life, which seemed to be overflowing with drama and colour – and yet there did not seem to be a particularly full or dispassionate written account of it.

I am extremely grateful to everyone who helped me in various ways with this book. At Buckingham Palace, I owe a particular debt of gratitude to Sir Brian McGrath, Prince Philip's extra equerry. While Sir Brian never pretended that my project was especially welcome, neither was he in the least bit obstructive. On the contrary, he was very helpful in enabling interviews with Prince Philip's friends and relations. Both he and Dame Anne Griffiths, Prince Philip's librarian and archivist, also helped with access to various papers at Buckingham Palace, the Royal Archives and the Hesse State Archives in Darmstadt, and took the trouble to read an early draft of my manuscript and suggest corrections of fact and interpretation. It should be stressed, however, that this biography is in no sense approved or authorized, and I was therefore under no obligation to omit things and incidents that might be deemed discreditable to Prince Philip or the royal family. It was never my intention to be sniping or mean-spirited. However, I knew that for the portrait to be credible to neutral readers, some of the foibles, or perceived foibles, needed to be given an airing alongside Prince Philip's finer qualities. I am equally confident that readers will respond more sympathetically towards him in consequence. I accept full responsibility for any errors there may be in the final version.

I am extremely grateful to all those who agreed to talk to (or correspond with) me about various aspects of Prince Philip's early life, including, in no particular order, Countess Mountbatten of Burma, Lady Pamela Hicks, Lady (Myra) Butter, Philip Ziegler, Kenneth Rose, The Hon. Mrs Janie Spring, Captain North Dalrymple-Hamilton, Lord Gainford, The Hon. Mrs Sarah Baring, The Dowager Countess of Cromer, Lady Macmillan, Lady Margaret Stirling-Aird, the Dowager Duchess of Devonshire, The Hon. Mrs (Oliver) Dawnay, Robin Dalton, Daphne Davie (née Brock), Major General David Alexander, Air Vice-Marshal Sir John Severne, Patrick Kidner, Sir Jeremy Chance, Clive Stewart-Lockhart, Landgrave Moritz of Hesse, Prince and Princess Ludwig of Baden, Professor Max Boisot, Peter Saunders, Leading Signalman Ted Longshaw, Lester May, Jimmy Taylor, John Wynne and the late Lord (Aubrey) Buxton.

Among the archivists who helped me, I am grateful to Pamela Clark at the Royal Archives, Windsor Castle; Professor Chris Woolgar, Archivist of the Mountbatten Papers at the University of Southampton; Professor Echart G. Franz at the Hesse State Archives in Darmstadt; Michael Churchill at Cheam; Michael Meister and Sophie Weidlich at Schule Schloss Salem; Louise Harvey at Gordonstoun; the staff of the National Archives at Kew in London; the staff of Churchill College Archives in Cambridge; the staff of the British Library; the staff of the newspaper library at Colindale, London; and the staff of the *Telegraph* newspaper library. I am also extremely grateful to the staff of the London Library, where the majority of this book was written.

I am greatly indebted to various published sources. Among these, Hugo Vickers's scrupulously researched authorized biography of Prince Philip's mother, *Alice: Princess Andrew of Greece*, was an invaluable source of otherwise unavailable family information and letters, many fragments of which I have cited.

Among the biographies of Prince Philip himself, those that I found most useful were by Basil Boothroyd (*Philip: An Informal Biography*), Queen Alexandra of Yugoslavia (*Prince Philip: A Family Portrait*), Tim Heald (*The Duke: A Portrait of Prince Philip*) and Gyles Brandreth (*Philip & Elizabeth: Portrait of a Marriage*). I also relied heavily on several of Philip Ziegler's books, principally his outstanding biography *Mountbatten*, and on the excellent royal biographies by Sarah Bradford (*George VI* and *Elizabeth*), Ben Pimlott (*The Queen*), Robert Lacey (*Majesty* and *Royal*), and William Shawcross (*Queen Elizabeth, the Queen Mother*). Other particularly useful books included Jonathan Petropoulos's *Royals and the Reich*, a study of the relationship between the Hesse family and the Nazi regime, and Graham Turner's *Elizabeth: The Woman and the Queen*.

My literary agent, Caroline Dawnay, was, as ever, a constant source of sound advice, excellent ideas and much needed encouragement. I was extremely fortunate to have as my editor at Harper Press Martin Redfern, who was a pleasure to work with and made numerous editorial suggestions which greatly improved the book. My thanks, too, to Richard Collins, for his painstaking copy editing, to Sarah Hopper, for her very willing and resourceful picture research, and to Christopher Phipps, for his exemplary index. I am particularly grateful also to Victoria Lane, who read and edited an early draft of the first half of the book, and did much to make it better, and to Robert Gray, who very generously agreed to read the whole manuscript, in the course of which he tightened a great many of my loose sentences and made countless perceptive comments.

Many thanks, too, to Oliver James, Robert Hardman, Richard Davenport-Hines, David Profumo, Abigail Napp, Anne de Courcy, Francis Wheen, Richard Ingrams, Lucy Cavendish, Annabel Price, Saffron Rainey, Violet Hudson, Kate Hubbard, Matthew Bell, James

Owen, James Kidner, Jane Stewart-Lockhart, Richard Mead, Richard Rycroft, Miranda Seymour, Alex von Tunzelmann, Fiammetta Rocco, Chelsea Renton, David Ford, Dan Renton, Kim Reczek, Zara D'Abo, Tom Faulkner, Epoh Beech, Rodolf de Salis, John Lloyd, Giles Milton, John McNally, Joachim von Halasz, Eloise Moody, Stephen Birmingham, Kitty Kelley, Michael Bloch, John Parker, Gyles Brandreth, Janie Lewis, Olivia Hunt, Helen Ellis, Minna Fry, Austin Mutti Mewse, Molly Guinness, Margaret, Viscountess Stuart, Nicky and Jasmine Dunne, Fiona and Euan McAlpine, Belinda and Patrick Macaskie, Jo and Richard Wimbush, my mother and father, and anyone else I may have forgotten to mention.

PROLOGUE

Autumn 1937

At around noon on 16 November 1937, Prince Philip's heavily pregnant sister Cecile set off on the short drive through the woods from the Hesse family's old hunting box at Wolfsgarten to Frankfurt aerodrome in order to fly to London for a family wedding. With her were her husband, George Donatus, or 'Don', who had recently succeeded his father as the Grand Duke of Hesse and by Rhine, his widowed mother, the Dowager Grand Duchess, their two young sons, aged six and four, who were due to be pages, a lady-in-waiting and the best man.[1] The only member of the Grand Ducal family left behind at home was their baby daughter Johanna, who was too young to go to the wedding.

By the mid-1930s, air travel had become sufficiently popular for Bradshaw's to begin publishing its monthly *International Air Guide*, looking much like a train timetable although unashamedly aimed at the travelling elite, with advertisements only for luxury hotels. However, it was still rare compared with travel by sea or rail and most Europeans considered it too risky and unpredictable, particularly in the high winds and dense fogs of late autumn. In December 1935, fourteen-year-old Philip's grandmother had pleaded in vain with him before one of his frequent continental trips to visit relations: 'This time I really think you had better not fly across, as it is such a stormy time of the year.'[2] Philip's sister Cecile shared their grandmother's misgivings. She was reputedly so terrified of aeroplanes that she always wore black when she flew. However, Don Hesse was a dedicated and fearless flyer, like his young brother-in-law, and with an aerodrome so close to home, he was not one to be put off by the potential hazards.

They took off just before two o'clock in bright sunshine in a three-engine Junkers monoplane operated by the Belgian airline Sabena and captained by one of its most experienced airmen, Tony Lambotte, the personal friend and pilot of King Leopold III, assisted by an engineer, wireless operator and mechanic. The plane had been scheduled to land en route near Brussels, but thick fog had swept quickly in from the North Sea and so they were instructed by wireless to proceed instead to Steene aerodrome on the coast near Ostend. There, too, fog had reduced visibility to a few yards, yet the pilot nevertheless went ahead with his descent, flying blind. The aerodrome staff fired three rockets to help him find his way, but only the first one worked.[3]

An eyewitness later described having seen the aeroplane coming down out of the fog and hitting the top of a brickworks' chimney, 150ft high, 'at about 100 miles an hour. One wing and one of the engines broke off, and both crashed through the roof of the works. The remainder of the aeroplane turned over and crashed to the ground in the brickfield about 50 yards further on, where it at once burst into flames.'[4] Fire engines and ambulances raced to the scene but they could not get near the burning wreckage until there was no hope of there being any survivors. Additional news from Ostend later added a poignant footnote to the tragedy. Firemen sifting through the charred wreckage of the plane had stumbled upon the remains of an infant, prematurely delivered when the plane crashed, lying beside the crumpled body of Cecile.[5] The discovery gave rise to the theory that the pilot had only attempted to land after he became aware that the Grand Duchess had begun to give birth.[6]

* * *

At Gordonstoun School in Morayshire it fell to the German émigré headmaster Kurt Hahn to break the terrible news to sixteen-year-old Philip, who would never forget the 'profound shock' with which he heard what had happened to his sister and her family.[7] Even before this latest tragedy, the young prince had suffered more than his share of blows during his short life and, perhaps thus fortified, he 'did not break down', so his headmaster later recorded. 'His sorrow was that of a man.'[8]

The next week, Philip travelled alone to Germany for the funeral at Darmstadt, the Hesse family's home town south of Frankfurt. As the coffins were borne through streets festooned with swastikas, he cut a distinctly forlorn figure walking behind them in his civilian dark suit and overcoat, his white-blond hair standing out against the surrounding dark military greatcoats. Beside him marched his surviving brothers-in-law – Prince Christoph of Hesse, the husband of Philip's youngest sister Sophie, the most conspicuous in his SS garb; and Christoph's brother Prince Philipp of Hesse walking alongside in an SA brown shirt. Philip's uncle Lord Louis 'Dickie' Mountbatten followed just behind in British naval dress.[9]

The streets of Darmstadt were lined with detachments of soldiers in Nazi uniforms and, as the procession passed, many in the crowd raised their outstretched arms in a full 'Heil Hitler' greeting[10] – a gesture that Philip had become accustomed to seeing as a schoolboy in Nazi Germany four years earlier and on regular visits there ever since. Don and Cecile had recently joined the Nazi party themselves. Hitler and Goebbels had sent messages of sympathy; Goering attended the funeral in person.

This strange and desperately sad occasion was also the first time that Philip's parents had seen each other since 1931, when his mother, who had been born deaf, had been committed to a secure psychiatric sanatorium after suffering a nervous breakdown. Shortly afterwards his father had closed down the family home near Paris and taken himself off to live in the South of France, leaving ten-year-old Philip to be brought up in Britain by his wife's family, the Milford Havens and Mountbattens. For almost five years he had heard nothing from his mother and he had become reacquainted with her only shortly before the disaster that befell Cecile.

Almost exactly a decade after the tragedy, Prince Philip married the most eligible young woman in the world, heir to the British throne. As he approaches his ninetieth birthday – two years after surpassing the record of George III's Queen Charlotte as the longest-serving consort in British history – still walking dutifully a pace or two behind his wife, emitting the odd robust remark, it is easy to forget what a turbulent time he had when he was younger.

ONE

Kings of Greece

Although he has been married for more than sixty years to the most enduringly famous woman in the world, Prince Philip's own origins have remained strangely shrouded in obscurity. 'I don't think anybody thinks I had a father,' he remarked ruefully in the 1970s. 'Most people think that Dickie [Mountbatten] is my father anyway.'[1]

The easiest way of understanding Prince Philip's paternal ancestry is to start with his grandfather, King George I of Greece. A dashing figure, seen in photographs sporting a range of spectacular moustaches, King George was born Prince William of Schleswig-Holstein-Sonderburg-Glücksburg in 1845 in Copenhagen, the younger son of an army officer whose meagre pay meant that his children grew up in comparative poverty. Their home, the Yellow Palace, was not especially palatial, with a front door that led straight on to the pavement,[2] their lifestyle scarcely regal, with William's mother doing much of the housework and his sisters sharing a room and making their own clothes. As a family, the Glücksburgs were loud and frivolous, informal and uncultured, apt to 'make funny noises and yell if they saw anyone trying to write a letter'.[3] They were also distinctly unspoilt and unpretentious, yet within a very short space of time they had 'colonised royal Europe', as one chronicler put it.[4]

In 1852, William's father was unexpectedly named as heir to the Danish throne, by virtue of being a godson and distant kinsman of the childless king, although for the time being this made no difference to his income and the family still struggled to make ends meet.[5] However, their status changed dramatically in 1863, when, within a year, the father succeeded as King Christian IX of Denmark, William's sister Alexandra married the Prince of Wales, destined to become King Edward VII, and a delegation from Greece came and asked seventeen-year-old William to be their king. Another sister, Dagmar, would shortly marry the future Tsar Alexander III of Russia, while yet another, Thyra, married the heir to the throne of Hanover – although that was soon dissolved by Prussia after the 1866 Anglo-Prussian war. Within the next half-century, the descendants of Christian IX would occupy no fewer than nine European thrones.[6] Only the descendants of Queen Victoria were more widely spread.

King George I, as William became on his accession, later maintained that he had accepted the Greek throne with great reluctance, since it meant abandoning his chosen naval career to go and rule a far-off country with a turbulent people and a language he did not speak.[7] Greece had only recently broken free from the Ottoman Empire as a result of the long and bloody war of independence that had claimed the life of Lord Byron among countless others. The new country – unstable, poor and less than half the size of what it was to become during George's reign – was formally recognized by the London Protocol of 1830, in which the protecting powers, France, Great Britain and Russia, stipulated that a hereditary sovereign should be chosen from outside the country to lessen the chances of internal disputes. In 1833 a young Bavarian prince called Otto had arrived in a British frigate to fill this vacancy, but his tactless and despotic rule caused countless insurrections. In 1862 he was deposed in a bloodless revolution and left Greece just as he had arrived, in a British warship.

Many Greek people had wanted to have as his successor Queen Victoria's second son, Prince Alfred, whose portrait was carried through the streets of Athens by a cheering mob. But Alfred was ineligible as a prince of one of the protecting powers; and besides, his mother did not like the idea. Several alternatives were suggested before eventually they settled on the young Danish prince as the least contentious candidate.

When he first arrived in Greece, he was still not yet eighteen and as he took the oath to the new constitution at the national assembly, the British ambassador was moved by 'the sight of this slight, delicate stripling, standing alone amidst a crowd of callous, unscrupulous politicians, many of whom had been steeped to the lips in treason, and swearing to observe, as he has so faithfully done, the most unworkable of charters, from which nearly every safeguard had been studiously eliminated'.[8]

Athens then was no more than a collection of villages, with a combined population of about 45,000, and the young king developed an endearing habit of walking alone through the streets, stopping every now and then to talk to passers-by. So determined was he to master the Greek language and customs that over the next four years he never left the country, travelling instead to all corners of his realm by ship, carriage, mule and on foot.

While he never entirely lost his slight Danish accent, King George's enthusiasm and lack of affectation were greatly appreciated by the Greek people. On Monday mornings, he was available to any of his subjects who wanted to come and air their grievances. He also gave an audience to any foreigner who requested one, provided they put on dress-clothes and white tie. The king tended to stand throughout these interviews and one of those who paid a visit, E. F. Benson, was disconcerted by his habit of continuously rising on his toes and rocking back on his heels. Benson found this 'as infectious as yawning' and it was only with the greatest effort that he could prevent himself from following the royal example. Aspirational American ladies began flocking to Athens because, as one of them remarked, 'The royal family of Greece is the easiest royal family to become acquainted with'.[9]

Affable and approachable the young King George may have been, but he still had to learn to stand up for himself against his wily ministers. Shortly after his arrival, a story was told of one cabinet meeting at which the boy king stood up and went over to a map to illustrate a point he was making. When he returned to his seat he noticed that his watch was missing. He looked around the table: 'Will whoever has my watch please return it?' he demanded. His ministers stared blankly back at him. 'Well, gentlemen,' the king continued, 'I'm not accustomed to this type of joke. I'd like to have my watch back.' Still nobody spoke. Adopting a sterner tone, the king announced that he was going to put out the light and count to sixty. 'If I find the watch again on the table, the incident will be closed,' he said. In the darkness he called the seconds out loud. When he turned the lights back on his silver inkstand had vanished as well.[10]

Apart from dealing with his ministers and frequent changes of government (forty-two in the first twenty-five years of his reign), he also had to re-establish the rather ramshackle court, train his own aides-de-camp, butlers, footmen and so forth, and set the appropriate tone, although to begin with his youthful demeanour made it 'sometimes difficult for his daily companions to maintain the respectful reserve and gravity due to a royal station'.[11] The young king was also regularly reminded by his counsellors of his dynastic responsibilities, to marry and produce a son born on Greek soil, and so in 1867, aged twenty-one, he visited his sister in Russia, where he hoped to find a wife.

Tsar Alexander II had persuaded George that his was the only country where he would find a girl with the requisite combination of royal breeding and Orthodox faith. The two-month trip would also enable him to see how the vast empire was run. He lost no time as regards his primary purpose and on a visit to the tsar's younger brother Constantine at Pavlovsk he promptly proposed to the Grand

Duke's fifteen-year-old daughter Olga, a shy and pretty girl with beautiful dark eyes, whom Queen Victoria had thought might do rather well for her son Alfred.[12] Engaged within a week of meeting, they were married shortly after her sixteenth birthday in an elaborate five-day ceremony at the Winter Palace.

For her arrival in Athens, Queen Olga thoughtfully wore a dress in the Greek national colours of blue and white which delighted the huge crowd and her 'fresh young beauty' soon won the hearts of her subjects.[13] With her came a Russian lady-in-waiting, a governess and a trunk full of dolls and teddy bears to complete the entourage. At times overwhelmed and frightened by the reception she received, the young queen was once found hiding beneath the palace staircase 'hugging her favourite Russian stuffed bear, and weeping bitterly'.[14] She never did entirely overcome her homesickness – whenever a Russian ship docked at Piraeus, she could scarcely keep away from it – but the marriage was extremely successful and as queen she won the enduring love of the Greek people.

Olga's first child, a son, was born barely nine months after the wedding and named Constantine after the last emperor of Byzantine Greece, an augury which prompted much rejoicing. She went on to have a further seven children, three girls (one of whom survived only three months) and four more boys. Philip's father, Andrew, known as Andrea, was the last but one, born in 1882 at Tatoï, the royal family's country estate, some thirty miles north of Athens. He was premature and so tiny that he spent his first few days in a cigar box being fed with a toothpick,[15] however after being wet-nursed by a 'pleasant-looking peasant from the island of Andros, called Athena',[16] he eventually grew into a tall and athletic figure, 'like a thoroughbred horse' according to Philip's aunt Marie Bonaparte.[17] By common consent he was the most handsome of the king's sons. It was from him that Philip inherited his high-domed forehead, his 'fine nose and lips and the narrow Mountbatten eyes' coming from his mother.[18]

Andrea grew up with his brothers and sisters at the gaunt royal palace which had been built by King Otto on a hill overlooking old Athens and was extensively ransacked after his departure. Nowadays used as the Greek parliament, during Andrea's childhood it was an 'excessively uncomfortable' family home, so his younger brother Christopher recalled, with only one bathroom where the taps emitted a dismal trickle of water and the odd defunct cockroach.[19] As a boy, Andrea suffered at least one bout of typhoid, presumed to have been caught from the palace drains.

Winters were especially spartan, with cold winds whistling through the long, dim galleries and countless unused rooms. King George seems to have grown sterner with fatherhood and whatever the weather bade his sons get up at six each morning for a cold bath and then lessons at 6.30 sharp. His sister Alexandra, who came to visit in 1893, when Andrea was eleven, noted that the king was 'rather tyrannical in the family' and failed to take his children into his confidence even when they grew up, which embittered them towards him.[20] However, he would occasionally unbend to lead bicycling or roller-skating processions around the palace with the whole family following in order of age.

He told his children: 'You must never forget that you are foreigners in this country, but you must make them [the Greek people] forget it.'[21] The eldest children spoke Greek to each other at home and English to their parents, who in turn conversed in German. Andrea was always more Greek than any of his siblings and as a boy flatly refused to speak any other language.[22]

Although George liked discipline and uniforms, he was in other respects a relatively down-to-earth monarch, and the atmosphere at his court was generally far more relaxed than elsewhere in Europe. The princes and princesses were known by their Christian names alone and often hailed as such in the street. They all grew up with a love of practical jokes. 'Anything could happen when you got a few of them together,' according to Philip. 'It was like the Marx brothers.'[23]

Court balls were notably democratic. A foreign guest once hired a carriage to drive him to the palace for one of these parties, only for his coachman to stipulate: 'Do you mind going rather early, because I'm going there myself and shall have to go home and change?' The foreign gentleman laughed at what he thought was a rather good joke; but later in the evening, there was his driver, resplendent in evening clothes, dancing with the wife of a minister.[24]

There was a fairy-tale quality to the whole set-up. When E. F. Benson visited in 1893 he recorded that on Sunday afternoons a small compartment was often reserved on the steam tram that ran between Athens and the coast at Phaleron; when it stopped opposite the palace, the king and his family would emerge to the sound of a bugler. If they failed to come at once, the driver would impatiently touch the whistle. Benson found Greece to be an

> astonishing little kingdom, the like of which, outside pure fiction, will never again exist in Europe … its army dressed in Albanian costume (embroidered jacket, fustinella, like a ballet skirt, fez, white gaiters, red shoes with tassels on the toes like the seeds of dandelions), its fleet of three small cruisers, its national assembly of bawling Levantines and its boot-blacks called Agamemnon and Thucydides, was precisely like the fabulous kingdom of Paflagonia in *The Rose and the Ring*, or some Gilbertian realm of light opera.[25]

Every other summer the family would travel to Denmark, where King Christian IX and his wife Queen Louise had their descendants to stay en masse at the vast Fredensborg Palace. With all the court attendants and personal servants, the house parties numbered up to three hundred, and apart from the Greek royal family, included the Prince and Princess of Wales and Tsar Alexander III and Tsarina Marie

Feodorovna (as King George's sister Dagmar had now become). Court etiquette was dispensed with during the day, when the tsar would take the children off to catch tadpoles or steal apples, but for dinner they all entered the big hall in a long procession arm in arm, preceded by the tsar, who offered his arm to Queen Louise, and the rest following according to rank.

There were also regular trips to Russia – across the Black Sea to Sebastopol where the luxurious imperial train awaited – and to Corfu, one of the Ionian islands given to Greece by Britain on George's accession to the throne, and where the municipality had presented the new king with a villa, Mon Repos, on a promontory just to the south of Corfu Town. But most of their time away from Athens was spent at Tatoï, Andrea's birthplace, the royal estate of 40,000 acres in the pine-scented foothills of Mount Parnés, high enough to be much cooler than the capital. After buying Tatoï in 1871, King George had established a vineyard to produce an alternative to the pine-infused retsina, which he detested, and a butter-making dairy farm with a range of Danish-style stone buildings. For those who were not well disposed towards their imported monarch there was evidence at Tatoï that he had not embraced his adopted country quite as wholeheartedly as he liked to make out.

By 1886, the king had replaced the original small villa with a replica of a hideous Victorian-style house that stood in the grounds of his wife's family home, Pavlovsk, and so Tatoï became the one place where Queen Olga never felt homesick; she celebrated her birthday there each year with a big party for all the estate workers. The family all grew to love Tatoï and most of them, including Andrea, are buried in the wooded cemetery there. But their white marble graves are seldom visited nowadays. Since 1967, when the last Greek king, Constantine II, went into exile in Surrey, the estate has become overgrown and the buildings are now mostly ruins. A few picnic tables scattered about the park hint at the symbolic gesture of giving Tatoï to the republican Greek people of today, but few visitors come here now and if you ask for directions from Athens, you are almost guaranteed to get a blank look.

Andrea's childhood was on the whole steady, but there were also events of great sadness. The first of these occurred when he was nine, when his sister Alexandra died while giving birth to her son, Dimitri, three years after her marriage to Grand Duke Paul of Russia. The whole family, including Andrea, travelled to Moscow, where the young Grand Duchess lay in state in a special room at the station, and then on to St Petersburg for the funeral. One of Andrea's elder brothers later recalled that it was 'all so unexpected and awful that the shock and sorrow overpowered us all'.[26] King George, who doted on his daughter, never got over it.

For all the king's personal popularity, Greece remained a turbulent and violent country, and he survived several assassination attempts. In 1898, while out driving with his daughter Marie – later Grand Duchess George of Russia – his carriage was attacked by two men who opened fire with rifles at close range. Marie had a red bow in her hat which her father thought would make her an easy target for them 'so he quickly stood up,' she recalled, 'put his hand on my neck and forced me down. With his other hand he menaced them with his walking stick.' Both horses were hit and slightly wounded and a footman was injured in the leg; however the king and his daughter were miraculously unscathed.[27]

When he was fourteen, Andrea began attending classes twice a week at the military college at Athens, where he was drilled by German officers and became quite friendly with the future dictator Theodore Pangalos,[28] an association that may later have saved his life. From the age of seventeen, he was privately tutored by another future revolutionary, Major Panayotis Danglis, who privately noted that his new charge was tall, quick and intelligent – and short-sighted.[29] The king was forever urging Danglis to increase Andrea's hours of tuition, and when the family went on holiday to Corfu in the spring of 1900 Andrea was made to stay in and attend to his military studies rather than go on many of the picnics and excursions.[30]

In 1902, aged twenty, Andrea was examined by a panel that included his father, his elder brothers, the prime minister, the arch-bishop, the war minister and half the teaching staff of the military academy. The king had been keen to ensure that the test was as rigorous as it could be, but they were unanimous in passing Andrea and he was duly commissioned as a subaltern in the cavalry. Shortly after this he met the beautiful seventeen-year-old Princess Alice of Battenberg, the girl who was to become his wife.

TWO

House of Battenberg

The House of Battenberg to which Alice belonged was slightly older than the House of Greece and equally romantic in its origins. Alice's grandfather was Prince Alexander of Hesse, officially the third son of the famously ugly Grand Duke Louis II of Hesse and by Rhine but widely assumed to have been sired by the Grand Duchess's handsome chamberlain, Baron Augustus Senarclens von Grancy, with whom the duchess had been openly living for three years by the time Alexander was born in 1823.[1] Alexander's younger sister Marie, who was thought to have the same biological father, went on to marry the future Tsar Alexander II. Hence, at the age of eighteen, Alexander joined the tsar's imperial army as a colonel, and was later promoted to major general when his sister produced an heir. However, his career faltered after he fell in love with Marie's Polish lady-in-waiting, Julie Hauke, who, although a countess, was deemed to be unacceptably beneath his rank.

Julie became pregnant and Alexander married her, with the result that he was banished from Russia. His Hessian family was equally dismayed by the match but his brother, Louis III, nevertheless revived the dormant title of Battenberg – a small town in the north of the Grand Duchy – for Julie, with the quality of countess, later raised to princess. Alexander remained a prince but it was stressed that no child of their morganatic marriage would have a claim to the Hessian throne.

Their eldest son was Alice's father, Prince Louis of Battenberg. From an early age Louis was determined to depart from the Hessian soldiering tradition and become a sailor, but there were only a handful of vessels in the German fleet at that time, so in 1868, aged fourteen, he set out for England to join the Royal Navy. Considering that he never entirely lost his German accent he had a remarkably successful career, culminating in his appointment as First Sea Lord, the pinnacle of his profession, in 1912. Tall and handsome, with dark, hooded eyes, Louis was also a good dancer and an entertaining raconteur, and as a young midshipman he had wooed a succession of pretty girls in the ports where his ship put in. His dalliances did not always require much effort. As an orderly officer in the suite of his cousin, the Prince of Wales, on his tour of India in 1875, he recalled one evening when after dinner each member of the prince's entourage was guided to his own private 'enormous divan with many soft cushions. Refreshments and smoking material were laid out on a little table. On the divan reclined a native girl in transparent white garments.' On another occasion, when the Maharajah of Jammu and Kashmir arranged for a well-born girl to be placed in the Prince of Wales's tent, Louis contrived to transfer her to his own.[2]

A few years later, while serving as an officer of the royal yacht *Osborne*, Louis fell in love with the Prince of Wales's mistress, Lillie Langtry, the beautiful Jersey-born actress. When she became pregnant, there were at least two other possible candidates for the child's paternity, but Louis believed that he was the father and gallantly told his parents that he intended to stand by Lillie.[3] His parents were anxious to avoid a scandal, however, and promptly arranged a financial settlement for her. Queen Victoria then fixed it for Louis to be posted to the frigate *Inconstant*, which was to undertake a voyage round the world under sail, 'a project designed to keep him out of harm's way for a long time'.[4]

Soon after his return he set his romantic sights on his young first cousin once removed from the main branch of the Hessian royal family, whom he married in 1884. His bride was twenty-year-old Princess Victoria, who had been born in 1863 at Windsor Castle, the eldest of seven children of Grand Duke Louis IV of Hesse and Princess Alice, Queen Victoria's second daughter. Princess Victoria had experienced profound sadness during her short life, losing her younger brother, Fritz, when he fell out of a window at the age of ten, and as a teenager unwittingly initiating an even greater family tragedy. In the winter of 1878, aged fifteen, she had fallen ill with diphtheria, but before the symptoms of her illness became apparent she had read aloud parts of *Alice in Wonderland* to her five younger siblings.[5] All but one of them had caught the disease, as had her father, the Grand Duke. Her mother, Alice, had insisted on nursing them all and, though urgently warned not to do so by her doctors, had hugged and kissed her son while telling him that his little sister May had died. A month later Alice, too, succumbed to the disease. She was thirty-five.

After their mother's death, young Victoria had taken charge of running the household and looking after her four surviving siblings – Ella, Irene, Ernie and Alix – supported from afar by her grandmother, Queen Victoria, who urged her to 'look upon me as a mother'.[6] By the time she fell in love with Louis, she was still only nineteen, he twenty-eight, tall, dashing and sun-tanned from his travels – 'a fairy-tale prince' according to at least one biographer.[7]

In some ways they seemed ill-suited. Despite his undoubted qualities, Louis was rather flashy, and loved dressing up in uniforms – he also boasted a large tattoo of a dragon stretching from his chest and to his legs.[8] Victoria was on the whole more self-effacing and was slightly embarrassed by Louis' sartorial flamboyance. She was also more of a free spirit, as well as being highly intelligent. 'Radical in her ideas,' wrote Philip Ziegler, 'insatiably curious, argumentative to the point of perversity, she leavened the somewhat doctrinaire formality of Prince Louis.'[9] Despite their differences, it proved to be an extremely successful marriage and produced four remarkable children.

Philip's mother, Alice, was the eldest of these, 'a fine sturdy baby'[10] born in 1885, at Windsor Castle, like her mother, in the presence of Queen Victoria, who from time to time helped the family out financially and did what she could to advance Louis' naval career.

Alice was a handsome child, tall and slender with golden hair and large brown eyes.[11] However, she was slow in learning to talk and often had a strange faraway look,[12] which her mother at first mistook for absentmindedness. It was not until she was four that an aurist pronounced her almost completely deaf due to a thickening of the Eustachian tubes, which at that time was deemed inoperable although nowadays it would be curable.[13] Her condition, which improved very slightly as she grew older, made her unusually self-reliant, able to spend hours happily absorbed in her own company. Her mother was adamant that she should not draw attention to her disability and she was thus forbidden from asking anyone to repeat what they had said.[14] Required to disguise her confusion as best she could, she soon became a brilliant lip-reader and, because the family moved about so much, following Louis' postings in Britain and Malta and summer holidays at the various Hessian schlosses, she learned to do so in several languages. Acquaintances often failed to notice any defect, as her mother would have wished, and so striking were her beauty, poise and accomplishments that the Prince of Wales reputedly remarked that 'no throne is too good for her'.[15]

In June 1902, she went to stay at Buckingham Palace for the coronation of King Edward VII, and met Andrea, Queen Alexandra's nephew, who appeared to her to be 'exactly like a Greek God', so she later told her grandson Prince Charles.[16] The coronation was delayed at the last minute when the king fell ill with appendicitis, but there was still time before the various guests dispersed for Andrea and Alice to fall in love and become privately engaged. Alice's mother Victoria later admitted that to begin with she was not in favour of this arrangement, thinking them too young.[17] It was also said – though she did not admit this – that she thought her daughter could do better than the fourth son of the insecure and impecunious King of Greece.

In July Alice and her mother returned home to Heiligenberg, from where she wrote to Andrea every day. On one occasion, when a week had gone by without a letter from him, a friend found her in tears, tormented by the thought that something must have happened to him or that he had changed his mind. The next morning she arrived at school glowing, having just received five letters in the post from Greece.[18]

After an emergency operation to remove his appendix, Edward VII was well enough to be crowned in early August and Andrea and Alice returned to Buckingham Palace and travelled in the same carriage to Westminster Abbey, together with Alice's mother and Andrea's elder brother, George. After the coronation there was a further separation while Andrea was away on military duty in Greece, but in May 1903 he returned, Edward VII gave his consent and their engagement became official. The announcement came as a shock to some of the snootier European royalty, the octogenarian Grand Duchess of Mecklenburg-Strelitz bemoaning 'the very youthful betrothal, so odd, no money besides!' She even questioned the attendance of Andrea's aunt, Queen Alexandra, at the wedding: 'Why? There is surely no reason for it, a Battenberg, daughter of an illegitimate father, he a fourth son of a newly baked King!'[19]

Still, the wedding at Darmstadt in October was a spectacular event and drew an impressive array of European royalty. Among those present was Tsar Nicholas II – Andrea's first cousin, son of his aunt Dagmar, and husband of Alice's aunt Alix – who gave the couple a Wolseley motor car and threw a bag of rice in Alice's face as the couple drove away in it.[20] Three hundred and fifty Russian detectives patrolled the town to ensure the tsar's safety.[21]

There were two religious ceremonies, Protestant and Russian Orthodox, the first preceded by a thirty-strong royal procession into the chapel, followed by Andrea and his parents, and lastly Alice with hers. During the nervous exchange of vows, Alice was defeated by the bushiness of the priest's beard and failed to lip-read the questions, so when asked whether she consented freely to marriage she replied 'No', and when asked whether she had promised her hand to someone else she said 'Yes'.[22]

They began their married life in a wing of the royal palace in Athens, spending summers at Tatoï or with her parents in England, Malta and Germany. Their first child, Margarita, was born in 1905, and that autumn they all moved to Larissa, a garrison town in Thessaly on the Turkish border, where Andrea was responsible for transforming mountain goatherds into cavalrymen.[23] Shortly after their return to Athens the following spring, their second daughter, Theodora, known in the family as Dolla, was born.

In 1907 the Greek royal family came under attack in the local press due to inflated estimates of the king's wealth and a rumour that the princes were to receive annuities. 'To be remunerated for doing nothing is the privilege of the Russian Grand Dukes,' snarled one newspaper. In another the princes were accused of failing to take the lead in times of trouble, and of 'loafing about the boulevards of Paris' while Salonika was set ablaze by Bulgarians in 1902.[24] The British ambassador Sir Francis Elliot considered the charge of indifference undeserved and the criticisms 'characteristic of this country where liberty is confounded with license, and disrespect for authority mistaken for independence'.[25]

The rumblings continued, though, and in August 1909 disgruntled officers launched a *coup d'état*, with the aim of installing the charismatic Cretan nationalist Eleftherios Venizelos as prime minister and preventing the sons of the king from holding any high commands in the army. Andrea had by then completed his staff college exams but, for their father's sake, he and his four brothers resigned their posts, leading to three years of demoralizing unemployment.[26] In 1912, though, he was able to resume his military career when Greece entered the First Balkan War against Turkey, with the aim of expanding Greek territory towards Constantinople and resolving the ownership of Crete. Andrea and his brothers made for Larissa to join the conquering army led by their eldest brother, Crown Prince Constantine, which then swept victoriously through southern and western Macedonia, repeatedly putting the Turks to rout. The campaign not only helped revive the popularity of the Greek princes but also provided Alice with the opportunity for what her biographer Hugo Vickers calls 'her finest hour'.

Alice was inspired to become a nurse by the example of the grandmother whose name she had been given and more recently by the extraordinary precedent of her aunt Ella, Victoria's younger sister. Ella was married to Tsar Alexander III's brother, Grand Duke Serge Alexandrovich, the reactionary and widely disliked governor-general of Moscow. In February 1905 Serge had been blown to pieces by a terrorist bomb thrown at his carriage in the Kremlin. Hearing the explosion, Ella had rushed to the scene and, kneeling in the snow, calmly helped gather up his scattered remains, though other parts were later retrieved from nearby rooftops.[27]

The murder brought about a profound change in Ella. Shortly afterwards she visited the assassin at the police station and vainly pleaded with him to repent. She withdrew from society, turned increasingly to her adopted Orthodox faith, became a vegetarian, gave away her jewels and furs, and – inspired by her mother's 'Alice Nurses' at Darmstadt – opened a charitable convent where she lived as the abbess, sleeping on a bare wooden bed with no mattress and one hard pillow, and tending patients herself in the hospital wing. She founded a home for consumptives and an orphanage, and during the October

Revolution in 1905 stole out of the besieged Kremlin each day to tend to the wounded in hospital.

Alice had seen for herself her aunt's work when she visited Russia, and it made a deep impression on her. Since first arriving in Athens she had spent much of her time at the charitable Greek School of Embroidery and at the outset of the First Balkan War she had the school make 80,000 garments for the troops and refugees.[28] Then, leaving her three young daughters – her third, Cecile, had been born in 1911 – she went with Andrea and his brothers to Larissa, where in a burst of manic energy she established a hospital after finding that the army had no plan for one. 'I myself forced the Military Authorities to fit out an operation room in 24 hours,' she wrote to her mother.[29] Realizing it was taking fourteen hours for the wounded to be transported from the front, she then moved her hospital to the recently liberated town of Elassona at the foot of Mount Olympus, requisitioning a school and raiding Turkish houses for mattresses and bedding for 120 men. Alice was in the thick of it, changing bandages on 'ghastly' wounds, helping the doctors in 'fearful operations, hurriedly done in the corridor amongst the dying and wounded waiting for their turn', with barely any light, the battle still raging all around them, and scarcely any time for sleep between each batch of arrivals. 'God! What things we saw!' she wrote. 'Shattered arms, and legs and heads, such awful sights – and then to have to bandage those dreadful things for three days and three nights. The corridor full of blood, and cast-off bandages knee high.'[30]

She soon expanded her hospital, taking over four more houses and later, as the Greek army advance continued northwards, she moved on to Kozani, where on one occasion she found herself assisting at the amputation of a leg, administering chloroform and preventing the patient from biting his tongue. 'Once I got over my feeling of disgust, it was very interesting, of course,' she assured her mother. When the operation was over, the leg lay abandoned on the floor of the ward and Alice suggested someone ought to take it away. Her assistant duly picked it up, 'wrapped it up in some stuff, put it under her arm and marched out of the hospital to find a place to bury it in. But she never noticed that she left the bloody end uncovered, and as she is as deaf as I, although I shouted after her, she went on unconcerned, and everybody she passed nearly retched with disgust – and, of course, I ended by laughing.'[31]

As the Greeks pressed on through the snowy mountains towards Salonika, the capital of Macedonia, determined to wrest it from Turkish control before the Bulgarians did, Alice remained constantly at or near the front. In each place she passed through she left a well-organized hospital, work for which she would later be personally thanked by prime minister Venizelos.[32]

On 12 November 1912 Venizelos accompanied the king and his heir as they rode in triumph through the streets of Salonika. There was great rejoicing throughout Greece, and Alice and Andrea went to stay with the king, who had installed himself in the Sultan's villa in the city. In March 1913 Janina, the capital of Epirus, also fell to the Greeks – witnessed by Alice who was again organizing the hospitals – and by the end of the Second Balkan War that summer, which began when the Bulgarians ill-advisedly attacked both Greece and Serbia, Greece had almost doubled in size and population, having gained southern Epirus, Macedonia, Crete and some Aegean islands.

After the tribulations of recent years, these territorial gains were a source of great relief and happiness to King George, and at lunch one day, on 18 March 1913, he announced that he now intended to abdicate on his golden jubilee in October, leaving his newly popular and auspiciously named son Constantine to succeed him. As the lunch party broke up, one of the generals present ventured to warn the king that his habit of strolling freely about the streets was perhaps more dangerous in Salonika than it was in Athens, to which the king replied that he did not wish for such a sermon. Later that afternoon, accompanied by his equerry and two policemen, the king set out for his usual walk to the White Tower. On his way back, as he passed a café, a man came out and shot him dead with a revolver. The assassin turned out to be an insane Greek rather than a Bulgarian or Turkish nationalist as had been feared, and he subsequently leapt to his death from a window while awaiting trial.

King George I's body was carried by sea to Athens, from where a train took the coffin to Tatoï. Crowds of peasants collected alongside the track and knelt as the train passed.[33] The British ambassador reported that

> Tragic as was the manner of the King's death, he was at least happy in the moment of it. He had seen the edifice he had laboured to construct for 50 years crowned by the victories of his army under the leadership of his son and successor. He had the assurance that his dynasty was at least firmly seated upon the throne which he had often during his long reign been tempted to abandon in despair. He had seen his aspirations realized beyond his wildest dreams. He will live on in the memories of his people as a martyr to the national cause.[34]

King George's son was now hailed in some newspapers as Constantine XII, successor to the last Greek ruler of Byzantium who had died during the siege of Constantinople in 1453, although in fact he ascended the throne as Constantine I. The British ambassador deemed him 'inferior in intelligence to his father, and wanting in his dexterous pliability', yet at the same time 'a man of stronger character' who 'may well be fitted to deal with the new problems which will arise in the new situation'.[35] His reign was to prove rather less happy and considerably less enduring.

One of Constantine's handicaps was that he had married Princess Sophie of Prussia, the sister of Kaiser Wilhelm II. On the outbreak of the First World War he was thus torn between loyalty to his wife and a feeling that Germany might win on the one hand, and pressure to join the Allies on the other. His decision to stay neutral placed Greece at odds with both sides and thereafter lowered the Greek royal family in the estimation of the British people.

The outbreak of the European war placed Alice, born a German princess yet with her father serving as Britain's First Sea Lord, in a similarly awkward position. Louis of Battenberg had been responsible for mobilizing the British fleet prior to the war and on 4 August 1914 he sent the signal: 'Admiralty to All Ships. Commence hostilities against Germany.'[36] By then he had served for forty-six years in the Royal Navy, yet his accent and mannerisms were still faintly German, and he kept German staff in his household. Within the navy, he was acknowledged as an exceptional sea officer and Fleet Commander, and a kind and courtly man; however, his insistence that there were certain things that were done more efficiently in his country of birth inevitably aroused hostility towards him.[37] Following the outbreak of war, the British popular press whipped up a wave of scurrilous anti-German paranoia, during which anyone or anything deemed to be of German origin was liable to come under attack. Shop windows were smashed, dachshunds were kicked in the street and innocent people with Teutonic-sounding names were arrested and imprisoned without trial. When two German cruisers mysteriously evaded a British force in the eastern Mediterranean and made it to Constantinople, it was whispered that a British admiral must have assisted them and that Louis Battenberg was a German spy. Of course, George V, too, had a German name and connections, and the wholeheartedness of his commitment to the Allied cause also came under scrutiny. On one occasion, Lord Kitchener 'had solemnly to assure the Cabinet that lights seen flashing over Sandringham during a German air sortie were caused by the car of the rector returning home after dinner'.[38] Winston Churchill, then First Lord of the Admiralty, attempted to make light of all the xenophobic hysteria, and when told off for drinking hock, he responded: 'I am interning it.'[39] Nevertheless, he worried about the effect of all the attacks on his First Sea Lord's powers of concentration, and soon decided that the country's best interests would be served by replacing Louis with the more dynamic Admiral 'Jacky' Fisher.[40] It was with some relief, therefore, that he accepted Louis' resignation on 29 October 1914, even though it deprived the Royal Navy of one of its shrewdest strategic brains.

The whole episode was a great tragedy for Louis. 'I feel for him deeply,' wrote George V in his diary, 'there is no more loyal man in the country.'[41] However, Battenberg's younger son, also called Louis but known in the family as Dickie, then a fourteen-year-old naval cadet at Osborne, casually remarked to a contemporary: 'It doesn't really matter. Of course I shall take his place.'[42] His vow to avenge the family's humiliation would propel him on a career path even more remarkable than that of his father.

During the early part of the First World War, Andrea was stationed at Salonika, but in 1916 his brother King Constantine sent him on a diplomatic mission to London and Paris to assure the Allies that Greece was not on the German side. Alice remained mostly in Athens, looking after their four daughters. The youngest of these, Sophie, had been born in 1914 and was always known in the family as Tiny, although she grew to be the tallest of the four sisters. Shortly after her birth her teenage uncle Dickie had written to his mother, Victoria: 'Please congratulate Alice from me, but it was silly not to have a boy for once in a way.'[43]

The political situation in Greece remained fraught throughout the war. Venizelos favoured siding with the Allies, thinking that they would win and be more sympathetic towards Greece's remaining territorial ambitions. He also considered the Allies' superior naval power vital to the protection of his maritime country. In 1916 he staged a coup and established a rival government in Salonika, which promptly declared war on Germany. When King Constantine continued to insist on Greek neutrality, the Allied fleet bombarded Athens.

Alice was at the embroidery school at the time and drove home 'through a rain of bullets' to find one of the nursery windows shattered by a shell. She quickly took her children down to the palace cellar, where Constantine's queen Sophie was also sheltering.[44] During the subsequent blockade they both worked in soup kitchens. Eventually, in June 1917, Constantine bowed to Allied demands that he leave the country, a humiliating finale to a reign that had begun with such high hopes.

While the banished king made his way to Switzerland accompanied by his eldest son, Crown Prince George, whom the Allies also considered too pro-German, he was succeeded by his second son, Alexander. The other brothers, including Andrea, were soon asked to follow Constantine into exile, and Andrea and Alice were thus condemned to another spell of kicking their heels, this time at a hotel in St Moritz and later in Rome.

Alice's parents in England, meanwhile, suffered further upheavals of their own. In the summer of 1917 George V decided to camouflage the royal family's Germanic associations by renaming his dynasty the House of Windsor. Absurdly, no one in Britain seemed able to agree on what the previous name was, although the Kaiser declared that he was looking forward to attending a production of 'The Merry Wives of Saxe-Coburg-Gotha' – one of his only recorded jokes. The king accompanied his change of name with a request that other members of the royal family relinquish all of their German names and styles and titles.[45] Alice's father, His Serene Highness Prince Louis of Battenberg, thus found himself relegated to being the Marquess of Milford Haven, while his family name was translated into English as Mountbatten. He admitted to finding the change 'a terrible break with one's past'[46] and while staying with his elder son Georgie when his new title was announced, he wrote sadly in the visitors' book: 'Arrived Prince Jekyll, Departed Lord Hyde'.[47]

Yet Louis' predicament was mild compared with the branch of his family in Russia, where the tsar had been forced to abdicate following the outbreak of revolution in March 1917. George V, the tsar's first cousin, briefly considered giving him sanctuary but then had second thoughts, fearful that his apparent endorsement of the old tsarist regime would antagonize Russia's new rulers, who remained Britain's allies in the war.[48] The offer of asylum was thus withdrawn.

In April 1918 the tsar and tsarina (Alice's aunt Alix, who had become deeply unpopular in Russia due to her perceived Germanic aloofness and devotion to Rasputin) and their teenage children were taken to Ekaterinburg in the Ural Mountains, where three months later they were executed. Alice's other aunt, Ella, had carried on with her selfless work, refusing all offers of asylum from abroad. In 1918 she, too, was arrested by Lenin's secret police and taken with other members of the imperial family and their retainers to the mining town of Alapayevsk, one hundred miles from Ekaterinburg. One night they were woken up and told to get dressed. They were then blindfolded and their hands tied behind their backs before being driven to the edge of a mine shaft, where they were thrown in. They were heard saying prayers until, it seems, they were eventually killed by a combination of hand grenades and burning brushwood. The martyrdom of Ella in particular (she was later recognized as a saint) would have a profound influence on the future course of Alice's life – and by extension that of Prince Philip.

The new Greek king, Alexander, had reigned for only three years when, in October 1920, he was out walking his wolfhound, Fritz, in the garden at Tatoï and the dog was attacked by a tame Spanish monkey. While trying to release the monkey from Fritz's teeth, the king was attacked by its mate and severely bitten in the leg. The wound was quickly cleaned and dressed but after two days a fever set in.

Three weeks after that the king died from blood poisoning, aged twenty-six, leaving a young and beautiful widow, Aspasia, who was five months pregnant with their daughter Alexandra, Philip's cousin, childhood friend and future biographer.

Winston Churchill later remarked that it was perhaps no exaggeration to say that 'a quarter of a million persons died of this monkey's bite' – an allusion to Greece's subsequent military campaign in Turkey, which was led by Alexander's father Constantine, who returned to the throne after his son's death. In the lead-up to this latest adventure, fearing Italian encroachment in the region, the Allies had agreed to the landing of Greek troops in Smyrna (now Izmir, on the west coast of Turkey), the wealthiest of Ottoman cities and the embodiment of that empire's reputation for cosmopolitanism and religious tolerance. Smyrna had more Greek inhabitants than Athens and had been a long-cherished objective of Greek nationalists. In June 1920 the Greeks had advanced further into Turkish territory and in August, under the Treaty of Sèvres, they had gained Thrace while their administration of Smyrna and its hinterland had been extended for a further five years – after which the region was to be annexed if the local parliament so decided. Venizelos's supporters boasted of having created a Greece of 'the two continents and of the five seas'.

After King Alexander's death, his younger brother Paul was invited by Venizelos to assume the throne, but he refused on the grounds that his father and elder brother had never renounced their prior rights. Venizelos then called a general election in November 1920 in which he offered the Greek people the freedom to vote for the restoration to the throne of Alexander's father, the exiled King Constantine. To the amazement and dismay of virtually all foreign observers they did so, decisively removing Venizelos and his government from office in the process.

Andrea, by now balding and wearing a monocle, was at last able to return to Greece from Rome with his family. On arrival at Phaleron

Bay he and his brother Christopher were 'borne on the shoulders of the populace, frenzied with joy' all the way to Athens, so Alice recorded, and he was then required to make a speech from the balcony of the royal palace 'to the vast crowds gathered below'.[49] A month later, on 19 December, King Constantine returned from exile to the throne amid much Greek rejoicing – although the Allies refused to recognize him.

Having previously criticized the campaign in Turkey, once in power it soon became clear that the new royalist government now planned to continue it with a spectacular offensive eastwards from occupied Smyrna towards the towns of Kutahya and Eski Shehir in the heart of Anatolia. 'The morale of the army, its spirit and its certainty of success are high,' wrote King Constantine. 'God grant that we may not suffer disappointment! It will be a very hard struggle, which will cost us enormous sacrifices; but what a triumph if we win!'[50] Andrea returned to the Greek army in the rank of major general and after years of depressing inactivity he was raring to go.

THREE

Boy's Own Story

Alice had by this time just become pregnant again. When she told her parents the news three months later, in February, she was reposing at Mon Repos, the Regency villa on the island of Corfu that Andrea had inherited from his father. Originally built for the British high commissioner, the house stood in grounds scented with eucalyptus and cypress, looking out across the Ionian Sea towards Albania and northern Greece.

Unoccupied during their three years away from Greece, it was sparsely furnished and almost entirely lacking in modern comforts – there was still no electricity or gas or running hot water or central heating – however, after the traumas of the past few years, its seclusion made it the ideal place for Alice to await the birth of her fifth child. Andrea had remained in Athens, imploring the military authorities to give him a command in Turkey, but Alice had their four daughters with her, along with a Greek cook and cleaner, an English couple who acted as housekeeper and handyman, and an elderly English nanny, Miss Roose, who had once nursed Alice herself and now ordered in stocks of baby foods and clothes from London[1] in anticipation of the new arrival, which everyone was hoping would be the longed-for boy.[2]

Alice went into labour on 10 June 1921 and was taken by the Corfiot doctor to the dining-room table, which he deemed the most suitable place in the house for this thirty-six-year-old princess to give birth. At 10 a.m., a baby boy was delivered. Registered in nearby Corfu Town under the name of Philippos, he was sixth in line to the Greek throne.

'He is a splendid, healthy child, thank God,' Alice wrote three weeks later to her aunt Onor[3] at Darmstadt. 'I am very well too. It was an easy delivery & I am now enjoying the pleasant fresh sea air on the chaise-longue on the terrace.' In Andrea's absence, she had to answer the 'piles of telegrams' herself, dictating three to four letters a day.[4] The housekeeper Agnes Blower later recalled Philip as 'the sweetest prettiest baby' with a healthy appetite. When he was a little older, she prudently 'put a stop to his being fed on those messy foreign dishes which the Greek cook concocted' and instead made him 'nourishing rice and tapioca puddings and good wholesome Scots porridge'.[5]

Andrea would have to wait several months before he saw his son. Having at last been given the command of a division, he had left Athens for Smyrna the day before Philip's birth, accompanying his brother, King Constantine, who had placed himself at the head of his troops.[6] Cut off from Greece, the once great city of Smyrna had fallen into decline and their arrival served as a symbolic boost to its inhabitants, who cheered as Andrea and Constantine, the first Christian king to set foot on Anatolian soil since the Crusades, marched through the streets. Like the crusading kings, Constantine expressed his desire to lead the Greek army into battle, although in reality he was to be no more than a figurehead.[7]

Andrea wrote despondent letters home about his own ill-equipped and inexperienced troops,[8] although he insisted that the Greeks as a whole would triumph in the end.[9] For a time his optimism seemed justified. With the Greek army sweeping all before it, the town of Kutahya, more than halfway towards Ankara, fell on 17 July. However, at this point the Turkish nationalist leader Mustapha Kemal (later better known as Atatürk) shrewdly withdrew his main army intact.[10] Ankara now 'beckoned like a mirage' for the Greeks[11] and their determination to capture it was to lure them into a treacherous wasteland and fatally overstretch their lines of communication. The consequences of their doomed venture dramatically changed the course of Andrea's and his family's life. But before Alice and the others on Corfu apprehended all this, they received sad news from England.

The summer of 1921 had been a happy one for Alice's sixty-seven-year-old father, Louis, who had been delighted by the birth of his grandson, Philip. In July he had chaired a Royal Navy Club dinner and hundreds of his brother officers had flocked from all corners of the country to what was usually a sparsely attended event. When he stood up to answer the toast there was a roar of cheering that lasted nearly five minutes, which so affected him that he was barely able to murmur his thanks. A fortnight later he learned that the king had promoted him to the rank of Admiral of the Fleet on the retired list, an honour accorded only once before. In late August, Louis went up to Scotland, where his younger son Dickie, then twenty-one, was serving in the battle cruiser *Repulse*. The week he spent on board at the invitation of the captain was his longest spell at sea for many years and he thoroughly enjoyed it. However, during the last three days he suffered from a chill and when he returned to London, his wife Victoria sent him to bed and called a doctor. While she went off to a chemist's to fetch the medicine that the doctor had prescribed, a maidservant came to collect Louis' tea tray, and found him lying serenely back on his pillows with his eyes closed. Victoria returned to be tearfully told. 'Oh dear, Ma'am, the Admiral is dead.'[12]

On hearing the news, Alice took Philip – who had thus been deprived of meeting the only one of his grandfathers still living at the time of his birth – over to England for the funeral. But they were still en route when Louis' coffin was carried in a great military procession from the private chapel at Buckingham Palace to Westminster Abbey, with seven admirals and a major general of the Marines acting as pall-bearers. After the service he was taken by special train to Portsmouth and thence by destroyer to be buried on the Isle of Wight, where Alice and her son caught up with the rest of the family. Their first sight of three-month-old Philip was a welcome distraction for the mourners and Alice's brothers took turns at cradling their future protégé in their arms. When they eventually got back to Corfu, Alice was surprised to find Andrea at home on leave, following an escalating series of disagreements with his commander-in-chief.

The auguries for Andrea had not been good ever since he had arrived at the front. In his account of the Greek campaign in Asia Minor, aptly entitled *Towards Disaster*, he later alleged that the deficiencies of his troops had been part of a republican ploy whereby his division 'would suffer disasters, in which case I would have borne the responsibility'.[13] To begin with his men had acquitted themselves surprisingly well, however, and in early August Andrea had been promoted to take command of the 2nd Army Corps. By this time, though, 'all military prudence had vanished', he wrote, and the 'prevailing idea of GHQ was that the enemy no longer existed, and that an advance to Angora [Ankara] was only a military promenade'.[14] Even after crossing the Anatolian Salt Desert and capturing the strategically important Kale Grotto range, Andrea felt that the victory had been Pyrrhic. They had very little ammunition left and still less food. The horses in his division were dying for lack of fodder and there was no firewood for his soldiers to cook with.[15] Meanwhile the enemy had succeeded in withdrawing without any losses in prisoners or materiel.[16]

The Greek military plans, drawn up by one Major General Stratigos, seemed to Andrea to be wrongheaded and contradictory. On more than one occasion he had deemed it prudent to carry out an alternative manoeuvre to that prescribed by headquarters. Eventually, however, when, during the battle of Sakaria, he refused to obey an order to attack, fearing it would be disastrous, his command-ing officer General Papoulas decided he had had enough: 'The only person competent to judge and decide is myself as Commander-in-Chief,' he barked.[17] When Andrea then asked to be relieved of his command, the staunchly royalist general would not hear of it.[18] However, as rumours about Andrea's supposed 'lack of fighting spirit' began to spread through the Greek ranks, Papoulas eventually granted him three months' leave, whereupon Andrea made his way straight to Corfu.

His spirits were temporarily lifted by seeing his son for the first time, but after two months he gloomily returned to Smyrna. From there, on New Year's Day 1922, he wrote to his friend Ioannis Metaxas bemoaning the impossibility of the exhausted Greeks holding their defensive line. 'Something must be done quickly to remove us from the nightmare of Asia Minor ... we must stop bluffing and face the situation as it really is. Because finally which is better? – to fall into the sea or escape before we are ducked?'[19]

Andrea avoided the denouement he dreaded as he was posted in the spring to Janina in the province of Epirus in north-western Greece. On his way there, he spent Easter on Corfu, where Alice's sister Louise and widowed mother Victoria had been helping to look after the children. The eldest, Margarita and Theodora, aged seven-teen and sixteen, were 'perfectly natural,' wrote Victoria, '& Alice brings them up really well'.[20] She thought that Cecile, nearly eleven, would 'certainly be the prettiest of the lot' while seven-year-old Tiny (Sophie) was 'great fun' and 'the precious Philipp the image of Andrea'.[21]

Aged eleven months, Philip could 'stand up alone now & sits with bare legs on the hard road & crawls on it without minding the stones. He is in fact as advanced & sturdy for his age as all the others were & has the same tow-coloured hair.'[22] Aunt Louise reported that her little nephew 'laughs all day long. I have never seen such a cheerful baby.'[23]

At the beginning of May, Alice accompanied Andrea to Janina and spent a couple of weeks there helping him to set up house.[24] Shortly after returning to Mon Repos, she travelled with her children on to London for the wedding of her younger brother Dickie Mountbatten to Edwina Ashley, granddaughter and heiress of the fabulously wealthy Jewish financier Sir Ernest Cassel. Dickie and Edwina had met in October 1920 at a ball at Claridge's, hosted by Mrs Cornelius Vanderbilt, shortly after Dickie's first love had broken off their engagement. Later that year they had been guests of the Sutherlands at Dunrobin Castle when Dickie received the news that his father had died. Within days Edwina's grandfather was dead, too, and their shared bereavements brought them closer.

When, soon afterwards, Dickie travelled to India in the retinue of his cousin, the Prince of Wales (the future Edward VIII), Edwina joined him at the Viceregal Lodge in Delhi, where their courtship intensified beneath the disapproving gaze of the Viceroy's wife, who, failing to foresee Dickie's glittering future, hoped that Edwina would find someone 'with more of a career before him'. At a St Valentine's Day ball held by their hosts, Dickie asked Edwina to marry him and she said she would.[25]

The magnificent wedding took place on 18 July 1922 at St Margaret's, Westminster, with the Prince of Wales as best man. The congregation included King George V and an assortment of royalty and nobility from across Europe. Philip's sisters were all bridesmaids, although Philip himself was left behind in the nursery of Spencer House.

A month later, on 26 August, they were all still in London when, with a thunderous roar of artillery, Atatürk launched his devastating assault on the overextended Greek front in Turkey. Within a few days, it had turned into a rout, with the bedraggled Greek forces hurriedly withdrawing to the coast. They evacuated Smyrna on 8 September and the ensuing Turkish occupation of the city was accompanied by a massacre of some 30,000 Greek and Armenian Christians, a great fire which only the Turkish and Jewish quarters survived, and the flight of more than a million Greek refugees. It was a national humiliation on an epic scale.

As the remnants of the Greek army regrouped on nearby Aegean islands, a handful of colonels took charge and called for revolutionary action to purge the national shame. Their leader was Nikolaos Plastiras, one of Andrea's least friendly subordinates during the campaign.[26] On 26 September an aeroplane flew over Athens demanding the resignation of the government and the abdication of King Constantine, a demand which Andrea advised his brother to accede to. Constantine was replaced by his eldest son, who ruled briefly and unhappily as King George II.

Andrea had been on leave in Athens as the disaster at Smyrna unfolded, and the British embassy reported that he had done his reputation with the Greek people no good by remaining 'absent from his command in Epirus while such tragic events are happening to his country'.[27] It was subsequently understood that Andrea would now accompany the king into exile, the British ambassador, Francis Lindley, warning that any delay would be 'most dangerous to their lives'.[28] However, when the king and queen slipped away from Greece in a grubby troopship bound for Palermo, Andrea was not with them.[29]

Instead he had returned to Corfu to be with Alice and the children on their return from Dickie's wedding, the revolutionary government having assured him that, providing he resign his commission, he and his family would be safe at Mon Repos. They soon found themselves more or less under house arrest, however, their movements and conversations monitored by police, their post opened and scrutinized. As the hunt for scapegoats for the Greek defeat intensified, they all worried about what might happen to Andrea.[30]

In Athens, the new government set up a commission of inquiry into the disaster in Turkey, presided over by General Theodore

Pangalos, Andrea's old classmate from military college and now a ruthless staff officer ready to throw in his lot with the revolutionaries. The British embassy considered Pangalos 'extraordinarily capable' yet also 'vindictive', 'a bad character', 'a fanatic'.[31] Eight of those held responsible for the military debacle – including two former prime ministers, ministers of the interior, war and foreign affairs and two generals – were soon arrested and on 23 October it was announced that they would be tried by a special court martial.

Three days later one of the revolutionary colonels came to Corfu in a destroyer and took Andrea back to Athens with him so that he could give evidence at the court martial. Andrea was told that he would be away for two days but after two weeks he had still not returned. Alice received a smuggled pencil note from him to say that he was being kept 'strictly alone' and was probably now going to be accused rather than appear as a witness.[32] He was being held under police guard at a private house and was allowed no visitors apart from his valet. All letters and parcels that arrived for him were confiscated and friends later reported that for three weeks 'there was always the disagreeable feeling that death might come suddenly, perhaps in his quarters'.[33] One old lady had sought to console him by sending a *foie gras* in aspic, but even that was hacked to pieces before he was allowed to eat it. His brother Christopher managed to smuggle in a letter on cigarette paper which he hid among other cigarettes in the valet's case, and in reply he received 'a short note, full of courage' describing a conversation Andrea had just had with his former schoolfriend. Out of the blue, Pangalos had asked, 'How many children have you?' When Andrea told him, Pangalos shook his head and sighed, 'Poor things, what a pity they will soon be orphans.'[34]

Meanwhile, the court martial of the other scapegoats began on 13 November 1922 in the parliament building in Athens, which was crammed with spectators, craning to catch a glimpse of the doomed men. They were all charged with high treason, for having 'voluntarily and by design permitted the incursion of foreign troops into the territory of the kingdom'. In view of the very high probability that they would be shot, the British ambassador threatened to break off diplomatic relations if the revolutionaries failed to exercise clemency. At the Lausanne peace conference, the British foreign secretary, Lord Curzon, urged Venizelos, the former Greek prime minister, who was now an envoy for the revolutionary government, to do all he could to avert this 'abominable crime'.[35]

Curzon also had very much in mind the grave danger now facing Andrea, first cousin of George V, and he would almost certainly have been made aware in their meetings of the discomfort that the king still felt over the way he had allowed expediency to prevent him from giving sanctuary to his other first cousin, the tsar, in 1918. While there seems to be no conclusive evidence that George V took the exceptional step of exercising the royal prerogative to order the rescue of Andrea – as has sometimes been suggested – the king nevertheless later expressed the view that his cousin's life had been saved 'through his [George V's] personal action'.[36] Whatever the precise nature of the king's 'personal action', the result seems to have been that one Commander Gerald Talbot was soon on his way to Athens on a mission to reach an accord with the rebels.

This imperturbable forty-year-old naval officer, who had impressed Compton Mackenzie with his 'great domed forehead' and 'the majestic stolidity of the demeanour it crowned', had the crucial advantage of being a good friend of Venizelos.[37] Talbot had got to know him well while posted to Athens between 1917 and 1920, ostensibly as British naval attaché although effectively a spy. Reputed to 'know more about the tortuous channels of Greek politics than most Greek politicians',[38] Talbot was now part of Curzon's delegation at Lausanne, with a specific brief to find out what his wily old Cretan friend was thinking.

When asked by Curzon what position he would be placed in, as the Greek government's representative at Lausanne, if the threatened executions were carried out, Venizelos replied that he had already sent Talbot to Athens 'to urge counsels of moderation on the revolutionary committee'.[39] Talbot, though, was presumably answerable to the Foreign Office rather than Venizelos, and he himself later maintained that he had undertaken his mission on the instructions of Curzon's adviser, Sir William Tyrrell.[40]

Wherever his orders came from, he was quickly on his way. When they got wind of this, the revolutionary government concluded the trial as quickly as possible, motivated partly by fears for their own safety if the defendants were not seen to be adequately punished.[41] The court martial opened on Sunday 26 November and at midnight on the Monday it rose to consider its verdict, which was delivered at 6.30 the next morning. All eight were found guilty of high treason. Six were sentenced to death, two to life imprisonment. By the time Talbot arrived in Athens at noon that day, 28 November, the condemned men were already dead. Their impassivity was 'absolute', according to one account. One former prime minister stared attentively at the firing squad; the former foreign minister put on his monocle after wiping it with his handkerchief; a general stood to attention; none of the six agreed to have his eyes bandaged.[42]

Too late to save these wretched men, Talbot concentrated his efforts on Andrea, whose own court martial was due to begin on 30 November and whose position Lindley, the British ambassador, now deemed 'much more dangerous' since the executions.[43] The ambassador left Athens that evening in accordance with his threat to break off diplomatic relations, but before going he met Talbot and they agreed that a show of force such as the presence of a British man-of-war would do more harm than good. Instead Lindley suggested that Talbot should consider the possibility of bribery.[44]

Talbot promptly went into a series of long and secret meetings with the rebel leaders, Colonel Plastiras and General Pangalos – by now minister of war. On 30 November the British counsellor was able to report that Talbot had obtained a promise from them 'that Prince Andrew will not be executed but allowed to leave the country in the charge of Mr Talbot'. The arrangements agreed upon were that:

Prince will be tried on Saturday and sentenced probably to penal servitude or possibly to death. Plastiras will then grant pardon and hand him over to Mr Talbot for immediate removal with Princess by British warship to Brindisi or to any other port en route to England. British warship must be at Phaleron by midday on Sunday, December 3rd and captain should report immediately to legation for orders, but in view of necessity for utmost secrecy, captain should be given no indication of reason for voyage. This promise has been obtained with greatest difficulty and Talbot is convinced it is essential that above arrangement be strictly adhered to so as to save Prince's life. As success of plan depends upon absolute secrecy of existence of this arrangement, even Prince and Princess cannot be given hint of [what is] coming. Talbot is convinced that he can rely on word given him and I see no other possibility of saving Prince's life.[45]

On 2 December Andrea went on trial in the parliament building, charged with disobeying an order during the battle of Sakaria and of abandoning his post in the face of the enemy. His commander-in-chief General Papoulas and another officer were called to give evidence, the latter asserting that the battle would have been won had the order been obeyed. During the course of the proceedings Andrea wore civilian clothes and one American journalist observed that he thus 'failed to give the impression of a virile general defending his actions during the war'.[46] The court martial found him guilty and he was sentenced to degradation of rank and banishment for life, escaping the death sentence only, as it was stated for public consumption, due to 'extenuating circumstances of lack of experience in commanding a large unit'.[47]

On the afternoon of Sunday 3 December Pangalos quietly escorted Andrea and Talbot to the quay at Phaleron, where Alice was already waiting aboard the British light cruiser *Calypso*. The departure had been arranged in the strictest secrecy, so there were no crowds to send them on their way, although a few boatmen recognized Andrea and greeted him.[48] Taking leave of the British counsellor who accompanied him to the pier, Andrea requested that he 'convey to His Majesty's Government his deep gratitude for their efforts on his behalf'.[49] The same counsellor later drew Curzon's attention to the 'great services' rendered by Talbot. 'I believe that he has succeeded in checking the Greek Government in their course of madness.'[50]

The next day, en route for southern Italy, they called in at Corfu to pick up their four daughters and young son, along with Nanny Roose, two maids and a valet.[51] Philip's youngest sister Sophie recalled their hurried departure as 'a terrible business, absolute chaos', and many years later she could still smell the smoke from the grates in every fireplace at Mon Repos as her elder sisters burned all their letters and documents before gathering together a few possessions and then being bundled into cars and then a small boat to the cruiser, anchored offshore.[52] Philip remembered nothing at all about the whole episode.[53]

FOUR

Family in Flight

During the passage to Brindisi, several officers of *Calypso* vacated their cabins for Andrea and Alice's family, and the crew fashioned a crib from a fruit crate for the eighteen-month-old Philip to sleep in. It was a rough crossing and some of them were sick, yet Andrea nevertheless struck the captain as 'delightful, and so English', and all the family were 'rather amusing about being exiled, for they so frequently are …'[1] Their apparent insouciance belied the strain that they had been under.

On arrival in Italy, they continued by train, with the infant Philip crawling all over the carriage and licking the window panes, oblivious to the drama. At Rome, they thanked the Pope for his help in securing their release.[2] The British ambassador lent them 14,000 lire and private arrangements were made for their entry into France, as they had no passports either.[3] An extra sleeping carriage was then attached to the overnight express to Paris, where they arrived on 8 December and went straight to the hotel apartment of Andrea's brother Christopher. Thereafter a tense Andrea 'denied himself to all callers', instructing the hotel management that no one be permitted even to send up a card.[4]

Talbot had promised Plastiras and Pangalos to take Andrea straight to London – or else more executions were threatened – but there was nervousness in London about members of the Greek royal family suddenly turning up, especially while Parliament was sitting, and the prime minister (Bonar Law) wrote urging George V not to encourage them to settle in England.[5] The king was only too happy to assent to this. As he saw it, he had already saved Andrea's life, and bearing in mind the antagonism directed towards him the last time the Greek princes came to London, during the war, he felt that Andrea and his family should not 'unduly estimate the inconvenience' of remaining in Paris until after Parliament had prorogued.[6,7] While they waited there, Talbot went on ahead to London to make his report, and was promptly knighted by the king for his role in rescuing his cousin.

On 17 December, with Parliament in recess, Andrea and Alice and their family slipped into Britain at Dover, their arrival going unnoticed by the British press. Likewise, when Andrea went to see George V two days later,[8] his visit was not advertised in the Court Circular. Their experiences over the past few months had visibly aged both him and his wife. Photographs from the time show the monocled Andrea looking far in advance of his years, his furrowed brow a manifestation of the ordeals he had been through, while Alice's sister Louise was shocked at how worn out she looked compared to the previous summer, when she had come over for Dickie's wedding.[9]

Still smarting at his treatment, Andrea told an American newspaper that he had

> ample documentary material for an appeal, and when the right time arrives I hope to publish the facts. Then the people of my country can judge for themselves whether I was rightly convicted. At present all the evidence that reaches me is convincing that the Greeks as a whole disagree with what has happened. I believe I can say without egotism that the nation is in sympathy with me, and I am confident that, when hot passion and political prejudice have subsided somewhat and my statement of my case is placed before them, the people will decide in my favour.[10]

However, the American chargé d'affaires in Athens said that it was 'a great mistake' that Andrea and his brothers were 'carrying on a kind of propaganda abroad against the present regime in Greece and abusing them quite openly wherever they go'. Not only did it annoy those in power and make them more hostile to the exiled princes' nephew, the king, but it was also particularly ill timed at a moment when private promises had been extracted through diplomatic channels to respect Andrea's property and possessions on Corfu.[11]

Andrea was still undecided as to where they were going to live, but planned in the meantime to visit his brother Christopher in America.[12] As guests of his brother, he and Alice could at least expect to be well looked after, not least since Christopher's wife, Nancy, was extremely rich, having inherited a fortune from her first husband, the tin-plate tycoon William B. Leeds, when he died in 1908.[13]

After spending Christmas with Victoria at Kensington Palace, Andrea and Alice sailed for New York in January 1923, leaving the two elder girls, Margarita and Theodora, with their grandmother in England[14] and the two younger ones and Philip with their uncle, Prince George of Greece, and his wife, Marie Bonaparte, in Paris. In mid-Atlantic news reached them that Andrea's brother, Constantine, had died in Sicily. The exiled king's death had met with a subdued reaction in Athens. 'A few weeping people were loitering outside the gates of the Palace the next day,' reported the British counsellor, but otherwise, 'tears were shed in private houses.' His name, wrote the counsellor, had been inextricably linked in the minds of the Greek people with the dream of Constantinople, and at one time he had acquired a popularity unattained by any of the other kings of Greece. But parallel to this, 'he was hated by a constantly varying number of his fickle subjects' and 'rightly or wrongly, he was accused of having sympathised entirely with Germany during the war'.[15]

Andrea and Alice arrived in New York dressed in mourning clothes. After they landed, Christopher took them straight up the Woolworth

Building, at that time the tallest structure in the world, for a panoramic view of the city. Andrea bought models of it to give to his children and to the waiting reporters he enthused about New York's skyscrapers. He also pronounced the outfits worn by American women 'very neat indeed'. The reporters were curious about their small entourage – consisting of only a valet and a maid – and when one of them asked Andrea why he did not have a gentleman-in-waiting to attend to social matters, he laughed and replied: 'I'm a democrat!'[16]

Andrea and Alice stayed in America for two months, during which time they travelled by train to Montreal to attend a memorial service for King Constantine,[17] and also spent time in Washington, DC, and at Palm Beach in Florida with Christopher and Nancy – who did not let on that she was dying of cancer – before sailing back across the Atlantic on 20 March. As he prepared to board the Cunard liner *Aquitania*, Andrea told the press that he would not 'risk the chance of being executed' by going back to Greece.[18] The prospect of living in Britain among a suspicious and rather hostile people did not greatly appeal either – George V would presumably have intimated to Andrea the difficulty of their staying there when he saw him in December – and so instead they decided to settle in Paris, which was already home to a cluster of Greek and Russian émigré royalty and would remain their base for the remainder of the decade.

To begin with they were lent a suite of rooms in a *palais* on the edge of the Bois de Boulogne, but Andrea found he could not afford the household that came with it, so they soon moved across the Seine to a small lodge in the garden of 5 rue du Mont-Valérien, in the smart hilltop suburb of St Cloud, six miles west from the city centre and commanding spectacular views eastwards towards Montmartre and the Eiffel Tower. Both properties belonged to Marie Bonaparte, Princess George of Greece, the wife of Andrea's elder brother, an intriguing figure known in the family as 'Big George'. His eventful career had included a spell in the Greek navy – during which he acquired a quarterdeck vocabulary in four languages[19] – and a period as high commissioner of Crete. Earlier he had saved the life of his cousin, the future Tsar Nicholas II, by parrying the sabre of a would-be assassin in Japan.

Marie herself was a restless, exotic woman, destined shortly to become one of Sigmund Freud's leading disciples and benefactors, and thus central to the establishment of psychoanalysis and sexology in France. She was the great-granddaughter of Napoleon's renegade younger brother Lucien, although her great wealth came from her maternal grandfather, François Blanc, who had accumulated a vast fortune from property in Monaco and as owner of the casinos at Monte Carlo and Homburg. She had been in love with the tall and handsome Big George when they married in 1907, she aged twenty-five, he thirty-eight, but she soon became disillusioned on account of his disinterest. For one thing, he refused ever to let her kiss him on the lips and their wedding night, she recorded, culminated in 'a short, brutal gesture' from him and an apology: 'I hate it as much as you do. But we must do it if we want children.'[20] By the time Andrea and his family came to live in the grounds of their large mansion at St Cloud, where Marie had been born, Marie and George were spending much of their time apart, she carrying on with a succession of lovers, most recently the French prime minister, Aristide Briand, he often away in Denmark with his father's younger brother Waldemar, ten years George's senior and the love of his life.

George had formed this unusual attachment after being entrusted to his uncle's care at the age of fourteen, when he enrolled at the naval academy at Copenhagen. Standing on the pier where his parents' ship was preparing to depart, he had suddenly been overwhelmed by feelings of abandonment, feelings which had then been allayed when Waldemar took his hand and walked with him back to his residence. 'From that day,' Big George later told Marie, 'from that moment on, I loved him and I have never had any other friend but him.'[21] On their wedding night in Athens, according to Marie, George came to her room having first visited that of his uncle, and she later wrote to her husband that 'you needed the warmth of his voice, of his hand, and his permission to get up your courage to approach the virgin'.[22] Waldemar accompanied them on the first three days of their honeymoon and George cried as they parted at Bologna. In later years, their children would become so used to seeing their father together with his uncle that they took to calling Waldemar 'Papa Two'.

The house that Marie lent Andrea and his family was pleasantly surrounded by apple trees and gravel paths but had barely enough room for the family and their small staff. (It has since been demolished, along with Marie's mansion, to make way for modern blocks of flats.) Philip's sister Sophie later remembered that 'there were always problems paying the bills', although George and Marie's son Peter was under the impression that his mother 'paid all their expenses for years'.[23]

The extent of the family's penury at this time is unclear. On arrival in London, Andrea told one newspaper that he had managed to bring some money with him from Greece,[24] although Philip later doubted that he had ever received his army pension.[25] He had a small bequest from his brother Constantine, and before that he had inherited an annuity from his father as well as Mon Repos, where the Blowers and their unfriendly dogs had stayed on as caretakers, antagonizing the local population by denying them access to the only good bathing spot near to Corfu Town.

Andrea continually worried about the threat of confiscation hanging over Mon Repos, however, and in May 1923 he wrote to his saviour Gerald Talbot refuting the notion that he was going about criticizing the revolutionary government in Greece. 'Since I am in Paris I see nobody and I go nowhere,' he pleaded. However, he suspected that others wish to believe or rather make others believe the story of my dark doings abroad in order that they may lay hands on my property. I am awfully sorry to bother you with all this, but you are the only one who can help me and I hope you can see your way to letting the Foreign Office in London know that I *flatly* and *absolutely* deny the charge of carrying on *any* kind of propaganda. It would be idiotic of me anyhow to poke spokes in [the British counsellor] Bentinck's wheels while he is trying his level best to save my house in Corfu![26]

On the same day, he shot off another letter to Bentinck in Athens, expressing himself 'astonished' by the American chargé d'affaires' suggestion that he had been spreading propaganda. 'I cannot think where he gets his information from. I went to America to recuperate, and I can assure you that I did what I could to forget politics, revolutions and wars. When I was asked by newspaper men whether I had been imprisoned and in danger of my life, I answered in the affirmative because I could not very well tell them that I had been perfectly free … I'm afraid you will have to take my word for it.'[27]

In the event, Mon Repos never was confiscated, although many Greeks continued to believe that it rightfully belonged to the Greek state, as it had originally been given to 'the King of the Hellenes', and was not transferable.[28] In 1926 Andrea leased the house to Dickie Mountbatten, providing a modest extra source of income, and in 1937, having won a legal case over its ownership, he sold it to his nephew, King George II.[29]

Alice, meanwhile, had inherited a tenth of her father's estate, but this had been substantially depleted by the Bolshevik revolution and the catastrophic inflation and currency devaluation in Germany – which effectively wiped out the proceeds from the recent sale of Heiligenberg Castle, where her father had spent his youth. She also received a small allowance from her brother Georgie. However, by royal standards, the family was certainly not well off.

Andrea was never comfortable about receiving handouts, but he was at least fortunate in having several close relations with considerable sums to spare. After Christopher's wife Nancy died in 1923, the money she left took care of the children's school fees and other items that Andrea could not afford.[30] Then there was Dickie Mountbatten's new wife Edwina, who had inherited almost half of her grandfather Ernest Cassel's estate, conservatively estimated at £6 million, and could thus be justly described as 'The Richest Girl in Britain'.[31] Edwina found subtle ways of helping without offending Andrea's pride – when ordering clothes, she stipulated extra wide hems so that they could be later handed down to her nieces and adjusted if need be[32] – and in 1924 she also took out an insurance policy for her nephew Philip.

According to his cousin Alexandra, as he grew up Philip was himself 'trained to save and economise better than other children, so much so that he even acquired a reputation for being mean'.[33] Alexandra – whose version of events was later disputed by Philip – was the originator of the Dickensian legends portraying the boy in patched clothes, making do with no toys and forlornly staying behind after school on wet days because he had no raincoat.[34]

Neither Alice nor Andrea had paid jobs in Paris. Alice volunteered in a charity boutique in the Faubourg St Honoré, called Hellas, selling traditional Greek tapestries, medallions and honey, with the proceeds going towards helping her fellow less fortunate Greek refugees. The shop did quite well, not least because its customers appreciated the novelty of being served by a princess.[35] Andrea tended to become restless and depressed when he had nothing to do, but, as an émigré Greek prince experienced only in soldiering, he was not especially employable in Paris. Instead he devoted much of his time to writing a personal account of the Greek debacle in Turkey, *Towards Disaster*, which was eventually published in 1930, translated into English from his original Greek manuscript by Alice. Designed to justify his actions at the battle of Sakaria and thereby redeem his reputation, the book's indignant tone served more effectively to show how embittered he remained almost a decade after the events in question.

Otherwise, he took the children for long walks in the Bois de Boulogne or motored into the centre of the city to meet fellow exiles and hear about the latest depressing developments in Athens.[36]

The death of Andrea's brother King Constantine had done little to quell anti-royalist feeling in Greece and in December 1923 Colonel Plastiras succeeded in persuading the cabinet that the continuance of the Glücksburg dynasty was 'a national stigma which should be blotted out'. King George II and his queen, Elizabeth, were thus required to leave the country in a steamer bound for Romania.[37] In February 1924, in the national assembly General Pangalos launched a scathing attack on Andrea, reiterating his responsibility for the defeat at Sakaria and saying he would have been executed but for the intervention of a 'semi-official British envoy' (i.e. Talbot) who had come to Greece with a 'sackful of promises'.[38] On 25 March the revolutionary constituent assembly issued a resolution proclaiming Greece a republic, forbidding the Glücksburgs 'their sojourn in Greece' and authorizing the 'forcible expropriation' of all property belonging to the deposed dynasty.[39] Any hope that Andrea and Alice might be able to return home was effectively extinguished at this point.

Unable to return to Greece, they put down more permanent roots at St Cloud, where another of Andrea's brothers, Nicholas, and his wife Ellen and their three daughters were also now living, as was Margarethe 'Meg' Bourbon, daughter of George and Andrea's uncle Waldemar, and her family. On Sundays Big George and Marie would often hold family lunch parties together but otherwise Marie tended to live with her father in the centre of Paris while pursuing her career as a psychoanalyst. Left on his own next door, Big George would come over each evening, we are told, to say his prayers with Philip and kiss him goodnight.[40]

*　*　*

Many of the earliest recorded glimpses we have of Philip are on holiday. In the summer of 1923, at Arcachon, on the coast south-west of Bordeaux, his aunt Louise found the two-year-old to be 'quite too adorable for words, a perfect pet, so grown up & speaks quite a lot & uses grand phrases. He is the sturdiest little boy I have ever seen & I can't say he is spoilt.'[41]

In the autumn of 1924, aged three and a half, he made his third trip to London, but the first one about which he could later remember anything. He was taken by train and boat from Paris by his nurse, and was met by Alice, who had gone on ahead to visit her mother, at Victoria Station. Philip was 'very pleased and excited', Alice recorded, and 'discovered the first policeman by himself & pointed him out to me. Also the buses were his joy, & I had to take him in one this afternoon. Of course he made straight for the top, but it was too windy and showery to go there, but he was reasonable and went inside ...'[42]

Philip was about four when he and two of his sisters and Miss Roose first went to stay with the Foufounis family, staunch Greek royalists and fellow émigrés from the revolution, who had a farm just outside Marseilles. Philip became great friends with the children, Ria, Ianni and Hélène, and was treated as part of the family. Their newly widowed mother doted on him to such an extent that Hélène recalled becoming 'terrified she would switch her affections completely from me to him ... the little blue-eyed boy with the most fascinating blond-white hair seemed to have everything I lacked. In my mind he became a great danger, and I became ridiculously jealous.'[43] For her own part, Madame Foufounis later recalled: 'He [Philip] was with us so often people used to ask, "Are you his guardian or his governess?" I was neither, yet much more. I loved Philip as my own.'[44]

Philip also spent summer holidays with the Foufounises at Berck Plage near Le Touquet in the Pas-de-Calais, where he and his sisters would go to stay for up to three months at a time. The eldest Foufounis girl, Ria, was in plaster up to her hips for four years as a result of a bad fall, and Hélène later described how Philip would sit for long periods next to her bed talking to her, refusing to be lured away by the other children. One day a spectacularly insensitive guest bought some toys for all the children except Ria, explaining to her that 'you can't play like the others'. The others were stunned by this, none more so than four-year-old Philip, whose eyes 'grew wider and bluer. He looked at Ria, who was trying very hard not to cry, then he ran out of the room and returned ten minutes later with his arms full of his own battered toys, and his new one, and he put them all on Ria's bed saying, "All this is yours!"'[45]

In other respects Philip was a boisterous, mischievous boy. Each day after lunch, he and Ianni would take Persian rugs from the drawing room through the French windows and lay them out in the garden for their siestas. One afternoon the boys disappeared with the rugs and after an hour's search they were found walking from door to door down the road with the carpets on their shoulders, emulating the Arab salesmen they had seen selling oriental wares on the beach.

Their various misdeeds earned them regular spankings from the Foufounises' governess, a fierce – and, incidentally, kleptomaniac – Scottish woman called Miss Macdonald although known to the children as Aunty. Hélène described how on one occasion after Ianni and Philip had broken a large vase, Ianni received his usual beating, whereas Philip vanished. Hélène eventually spotted his frightened blue eyes behind a French window and heard him call out to Miss Roose: 'Nanny, let's clear.' When Aunty heard this, too, she rushed towards Philip, who 'straightened himself, looked her squarely in the eye, and said: "I'll get my spanking from Roosie, thank you". And he did.[46]

Other holidays were spent at Panker, the Landgrave of Hesse's summer house on the Baltic coast, with Philip's Prussian aunt, Sophie, Constantine's widow, and a collection of royal cousins, including the deceased King Alexander's young daughter Alexandra, whose first memory of Philip was as

> a tiny boy with his shrimping net, running eagerly, far ahead of me, over a white expanse of sand towards the sea, [then] splashing merrily in the water, refusing to leave it, running and eluding every attempt to capture him. Long after I have returned to my nannie and the waiting towel, Philip is still there until he is finally caught and dragged out forcibly, blue with cold, yelling protests through chattering teeth.[47]

Like the Foufounises at Villa Georges, they kept pigs at Panker, and Philip loved feeding them, although he later professed to have 'absolutely no recollection' of an occasion recounted by Alexandra in which he was said to have released the pigs from their sties and herded them up to the lawn where they created havoc with the adults' tea.[48]

About an hour away from Panker, his great-aunt Irene (Victoria's sister) and her husband Prince Henry had their country property, Hemmelmark, where Philip jumped off a hay wagon and broke a front tooth. 'Of course he was a great show-off,' his sisters Margarita and Sophie recalled. 'He would always stand on his head when visitors came.'[49] By their account, as he grew older, he also became 'very pugnacious and the other children were scared to death of him'.[50]

Philip and his sisters also went to stay with their cousin, Queen Helen of Romania (daughter of their uncle King Constantine of Greece and deserted wife of King Carol), and her son Michael, at the dilapidated Cotroceni Palace near Bucharest, repairing in the heat of high summer either to their castle at Sinaia high up in the Carpathian Mountains or to the newly built Mamaia Palace at the mouth of the Danube on the Black Sea, which had quickly become the centre of a thriving resort, where Philip first experienced pony riding on the beach. Michael, a more taciturn child, was a few months younger. In 1927, at the age of five, on the death of his grandfather Ferdinand, he was proclaimed King of Romania under a regency. When he asked his mother the next day why people were calling him 'Your Majesty', she thought it best to tell him, 'It's just another nickname, dear.'[51] Philip and his two elder sisters, Theodora and Margarita, stayed at Mamaia the next year[52] but Michael's new status seemed to make no difference to the children's play 'except that there were always many more people about', wrote Alexandra, and the three of them never quite seemed able to wander off by themselves. Michael, though, 'fully realised he was King and early adopted courtly little ways', once telling Alexandra's mother: 'I am most pleased with Sandra. She suits me very well.'[53]

The anecdotal evidence gives the impression that Philip saw little of his own parents in the course of his nomadic wanderings as a small child. While Victoria Milford Haven's biographer asserts that Alice often travelled about with him and enjoyed 'showing him things and watching his alert intelligence growing',[54] her nerves had been badly strained by all the anxieties surrounding the family's exile from Greece, and because of this the children were regularly packed off to friends and relations for long stints without their parents, while the family home at St Cloud was shut up. 'Philip goes to Adsdean [Dickie and Edwina's country home],' wrote Victoria to her friend Nona Kerr in June 1926, 'where they can keep him until autumn if desired, only for Goodwood week his room will be needed for guests, so if you [Nona] still would like & could have him & Roose that would be the time for his visit to you.'[55] Philip went regularly to Nona Kerr over the years and he took to calling her 'Mrs Good … because she is good and that is the right name'.[56]

There are several indications that from an early stage in their new life in Paris, all was not well between Alice and Andrea. Prominent among them is the story of Alice's infatuation with an unnamed, married Englishman, whom she fell in love with in 1925 when she was forty and Philip four. According to the account given to Alice's doctor by her lady-in-waiting, it never amounted to an actual affair, and

Alice eventually gave up, consoling herself that they would 'meet again in another world'. Her biographer suggests that in any case Alice's strictly conventional background and 'high moral principles' would have prevented anything improper from happening, pointing out that 'nothing in her life was flighty or flippant'.[57] However, the mere fact of this infatuation suggests that she and Andrea had already begun to grow apart.

In 1927, aged six, Philip started at a progressive American kindergarten housed in Jules Verne's former home – a rambling old St Cloud mansion (also since demolished) at 7 Avenue Eugenie just above the Seine, opposite the western end of the Bois de Boulogne, and shaded by the large trees which gave the school its name, the Elms.[58] His uncle Christopher paid the fees.[59]

The accounts we have of Philip's time at the school all emerged after his engagement to Princess Elizabeth and thus they may have been embroidered with the benefit of hindsight. One of his teachers, though, remembered being struck by the young prince's precocious sense of responsibility.[60] Having walked to school with his nanny, she recalled, he usually arrived there half an hour early, and he would fill in the time cleaning blackboards, filling inkwells, straightening the classroom furniture, picking up waste paper and watering the plants. Another tale was later told how, on his first day, some of the other boys had demanded that Philip 'fight it out' with another new boy. After a brief scuffle, he whispered to his opponent, 'Are you having fun?' When the other boy admitted he wasn't, Philip said 'Let's quit', which they did.[61]

By all accounts, he settled in quickly, although he was teased for having no last name. Asked to introduce himself in class he insisted at first that he was 'just Philip', before eventually awkwardly admitting that he was 'Philip of Greece'.[62] The school's founder and headmaster, a thirty-one-year-old native of New England, Donald MacJannet, known to the boys as 'Mr Mac', later recalled the young prince as exuberant and sometimes rowdy yet at the same time polite and disciplined: he regularly repeated the mantra learned from his elder sisters: 'You shouldn't slam doors or shout loud'. He 'wanted to learn to do everything', including waiting at table,[63] his mother having taught him that 'a gentleman does not allow a woman to wait on him'.[64] He also appeared to take for granted his mother's insistence on hard work: Alice made him do extra Greek prep three evenings a week, and asked the school to set him a daily exercise for the holidays.

When Philip first arrived at the Elms, Alice had told the headmaster that her son had 'plenty of originality and spontaneity' and suggested that he be encouraged to work off his energy playing games and learning 'Anglo-Saxon ideas of courage, fair play and resistance'. She said she envisaged him ending up in an English-speaking country, perhaps America, so she wanted him to learn good English. Philip later recalled that at that time 'We spoke English at home ... but then the conversation would go into French. Then it went into German on occasion ... If you couldn't think of a word in one language, you tended to go off in another.' Alice also wanted him to 'develop English characteristics', although she was thwarted in this for the time being.[65] For one thing, Philip's two best friends at the school were Chinese – Wellington and Freeman Koo, sons of the prominent diplomat V. K. Wellington Koo, then ambassador to Paris, later foreign secretary, acting premier, interim president of China and ultimately judge at the International Court at The Hague. Their mother, Hui-Lan Koo, was one of the forty-two acknowledged children of the sugar king Oei Tiong Ham and much admired in 1920s Parisian society for her adaptations of traditional Manchu fashion, which she wore with lace trousers and jade necklaces.

The two Koo boys had each been robustly introduced to Philip at the Elms as 'Ching Ching Chinaman'[66] but they proved well up to looking after themselves, and their knowledge of jiu-jitsu came in useful whenever Philip found himself outnumbered in playground tussles. He often spent the weekend at the Koos' residence in Paris, where, invariably spurred on by Philip, the boys all ran steeplechases and played other raucous games amid the Chinese embassy's precious artefacts. The ambassador's wife admitted to Alice that however much they enjoyed having her son to stay, they were always a little relieved when the time came for him to go and nothing had been broken.[67]

Other friends at the Elms during his time included his Franco-Danish cousins Jacques and Anne Bourbon, who later married King Michael of Romania. But the majority of his classmates were American and Philip picked up something of their drawl and learned to play baseball before he played cricket. He coveted anything that came from the New York department store Macy's and was only too pleased to swap a gold bibelot given to him by George V for a state-of-the-art three-colour pencil belonging to another boy.[68]

FIVE

Orphan Child

However much Philip enjoyed his first school, his restless energy still made him a handful for his parents when he came home each afternoon. Another option would have been for him to board at the Elms, but Alice told him they could not afford the fees.[1] She was nevertheless determined that her son remain active and stimulated, and she wrote to MacJannet at the start of the autumn term of that year requesting that he form a Cub Scout group. Alice explained to the headmaster that Philip was 'too young to be a scout and his character and clever fingers will fit him well to be a cub, and the training would have such an excellent influence on him, in turning his great vitality to good use'. She would be 'infinitely grateful' if he could manage it as soon as possible.[2]

Alice's letter has a slightly desperate tone, but she was not herself at the time. She was, as it soon became clear, on the verge of a serious nervous breakdown. The rapid deterioration in her mental state overshadowed not only Philip's last year at the Elms but also the remainder of his early life. He has since always robustly played down the ramifications of his mother's illness; however it can scarcely have failed to have had an effect on him.

Alice's illness has often been described as a 'religious crisis', and indeed the most obvious sign of her decline was her increasingly eccentric religious fervour, and her attendant interest in spiritualism and the supernatural. As long ago as 1912 she had performed auto-matic writing at Tatoï with Andrea's brother Christopher, placing a finger on a glass and then watching as it slid about the table, spelling out a message from the spirit world. Her mother later described how Alice read extensively about this then fashionable activity and prac-tised it whenever she had an important decision to make. She grew more and more superstitious and was forever dealing herself cards to obtain messages.[3] The murders of her aunts in Russia and the trauma of the family's flight from Greece further steered her towards the spir-itual, as apparently did her hopeless love for the mysterious Englishman in 1925, after which her biographer concludes that she turned to religion as a 'safe outlet' for her repressed feelings of unful-filled desire.[4]

Another equally plausible suggestion is that Alice suffered from manic depression – or bipolar disorder.[5] Besides her various spiritual interests, her wartime nursing activities had also been pursued with a fairly manic energy. As was her chimerical scheme to have Andrea installed as President of Greece – a plan hatched in 1927 after a chance encounter with an American banker, who persuaded her that Andrea's presidency would not only suit moderate republicans and royalists, but would also boost the chances of Greece obtaining a large loan from the League of Nations. To this end, Alice dashed about canvassing politicians and diplomats, and even arranged an audience at Buckingham Palace with George V, who was horrified by her idea and promptly scotched it, observing tersely that 'Ladies get carried away', and that it would be 'most unwise for Prince A to go near Greece'.[6]

In October 1928, a fortnight after she and Andrea celebrated their silver wedding anniversary at St Cloud, Alice quietly converted to the Greek Orthodox faith, a move that did not greatly alarm the Anglican members of her family, given that this was the church into which her husband and her children had been baptized. But the next spring,

1929, her behaviour grew more peculiar. She took to lying on the floor in order to develop 'the power conveyed to her from above'[7] and became convinced that she had acquired the power of healing with her hands, which she deployed to no obvious ill effect on Nanny Roose's rheumatism and later at a small clinic. She could stop her thoughts like a Buddhist, she said, and was getting messages about potential husbands for her daughters, whose marriage prospects were beginning to preoccupy her. By November she was no longer speaking to her family.[8]

Realizing that she was ill, she took herself off with a maid to spend Christmas in a hotel at Grasse on the French Riviera, leaving Andrea, Philip and the girls to fend for themselves at St Cloud. She suffered from terrible headaches, barely ate and spent the best part of Christmas Day in a hot bath. Much of the time she felt thoroughly worn out and depressed; at other moments she was inappropriately elated and talkative. When she eventually came home, she declared herself a saint and 'the bride of Christ'. She lay about the house with a seraphic smile and affected to banish evil influences with a sacred object she carried about with her.[9]

When her mother Victoria came over to visit in January 1930, she told her lady-in-waiting, Nona Kerr, that Alice was 'in a quite abnormal state mentally & bodily', and looking 'frail & exhausted'. She had had visions of Christ and had told Andrea's cousin Meg Bourbon that within a few weeks she would have a message to deliver to the world. 'She wanders praying about the house at times,' wrote Victoria. 'She told Meg she was in bliss & to me too she said she is happy. I think she has anaemia of the brain from too much contemplation & starvation & is in a critical state.'[10]

Among those to whom the family turned for advice was Andrea's sister-in-law, Marie Bonaparte, who had recently undergone psychoanalysis with Sigmund Freud with the object of practising herself. She had also been helping to finance a new sanatorium at Tegel, on the outskirts of Berlin, established by a fellow Freudian, Dr Ernst Simmel. Tegel was the first clinic in the world designed to use psychoanalysis to treat patients and it was there that Marie recommended that Alice should go.

After several sessions, Simmel diagnosed Alice as 'paranoid schizophrenic' and suffering from a 'neurotic-pre-psychotic libidinous condition'. During their discussions, she said that she believed that she was the only woman on earth, was married to Christ and 'physically involved' through him with other great religious leaders such as Buddha. Simmel consulted his friend Freud, who proposed 'an exposure of the gonads to X-rays, in order to accelerate the menopause' – the idea being that this would help to calm her down and subdue her libido. It is unclear whether or not she was ever consulted about this procedure, but it was carried out nevertheless. Shortly afterwards she began to feel better.[11]

As she felt stronger so she also began to feel bored, restless and homesick. At the beginning of April she discharged herself and went back to Andrea and the family at St Cloud. 'I found everybody looking very well indeed and the season far more advanced than in Berlin,' she wrote to her daughter Cecile. 'The fruit trees are blossoming & the leaves beginning to come out, & the air is very mild & I must say I am truly delighted to be back after 8 weeks absence.' She went on to say how nice it was of uncle Ernie 'to invite us all for Easter & we are looking forward to it so much – I fancy Philip & I will come by train & the others by car, Fondest love & au revoir soon, your ever loving Mama.'[12] Up the side of the letter she had scrawled 'God Bless You' and in the top left-hand corner she had drawn a cross.

However, it was soon clear to her family that she was little better than before she went away. In desperation, Andrea went to London and with Victoria saw two more doctors, who both advised that she should be interned in a secure sanatorium. 'Andrea & I feel that it is the only right thing to do,' Victoria told Nona Kerr, 'both for Alice and her family. How hard it has been to come to this decision & what we feel about it you know. This Easter will be a miserable one.'[13]

Victoria's brother Ernie, the Grand Duke of Hesse, had asked the whole family to the Neue Palais at Darmstadt for Easter. However, what should have been a happy few weeks' holiday was, as Victoria had foreseen, overshadowed by their anxiety about Alice.

Soon after reaching Darmstadt, Victoria went to Heidelberg, the nearby picturesque university town, to consult a noted expert on insanity, Karl Wilmanns, about a suitable sanatorium for her daughter. Wilmanns recommended the Bellevue private clinic at Kreuzlingen on the south-western shore of Lake Constance, run by a pioneer in the field of existential psychology, Dr Ludwig Binswanger, who had studied under both Jung and Freud. He was especially interested in subjects with unusual creative ability – his patients included the expressionist painter Ernst Ludwig Kirchner and the Russian dancer Nijinski, who was being treating at Bellevue for schizophrenia at that time.

Victoria was reassured by the fact that the proposed clinic lay 'in a fine park of its own & has 3 separate establishments for closely interned patients, semi-interned & a so-called free section where the patients can go into town etc with a nurse. The patients are all higher class, educated people, so if Alice likes to make the acquaintance of any of them, she will find suitable companionship …' Yet still she agonized over whether this was the right place for her daughter, who had arrived in Darmstadt looking physically healthier than she had been for some time and had behaved in many respects perfectly normally. 'When she is enjoying being amongst us, I feel a brute,' wrote Victoria to Nona Kerr, '& then again come moments when I clearly realize the need of her going away.'[14]

She wrestled with her dilemma for nearly three weeks before finally asking Professor Wilmanns to come and take Alice away. When he arrived at the Neue Palais, Alice was alone. Andrea and two of the girls had already left Darmstadt and Victoria had made sure to take all those who remained – Philip, Theodora, Cecile, Ernie and Onor – out for the day. Alice at first greeted Wilmanns warmly, but the atmosphere changed as soon as he told her what he had come for. When she tried to escape he restrained her and injected her with morphium-scopolamine to sedate her. She was then bundled into a car and driven south for several hours to Lake Constance, arriving at the Bellevue sanatorium at eleven o'clock that night.[15]

Alice's committal on 2 May 1930 marked the end of their family life, although the children would not have realized this when they arrived back that evening to find their mother gone. Alice and Andrea's marriage had been under strain for several years but it effectively finished at this point. They hardly saw each other from then on and, although they would never divorce, Andrea 'relinquished his role as husband', as Hugo Vickers puts it.[16] He liberated himself from many of his responsibilities as father, too, shutting up their family home at St Cloud and thereafter leading a rather aimless life, drifting between Paris, Monte Carlo and Germany, interspersed with sporadic interventions in Greek affairs. He saw Philip now and again during the school holidays, but otherwise left him in the care of Alice's family, the Milford Havens and Mountbattens.

The girls were by this time aged between sixteen and twenty-five, and they would all be married within eighteen months, so the disappearance of both their parents was of far less consequence for them than it was for their eight-year-old brother. Up until now, Philip had been doted on by both mother and father, to the extent that the girls had often felt the urge to squash their overindulged little brother.[17] Alice had given him much of her attention, knitting him woollen jumpers, sleeping with him in the nursery when his nanny was away and telling another of his nursemaids in 1928 that 'Philip is always very good with me'.[18] Andrea, too, appeared to adore his only son, as the girls were made only too aware by the gales of laughter whenever they played together.[19]

In those days, fathers of Andrea's background had a rather more hands-off approach to child rearing than they do today, when more is expected of both parents, even those from the upper classes. But even so, his virtual abandonment of his young son at this critical time is surprising. The most likely explanation seems to be that he had been so traumatized by his treatment at the hands of the Greek revolutionaries and depressed by his subsequent exile that he did not feel up to the task of raising Philip on his own after this latest crisis. He may also have felt, not unreasonably, that his son might be better off with Alice's family in England than he would be with his father in his jaded frame of mind.

In recent years, as Alice's mental health had begun to give cause for concern, her mother Victoria had already started to arrange many of the practical aspects of her grandson's upbringing, such as where he was to stay at various stages during the school holidays. After the closure of the family home in 1930, Philip went to stay for a time with his grandmother at her apartment in Kensington Palace. However, another of the residents there, Philip's seventy-three-year-old great-aunt, Princess Beatrice, Queen Victoria's youngest daughter, was far from thrilled about the new arrival, muttering that the palace was not the right place for the 'younger generation'.[20] For this reason it was soon decided that Alice's elder brother, Georgie, who had succeeded his father as the second Marquess of Milford Haven, should also take Philip in.

Georgie's younger brother Dickie Mountbatten is more often thought of as Philip's surrogate father, but although Philip would occasionally go and stay with him and Edwina at Brook House in London and Adsdean in Hampshire when he was young, it was only later that Dickie took on that role. From when Philip was nine until he was sixteen, it was Georgie who acted as the boy's guardian, officially and in practice, turning up *in loco parentis* at school prize-givings and sports days, and providing a home for him during the shorter school holidays at Lynden Manor, the Milford Havens' house on the Thames at Holyport, between Windsor and Maidenhead.

A relatively obscure figure in all published accounts of the Mountbatten family, in terms of sheer intelligence and ability and charm Georgie was as remarkable as any of them. From the age of ten he had had a workshop in his father's castle at Heiligenberg, with lathes and a forge and foundry; by fifteen he was designing and constructing his own working models of steam engines – he later laid out a spectacular model railway at Lynden. He was said to solve problems of higher calculus 'for relaxation',[21] and at Dartmouth the second master pronounced him the cleverest and at the same time the laziest cadet he had taught. As a young naval officer he was supremely inventive, although his inventions were, as Philip Ziegler puts it, 'as likely to be directed to the comforts available in his cabin as to the wider interests of the Royal Navy'.[22] Among his creations was a system of fans, radiators and thermostats for air-conditioning his quarters when afloat, and a device controlled by an alarm clock for making his early morning tea, twenty years before any such contrivance appeared on the market. His enthusiasm helped fire his nephew's budding interest in invention and design, and when Philip grew up he, too, would be forever in search of the latest gadgets.

Georgie's technical expertise was allied to great resourcefulness and skills of organization, and those who knew him best confidently predicted a brilliant career, and that he would, like his father, eventually succeed to the position of First Sea Lord. However, he did not have the obsessive ambition of his more dazzling younger brother, nor such a rich wife. So in the late 1920s, with German inflation having more or less wiped out his inheritance, and the Great Depression threatening everything else, he left the Royal Navy in order to make some much-needed money in business. After a spell at a brokerage house on Wall Street, he went on to become chairman of the British Sperry Gyroscope Company, and a director of Electrolux (of which his brother-in-law, Harold Wernher, was chairman), Marks & Spencer and various other companies.[23]

His business career was partly necessitated by the extravagance of his wife Nada, who once ordered a tub of champagne to soothe her feet after winning a Charleston contest in Cannes, whereupon her hostess was presented with a huge bill which read 'Champagne for Marchioness of Milford Haven's feet'.[24] Nada was the great-grand-daughter of the Russian poet Alexander Pushkin (after whose mother she was named), and daughter of Grand Duke Michael Mikailovich, who had been banished from Russia on account of his morganatic marriage and thereafter divided his time between the stately Kenwood House on Hampstead Heath, from where Nada was married,[25] and a lavish villa at Cannes, where he was remembered for distributing 'lovely Fabergé things' and for introducing Edward VII to Alice Keppel, his mistress-to-be. To begin with he could afford to give his daughters substantial allowances – £2,000 a year, with extra for jewellery and travel expenses – although the flow of funds dried up with the Russian Revolution.

Dark and attractive, Nada was an engaging character, outgoing, rebellious, full of life and verve. Her niece Myra Butter remembers her as 'off the wall, the best fun, completely different, very bohemian'.[26] Even her grandchildren occasionally found her too boisterous, such as when she was 'squirting you with the garden hose or pouring a night pot full of water on people out of the window'.[27] Among other attributes, she also gained a reputation for her fluid sexuality: her girlfriends included Gloria Morgan Vanderbilt, the American society beauty who regularly stayed at Lynden while Philip was there.[28] Nada and Georgie were nonetheless devoted to one another, both of them by nature adventurous and risqué, and both dedicated to the good life. They smoked cigars together after dinner, took their son David, who was two years older than Philip and became a great friend, to a brothel in Paris when he was seventeen to round off his education and amassed one of the largest collections of pornographic books in private hands – an extensive library of 'blue' literature, photograph albums and marked catalogues for such enticing titles as *Lady Gay: Sparkling Tales of Fun and Flagellation* and *Raped on the Railway* – 'a true story of a lady who was first ravished and then flagellated on the Scotch express'.[29]

The Milford Haven ménage was completed by their mentally retarded daughter, Tatiana, born in 1917, for whom they later retained an elderly woman to act as her companion.[30] There were also extended visits from Nada's younger brother, Count Michael 'Boy' de Torby, who had great charm and painted well, often on rice paper or silk, but whose bipolar illness occasionally rendered him 'decidedly odd, mooching about'. He complained of all the 'terrible pills fighting inside me' and when he felt his depression returning he would say 'I'm afraid I must go back', and have to be rushed to Roehampton.[31] All in all, Lynden Manor was unlike any home that Philip had previously experienced.

Alice was visited from time to time at Bellevue by various members of the family and at other times they kept in touch by letter. Three weeks after her admission, she learned that Philip would be going to prep school at Cheam in England that autumn and, according to Cecile, although initially nervous, he was now 'thrilled' at the prospect.[32] In the meantime, Philip was to spend his ninth birthday with the Hessian side of his family at Wolfsgarten, which had originally been built as their hunting lodge yet was nevertheless equivalent in size and layout to that of an average Oxford college. He relished the more relaxed and jollier atmosphere he encountered, in contrast to the regime of his grandmother Victoria, who tended to be quite stern with him.[33]

On this occasion the family was gathering to celebrate the engage-ments of the younger two of Philip's sisters. The youngest, Sophie, a very pretty girl, was not yet sixteen when she agreed to marry Christoph of Hesse, her handsome second cousin once removed, with whom she had fallen in love while staying with her great-aunt Irene at Hemmelmark on the Baltic. Thirteen years Sophie's senior, 'Chri' was charming, extroverted and amusing. He had studied agriculture and spent the so-called 'golden years' of the Weimar Republic floating between various family schlosses, lending a languid hand to the running of their estates. He was a keen horseman and talented dres-sage rider, competing across Europe, but above all he was obsessed with flying and with motorcycles and cars – his passion was such that he would often sleep in a new car for the first few days after acquiring it. Recently laid off from a job in a factory producing engines, he was now reluctantly selling insurance in Berlin. While the marriage offered Sophie a welcome sanctuary after the break-up of her own family, for Christoph it represented a safe harbour after a series of stormy love affairs during the 1920s.[34] There was nothing arranged about their union and it proved to be one of lasting mutual devotion, undimin-ished by his subsequent staunch attachment to the National Socialist cause.

In 1939, shortly after reporting for active service with the Luftwaffe, he would write to tell her:

I miss you and long for you. It is simply terrible. I am so depressed and so miserable that I shall be pleased to get away from this house [their Berlin-Dahlem home] in which we have spent those lovely happy years together and enjoyed having our little Poonsies [their children]. Oh darling if only you were here! When I enter the house I think how often the door used to open like with magic and then you angel were there waiting for me smiling or laughing and giving me a thrill of happiness I feel a lump in my throat to think of it. I love you, love you,

love you, my angel, and you mean everything to me … lovingly as your
old adoring Peech [Christoph].[35]

Philip came to know Christoph well while visiting Sophie during
holidays in Germany before the war and years later described him as
'a very gentle person, interestingly enough [in view of his politics],
and very balanced actually. He was kind and had a good sense of
humour. So he actually was the complete opposite of what you'd
expect, I suppose.'[36]

Sophie's eighteen-year-old sister, Cecile, meanwhile, had been
snapped up by another cousin, Grand Duke Ernie's twenty-three-
year-old son and heir, George Donatus of Hesse, known in the family
as 'Don', like Christoph an avid sportsman and a fan of fast cars and
aeroplanes. Though in Alice's estimation 'such a sensible, dear boy',[37]
he, too, was to join the Nazi party, in 1937, along with Cecile.

Alice felt understandably wretched at being excluded from all the
celebrations and when she received flowers from her daughters as a
token of their engagements she spent much of the day crying. Five
days after Philip's birthday, Cecile wrote to her from a 'terribly hot'
Wolfsgarten, reporting that they had been bathing 'everyday at least
twice including Philipp [she used the German spelling of his name]'.
Andrea had arrived looking 'rather tired' and in due course had left
for Marienbad, the spa town in Bohemia, 'already much fatter and
browner'. Philip was

quite blissful … U Ernie and A Onor gave him a new bicycle for his
birthday and he rushes about on it all day. In the evening from the
moment he has finished his bath till he goes to bed he plays his beloved
gramophone which you gave him. He got really lovely presents this
year. Dolla and Tiny gave him pen-knives, and Don a big coloured ball
for the swimming pool, and I gave him a rug to lie about on in the
garden. He is very good and does just what A. Onor tells him.[38]

In another letter, Cecile described how 'Philipp appeared in his uniform and looked adorable, everybody was delighted, especially A Sophie who worships him'.[39]

Alice was especially grateful to Cecile for describing her son's birthday, 'particularly thoughtful of you … as no one else has done so',[40] and she remained eager for news of him, urging him the next month to 'write me a postcard and tell me what you are doing'.[41] Around the same time Philip's former nanny, Nana Bell, herself wrote to Philip: 'I know how difficult it is to write letters on holiday [but] you must write to your dear Mama often.'[42]

Philip was taken to see his mother a handful of times over the next two years, and otherwise received only occasional letters and cards from her. For the five years after that, from the summer of 1932 until the spring of 1937, he neither saw nor heard from her at all. He was subsequently at pains not to overstate the effect of all this. 'It's simply what happened,' he told one biographer. 'The family broke up. My mother was ill, my sisters were married, my father was in the South of France. I just had to get on with it. You do. One does.'[43] Yet while he was never one to make a meal of the various vicissitudes that came his way in life, being separated from his mother for five years at such a critical stage of his upbringing must have left its mark on him. It is certainly true that he grew extremely fond of his grandmother, and of Georgie and Nada, and was deeply appreciative of the homes that they provided for him, but at the same time they could never fully make up for the one he had lost. When, years later, an interviewer asked him what language he spoke at home, his immediate retort was, 'What do you mean, "at home"?'[44]

As far as Philip's future wellbeing was concerned, it was fortunate that he had previously felt loved by both his parents and his nanny, and that he was thus a self-assured and happy child. According to the child psychologist Oliver James, this would have protected him to some degree from the psychological fallout of his mother's breakdown and his father's subsequent absence. 'It would mean there was a kernel there, the basis for him to have been able to develop a more intimate and decent personality than is generally believed.' However, James would still be inclined to question

whether having been part of a close family and having the whole thing smashed to pieces might have rather diminished his capacity to have faith in intimacy or love or closeness. The impact of having a mother go mad on you is to make you scared and also possibly fearful that the same thing is going to happen to you. If you throw in the disappearance of his father and being packed off to boarding school, which were pretty scary places in those days, you have a triple whammy, and there's a fairly high probability that he would have developed what psychologists call a highly defended personality. That's to say he doesn't want to know about his emotions or other people's emotions and he's basically in survival mode – either he develops a pretty hard-nosed approach to life or he cracks up. He has to develop a false self to hide behind in order to avoid people knowing what he's really feeling, and for himself, as he doesn't want to know what he's really feeling either. Obviously he was very handsome and no doubt he developed a very charming and attractive persona because he was probably all too aware that was necessary. But people like that, unless they're very lucky, live in isolation all their lives although they don't even know they're doing it.[45]

Philip would perhaps take issue with this analysis. However, in years to come, deprived of the constant loving attention of his parents, his emotional reserve would become as noticeable to friends as his bluff, controlled, no-nonsense exterior. His tendency to hide his feelings also meant that his occasional bouts of sensitivity and touchiness could take even those who knew him well by surprise.

SIX

Prep School Days

Boarding school offered one solution to the sudden dissolution of Philip's family life. Andrea had wanted to send his son to school in England, hoping that he would receive a better education there than the harsh Greek military one he had experienced, but the actual choice of Cheam, England's oldest prep school, was made by Philip's new guardian, Georgie Milford Haven, whose father Louis had been sufficiently impressed by the manners of two Cheam old boys serving with him in the navy to send Georgie there, although not his younger son Dickie.

Georgie had in turn sent his son David to Cheam, and when Philip arrived his cousin was two years above. Listed on the register under his courtesy title, Earl of Medina, David was the only titled boy at the school at that time, although generations of nobility had attended the school since its foundation in 1645. One mid-nineteenth-century headmaster, Robert Tabor, had even gone to the trouble of devising graded modes of address for his various charges: when speaking to a peer, he would begin 'my darling child'; with the son of a peer, it was 'my dear child'; and with a commoner simply 'my child'.[1] The more illustrious Cheam old boys included one prime minister, Henry Addington, one speaker of the House of Commons, two viceroys of India and Lord Randolph Churchill, the father of Winston, who was 'most kindly treated and quite contented' at the school, according to his son.[2]

Perhaps not surprisingly, no great fuss seems to have been made of either of the royal children at the school while Philip was there, although, if anything, more was made of David Medina, as being more obviously one of the English royal family and aristocracy, whereas Philip was deemed to be foreign and therefore somehow slightly inferior.

Philip's time there coincided with the school's last years at Tabor Court in the Surrey village of Cheam, before the railway station and encroaching urbanization prompted the headmaster to sell up and move his school to its present site in the midst of the Berkshire countryside. His headmaster was Harold Taylor, a cheerful clergyman with a deep-seated affection for his boys. Forty when Philip arrived, Taylor was a product of Marlborough and Trinity College, Cambridge, a fine all-round athlete – albeit a heavy smoker – powerful swimmer and fearless horseman. He had served as a chaplain during the war in France, returning with shell shock and a military OBE. The boys called him by his initials, pronounced *HMS T* in line with the school's strong naval tradition and his rolling gait which was said by some to resemble that of a ship in heavy seas.[3]

After buying Cheam in 1921, Taylor and his vibrant wife Violet had insufficient funds to improve the spartan living conditions – prison-style beds, communal baths, 'dog baskets' to store the boys' clothes – but they set about making it a more humane place in other ways. Boys with experience of the previous regime of Arthur Tabor were soon remarking on the 'incredible change to friendliness' after the Taylors took over. Philip himself retained fond memories of such school characters as Jane, the warm-hearted housemaid who scrubbed the boys' backs at bathtime and made sure that their ears were clean; Major C. H. M. 'Chump' Pearson, Taylor's unofficial deputy who 'was far from scrupulous about his dress and habits' and often taught lying back on the radiator with his feet on his desk; and W. J. 'Molly' Malden, the most popular of the masters, partly on account of his all-round athletic prowess, partly because he drove fast cars and flew a Puss Moth.[4]

Taylor himself took games very seriously, but, with only seventy boys to choose from, Cheam struggled to compete against other schools. On the bus home from away matches the mood was often sombre as the headmaster brooded over yet another heavy defeat.[5] He had more success organizing non-sporting exercises for the whole school, such as pumping out the school swimming pool with an old manual fire-engine pump or beating for pheasants in the woods at Headley.[6]

For all his bonhomie, Taylor was also a staunch disciplinarian, declaring sloth, dirtiness and untruth to be deadly sins, and resorting to corporal punishment at least as often as his peers, using a cane for daytime offences and a sawn-off cricket bat for those caught pillow-fighting after lights out. It was generally conceded that he beat 'without rancour', though some boys thought that he joked on the subject a little too readily. It was indicative of his reputation that when, shortly after Taylor retired, his one-time charge became engaged to the future Queen of England, the former headmaster was sent a rough rhyme:

> Whoever of his friends then thought,
> When, venturing, Cheam School he bought,
> He'd lay his cane athwart
> The bottom of a Prince Consort.[7]

His first taste of this punishment as a new boy prompted Philip to ask the headmaster's wife, 'Do you like Mr Taylor?' The experienced Mrs Taylor countered expertly, 'Do you, Philip?' she asked. 'No,' said the young boy unequivocally, 'I do not.'[8]

However, as time passed, Philip grew to like not only Mr Taylor but also everything else about Cheam, whose tough regime he later extolled in a preface to an exhaustive history of the school, published in 1974: 'Children may be indulged at home,' he wrote, 'but school is expected to be a spartan and disciplined experience in the process of developing into self-controlled, considerate and independent adults. The system may have its eccentricities, but there can be little doubt that these are far outweighed by its values.'[9]

His son, Prince Charles, who had a miserable time at Cheam, may not have entirely agreed with this credo, but Philip himself settled quickly into his new school. The headmaster's son, Jimmy Taylor, who was at Cheam at the same time, says the fact of having arrived late (aged nine rather than the normal starting age of eight), with a 'strange name and a shock of white hair' ought to have made life difficult for the prince. There was an aura about him of 'having arrived in England virtually an orphan and more or less friendless and speaking or certainly writing French better than he did English. So he was distinctly different from the other boys and must have been aware of that … But he was good at games so he was soon accepted.'[10] He remained, though, 'quite private, not much given to confiding in others'. He was also physically strong and had a fairly quick temper, which deterred too much teasing, although he did get landed briefly with the nickname Flip-Flop. Another contemporary, John Wynne, remembers Philip as 'extremely gifted' but that he 'didn't show off his talents'. He was 'a most charming person, very popular'.[11] 'When you think of all the problems he had being shovelled around, it was a remarkable achievement. He wasn't bullied. Nobody would ever have had a poke at him, because they'd have got one back!'[12] Wynne remembered thinking that Philip had 'tremendous confidence from somewhere', and later, just before they left Cheam, while they were unpacking, seeing a photograph of George V beneath a pile of clothes in Philip's trunk signed 'From Uncle George' which he had never displayed.[13]

* * *

At the end of his first term at Cheam, Philip spent the 1930–31 Christmas holidays in Germany, where the festivities got under way on 15 December with the wedding of his sister Sophie and Christoph Hesse at Schloss Friedrichshof (now a five-star hotel) in the town of Kronberg in the Taunus foothills. Philip joined his sisters in helping to dress the excited Sophie in her room before the two ceremonies, Orthodox and Protestant, during which he carried her train. Their mother Alice was not there, feeling 'not strong enough & too shy of strangers', so Victoria told her lady-in-waiting, and after everything that had happened everyone felt sorry for Andrea, who 'behaved splendidly', reported Louise, although he 'had the greatest difficulty not to break down'.[14]

The wedding took place against a backdrop of deepening political crisis in Germany, Hitler's National Socialists having established themselves as the main party of opposition in the Reichstag elections that autumn. Sophie's bridegroom Christoph had long grown disillusioned with the Weimar Republic, whose laws repeatedly challenged the Hesses' property and position, and his elder brother Philipp had signed up to the Nazi party in October 1930 – he would eventually come to be regarded as Hitler's second closest friend after Albert Speer.[15] To begin with Christoph resisted following Philipp's example, but he was just the sort of dashing type whom the Nazis proved so successful in recruiting – Hitler was obsessed with fast cars and planes, which sped him about between rallies, and National Socialism's association with sports, adventure and modernity were big attractions to Christoph.[16] Within a year of his marriage to Sophie, he, too, had joined as a clandestine member, and by early 1932 he was in the SS and beginning to demonstrate 'a discipline and a commitment to a cause that was unprecedented in his life'.[17]

* * *

These developments doubtless seemed rather less sinister at the time than they do in retrospect and in any case they would almost certainly have meant very little to nine-year-old Philip, although they would have some bearing on his future – not least when it came to the question as to which of his family would be invited to his wedding. For the time being, after spending Christmas Day 1930 with uncle Ernie and aunt Onor at Darmstadt, on Boxing Day Philip was taken to see his mother at her sanatorium, he and his grandmother staying for a few days at a nearby hotel. The visit went smoothly enough, although Alice confided to Victoria that she did not think she had long to live.[18]

A month later, on 8 February 1931, Philip attended the next family wedding, that of his other younger sister, Cecile, and Don Hesse. Some fifty relations gathered for the event at Darmstadt amid a densely packed and enthusiastic crowd of townspeople, who blocked Andrea and Cecile's route to the church, and afterwards cheered the bride and groom on the balcony. 'It seemed funny in a "republic",' wrote Victoria, 'but was a nice sign of the affection of the people for Uncle Ernie & his family.'[19] Afterwards, Dickie Mountbatten took Philip back to school in England.

In the Easter holidays, he again travelled over to Germany with his grandmother, this time for the wedding of his eldest sister, Margarita. En route he was again taken to Kreuzlingen to see his mother. Alice gave no particular cause for concern during the first two days of their stay, but on the third she started complaining about the violent means by which Victoria had organized for her to be taken away from Darmstadt. From then on, she increasingly blamed Victoria for her detention and even wrote to the British Consul-General in Zurich to complain that she was being held against her will. She was not allowed to go to Margarita's wedding, nor would she be permitted to attend Theodora's later in the year, but she was instead visited by the bride and groom, and also by Andrea, the first time they had seen each other since her internment. The fact that he never visited her again is further evidence that they had already drifted apart before Alice's breakdown. The assertion in one biography that by 1929 Andrea had already 'moved to Monte Carlo, where he had a mistress', is not supported by any clear evidence, yet at the same time it appears perfectly plausible.[20]

Margarita's marriage, meanwhile, strengthened family ties with the House of Coburg, her bridegroom being Gottfried 'Friedel' of Hohenlohe-Langenburg, grandson of Prince Alfred, Queen Victoria's second son and Philip's immediate predecessor as Duke of Edinburgh. Heir to Weikersheim, an almost perfect example of medieval architecture, and Langenburg, as large and impressive as Buckingham Palace, Friedel was an old friend of Philip's aunt, Nada, and had preceded her as the lover of Gloria Morgan Vanderbilt, the sultry American widow whom he had met on the way over to New York in 1926. Eight years later, in the sensational Vanderbilt custody trial, Gloria's nurse was to testify that Friedel and Gloria had been in and out of each other's bedrooms for two years and that he had read to her 'vile books!'[21] The proposed match eventually foundered, however, amid far-fetched whispers (spread by Gloria's hysterical mother) that Friedel intended to murder Gloria's daughter for her inheritance from the Vanderbilt railway fortune. Fearing that her allowance would be cut off, Gloria got cold feet and broke off the engagement, leaving poor Friedel heartbroken.

It was shortly after this, in 1929, that Gloria first met Nada at Cannes, where the Milford Havens went to disport themselves each summer. The 'startlingly alive' and 'entirely Russian' Nada made an instant impression on the comparatively shy and inarticulate Gloria.[22] Their ensuing relationship would later also come under the spotlight at the Vanderbilt custody trial, in which a maid from the Miramar Hotel in Cannes testified that she had seen Nada kissing Gloria 'just like a lover' while sharing a room there in the summer of 1931.[23]

Wallis Simpson had also been on that holiday, but evidently the lesbian atmosphere had not appealed to her and she had left early.[24]

It is, of course, doubtful that ten-year-old Philip would have known much about any of this at the time, although he often came across Gloria at Lynden with Georgie and Nada. Another regular visitor to the house was Gloria's identical twin sister, Thelma, Viscountess Furness, wife of the philandering shipping tycoon Marmaduke Furness, and chief mistress of the Prince of Wales from 1929 until 1931. As a friend of Wallis Simpson, Thelma was also responsible, to her eternal regret, for inadvertently introducing the prince to her successor. Dickie Mountbatten later maintained that the fateful first encounter between the prince and Mrs Simpson had taken place over lunch with the Milford Havens at Lynden, but most historians now agree that they first met in early 1931 at Burrough Court, Thelma's country house near Melton Mowbray. The prince seemed to be far from bowled over on first acquaintance, however he soon fell for Wallis's quick wit and forthright manner. Within a few weeks, according to Mountbatten again, they had somehow 'reached a position where they went to bed. From that moment he lost all sense of reason.'[25] Their love affair and the eventual abdication of Edward VIII, as the prince had by then become, would have profound consequences for Philip's future.

Meanwhile, during the summer holidays of 1931, he again went to Germany for another family wedding, this time that of his twenty-five-year-old sister Theodora and Berthold, the Margrave of Baden. After the ceremony in the spa town of Baden-Baden, he travelled north to stay at Wolfsgarten with various members of the family, including his sister Sophie and brother-in-law Christoph, his grandmother Victoria and his father, Andrea, who seemed more cheerful than he had been for a long time.[26]

Theodora's new home was to be Schloss Salem, the sprawling former Cistercian monastery which had come into the Baden family after Secularization in 1803. More recently, in 1920, a wing of it had been made into a progressive boarding school, founded by Theodora's late father-in-law, Max of Baden, the last imperial chancellor of Germany who had retired to Salem after the Treaty of Versailles with the ambition of educating a more peaceful young German elite to help rebuild his shattered country.

Set amid rolling farmland just north of Lake Constance, Salem was to play a big part in Philip's upbringing, in so much as he would shortly go to school there. But before that he also spent part of his school holidays staying with his sister and brother-in-law at the castle, a convenient hour and a quarter's drive from Alice's sanatorium at Kreuzlingen.

Visiting his mother was liable to be a disquieting experience. Alice had become increasingly prone to violent mood swings and eccentric behaviour, such as going about barefoot, holding her hand in blessing over her teacup and hiding things in her room.[27] Her tolerance finally snapped in July 1932, when she leapt from a window at the Bellevue with a bundle of laundry and made it as far as the railway station, only to be arrested aboard a train and returned to the clinic. During that summer holidays, Theodora took Philip to see their mother, but they found her 'so depressed that she hardly talked at all'.[28] After two and a half years, she was badly in need of a change of scene, and even Dr Binswanger, whom she smacked across the face on one occasion, conceded that her stay at the clinic might be having a detrimental effect.

Victoria realized this, too, and, overriding the objections of Professor Wilmanns, organized Alice's transfer to the Martinsbrunn Sanatorium in the south Tyrol, where she responded well to the much freer regime. When Victoria visited her in December, she found her 'much improved' and enjoying the friendship of a Swedish lady, 'a masseuse and physiotherapist of late middle age', who 'acted as her secretary and was happy to discuss philosophical ideas with her'.[29] Alice still felt badly let down by her family, however, and told her mother that from now on she wanted to have nothing to do with any of them. Philip, by then aged eleven, was possibly not told of her decision, but he would neither see nor hear from his mother for the next five years.

Philip now came to depend more than ever on Georgie and Nada Milford Haven and on his grandmother, Victoria. She visited him during term time at Cheam, and had him for half-terms with her at Kensington Palace, which he later recalled as 'a sort of base where I kept things'. As time passed, he became extremely fond of her and he later credited her with having 'the right combination of the rational and the emotional' in her approach to bringing up children. But while Victoria excelled in many aspects of motherhood, showing warmth was not her strongest suit. Many years earlier, her own grandmother, Queen Victoria, had perceived 'a certain coolness and detachment, springing perhaps from her mother's death and too much responsibility borne too young', and felt that she failed to show sufficient love and affection towards her husband.[30]

Philip soon got used to never knowing at the start of each school holidays where he would be spending them and to always being on the move, but he did not complain. Victoria rearranged her own life so that she could supervise his, a task she tackled with the same dedication she had exercised on her own sons. Occasionally, to broaden his entertainment, the Mountbattens' footman Charles Smith would be prevailed upon to take him to the cinema. When they went to see *Treasure Island* at the Metropole, Philip sneaked out with a pile of 'Reserved' labels, which Smith only became aware of on the bus ride back to Kensington as passengers searched in vain for an unreserved seat. The next morning the stickers were on every lavatory door at Kensington Palace.[31]

With Andrea spending much of his time in Paris or Monte Carlo, having freed himself from his day-to-day paternal responsibilities, other father figures, besides his uncles, began to take his place in Philip's life. One of those who held a watching brief was Sir Harold Wernher, the husband of Nada Milford Haven's sister Zia, who together came to be looked on by Philip as honorary uncle and aunt.[32] Harold was the son of the German-born 'Randlord' Sir Julius Wernher, one of the creators of modern South Africa. Having amassed a fortune from mining diamonds and gold, Julius was reputed to have been the richest man ever recorded by Somerset House, leaving £5 million on his death in 1912. A man of great drive and energy, and not a glad sufferer of fools, Harold exerted a considerable influence on the young Philip, who relished their long discussions and would often arrive with a list of questions for advice.[33] Harold and Zia, a far more straight-laced character than her sister, may well have seen themselves as a useful corrective against the louche milieu that Philip encountered with the Milford Havens at Lynden. Zia was apparently 'shocked to the core' by reports that Nada was frequenting lesbian bars in Cannes and making women friends with the likes of Gloria Vanderbilt.[34] Zia herself was a formidable character, 'frightfully strict' with her own children, according to her daughter Myra, though less so with Philip, and in the habit of keeping a silver-edged pad by her plate on which she noted down the faults and mistakes of her servants, who nonetheless worshipped her.[35]

Before moving to Luton Hoo, the Wernhers lived at Thorpe Lubenham Hall near Market Harborough and it was here that Philip came to stay for long periods during the 1930s, making great friends with the Wernher children, Alex, Gina and Myra. Myra (later Lady Butter) remembers him at the time as 'a very good-looking young Viking'. Although she was somewhat younger, Philip was 'always kind, paid attention to one'. At other times he could be 'very boisterous – pushed Gina down the stairs once – awful sometimes, very alpha male'. He was 'frightfully neat and tidy with his room and used to fold his grey flannel trousers under the mattress because that pressed them'. And although he had 'nothing' he never felt sorry for himself. '"You are where you are in life so get on with it" is his philosophy … he was never beholden to anyone, which he would have hated, and never let misfortune cloud his life as far as I could see.'[36] Philip was particularly close to Alex, whom he came to look upon as a substitute elder brother, and to Gina, whom he accompanied to parties even though they had been forbidden to go by Zia.

But his closest friend was probably the Milford Havens' son, David, Earl of Medina, who was later destined to become his best man, although they subsequently fell out over David's lapses of judgement after the wedding. During the holidays from Cheam they played endless games of roller-skate hockey at Lynden and sped about on two-stroke motorbikes. In 1932, the young earl was made head boy for his last term at Cheam, and in his final report the headmaster wrote that he was 'incapable of doing anything flashingly' (he developed the capability later) and that he had led 'by his example rather than by his command, and has won the respect of every boy in the school'.[37]

Philip, meanwhile, having arrived late at Cheam, had made his mark by winning the prize for mathematics in his first year, and one for French the next. He also won the under-12 hurdles, high-jump, swimming and diving trophies, caught the eye playing football as a goalkeeper and by the early age of eleven had made it into the first school team for cricket.[38] But he did not stay long enough to reach the top of the school, leaving in the summer of 1933, a year before the normal leaving age of thirteen, in order to continue his education at his brother-in-law's school at Salem in Germany.

Philip later recalled that this move was the result of 'a family decision', taken after only a token consultation with his two Mountbatten uncles, and that he felt vaguely coerced.[39] The principal impetus seems to have come from his sister, Theodora.[40] Given that Hitler had become chancellor of Germany in January that year and the school to which Philip was going was now being steadily Nazified, it seems a strange decision in hindsight. However, at the time many relatively moderate people in Germany – several of Philip's relations among them – regarded the advent of the National Socialists as a necessary step on the road to national recovery after the humiliation of the last war. 'The coup d'état is very popular here,' wrote Philip's grandmother Victoria from Darmstadt in the spring of 1933 shortly after Hitler's seizure of power. 'There was an enormous torchlight procession last night, which passed without any disturbances & now normal life has returned, after a week's holidaying, when all the town was out on the streets. The fine dry weather & warm sun increases the holiday feeling.'[41]

SEVEN

Dodging the Hitler Youth

When Prince Max of Baden founded his school at Salem in 1920, his stated aim was to 'train soldiers, who are at the same time lovers of peace' and to 'build up the imagination of the boy of decision and the will-power of the dreamer, so that in future wise men will have the nerve to lead the way they have shown, and men of action will have the vision to imagine the consequence of their decisions'.[1]

The job of interpreting and fulfilling these aims fell to Salem's first headmaster, Kurt Hahn, whose philosophy would shape the remainder of Philip's education. Philip had first come across Hahn in the summer of 1932, while spending his summer holiday with Theodora and Berthold. Venturing one day into the former monks' quarters occupied by the school, the eleven-year-old prince beheld a 'large figure,' he later recalled, 'head bowed and covered by a very wide-brimmed grey felt hat with a handkerchief clenched in his teeth'.[2] There was an air about him which 'commanded instant wariness and respect'.[3]

Hahn had worn the hat outdoors ever since suffering from severe sunstroke in 1904, which led him to have the occipital bone at the back of his skull removed and affected his health throughout his life.[4] His attire matched his overall eccentricity. One biographer encountered him 'swaddled in black, with protective glasses that seemed more like goggles. He was an extraordinary sight scuttling indoors to escape the sun's rays like an old crow pursued by hawks.'[5] Often lost in his own world, Hahn was once observed offering to cut up the meat of an incapacitated neighbour at dinner, then absent-mindedly eating it himself. On another occasion, late for an appointment, he leapt into a London taxi and shouted his telephone number in Scotland to the driver.[6]

Hahn was born in Berlin in 1886 into a German-Jewish family of industrialists and shortly before the First World War won a Rhodes Scholarship to read Greats at Oxford. There he became a keen student of Plato (studying under Professor J. A. Stewart, the leading Platonist of his day) and an ardent admirer of the English public school system. Still at Oxford when the First World War broke out, he slipped back to Germany via Scotland and Norway. Excused from military service on health grounds, he instead worked in intelligence, principally as an authority on the British press and on the psychology of British warfare.[7] At the end of the war he became private secretary and principal adviser to Max of Baden, and at Versailles he is thought to have written the famous line for Count Brockdorff-Rantzau, leader of the German delegation, that for Germany to admit sole responsibility for causing the war 'would in my mouth be a lie!' He thus inadvertently helped to justify the subsequent clamour among German nationalists for revenge and rearmament which eventually led to the creation of the Third Reich.

Salem started in 1920 with just twenty pupils, boys and girls, although the girls seem to have been included solely as a means of enriching the education of the boys, and were very rarely mentioned in Hahn's educational writings.[8] By 1933 there were 420 pupils and it ranked among the leading schools in Europe. Hahn proudly admitted that there was nothing original in its concept, that he had 'cribbed and copied' from Plato, from Thomas Arnold of Rugby, from Eton, from progressive schools such as Abbotsholme and from a wide variety of other educationalists.[9] 'In education as in medicine, you must harvest the wisdom of a thousand years,' explained his patron, Prince Max.[10]

Hahn believed that, surrounded by a 'sick civilisation', young people were 'in danger of being affected by fivefold decay: the decay of fitness, the decay of initiative and enterprise, the decay of care and skill, the decay of self-discipline, the decay of compassion'. He held that his charges should confront their weaknesses as a prelude to overcoming them. Great emphasis was placed on their health. They ran a quarter of a mile before breakfast (preferably on their toes), drank milk at meals, had a forty-five-minute mid-morning break for athletics and a forty-five-minute rest after lunch, lying flat on their backs on the floor while a grown-up read to them aloud.[11] In the track and field exercises, each child competed only against his or her previous record. Hahn considered high jump to be 'specially fitted to develop the power of decision' and particularly beneficial to stammerers and others of 'refined intellect and high sensitiveness'. He claimed that 80 per cent of those who left Salem were able to clear five feet.[12]

To divert energy away from the 'poisonous passions' of adolescence, Hahn sought to give each boy the chance to discover a consuming interest. On Saturday afternoons, 'guilds' of explorers, farmers and artists would set out in pursuit of their 'grande passion'. 'When a child has come into its own,' wrote Hahn, 'you will hear a shout of joy or be thrilled by some other manifestation of primitive happiness.'[13] These wholesome passions, once discovered, would become the 'guardian angel' of adolescence,[14] responsible according to Hahn for the 'gleam' in Salem boys' eyes and the clear texture of their skin.[15]

For their first term at Salem, new pupils wore their own clothes and only in their second would they be given their uniform – grey shirts and shorts – as an outward sign that they were now members of the school community. The uniform could then be taken away at any time for infringements such as cheating or lying.[16] Two days a week, they had to do certain estate duties – working on the farm or carrying out other jobs necessary to the running of the school.[17]

Two afternoons a week were given over to field games, with hockey, Hahn's speciality, being the main team game. But no practising was allowed at other times and there was no coach as Hahn did not want a passion for games to stifle other interests.[18] Concerted action rather than brilliant individual performances were what the headmaster wanted. One of his 'Seven Laws of Salem' was that the children should be made to 'meet with triumph and defeat'. However, his rigorous regime ensured that Salem's athletics team soon became more accustomed to winning than losing, carrying off the public schools athletics trophy at White City in 1935, 1936 and 1937.[19]

Judged by almost any criteria, the autumn term of 1933 was not a good time for a new boy to arrive at Salem. During Hitler's rise to power, Hahn had applauded the Führer's angry patriotism and under-estimated his capacity for evil.[20] However, when, in August 1932, Hitler condoned the savage murder of a communist by Nazi storm troopers at Potempa, Hahn wrote a circular letter to all Salem old boys, demanding that they break with Hitler or with the school: 'Salem cannot remain neutral,' he declared.[21] 'Germany is at stake, her Christian civilization, her reputation, her military honour.'

He subsequently became a marked man, especially after Hitler became chancellor in January 1933. During the arbitrary arrests that followed the Reichstag fire that February, Hahn was seized by the local police and imprisoned. Only after a personal appeal to the German foreign secretary by the British prime minister Ramsay MacDonald (whose private secretary Sir Nevile Butler had been looked after by Hahn during his internment in Germany in 1914) was he released, although he was barred from the province of Baden and the local newspaper *Bodensee Rundschau* drew attention to the 'Sinister Operations of the Jew Hahn'.[22] In July he fled to Britain, shortly before Philip made his way in the opposite direction.[23] A month after his departure and shortly before the arrival of Philip the first concentration camp opened at Dachau.

Over the summer holidays, Hahn's arrest and banishment had prompted many parents to withdraw their children from Salem, and Philip's brother-in-law Berthold had sought assurances from Hitler about the school's future, to which the Führer angrily retorted: 'Why don't you aristocrats get rid of your *Hofjuden* [Jewish courtiers]?'[24] The Baden family were far less enthusiastic about the National Socialists than Philip's other brothers-in-law, nevertheless Berthold persuaded Theodora to enrol Philip at the school as a means of increasing his bargaining power with the Nazi regime – which still valued Salem for its ties with Britain at a time when many parents were withdrawing their children from the country.[25] The dream of an alliance with Britain was closer to Hitler's heart than almost any other goal of Nazi foreign policy, although one Salem parent, General von Brauchitsch, warned the Führer in 1933 that the English would almost certainly not send their children to the school 'if it became officially committed to National Socialist training'.[26] Salem was thus allowed to survive without completely adopting the Nazi programme in order to act as a bridge to Britain's elite. The presence of young Prince Philip at the school served the interests of both Berthold and Hitler.

For Theodora, meanwhile, there was the added benefit of being able to keep a closer eye on her younger brother now that their mother had so decisively cut her family ties, and to give him a more settled family life than the one he currently had being shunted about between various relations in England, some of whose rakish behaviour may have alarmed her. He would also get the benefit of the education which she still believed Salem provided, despite the Nazis' efforts to corrupt or destroy it, and at no cost.

When Philip began his first term at Salem's junior school, Spetzgart, on the northern shore of Lake Constance, many pupils had been withdrawn and several members of staff had denounced Hahn to ensure their own safety. That October, Hitler took Germany out of the League of Nations and Spetzgart witnessed a 'feverish stitching of uniforms for the *Hitler-Jugend* [Hitler Youth]',[27] according to Philip's school friend Martin Flavin, son of the Pulitzer Prize-winning American novelist of the same name. The new Nazi Kommissar, a short, pudgy SA officer, had brought about an unwelcome change in school life, leading its contingent of Hitler *Jungvolk* and supervising their *Wehrsport* ('military athletics') and close-order drill, which the boys found decidedly tedious. His job was also to promote ideological indoctrination and he insisted on regular school assemblies to listen to the Führer's interminable radio talks.[28]

One of two new boys to have arrived from England, Philip was known by his first name by the English and American boys, whereas the Germans addressed him simply as 'Greece'. Some of his high spirits, at least, seem to have survived the journey from England and that October he was a willing combatant in the school's three-day 'water bomb war'.[29] Martin Flavin remembered that, although Philip was a year younger, he thought of him at the time as older and more adventurous,[30] and persuasive in his love of pranks. Overall, though, Philip found his new school a lot less congenial than Cheam, the superabundance of 'ghastly foot-slogging'[31] far outweighing any benefits of its being on his sister's estate. When, after a term, he moved to Salem proper, he lived with his sister and brother-in-law, but that arrangement was still far from ideal. 'He wasn't really integrated into the community,' recalled one of his masters. 'He had little opportunity to make real friends, and he spoke very little German. He was really very isolated.'[32]

He was, of course, too young to have much of an opinion about Nazi politics, but he was evidently amused by their ridiculous strutting, and we are told that he laughed whenever he saw the Nazi goose step or '*Heil Hitler*' salute, entertained by the fact that Cheam boys had made a very similar gesture when asking permission to go to the lavatory.[33] It was greatly to his relief when, at the end of that term, shortly after Hitler's Night of the Long Knives, he was sent back to Britain to resume his education there. 'We thought it better for him,' explained Theodora, 'and also for us.'[34]

Nothing could be settled about his future before his father had been consulted, however, and in the meantime, in July 1934, Philip went to stay at Wolfsgarten with several of his family, including his grandmother, Victoria, Cecile and her children, and Margarita and Friedel. 'She [Margarita] is decidedly fat,' wrote Victoria to Georgie, 'but quite well and cheerful and has remained on here, after he left, to see Andrea, who is due to arrive any day now.'[35] But Andrea was, as so often, delayed and Philip's movements and school plans remained in limbo for some weeks. When Andrea did eventually turn up ('we suppose en route for a rest cure at Marienbad,'[36] sighed Victoria), it was resolved that Philip would go in the autumn term to Gordonstoun, the Scottish public school that Kurt Hahn had recently established in Morayshire.

EIGHT

Off to Gordonstoun

As a prominent Jewish refugee from Nazi Germany, Kurt Hahn had been assured of a warm welcome by progressive circles in Britain. However, his attitude towards Hitler had remained ambivalent. At the end of 1933 he was still describing the Führer as having 'a warm, even a soft heart, which makes him over-sensitive to suggestions that he is not hard enough ... he does not want war, but he wants a peace in freedom, not a peace in impotence'.[1] Hahn later put these opinions down to his 'homesickness' in exile and 'wishful thinking', and he denied the suggestion that he had advised the appeaser Lord Lothian.[2] He claimed to have had his illusions finally shattered by the Night of the Long Knives in June 1934, after which he became an advocate of the dual policy of offering Germany peaceful revision of the Versailles Treaty so long as the Nazis were removed from power.[3]

Meanwhile, ever since his arrival in Britain, Hahn had been busily promoting his educational ideas, and in early 1934 the writer and disenchanted schoolmaster T. C. Worsley saw him lecturing beneath the banner of the liberal New Education Fellowship. 'He instantly struck me as in a different category from the others [in the NEF],' Worsley recorded.

They were enthusiastic, charming, rather dotty and somewhat amateur … while he was grave, serious and profound. His lectures made a considerable stir, less I think for what they said, than for what he was. For whatever you might think of Hahn as an educator, you could hardly deny that he had many of the attributes of a Great Man. He gave off personality in thick waves, and the personality had a solid, Germanic weight behind it. He had a full, wide face with a small resolute chin, jutting firmly out. His pronouncements had a ring of both wisdom and authority; they were aphoristic and seemed to dig deep. I can't, for the life of me, remember any of them now, but I still remember the flavour of them, and the aroma of profundity with which he invested them.[4]

Not everyone was so impressed by Hahn. The headmaster of Dartington Hall, W. B. Curry, warned his friend Clifford Allen, the socialist politician and educationalist, against being 'converted'.

Unless I am very profoundly mistaken … the education which Hahn advocates is incompatible with a really liberal civilization. It seems to me … to be the product of the tortured German soul … most Germans at present are incapable of even understanding the meaning of personal liberty, so strong have been the traditions of the last generation. I can understand that Hahn's views might seem liberal in Germany. What shocks me is that they are thought liberal in England. I grant that he is a man of immense power and vitality and of considerable intellectual ability. I also insist that his psychology has far more roots in his own emotional nature than in the nature of other human beings.[5]

Allen, though, leapt to Hahn's defence, replying that he was 'fairly confident that he [Hahn] is more likely to produce children of the dynamic outlook on life and a high standard of value than the more extreme freedom of some of the other schools'.[6] Allen's favourable opinion was shared furthermore by an impressive group of friends and sympathizers, including the Archbishop of York, William Temple (soon to head Gordonstoun's Board of Governors), the novelist John Buchan (Lord Tweedsmuir), the historian G. M. Trevelyan, the headmaster of Eton, Claude Elliott, and Geoffrey Winthrop Young, the mountaineer and poet. Collectively they urged Hahn to set up a school in Britain to continue his Salem experiment there.

While at Oxford before the war, in order to escape the summer heat Hahn had spent holidays in Morayshire and developed a lasting attachment to the landscape and people there. In the summer of 1933, just after his flight from Germany, he had returned to Scotland and began tutoring boys at The Doune of Rothiemurchus, a Georgian-fronted manse deep in the Cairngorms. 'I have a dwarfish school at present, numbering five boys,' Hahn wrote to the parents of one prospective pupil, Adam Arnold-Brown, who had been attending Abbotsholme, Britain's first progressive public school.[7]

In the spring of 1934 Hahn moved north towards his beloved Morayshire coast and leased Gordonstoun House and 300 acres of grounds at a low rent from his old friend Sir Alexander Gordon-Cumming – whose father, Sir William, had been famously ostracized by Victorian society for allegedly cheating at baccarat with the Prince of Wales at Tranby Croft and then losing a libel action against his accusers.

Gordonstoun lies half a mile inland from the Moray Firth, close to Elgin and Lossiemouth, with the harbour of Hopeman village a mile or two away in one direction and the small eighteenth-century Michael Kirk (where Sir William Gordon-Cumming had been buried in 1930) a mile away in the other, the Cairngorms rising up to the south, and the north-west Highlands visible across the blowy firth in Sutherland and Caithness. The house itself at first appears not unlike a French château, with a turret at each corner, but it is built of such heavy grey stone as to be not French at all, but bleakly and unmistakably Scottish. Writing about her isolated childhood there, Sir William Gordon-Cumming's daughter Elma recalled it as 'old and grey and full of evil', and 'grimly defiant to change'.[8]

Hahn moved into his new school premises in early May 1934 with thirteen boys,[9] the first of whom largely came either from a small group of families who knew all about the headmaster and his work or else had been failures or misfits at their previous schools. Those joining with Philip for the second term, in September 1934, included sixteen-year-old Jim Orr, recently removed from Harrow and destined one day to become Philip's private secretary; and Orr's cousin Teddy Sale, another dropout from St Edward's, who was to be killed in action in 1943. Another boy, Reggie Hoare, from the banking family, had lost a leg below the knee but was nevertheless made to play games and developed into a 'first-rate goalkeeper', while another, Sandy Kennedy, had polio and had to be carried everywhere on a stretcher – but nonetheless became a prefect.[10] The school was 'comprehensive' in its acceptance of children with a wide range of abilities and financial circumstances.

Among the first members of staff were Lt Commander J. H. Lewty, a pipe-smoking retired naval officer whose job it was to teach the boys seamanship, and Robert Chew, one of a handful to have come from Salem, who took charge of 'character building'. Chew became Philip's housemaster and was headmaster by the time of the arrival at Gordonstoun of his son Prince Charles, who found him 'a remote and austere character who adhered to the founder's beliefs with the conviction of a true disciple'.[11]

There were only twenty-seven boys when Philip joined the school, but expansion was quick as Hahn set himself the target of adding thirty new boys each year, and so by the time Philip left there were a hundred and thirty-five. In establishing Gordonstoun, the headmaster faced a very different set of challenges from those he had confronted at Salem, where the buildings and estate had been carefully maintained for centuries. Gordonstoun, by contrast, had long been neglected due to a sharp fall in the Gordon-Cumming family fortunes, and the house and grounds were in urgent need of repair. From the outset Hahn demanded that the boys do their share of estate work, deeming it not only educational but also a financial necessity.

Philip's intake thus became pioneers in a very hands-on sense, helping with the farming and gardening as well as building and decorating classrooms, a school library and the draughty dormitories in the curious circular stable block known as the Round Square. In keeping with Hahn's spartan vision, creature comforts came low on the list of priorities. Several decades later, one of Prince's Charles's contemporaries at Gordonstoun, the writer William Boyd, recalled with 'retrospective revulsion' the 'concrete and tile washrooms and lavatories, the pale-green dormitories with their crude wooden beds';[12] another, the journalist Ross Benson, described how windows were 'kept open throughout the night, which meant that those closest to them were likely to wake up with blankets rain-soaked or, in winter, covered with a light sprinkling of snow'.[13]

In Philip's time, the boys were also expected to do their fair share of domestic tasks. As a thirteen-year-old, Philip was no keener on these chores than any other boy but he was observed to perform them quickly in order to free himself for more congenial pursuits.[14]

Jim Orr's first memories of Philip, who was listed simply by his Christian name on the school register, were of his 'white, white hair', his friendliness and sense of fun, and the fact that he 'never swanked about his relatives'.[15] Another contemporary remembered that the young prince was initially rather sulky and slightly cheeky towards his headmaster, but that Hahn 'brought him down with a bump'.[16] Over time, though, there developed a deep mutual respect between the headmaster and his most prized protégé. In a piece written for the news agency Reuters in 1947, shortly before Philip's engagement to Princess Elizabeth, Hahn recalled that Philip's most marked trait on his arrival at Gordonstoun was

> his undefeatable spirit; he felt deeply both joy and sadness, and the way he looked and the way he moved indicated what he felt. That even applied to the minor disappointments which are inevitable in a schoolboy's life. But for the most part he enjoyed his life, his laughter was heard everywhere and created merriness around him. He had inherited from the Danish family a capacity to derive great fun from small incidents.

In his work, meanwhile, Philip 'showed lively intelligence, but also a determination not to exert himself more than was necessary'. However 'in the community life he followed a different rule. Once he had made a task his own he showed meticulous attention to detail and a pride in workmanship which was never content with mediocre results'.[17] When he was in the 'middle-school', he 'got into a fair number of scrapes through recklessness and wildness'. But while he was 'often naughty', he was 'never nasty'. Philip's chief faults seem to have been intolerance and impatience, but overall Hahn's educational philosophy, together with the school motto, 'More is in you', seemed well-suited to the young prince's inclinations.

Keen to instil in his boys pride in their physical condition – which Philip was to demonstrate throughout his life – Hahn devised a uniform exposing as much of their limbs as was decent: an open-necked grey shirt, pullover, shorts and stockings. He saw it as his duty to build up the fitness of every child under his care. Hence the Gordonstoun timetable was very similar to Salem's, crammed with physical activities and leaving little free time. The boys got up at 6.30 for a bracing cold shower and run. From 10.30 to 11.15 they had a break from lessons for running, jumping and javelin throwing. 'They ought to do [these activities] all year round, four or five times a week,' Hahn held. 'In 90 per cent of the cases you will help them to become resilient, quick of resolution and able to tap their hidden reserves. Many of them do not like their training at first; nearly all do in the end. I should think as little of asking them whether they want to train, as I should think of asking them whether they feel in the mood to brush their teeth.'

After lunch, at 1.30, there was a rest period, as at Salem, during which the boys lay on their backs while an adult or senior boy read to them. Games were played on two afternoons a week, but prohibited at all other times.[18] On another two afternoons the boys learned seamanship, on another two they performed a 'common task' and on the remaining afternoon they did a 'project' such as building, gardening, art or music.

At 4.30 they had a warm wash and cold shower, followed by tea and then prep. After supper at 6.30, at which meat was never served, in the summer senior boys played tennis, which Hahn joined in with considerably more enthusiasm than skill, yet so hated being beaten that the boys had to be instructed not to win.[19] At 9.15 there was quarter of an hour's silence, to enable the boy to 'glean the harvest from his manifold experiences'.[20] Then it was lights out.

Pinned to the inside of each boy's dormitory locker was his training plan, ruled into columns for each day of the week, each line on the left marked with phrases such as: Teeth brushed, Rope climbed, Skip 60 times, Press-ups, Cold shower, and so on. As well as the exercises to be carried out, there were 'Great Temptations' to be resisted, for example EBM (Eating Between Meals). The housemaster could add other temptations to the list as he saw fit. Hahn claimed that the training plan was responsible for curing habits like the biting of nails, and also argued that it promoted 'self-honesty' among the boys, although some thought that it was more likely to make the boys overly conscious of their own failings. Boys were given the training plan after a 'trial' of a year or so. Similarly, they were not granted the 'privilege' of wearing the school uniform until after their first term.

Hahn awarded colours not for proficiency in sports, but, rather, to boys he saw as the most virtuous representatives of the school. Recipients of white and purple stripes on their pullovers were known as 'colour bearers', from which body was chosen the 'colour bearer council', self-electing like the Eton Society, and charged with preserving the moral tone of the school. From this group the headmaster then appointed his 'helpers' (prefects) and 'guardian' (head boy), both titles coming from Plato and seen by Hahn in the Platonic sense as boys of superior virtue who would also act as protectors. Lower down the school, the attempt to diffuse responsibility as widely as possible and give each boy a sense of his own importance was reflected in such titles as captain of lost property, captain of bicycles and captain of the linen room. Philip himself was to progress all the way through the ranks from room leader (dormitory captain) to guardian.

Though no seaman himself, Hahn decreed that every boy at Gordonstoun had to learn to sail.[21] On seamanship afternoons the boys would put on long navy-blue trousers and sweaters and cycle the three miles to the village of Hopeman, where they built, maintained and sailed a variety of craft over the years. Philip tended to cycle down there 'regardless of safety rules', wrote Hahn, and on one occasion 'he avoided a clash with a baby in a perambulator by inches, thanks to his unusual agility; he appeased the mother by an apology which was irresistible'.[22] Devotion to speed would characterize Philip's later motoring career, during which he had several accidents and was fortunate to escape relatively unscathed. At Hopeman he also made friends with the fishermen, accompanying them on at least one all-night fishing trip, and spent much of his free time pottering about the harbour and working with the boat-builder, Mr Findlay.[23] It was the beginning of a lifelong love affair with the sea and of sailing.

The first voyage of any significance for the Gordonstoun boys was across the Moray Firth by cutter to Dornoch, in June 1935, and Philip later took part in expeditions farther afield to the Outer Hebrides, Shetlands and Norway, often given the job of cook because he seemed to be immune from seasickness.[24] Writing in 1938, Lewty described him as one of the most efficient members of the Gordonstoun Seamanship Guild, which took the place of an Officers' Training Corps. He could be trusted to take charge of a cutter under oars and sails, and on expeditions had 'proved himself to be a cheerful ship-mate and very conscientious in carrying out both major and minor duties'. Lewty added that Philip was 'thoroughly trustworthy and not afraid of dirty and arduous work'.[25]

In 1935 the boys also built a log cabin on a clifftop to house the school coastguard service and whenever rough weather threatened a Watcher's Corp manned the school lookout point on the rocky coast.[26] A fire service and mountain rescue were later added, and each boy was required to join one of the three and undergo the appropriate life-saving training. Hahn maintained that the provision of public service to the local district was vital for the spiritual health of his 'community of adolescent males'.[27]

With his parents still absent abroad, Gordonstoun provided Philip with a much-needed sense of stability, although, when it came to the holidays, there was always still the question as to where he would spend them. Much of the time he still tended to stay with Georgie and Nada Milford Haven at Lynden, where a calm atmosphere did not always prevail. The period just before Philip's first term at Gordonstoun was particularly tumultuous, in that much attention was focused on the pending involvement of various members of Philip's family in the custody trial in America for ten-year-old 'Little Gloria' Vanderbilt, which began on 1 October 1934 amid a blaze of publicity.

Little Gloria was the daughter of Nada's close friend, Gloria Morgan Vanderbilt, and on the death of her father when she was aged fifteen months, the girl had become beneficiary of a trust fund worth $5 million. While Little Gloria remained a minor, the rights to control the trust belonged to her mother, and mother and daughter travelled to and from Paris, often accompanied by big Gloria's sister Thelma, spending freely wherever they went. Eventually the girl's paternal aunt, Gertrude Vanderbilt Whitney (sculptress and founder of the Whitney Museum of American Art in New York), sued for custody of Little Gloria, alleging that her mother's raucous lifestyle made her an unfit parent.

After the opening day of the trial, the New York *Daily News* reported that, 'Mrs Gloria Morgan Vanderbilt ... listened to a tight-lipped nurse denounce her with virtuous relish as a cocktail-crazed dancing mother, a devotee of sex erotica, and the mistress of a German Prince [Philip's brother-in-law Friedel Hohenlohe] ... it was a blistering tale no skin lotion could soothe'.[28] Gloria's lawyer made it clear that he wanted to bring Nada from England to deny on the witness stand the accusations that she and Gloria had behaved like lovers at the Miramar Hotel in 1931.

Unaccustomed to public allegations of lesbianism on the fringes of the royal family, the British press stopped short of naming Nada, yet, as the news broke in America, she was mobbed by reporters at Croydon airport. 'What you have heard are a set of malicious lies,' she said, tears running down her cheeks. 'I cannot say definitely whether I shall go to the United States. What I can say is that I shall stand by Mrs Vanderbilt to the bitter end.'[29] Eventually, though, she was persuaded against going by King George V and Queen Mary.[30]

Philip's sister Margarita and her husband Friedel did, however, travel to New York as character witnesses on behalf of Gloria, who had stayed with them at Langenburg that summer. Margarita's presence disarmed the waiting reporters, who found it difficult to question the prince about his supposedly improper conduct with his former fiancée while his wife was present.[31] They also failed to make the connection between Margarita (whom they described inaccurately as a 'German woman') and Nada Milford Haven and to grasp that the main reason she, Margarita, wanted to exonerate Gloria was that Nada was her aunt. In court, Friedel and Margarita did their best to defend the good names of both Nada and Gloria, Margarita calling Nada 'a very cheerful, gay person' and Friedel staunchly refuting the notion that Gloria had ever indulged in 'excessive drinking ... impropriety ... drunkenness ... lascivious or indecent acts'.[32] Friedel, in particular, endeared himself to the judge with his admirable frankness. When asked what work he had been doing between the summer of 1927 and the end of 1928, he replied: 'From the summer of 1927 to the end of 1928 I was doing nothing.'[33] But their efforts were to no avail, and eventually, on 21 November 1934 custody of Little Gloria was granted to her aunt Gertrude Whitney.

A week after the conclusion of the Vanderbilt case, and after a whip-round among the Gordonstoun boys for collar studs and cufflinks, Philip came south to attend the wedding of his cousin Princess Marina of Greece, the twenty-seven-year-old daughter of his uncle Nicholas. Philip had known her well since their exile together in Paris, and she would remain one of his closest confidantes. Marina's bridegroom was Prince George, Duke of Kent, George V's fourth son, thirty-one, handsome, intelligent, artistic and, as Philip Ziegler puts it, 'disastrously ready to sample any delight that might be laid in front of him'.[34] During his drug-addled, bisexual bachelor days, he is said to have remarked to Nada Milford Haven, 'I suppose I've got to get married one day, but all the princesses I know are so damned ugly.'[35] Nada had promptly suggested the chic and sophisticated Princess Marina, who was also reputed to be one of the most beautiful women in Europe. Their courtship developed as guests of Marina's brother-in-law, Paul of Yugoslavia, at his castle in the Slovenian Alps, swimming in icy lakes and galloping along mountain paths.[36] Despite the forebodings of many of their friends, it proved to be one of the happiest of all royal marriages. Their home at Coppins in Buckinghamshire was henceforth added to the list of places where Philip regularly stayed during the school holidays.

The Kents' spectacular wedding at Westminster Abbey was preceded by a Greek Orthodox service, at which the Prince of Wales 'caused a mild furore when he not only absent-mindedly pulled out a cigarette but lit it on a candle held by a priest'.[37] The day held a special significance for Philip, although he would not have known it at the time, in that the bridegroom's niece, Princess Elizabeth, then aged eight, was one of the bridesmaids. This was almost certainly the first time that she and Philip had come across one another.[38] Also present was Philip's Parisian aunt, Marie Bonaparte, who possibly did not let on to the other guests that she had taken the opportunity of her trip to London to lecture the British Psycho-Analytical Society on female sexuality.[39]

Philip spent the Christmas holidays of 1934–5 back in the very different atmosphere of Nazi Germany, this time staying with his sister Sophie and brother-in-law Christoph, who were far more amenable to the new regime than the Badens at Salem. Indeed, Christoph's previously lacklustre career had taken off ever since Hitler's seizure of power. He had given up his hated job in insurance for a post in the new government, initially first secretary in the Prussian state ministry, but soon becoming head of Goering's 'Research Office' in Berlin, whose snooping assignments included monitoring Mussolini's calls to his mistress when Il Duce came to Berlin and tapping the phones of the Duke and Duchess of Windsor when they visited Salzburg in 1937.[40] At the same time, Christoph had also been given command of his own SS company of some 160 men, with which he helped to protect Nazi party rallies in what remained a climate of political violence.[41]

Sophie, too, enthused about the movement, writing to her mother-in-law after a rally in the spring of 1933: 'It was wonderful to see all the civil servants march with their flags; the customs men, the train men, bus men, etc. The policemen wore swastika bands on their arms and sang the *Horst Wessel Lied* as they marched! Oh glorious feeling …'[42] However, it was not until 1938 that she joined the Nazis' women's auxiliary, the *NS-Frauenschaft*.[43]

Philip's grandmother Victoria continued to organize his holiday movements. He kept a trunk or two of his belongings at her apartment and tended to stay there before heading on to his next destination. 'You might spend the few days after leaving Gordonstoun & starting for abroad with me at Kens. Pal.' she wrote to him before the start of the summer holidays in 1935. 'Write me a line in time to let me know when you will arrive at K.P. & when you will leave.'[44]

A compulsive organizer, Victoria was forever sending her grandson advice on his travel arrangements, as well as guidance on manners. In February 1935 she wrote to him at Gordonstoun suggesting that he send one of the photographs that Theodora had sent her 'to the kind man who gave you dinner in the train & the wrist watch … I think it will be enough if you write on the back of the card:

> To –
>
> in kind recollection
>
> from Philip, Prince of Greece, & date

I think the one with your hands in your pocket is the most suitable, but that is for you to decide.' The letter ended by asking Philip: 'Don't forget to let Georgie know in time when your Easter holidays start. You can come round here to repack. The things you left with Tiny [Sophie] have arrived here, she sent them off at once.'[45]

Every so often, Andrea came over to London to discuss his son's future with his mother-in-law, and, on one such visit, in October

1935, he told her that he had decided he wanted Philip to finish his schooling at Gordonstoun and then go into the Royal Navy '& be allowed to serve for a few years'. This, Victoria told her son Dickie, 'will be the best training for the boy & Philip is quite keen about it. The naval officer [Lewty], who is sports master etc. at the school will work him up.' Victoria was delighted by the idea that he would be following in the footsteps of her husband Louis.[46]

Andrea was still based in Monte Carlo, where he frequented the casino and befriended Gilbert Beale, a sybaritic bachelor and playboy who had made a fortune from Carter's Tested Seeds and golf courses in England and was now spending it on yachting and philandering on the Riviera.[47] An ebullient character, he later established a wildlife reserve – Beale Park – in Berkshire, and only gave up driving at the age of ninety-four after his Rolls-Royce, carrying four friends, careered into the River Thames in 1962.[48] Andrea's leisured existence had its compensations, but he was not temperamentally well suited to prolonged spells of idleness. A big part of him longed to return to his old life in Greece. Periodically he was quoted in the Greek press calling for the reinstatement of the monarchy, in the absence of which, between 1924 and 1935, the country had lurched from one crisis to the next, undergoing twenty-three changes of government, one dictatorship and thirteen coups.

In January 1935, Andrea told one newspaper that the movement for the restoration of the monarchy was spreading 'throughout the country' and he predicted that it would be reinstated 'within the coming year'. 'We shall not return as avengers,' he declared, 'but as symbols of the love of the people on whose will alone the restoration will be founded.' The British ambassador, Sir Sydney Waterlow, considered his assessment of the situation to be 'as unreliable as the channel through which it is imparted is disreputable'.[49] However, Andrea was vindicated when, in November 1935, General Kondylis staged a plebiscite which resulted in a vote of 1,491,992 to 34,454 in favour of the restoration of Andrea's nephew, King George II, who returned to the Greek throne later that month after twelve years of exile, the latter part of which he had spent living at Brown's Hotel in London.

The British ambassador warned that the experiment would 'almost certainly be doomed to fail' if the king were to insist on installing Andrea and his brother Nicholas in the country.[50] George II understood this and Andrea, too, professed to be happy that his nephew did not want 'the older generation' of the royal family to settle in Athens. At the same time, though, he was determined to follow the king to Athens 'to show himself & to be received well, to wipe out the shameful departure after the mock court-martial'.[51] In January 1936, the decree by which Andrea had been banished in 1922 was revoked,[52] and in May he arrived back in Greece aboard the yacht *Davida*, which belonged to an Australian friend of his in the South of France. Within ten days of his arrival, Waterlow reported that Andrea had undermined 'the work of conciliation' by airing his well-known royalist sentiments at a political meeting at Halandri. This 'fresh incursion into party politics cannot but be considered unfortunate', wrote Waterlow.[53] However, despite the ambassador's concerns, by the autumn Andrea was back living at the palace in Athens as principal aide-de-camp to the king.

In November 1936, George arranged for the remains of his father, King Constantine, his mother Queen Sophie, and his and Philip's grandmother, Queen Olga, who had all died in exile to be brought from a crypt at the Russian chapel in Florence for reburial in the family ground at Tatoï. This complicated operation offered, as the British ambassador drily observed, 'ample opportunity for the confusion that has hitherto been the rule on all ceremonial occasions in Greece'. And yet, 'not only was there no confusion, but there was presented to the public a series of spectacles which, for seemliness, order and even magnificence at the appropriate moments, would have done credit to any country. Greece has never seen anything like this before.'[54] As if to affirm with all possible emphasis the settled character of the restoration and to make it plain that the fortunes of Greece were indissolubly bound up with the dynasty, King George II was surrounded by nearly all the members of the Greek royal family. Fifteen-year-old Philip was given leave from Gordonstoun to attend the great occasion, the first time he been back on Greek soil since the family's enforced departure in 1922. His cousin Alexandra had not seen him since he had started at Gordonstoun and she now 'gazed in amazement at my blond, handsome cousin. He had suddenly shot up; he was thin without being gangling ... a new up-and-coming member of the family to please and interest some of the elders.'[55] At dinner, Philip ate a bad lobster and the next day, on the way from the funeral service to the palace, he was sick in his top hat, which he then calmly handed to an unsuspecting aide as he got out of the car.[56]

At this time, it was still perfectly possible that Philip might one day succeed to the Greek throne himself. George II had no children, Philip's father and surviving uncles were by now all visibly ageing, and the two ahead of Philip in the line of succession, George II's surviving brother Paul and Big George's son Peter, were both bachelors. At this great gathering of the Royal House of Greece, Alexandra recalled Philip's imagination being 'caught by the pomp and panoply of royalty as never before', and in seeking to ascertain 'precisely who was who' he 'asked one of our aunts so many questions that she had to ask him to stop'.[57]

Andrea came under pressure from George II to enter Philip for the Greek Nautical College; however, he was resolutely opposed to the idea, still bridling at the ignominy of his trial and banishment. 'Never the Greek Navy!' he told Victoria. 'In the Greek Navy after a bit they would throw him out – that's what they did to me, not once, as you know, or twice, but three times!'[58] Kurt Hahn later maintained that the 'lure of early and undeserved importance was keenly felt' by Philip and that there was 'no doubt that for a short time he was tempted both by the hazards and comforts likely to come to a Prince of Greece in residence at Athens'. But he nevertheless 'came back determined to sit the Special Entry Examination for the Royal Navy [saying] "England is my home"'.[59]

NINE

Blow after Blow

By the autumn term of 1936 there were 105 boys at Gordonstoun and fifteen-year-old Philip was one of eleven boys in Form Vb, the third from top.[1] Academically he did not stand out, but he was praised for his seamanship and for his 'ball sense and pluck',[2] which earned him a place in the first teams of his age group in rugby, hockey and cricket. With relatively few boys to choose from and stony pitches to practise on, Gordonstoun teams, like those of Cheam, barely competed with other schools, and in 1935 the school even resorted to playing its second XI against the ladies of nearby Elgin Academy. Philip, who was junior hockey captain at the time, wrote waggishly in the *Gordonstoun Record*: 'We hope that soon we shall be among the best Scottish girls' teams.'[3] Standards gradually improved, however, and during the 1936–7 hockey season, Philip scored the winning goal in their 3–2 away victory against Wellington, a result pronounced 'historic' by the school magazine.[4]

Throughout this time he had still had no contact with his mother, who was by now living quietly in a rural boarding house near Cologne in the west of Germany. Towards the end of 1936, however, she was beginning to show definite signs of regaining her equilibrium.[5] Just after Christmas, Alice wrote to Cecile, thanking her for sending photographs of her 'sweet and chubby' new baby daughter, Johanna, and particularly of Philip, whom she wistfully admitted she 'barely recognised, he is so changed'; she asked Cecile to 'Give him my love please'.[6] Philip spent part of that Christmas holiday staying with his cousin the young King Michael of Romania and his mother, Queen Helen, at the Villa Sparta in Florence.[7]

Alice's recovery continued into the spring of 1937, during which she was visited by Victoria, who returned to London heartened by her daughter's progress. When Philip stayed with Cecile and Don at Wolfsgarten during the Easter holidays, they felt confident enough of Alice's stability to take him to lunch with her in Bonn. It was the first time any of her children had seen Alice in almost five years and, finding her 'affectionate, bright and cheerful', they came away 'delighted with their meeting'.[8] How Philip responded to this encounter is not recorded, but one assumes it was an emotionally intense and confusing experience for him. Now fifteen, he was no longer the small boy he had been when he had last visited her five years earlier, and in the intervening years other mother figures had taken Alice's place in his life.

In June, Alice went to stay with Theodora at Schloss Kirchberg, another Baden castle on Lake Constance, from where she sent Philip a card for his birthday for the first time in many years, regretting that he was celebrating it 'at school and not here'.[9] The next month she visited Margarita at Langenburg. Her daughters were delighted by how well she seemed, although Cecile was worried about her latest plans to found an order of nuns in Greece and what she saw as her unrealistic hopes of living with their father again.[10] Even as they began to believe her completely recovered, Dr Binswanger warned Victoria that she would 'always need to be discreetly watched over & guided'.[11]

After spending the first three weeks of the summer holidays cruising around the Norwegian fjords as lamp trimmer aboard Gordonstoun's 75-ft wooden ketch *Henrietta*, Philip disembarked in mid-August to proceed via Oslo to visit his sisters in Germany.[12] In September he went to Wolfsgarten, where his grandmother Victoria had spent much of the summer nursing her sixty-eight-year-old brother, Ernie, the Grand Duke, who had been ill since the start of the year with lung disease. With Philip came his father Andrea, who was still acting as George II's ADC, although Victoria noticed he was 'getting very grey and rather deaf' despite his only being fifty-four.[13]

It had been hoped that Ernie would at the very least live long enough to see his younger son Ludwig ('Lu') married to Margaret (Peg) Geddes, whom he had met on a skiing holiday in Bavaria. But he faded far faster than expected and after lapsing into a coma he died on 9 October, two weeks before Lu's wedding had been due to take place. No one in the family told Alice, for fear that the news about her beloved uncle would jeopardize her fragile recovery, but she saw it anyway in a newspaper and promptly made her way to Darmstadt for the funeral, which took place on 12 October 1937.[14]

Ernie had disdained anything to do with the Nazis, but in May that year, when the party rolls had been reopened for certain individuals, his son and heir, Don, and daughter-in-law, Cecile, had both followed the earlier lead of Christoph (Sophie's husband) and joined. So, too, had Don's younger brother Lu,[15] who was already secretary to Joachim von Ribbentrop at the German embassy in London, and Philip's other brother-in-law, Friedel Hohenlohe-Langenburg, who offered to help introduce the Nazi leaders to the British royal family.[16] Hence it was only to be expected that Hitler would send a message of sympathy to the Hesse family on the Grand Duke's death and that the horse-drawn gun carriage which bore Ernie's coffin would make its way through lines of soldiers giving the Nazi salute.

From Alice's perspective, the event was probably more memorable for the fact that she saw her sister Louise (who had been married to Crown Prince Gustav of Sweden since 1923) for the first time in five years, and her brother Georgie for the first time in seven, though not Andrea, who was at that time accompanying George II of Greece to London, or Philip, who was by then back at Gordonstoun. Philip had written a letter of sympathy to his grandmother, though, to which she replied: 'As you say, it is no good dwelling on what one feels, but it is a comfort to me that you understand & join in my sense of loss.'[17] She also told Philip

> how Mama unexpectedly joined us for [the funeral] & spent a week with us all at Wolfsgarten. She was quite her old self again, like before she fell ill, and it was a great joy to Uncle Georgie and Aunt Louise to see her again after such a long time … She hopes to visit Aunt O, Cecile etc at Wolfsgarten after the new year, before Cecile's baby is expected. If you have any plans which are settled for your Xmas holidays, you might let her know. I am sure she would like to hear from you.[18]

Lu Hesse's marriage, which had been postponed when his father died, was now set to take place six weeks later in London, on 20 November. But what ought to have been an occasion to cheer the family in mourning was destined to be overtaken by a far greater catastrophe.

It was four days before the rescheduled wedding that Lu's brother Don, the new Grand Duke, and his pregnant wife Cecile, Philip's sister, set off on their fateful journey to London, accompanied by their two sons, Ludwig and Alexander, Cecile's lady-in-waiting, Alice Hahn, Don's widowed mother Onor and the best man, Joachim von Riesdesel. Lu and his bride-to-be had been awaiting the arrival of the party at Croydon airport. As they anxiously paced up and down the tarmac, at first they were told there was some delay, until eventually an official discreetly beckoned Lu to come inside the Sabena office, where he told him what had happened.*[19]

Don and Cecile and their children were to have stayed with the Mountbattens at Brook House, and their daughter Patricia (now

---

* The plane crash is described in the Prologue. After an inquiry, an employee at Steene aerodrome was found guilty of 'homicide by imprudence' for failing to transmit a message to the pilot telling him not to land at Steene but go straight on to London.

Countess Mountbatten) remembers 'walking home from school when I saw the poster saying that the plane had crashed, I was going home as I thought to meet them'.[20] Dickie Mountbatten had sent two cars to the airport, which now returned only with the engaged couple, 'prostrated with grief,' as he recalled. 'We all went round to Peg's father's house and had a ghastly family meeting. My mother said the wedding ought to go ahead, not in four days' time with all the formality and publicity, but the very next day while they were still in a state of shock.'[21]

The ceremony duly took place sombrely the next day at St Peter's, Eaton Square, with the bride, who had been intending to wear Bavarian peasant dress, instead wearing a black coat and skirt and veil. Dickie stood in for the best man who had been killed in the plane crash.[22] Among the very few present was Lu's boss, Ribbentrop, who had recently created a diplomatic incident by directing a Nazi salute at George VI,[23] yet on this occasion behaved with uncharacteristic sensitivity, doing what he could to comfort the stricken prince, and eventually signing the register.[24] Beforehand, the father of the bride, Sir Auckland Geddes, had asked the press to 'respect the deep grief of both Prince Ludwig and my daughter'. 'Prince Ludwig has just lost his father,' he explained. 'Today his mother and his only brother and sister-in-law and their children have been killed. The family has been practically wiped out and he is left to face the situation.'[25]

That same evening the newlyweds crossed the Channel to Ostend in rough weather to identify the remains of Lu's family, who had been laid out in eleven coffins in a local hospital and covered with flowers by the nuns there. The next day they accompanied the coffins on the funeral train back to Darmstadt, where they immediately adopted Don and Cecile's orphaned daughter Johanna. They were to have no children of their own.

At the funeral itself, Philip's parents saw each other for the first time since Andrea had made his one and only visit to the Bellevue clinic in 1931. Reunited in their shared grief, Alice hoped that they would now get back together for good; however shortly after the funeral they went their separate ways, destined to meet only occasionally thereafter.

Cecile had been Andrea's favourite daughter and her death came as 'a very, very hard blow,' he told Victoria that December, 'and the weight of it becomes heavier as time passes'.[26] Alice, by comparison, seemed to deal with the tragedy far better than her husband, and a decade later Theodora went so far as to tell Alice's psychiatrist, Dr Binswanger, that it had 'completely cured' her mother of her breakdown. Binswanger concluded in his notes that the plane crash that killed her third daughter and family had served as Alice's 'first curative shock', and that 'contrary to what was expected it apparently tore her out of everything'.[27]

If the previous traumatic experiences in Philip's childhood had caused him to seal himself off emotionally, in some respects he, too, might have been better equipped than he otherwise would have been to deal with this latest disaster, if not in a profound sense.[28] This may explain why, when Hahn broke the news to him in his study at Gordonstoun, 'his sorrow was that of a man'.[29] However, Philip had clearly been extremely fond of Cecile and Don,[30] and when he spent the desperately sad Christmas after their funeral staying at Lubenham with the Wernhers,[31] their daughter Gina noticed how deeply their deaths had affected him. 'He was very quiet. He didn't talk much about it, but [later] he showed me a little bit of wood from the aeroplane. It was just a small piece, but it meant a lot to him.'[32]

At the beginning of January 1938, Philip joined his father in Rome, en route for a reunion in Athens of his Greek relations, including two of his surviving sisters, Margarita and Theodora, at the wedding of Crown Prince Paul of Greece to Princess Frederika of Hanover. Sixteen-year-old Philip shared the duties of best man with his cousins

Prince Peter of Greece and King Michael of Romania. It was a happy interlude but a brief one. As Philip began the Easter term at Gordonstoun, sadness once again descended on the family.

In early December Philip's uncle and guardian Georgie Milford Haven had slipped on a marble floor and broken his thigh after dining with friends in London. At first this caused no great alarm, but after a month it was noticed that the fracture was taking a long time to heal. His brother Dickie was by that time away captaining an English polo team in Jamaica, and at the end of January he heard from a distraught Nada that Georgie had bone marrow cancer and there was nothing that could be done. His doctors preferred not to tell him, fearing the news would only hasten his decline, so poor Dickie was obliged to carry on with his polo tournament as if nothing was wrong.[33] He told his mother, who spent hours by Georgie's bedside, that he was 'utterly miserable and wretched to be prevented from returning at once ... Mama dear, I've been just like a baby. I cry myself to sleep almost every night.'[34]

Victoria wrote to Philip at Gordonstoun at the beginning of February, telling him that Georgie had been 'moved to a nicer nursing home, where he can have treatment. Such a lot of worries all on top of one another.'[35] When Dickie eventually made it back to England at the end of February, he found Georgie 'cheerful and uncomplaining but in intense pain'.[36] He held on for a further six weeks 'often wandering in his mind but assured by all around him that he was well on the way to recovery',[37] before finally succumbing to the inevitable on 8 April. 'The sweetest natured, most charming, most able, most brilliant, entirely loveable brother anyone ever had is lost,' wrote Dickie in his diary: 'Heartbroken.'[38] For Philip, the sweet-natured Georgie had come as close as anyone to providing him with a sense of stability after his mother's breakdown, and his death caused him profound sadness. Yet he again dealt with the blow quietly. 'I suppose he just buried his feelings,' remarked one of his fellow pupils at Gordonstoun.[39]

As far as Philip's future was concerned, the most important conse-quence of Georgie's death was that his younger brother Dickie Mountbatten now stepped in and took over what remained of the job of bringing his nephew up. The death of one father figure thus cleared the way for another, of far greater influence and ambition. Mountbatten had long recognized Philip's talents, and he had his own ideas as to what could be done with them.[40]

TEN

The Man with the Plan

Dickie Mountbatten's transition to chief mentor did not happen overnight. Much of Philip's holiday time was still spent with his sisters in Germany, most often at Salem with Theodora and Berthold, who taught his young brother-in-law to drive and to fish for trout with a dry fly.[1] And whenever he was in London he was as likely to stay with his grandmother at Kensington Palace as he was with Dickie and Edwina at Brook House, their mansion on Park Lane.[2] But he increasingly spent weekends and some of his holidays with them at Adsdean, the Gothic pile near Portsmouth that served as their country house until Edwina inherited Broadlands just before the war.

The Mountbattens lived on a far more opulent scale than the Milford Havens — Adsdean's amenities included a polo practice ground, golf course, three tennis courts and 800 acres of shooting[3] — yet there were striking similarities between the families in other respects. For one thing, the vivacious Edwina was every bit as much of a 'goer' as Philip's other aunt, Nada: 'Restless, dissatisfied, rapacious for new experience,' writes Philip Ziegler, 'it is unlikely that any one man could have given Edwina all she needed. Certainly her husband proved inadequate.'[4] Early in their marriage she had embarked on a string of indiscreet affairs and Charlie Chaplin claimed that she had even made a pass at him while on her honeymoon. A story in the *San Francisco Chronicle* in 1926 headlined 'Royal Spanking for Gay Lady

Mountbatten' was not as colourful as it now sounds, concerning only a rebuke by Queen Mary for having danced a Charleston with Fred Astaire, but there was plenty of gossip linking Edwina's name with other men and women.[5]

Her liaisons were facilitated by Dickie's long absences away at sea during the 1920s and 1930s, when, as one of the Royal Navy's rising stars, he was busy fulfilling the insouciant pledge he had made when he was fourteen to remedy the humiliation suffered by his father. Dickie's postings also limited his opportunity to keep tabs on his adolescent nephew, and his letter to Edwina in the spring of 1938, when Georgie was dying, suggests that they were not then nearly as intimate as they later became. 'Philip was here all last week doing his entrance exams for the Navy,' wrote Dickie. 'He has his meals with us and he really is killingly funny. I like him very much.'[6]

He nevertheless maintained that he had already marked Philip down as 'an exceptional person', the telling moment having been 'out shooting one day, when he was eight or nine. It was rough. The way he coped told me.'[7] The fact of having no son of his own inevitably helped focus Dickie's attention on his nephew. His daughter Patricia recalls that 'he [Philip] just appeared for the holidays so to speak. He was always very good looking and full of fun and games and quite a tease ... so he was always someone one was pleased to see when they arrived.'[8]

In due course, Philip would become like a son to his uncle. When Chips Channon met Mountbatten in 1942 he recorded that 'only when I talked of his nephew, Prince Philip of Greece, did his sleepy strange eyes light up with an affectionate, almost paternal delight'.[9] Philip may have bridled at the assumption of parental responsibility by his younger uncle, but Mountbatten is nonetheless often credited with having steered him towards the navy, in line with family tradition, and away from his original ambition to become a fighter pilot. As Philip Ziegler notes, this probably saved his life because otherwise 'he would have achieved his aim in time to fight in the Battle of Britain, with all the appalling risks that would have entailed'.[10] Philip's sister Theodora, however, maintained that to begin with her brother had wanted to join the Greek navy. 'Dickie did not stop him,' she said. 'I did, and persuaded him to enter the Royal Navy.' As she remembered it, 'it was only when he [Dickie] noticed that Philip and Elizabeth were falling in love that he started paying attention to Philip'.[11]

In order to help prepare Philip for the special entrance exam into Dartmouth, Mountbatten arranged for him to go and stay in Cheltenham with a naval coach and his wife,[12] who found the prince 'intensely eager to get on' and also very short of pocket money. According to Alexandra, apart from 'Saturday night visits to the movies, and radio or record sessions with the daughter of the house', Philip kept his nose to the grindstone, and when he sat the exam he was placed sixteenth out of the thirty-four candidates who qualified.[13]

Philip spent the summer term of 1938 at Gordonstoun as captain of cricket and helper of games, and afterwards travelled out to Venice at the invitation of Aspasia of Greece, who had lived there ever since her husband, King Alexander, had fallen victim to the monkey bite in 1920. Aspasia's daughter, Alexandra, was there at the same time and recalled how Philip had relished letting his hair down at last after such a harrowing year.[14] Reminding Aspasia beforehand that his son still had exams to pass, Andrea pleaded with her to 'keep him out of girl trouble'. Yet by Alexandra's account 'blondes, brunettes and redhead charmers, Philip gallantly and I think quite impartially squired them all'.

Approaching seventeen, tall and athletic, Philip was already very attractive to women. He was also fun to be with, 'very amusing, gay, full of life and energy and a tease,' according to a cousin.[15] He reminded Alexandra of 'a huge, hungry dog; perhaps a friendly collie who never had a basket of his own and responded to every overture with eager tail-wagging'.[16] He was also 'immensely gregarious,' she wrote, 'so quickly ready for each new experience', and he was showered with invitations from Venetian society hostesses. At one party, Philip overdid the Italian wine and amused the other guests by 'dancing about the terrace like a young faun' and 'swinging from the pergola', which then collapsed and he 'disappeared under the greenery'.

At each gathering, by the time his aunt told him she wanted to go, 'there was invariably some lovely young thing in tulle or organdie' to whom Philip had offered a ride home. 'No need to keep the driver, Auntie Aspasia,' he would say, 'I'll take over. The boatman's had a long day.' Aspasia complied on the condition that he came back within twenty minutes.

Eventually one girl began to stand out from the rest and Philip begged his aunt to be allowed to stay out in the boat a little longer. 'Very well,' she agreed. 'But you are to cruise round and round the island and don't stop the engine! I shall be listening.' Alexandra was listening, too, and wrote that after three or four circuits the engine suddenly went silent and remained so for the next five minutes – 'which we filled with surmise' – before starting again. When eventually they returned, Philip sheepishly explained that they had had 'trouble with the sparking plugs'.

Alexandra did not identify this particular girl but all the evidence points to her being Cobina Wright, the budding American actress whose mother, also called Cobina, was among those who entertained Philip during his time in Venice. Cobina Wright Senior was a socially pushy organizer of debutante parties in New York and was intent on grooming her daughter for a film career capped by a spectacular marriage. Cobina Junior was two months younger than Philip – they both turned seventeen that summer – and very striking: tall, slim and

Philip's paternal grandparents, King George I and Queen Olga of Greece.

His maternal grandparents, Prince Louis and Princess Victoria (centre) of Battenberg, with their children, from left, Louise, Georgie, Dickie and Alice, Philip's mother.

Philip's parents, Prince Andrew (Andrea) of Greece and Princess Alice of Battenberg, at the time of their marriage in 1903.

Mon Repos, the villa on Corfu where Philip was born on the dining room table in 1921; the family was forced to abandon it eighteen months later, never to return.

Alice with three-month-old Philip on a visit to England in September 1921 for the burial of his last surviving grandfather, Louis, Marquess of Milford Haven (as he had latterly become).

Philip's family, happy at Mon Repos, Corfu, Easter 1922, eight months before they were driven into exile: (left to right) Alice, Theodora, Cecile (in front), Philip, Andrea, Sophie and Margarita.

Five-year-old Philip
with his uncle and
mentor of later years
Dickie Mountbatten,
Adsdean, July 1926.

Aged seven in Paris,
winning a biscuit-eating
competition and in
Greek national costume.

The odd couple: Philip's unconventional aunt and uncle, Princess Marie Bonaparte and Prince 'Big' George of Greece, the family's landlords and benefactors at St Cloud.

Philip's sister Sophie on her marriage in 1930 to Prince Christoph of Hesse, later a member of the SS.

As a schoolboy at Salem in Germany in 1934, aged 12,
with his elder sister Theodora and her daughter Margarita
in the pram being inspected by another Salem pupil.

Salem pupils picnicking beside Lake Constance:
Philip is standing on the right, hand on hip.

Philip's uncles and aunts on his mother's side, in 1928: (left to right) Dickie and Edwina Mountbatten, Aunt Louise, Nada and Georgie Milford Haven.

Nada Milford Haven with her son David and daughter Tatiana at Lynden Manor, where Philip spent most of his school holidays between the ages of nine and sixteen.

Philip's sister Cecile with her husband George Donatus, 'Don', of Hesse and their three children, shortly before the Steene air disaster in 1937. Their funeral procession at Darmstadt (below) was led by Ludwig, 'Lu', of Hesse, who succeeded Don as Grand Duke, followed by (left to right) Friedel Hohenlohe, husband of Philip's sister Margarita; Sophie's husband Christoph of Hesse, in a SS uniform; Christoph's brother Philipp of Hesse, in a SA uniform; Philip, in a civilian suit; and his other surviving brother-in-law, Berthold of Baden. Dickie Mountbatten is in the row behind, in a naval peaked cap.

blonde, with huge blue eyes and a radiant smile. By 1938, she was already under contract with 20th Century Fox, while also modelling and singing in nightclubs. The next year she won the title of 'Miss Manhattan'[17] and was named the 'most attractive and talented New York girl of the 1939 season'.[18] Her first meeting with Philip took place at Harry's Bar, a favourite haunt of his aunt Aspasia, and Cobina later remembered that, on seeing the prince, her mother had 'shoved her into his arms'.[19]

Over the next three weeks Philip escorted Cobina around Venice, spending 'passionate evenings in gondolas on the Grand Canal' according to one account, before following her back to London for another week with her there, 'dining, dancing, and walking London's streets, hand in hand'. When mother and daughter left for America, he vowed to follow and was reported to have cried as he kissed the younger Cobina goodbye. Her friend Gant Gaither, the Broadway producer, later maintained that Philip then wrote her 'impassioned love letters. He said he planned to woo her to marriage, no matter what. He desperately wanted to marry her, but [in the end] Cobina Jr. just wasn't all that interested.'[20] In 1941 she fell in love with a wealthy American corporal, Palmer Beaudette, and married him instead. Interviewed by the American *Town and Country* magazine in 1973, she admitted that 'I met him [Philip] in Venice and he followed me to London'. She also revealed that in her bedroom she kept three photographs of 'the three loves of my life' – one of them being Philip. They were still 'good friends', she said, and wrote to each other often.[21] Friends of Philip, meanwhile, confirm that he had 'fallen very heavily' for Cobina.[22]

When Philip returned to Gordonstoun in the autumn, he was made house helper and helper of organization. Any romantic frustrations he might have felt he could take out on the playing fields. As hockey captain and centre forward he was 'an energetic player, who inspires the team to effort', reported the *Gordonstoun Record*, although he was sometimes 'too eager to follow his own pass'.[23] In the rugby XV, meanwhile, he was 'still inclined to tackle a little high, and to run in to the forwards rather than make openings for his wing', but he was 'improving every game' and had 'greatly strengthened the three-quarter line'.[24]

In his end-of-term report in December 1938, Hahn told Philip's parents that he had made their son guardian (head boy) for the Easter term. 'He is universally trusted, liked and respected,' the headmaster wrote. 'He has the greatest sense of service of all the boys in the school.' He was 'a born leader' but would 'need the exacting demands of great service to do justice to himself. His best is outstanding – his second best is not good enough.' Hahn predicted that Philip would 'make his mark in any profession where he will have to prove himself in a free trial of strength. His gifts would run to waste if he were soon condemned to lead a life where neither superior officers nor the routine of the day forced him to tap his hidden reserves.'[25]

The report also included Hahn's assessments in various categories, mostly to do with character, which in Philip's case amounted to a virtual paean. His public spirit was 'exemplary'; his sense of justice 'never failing' – although when baulked in his plans he was 'still inclined to jump to angry conclusions'. He could always be relied on to state facts precisely, had a 'marked power' for gathering and giving precise evidence, and 'hates subterfuges'. He had demonstrated 'unusual courage and endurance' in the face of discomforts and hardships and 'does not know what boredom is when intent on discharging his duties'. He had the 'courage of his tastes and his convictions' but 'the lure of the moment remains his danger'. He had the making of a 'first class organiser' and was 'both kind and firm', although 'as a leader of games he is at times too irritable'.

In dealing with younger boys, Philip had 'a natural power of command' and his 'sense of humour and a rapid understanding of human nature have proved a great help to him in tasks of leadership'.

Where a task in hand interested him he had the 'power of meticulous application', but where it did not 'he will only do his best under pressure'. Nevertheless his conscientiousness in everyday affairs and in tasks with which he was specially entrusted was 'exemplary'. In addition he had 'a natural courtesy'; his manual dexterity was 'very well developed', his physical endurance 'quite outstanding'; he was 'musical and has good taste' and his 'practical [art] work' was 'marked by energy, enterprise and care'.

One brief paragraph alone was devoted to how he had done in the academic subjects, crediting him with 'literary appreciation' and 'an unusual grasp of cause and effect in human affairs ... particularly evident in his historical studies'; he had 'a great talent' for languages, his understanding of mathematical problems was 'sound', and in scientific work he showed 'definite powers of observation'.[26]

Philip's mother Alice received this report while staying with Victoria at Kensington Palace, having recently returned from her first visit to Greece since the family's flight in 1922. Her plan was to create a base in Athens not only for herself – her first real home since her breakdown – but also for Philip when he left school the next year. She wanted to enable her son to spend time there and get to know the people whose prince he was. It was perhaps not the ideal time for him to settle in the country, which was by then under the dictatorship of General Metaxas, an outspoken admirer of Hitler and Mussolini, although on the other hand Metaxas was a staunch monarchist and had long been on friendly terms with Philip's father Andrea.[27] 'I have taken a small flat just for you and me,' Alice wrote to Philip from Athens:

Two bedrooms, each with a bathroom and two sitting rooms, a little kitchen & pantry. I found some furniture stored away in various places in the Old Palace, which I had not seen again since 1917, a most agree-

able surprise & the family here are giving me things to complete it …
Dickie tells me there is a chance of you having a long holiday in Spring
so I am looking forward to your living in our flat.[28]

Before that, Philip spent his last term at Gordonstoun as guardian.
Another boy at the school at that time, Joseph Pease (later Lord
Gainford), remembers that he had a 'natural authority – he just said
what needed doing and it was done, he never had to raise his voice'.
However, he also had 'quite a bit of the devil in him' and played several
memorable pranks on the other boys, encouraged by Hahn, who was
all in favour of practical jokes.[29]

At the end of term, Philip travelled out to Athens to join Alice in
her flat, although because Kurt Hahn and Dickie Mountbatten both
had qualms about his living with his mother, a Greek naval officer was
seconded to keep 'a paternal eye on him', so Alice reassured Dickie.[30]
In May he returned to England and entered Dartmouth as a cadet in
the Royal Navy 'consequent on a request from Buckingham Palace'. It
was not intended that he remain in the navy after he had reached the
rank of acting sub-lieutenant, but he would nevertheless do the
normal special cadets' training, spending two terms at Dartmouth
and two in the training cruiser.[31]

While he was at Dartmouth, another family tragedy struck. In June
Alice was on her way back to England to visit Philip when she was
intercepted with the news that her granddaughter Johanna, Cecile's
only surviving child, was critically ill with meningitis at the Alice
Hospital in Darmstadt. She rushed there to join the family vigil by
Johanna's bedside but soon after she arrived the little girl died.
Afterwards, she wrote to Philip describing the 'sweet picture before
our eyes of a lovely sleeping child with golden curls, looking for me
so very like Cecile at that age that it was like losing my child a second
time and I was thankful that Papa was away travelling and did not see
that, for Papa adored Cecile when she was small and could never bear

to be parted from her'.[32] A week later, she admitted to Philip that she herself was 'quite exhausted by the strain and sadness of it all'.[33]

It was only a month after Johanna's death that Philip had his first encounter of any significance with the young Princess Elizabeth, who was by then aged thirteen. Her family had known him since he was a small child, when his parents took him to tea at Buckingham Palace with Queen Mary, who later remembered 'a nice little boy with very blue eyes'.[34] Philip and Elizabeth had both been present at various family gatherings over the years, including the Kents' wedding in 1934 – where George V had exclaimed 'You're Andrew's [Andrea's] boy!' – and at the coronation of Elizabeth's father, George VI, in 1937, a year after the Abdication that had sprung the princess into the unexpected and unwanted position of being heir to the throne. Philip's name had even appeared in the newspapers as one of a select band of suitable potential bridegrooms for her. However, it is doubtful that either of them had given much thought to the other until 22 July 1939, when Mountbatten attended the royal family on a visit to the naval college at Dartmouth in the royal yacht, and engineered several encounters with his young nephew. 'Philip accompanied us and dined on board,' he noted in his diary at the end of the first evening. The next day, the 23rd, he recorded: 'Philip came back aboard V & A for tea and was a great success with the children.'[35] As Mountbatten's biographer suggests, 'it is hard to believe no thought crossed [Mountbatten's] mind that an admirable husband for the future Queen Elizabeth might be readily available'.[36]

At the time of the royal visit, the college was in the grip of a combined outbreak of mumps and chickenpox, so to avoid the risk of infection the princesses were sent off to be entertained at the house of the Captain of the College, Queen Elizabeth's old friend Freddy Dalrymple-Hamilton. His son North, then aged seventeen, later executive officer of the royal yacht *Britannia*, recalls being asked to 'get my toy trains out and god knows what' for the princesses to play with and that 'Prince Philip [who was uninfected] came along to assist looking after them – I think Mountbatten rather fixed it that he should ...'[37]

The princesses' governess, Miss Crawford – known to the girls as Crawfie – later described how, while they were playing with the clockwork railway laid out on the nursery floor, in came 'a fair-headed boy, rather like a Viking, with a sharp face and piercing blue eyes'. 'He was good-looking, though rather offhand in his manner,' she remembered. 'He said, "How do you do," to Lilibet [the family's name for Elizabeth] and for a while they knelt side by side playing with the trains. He soon got bored with that. We had ginger crackers and lemonade in which he joined, and then he said, "Let's go to the tennis courts and have some real fun jumping the nets."'[38]

By Crawfie's account, he made quite an impression on Elizabeth: 'She never took her eyes off him the whole time. At the tennis courts I thought he showed off a good deal, but the little girls were much impressed. Lilibet said, "How good he is, Crawfie! How high he can jump!" He was quite polite to her, but did not pay her any special attention. He spent a lot of time teasing plump little Margaret.'

There is no indication that Philip was bowled over by the meeting, or reason why he should have been. At that age Elizabeth was shy and rather solemn, like her father, and physically not as mature as many other girls of her age. As Crawfie put it, 'when so many are gawky, she was an enchanting child with the loveliest hair and skin and a long, slim figure'. The fact that she was still made to wear the same clothes as her nine-year-old sister Margaret – identical double-breasted tweed coats, dark berets, knee-length white socks and sensible walking shoes – only served to accentuate her child-like appearance. It can hardly have escaped Philip's notice that when he came aboard the royal yacht for dinner later that evening, Elizabeth had already been sent to bed in accordance with the nursery schedule.

The next day, though, Elizabeth was still visibly smitten with the dashing young prince. When Philip again joined the royal family with his fellow cadet captains for tea on their yacht, she was observed to ask him eagerly, 'What would you like to eat? What would you like?' and then watch with admiration as Philip tucked in to several plate-fuls of shrimps and a banana split.

The king, on the other hand, seemed barely to have noticed Philip until the time came for the royal party to leave and the high-spirited cadets commandeered a flotilla of small craft to send them on their way. Gradually they all fell back until one solitary blond oarsman was left, still rowing furiously in their wake, while Elizabeth watched him avidly through binoculars. Then the king saw him. 'The young fool!' he cried. 'He must go back!'

ELEVEN

A Good War

Shortly after the royal visit to Dartmouth, at the end of term Philip was again reunited with his mother at Kensington Palace, where Victoria found Alice 'so well & calm in her nerves'.[1] On 11 August mother and son departed together for Paris, spending three days there before continuing by train down to Italy and on by boat to Greece, arriving shortly before Britain and France declared war on Germany on 3 September 1939.

The outbreak of war placed Philip in a quandary. On the one hand he was keen to continue with his naval training in England, which he now regarded as home, and to fight on that side – even though his sisters were all married to Germans and living in Germany. At the same time he was a prince of Greece and, as things stood, the eventual heir to that throne. And as Alice explained to Dickie, he felt 'such an utter stranger to the language and people' there that if he did not now spend some time in the country and try and re-establish a bond with the people it would be much harder to do so in years to come.[2]

In September, unbeknown to Philip, he had moved even closer in line to the Greek throne after Big George's son Peter disqualified himself from the succession by marrying a Russian divorcee out in India, after which Big George, rather immoderately, refused to have anything to do with his son again. As Alice warned Philip in December, if Crown Princess Frederika had only daughters, Philip was next in line after the crown prince.[3] However, the possibility of his succeeding receded again on 2 June 1940, when Frederika had a boy, Constantine, who would eventually succeed to the throne, in 1964.

By that time, Philip had been saved from his deliberations by King George II, who asked him to go back to England and finish his training. Philip was surprised by the king's request[4] and his grandmother Victoria went so far as to suggest at the time that it would have been better if he had stayed in Greece 'where he belongs'. 'War is too serious a matter for boys of foreign countries to have to undergo the risks,' she wrote to Dickie, '& they can only be an encumbrance & of no real use to our country.' Nonetheless, she hoped that he might be appointed to 'some battle-ship' and receive 'the training and schooling we all agreed he could get better in our Navy, & fairly safely, which for poor Alice's sake I hope you may be able to arrange for him'.[5]

Philip returned to Dartmouth for his second term in the autumn with his future still uncertain. In late November the new captain of the college wrote to Mountbatten asking what was to happen to him after this term. 'Do you know what the answer is? The boy is anxious to know so that he can make arrangements for his leave etc. I gather that he, being a most enterprising young man, is full of ideas as to his future movements. I am told that he has done extremely well here and is one of the most outstanding cadets of his term.'[6]

Within weeks of the letter being written, Philip was awarded the King's Dirk as the best all-round cadet of his term and the Eardley-Howard-Crockett prize for the best cadet at the college. For the latter he was up against cadets who had been at Dartmouth since the age of thirteen, so it was quite an achievement, and it seems to have come at some cost to his popularity, some disgruntled fellow cadets later describing him as 'a bit of a bully' with 'that Germanic arrogance of command'. Yet even his detractors conceded that he had been 'saved from priggishness by his sense of humour – he could even laugh at himself'.[7]

Despite the laurels heaped on him at Dartmouth, as a 'neutral foreigner' Philip was for the time being barred from serving in a theatre of war and he was told that his application for naturalization as a British citizen could not be decided until after the war, the procedures having been suspended for the time being. It therefore fell to his uncle Dickie to pull the necessary strings to allow him to continue with his naval career. After suggesting to George VI that he could be sent to a ship on the China Station,[8] Mountbatten asked his former flotilla commander, H. T. Baillie Grohman, if as a favour he would be prepared to take his nephew aboard his ship *Ramillies*. So it was that, rather to Philip's frustration, on New Year's Day 1940 he was posted as a midshipman to this lumbering old battleship escorting convoys of Australian and New Zealand troopships bound for Egypt.

After taking passage on HMAS *Hobart*, he joined *Ramillies* on 22 February 1940 at Colombo. Although he would be supposedly out of the firing line, it was not an especially cushy posting. For one thing, *Ramillies* was unbearably hot at night when the ship was darkened and every scuttle was shut with deadlights. As 'Captain's doggie', it was also Philip's duty to brew the cocoa which hardly improved matters for him.[9] On 15 March they reached Sydney, where a general refit of wirings and gun mountings afforded time to venture up country, Philip recording in his midshipman's journal how he had gone to a sheep station four hundred miles inland and spent four days working as a jackaroo. Afterwards, *Ramillies* made for Aden, 'crossing the line' on 1 April when, for the benefit of those who had not qualified for 'a certificate from King Neptune, the ceremony of lathering and ducking was carried out on the quarterdeck'. Philip and the other initiates were left 'gasping and choking' as they were repeatedly ducked 'face down and feet up' in soapy water.[10] On the plus side, on entering the tropics, swimming pools were rigged on the decks and 'the issue of lime juice commenced'.[11]

When *Ramillies* reached Aden in May, Philip heard he was to be transferred to the county-class cruiser *Kent*, flagship of the China Station, a disappointment since he was 'just beginning to settle down and get accustomed to a definite routine'; the officers had been 'very good' to the junior group, and 'many irksome peacetime regulations had been neglected'. However he was thankful that 'the ventilation is so very much better [in *Kent*] that it is quite possible to sleep below decks in comfort' and there was 'no danger whatsoever of hitting one's head on the deck head or beams'.[12] The news that they were to be lumbered with 'royalty' had initially elicited groans from *Kent*'s ratings, who wanted nothing more than an uncomplicated passage home after a two-and-a-half-year-long tour of duty. However, one biographer maintains that Philip quickly won them over by 'running all over the ship trying to obey instructions' and 'smiling and being cheerful to everyone'.[13]

Their route took them via the Chagos Islands to Bombay, where it was the monsoon season and 'everybody had gone to the hills'. From there they convoyed eight battalions of British troops on their way home round the Cape, and at Durban 'began one of the pleasantest weeks spent by anyone for a very long time', wrote Philip; the South Africans' 'grand unselfish hospitality' would 'live in our memories for years to come, and the fact that so many hearts were left behind in Durban is not surprising'.[14] Whether or not he left his own heart there, he did not say.

Action continued to prove elusive. Shortly after leaving Durban, Philip's journal records, 'We have something to look forward to, there is an enemy raider in the Indian Ocean, and there is just a chance that our tracks will cross.'[15] But they did not. The greatest excitement was provided by the trade winds en route to Colombo, when 'a particularly heavy sea completely smothered the bridge and platform' and 'a lot of innocent fun was had in the mess, watching the Goanese stewards diligently laying the table, and then the plates, knives, forks, spoons, butter dishes, toast racks and marmalade landing in a heap on the deck'.[16]

In August he left *Kent* at Colombo and after three days at the festival of Buddha's Tooth up in the hills at Kandy, another weekend on a tea plantation and five weeks on a shore station, he was posted to *Kent*'s sister ship, *Shropshire*, for convoy duty in the Red Sea and down the east coast of Africa as far as Durban.

Italy's entry into the war in June 1940 had by this time advanced the prospect of Philip seeing action. To begin with, Metaxas had hoped to be able to keep Greece out of the fighting, while maintaining a benevolent neutrality towards Britain. However, Mussolini was anxious to demonstrate to Hitler that he, too, was capable of spectacular victories and had set his sights on Greece, as what he wrongly thought would be a soft target. On 15 August 1940 an Italian submarine had torpedoed a Greek light cruiser, killing nine sailors, and on 28 October Italian forces invaded Greece from Albania. With Greece now at war on the Allied side, it was no longer imperative for the Admiralty to keep Philip out of harm's way.

Thus, in mid-December, he heard that as soon as was convenient he was to join the newly modernized battleship *Valiant*, part of the Mediterranean Fleet.[17] After spending New Year's Eve at Port Said, with its 'rather limited facilities for celebration', he took a train to Alexandria, where he joined *Valiant*, his fourth ship in eleven months.[18] He did not have to wait long to experience the 'hot war' he had yearned for.

Three days later, at dusk, the battle fleet put to sea and shortly afterwards they were told they were going to bombard Bardia on the Libyan coast – a prelude to General Wavell's first advance into Cyrenaica. 'We arrived off the coast on Thursday morning at dawn,' Philip recorded in his journal, 'and in the dark the flashes of the guns could be seen a long way out to sea. We went to action stations at 07.30, and at 08.10 the bombardment commenced … The whole operation was a very spectacular affair.'[19] Next, they moved on towards Sicily, where he witnessed one British destroyer, *Southampton*, 'blowing up in a cloud of smoke and spray', another, *Gallant*, hitting a mine so that 'her bow was blown off, and floated slowly away on the swell …' and then 'two torpedo bombers attacked us, but a quick alteration of course foiled their attempt, and their fish passed down the port side. Shortly after this sixteen German dive-bombers attacked the *Illustrious*. She was hit aft and amidships and fires broke out. Then the bombers concentrated on us and five bombs dropped fairly close.'[20]

One of Philip's shipmates was the future Admiral of the Fleet, Terry Lewin, who had already made his mark with his skilful direction of *Valiant*'s close-range anti-aircraft armament. Lewin later recalled that from 'not knowing what to expect' from Midshipman Prince Philip of Greece, the gunroom had soon found him to be an excellent messmate.[21]

By mid-January 1941, Philip was enjoying a convivial shore leave with friends and relations in Athens, staying partly with his mother, who was doing charitable work helping the families of Greek soldiers and was delighted to see her son looking so well and happy,[22] and partly with George II, who for his own safety was living at Tatoï but came up to the capital most days to 'picnic' at the royal palace. Earlier that month the American-born MP and socialite Henry 'Chips' Channon had shared the king's picnic tray and found him to be 'kindly, gentle and loyal', albeit lonely and 'a mild bore'. During his stay in Athens, Channon also met Philip, describing him in his diary as 'extraordinarily handsome'. 'He is to be our Prince Consort,' Channon famously confided after a conversation with Philip's aunt, Princess Nicholas of Greece, 'and that is why he is serving in our Navy. He is charming, but I deplore such a marriage; he and Princess Elizabeth are too inter-related.'*[23] Even on Princess Nicholas's part,

---

* They were in fact second cousins once removed as descendants from Christian IX of Denmark and third cousins by descent from Queen Victoria.

this prophecy seems to have been speculative to say the least – even though Alice was 'inclined to dwell on potential dynastic alliances' for her children, as her biographer puts it, and an alliance with the British royal family would surely have been very high on her wish list, as it would on that of the rest of the beleaguered Greek royal family.

Channon also heard all about the rest of the 'peculiar' Greek royal family. Philip's mother Alice, he gathered, was 'eccentric to say the least'; and his father Andrea, meanwhile, 'philanders on the Riviera'.[24] Andrea had in fact been stranded in Monte Carlo after the fall of France the previous summer, but would have far preferred to have been back in Greece. Whether or not he deserved his reputation as a ladies' man is difficult to establish at this distance, but in any event he had by then struck up a steady relationship with an actress going by the name of Comtesse Andrée de La Bigne. They lived together aboard the 167-tonne yacht *Davida*, which he had now bought, but were cut off from outside news as his radio had been confiscated.[25]

During these five weeks spent in Athens, Philip's cousin Alexandra recalled him bounding up to their house 'ready for gramophone records and fun, and dancing with a whole new group of friends'.[26] During air raids he would contribute a running commentary 'amid the bark of ack-ack guns' and he attacked the Greek food with his usual gusto, although she implies that he used his naval duties as an excuse to be noncommittal when it came to dinner invitations – reading between the lines of her book one gets the impression that she was rather more eager for his company than he was for hers.[27] During this time, Philip also attended the funerals of his uncle Prince Christopher and General Metaxas, both of whom died while he was on leave.

At the beginning of March he returned to *Valiant*, which was now engaged in convoying British troops from Alexandria to Crete and Piraeus in order to bolster Greek defences ahead of the expected German landings. The only enemy force capable of disrupting these convoys was the Italian navy, but the British fleet possessed the advantages of air cover, radar sets and, most crucially as it turned out, experience in the art of night fighting, of which the audacious commander of the Mediterranean Fleet, Admiral Andrew Cunningham, was the navy's foremost expert.

On 27 March Philip recorded that 'there were to have been three nights of all night leave so that the whole ship's company could get ashore in Alexandria, but by Thursday forenoon there was a buzz going around the ship that some Italian cruisers had gone to sea'.[28] After darkness had fallen that evening they slipped out of Alexandria harbour, following Cunningham's flagship *Warspite*, the aircraft carrier *Formidable*, another battleship, *Barham*, and nine destroyers. Their objective, though they did not yet know this, was to intercept the Italian fleet which Ultra code-breakers had learned was threatening an Allied convoy to Piraeus. The next morning, Cunningham's reconnaissance planes located the Italian force – a battleship, eight cruisers and three destroyers – south-west of Cape Matapan, the central claw of the Peloponnese, and after several long-range exchanges of fire the Italians began to withdraw. In the ensuing chase that afternoon, torpedo strikes severely damaged the Italian flagship *Vittorio Veneto* and crippled their heavy cruiser, *Pola*, whereupon the Italian commander made the fateful decision of ordering a squadron of cruisers and destroyers to return and escort the stricken *Pola*. Cunningham now boldly decided to risk a fleet encounter at night, relying on the British skill at night fighting, honed in the Mediterranean in the 1930s. None of the Italian ships was equipped for this, and when they were detected on radar shortly after 10 p.m., *Valiant* and the other battleship, *Barham* opened fire at only 3,500 metres and in five minutes annihilated the two Italian heavy cruisers that had been sent to protect *Pola*. In the melee that followed, a further two Italian destroyers were sunk, along with the crippled *Pola*.[29]

Philip's role in the battle had been to operate the searchlights so that if any British ship illuminated a target he was to switch on

Valiant's midship light which 'picked out the enemy cruiser and lit her up as if it were broad daylight', he recorded. After the flagship and *Valiant* had set the target well ablaze, the captain and gunnery officer shouted from the bridge for the searchlights to train left, but 'the idea that there might have been another ship never entered my head, so it was some few moments before I was persuaded to relinquish the blazing target and search for another one', he wrote. Eventually, training to the left, his light picked up the other cruiser 'ahead of the first one by 3 or 4 cables. As the enemy was so close the light did not illuminate the whole ship but only ¾ of it, so I trained left over the whole ship until the bridge structure was in the centre of the beam. The effect was rather like flashing a strong torch on a small model about 5 yards away ... She was illuminated in an undamaged condition for the period of about 5 seconds when our second broadside left the ship, and almost at once she was completely blotted out from stem to stern.' After several broadsides and secondary armament fire, he estimated that 'more than 70% of the shells must have hit. The only correction given by the control officer was "left 1 degree", as he thought we were hitting a bit far aft. When the enemy had completely vanished in clouds of smoke and steam we ceased firing and switched the light off.'[30]

The battle of Cape Matapan effectively scuttled the possibility of any future substantial operations by the Italian fleet and confirmed Cunningham's reputation as the outstanding seaman of the war. The admiral mentioned Philip in his dispatches for his skill with the searchlights, his captain having reported that 'the successful and continuous illumination of the enemy greatly contributed to the devastating results achieved in the gun action'[31] and that 'thanks to his alertness and appreciation of the situation, we were able to sink in five minutes two eight-inch-gun Italian cruisers'.[32] George II also awarded Philip the Greek War Cross, although when Alexandra congratulated him, 'he simply shrugged'.[33] Later he told her: 'It was as near murder as anything could be in wartime. The cruisers just burst into tremendous sheets of flame.'[34] Immediately afterwards, Alexandra writes, Philip's searchlights had been 'scouring the ocean for survivors'. There is no mention of this in his midshipman's journal, in which he records that it was not until the next morning that they steamed back towards the scene of the action where Philip 'counted 40 rafts containing survivors and there must have been a good many empty ones as well'.[35]

Although Cape Matapan could be counted a significant victory, in its aftermath the British Mediterranean Fleet became increasingly hard-pressed. Within ten days of the battle the German armies had begun their advance through Greece and Rommel was pushing the British forces back towards Cairo. The Germans soon established air superiority over the central Mediterranean, besieged Malta, and on 20 May began an all-out assault on Crete. *Valiant* was among the vessels ordered by Cunningham to intercept the German seaborne landings, and quickly found itself in the thick of the action. Philip's journal entry for 22 May 1941 records:

As we came in sight of the straits we saw *Naiad* and *Carlisle* being attacked by bombers. We went right in to within 10 miles of Crete and then the bombing started in earnest. Stukas came over but avoided the big ships and went for the crippled cruisers and destroyer screens. *Greyhound* was hit right aft by a large bomb, her stern blew up and she sank about twenty minutes later. *Gloucester* and *Fiji* were sent in to help them … Three Me 109s attacked *Warspite* as dive-bombers, and she was hit just where her starboard forrard mounting was … When we had got about 15 miles from the land 16 Stukas came out and attacked the two cruisers. *Gloucester* was badly hit and sank some hours later. The fleet then had some more attention, and we were bombed from a high level by a large number of small bombs dropped in sticks of 12 or more. One Dornier came straight for us from the port beam and dropped 12 bombs when he was almost overhead. We turned to port and ceased firing, when suddenly the bombs came whistling down, landing very close all down the port side.[36]

It was only some time later that I discovered we had been hit twice on the quarterdeck. One bomb exploded just abaft the quarterdeck screen on the port side ... The other landed within twenty feet of it, just inboard of the guard-rails, blowing a hole into the wardroom laundry ... there were only four casualties [one killed and three injured].[37]

The damage to *Valiant* entailed a week of refitting in Alexandria, which again reunited Philip with his Greek relations. A month earlier, on 29 April, most of the Greek royal household had fled the advancing Germans by flying boat from Phaleron to Crete, only Philip's mother Alice and Princess Nicholas remaining in Athens, where they stubbornly stayed on throughout the German occupation. The royal party in flight included the king's dachshund, Otto, and his mistress, Mrs Joyce Britten-Jones. 'The very best sort of Army wife', according to the diplomat Harold Caccia, Mrs Britten-Jones had been flown out to Athens on Churchill's orders 'to stiffen the King of Greece', as the prime minister put it, and was by now designated as lady-in-waiting to Crown Princess Frederika.[38] After a few days, most of the party had carried on to Alexandria, though not the king, who remained on Crete for three weeks to offer a rallying point for his people, before finally escaping by donkey over the White Mountains in full service dress with medal ribbons to the awaiting destroyer *Decoy*, in Suda Bay. On the morning of 23 May, as *Decoy* skirted the western tip of Crete before heading south-east for Alexandria, the royal evacuees might have glanced through the portholes to see *Valiant*, with their kinsman Philip aboard, accompanying them.[39]

Also in the vicinity that morning was Philip's uncle, Dickie Mountbatten. As captain of the destroyer *Kelly*, Mountbatten had been immensely popular with his crew, albeit at times a little too fearless. 'If a destroyer could leave skidmarks,' wrote his biographer Philip Ziegler, '*Kelly* would have disfigured every sea in which she set sail.'[40] Her most serious mishap, though, could not be fairly attributed to her captain's impetuosity. In late May 1941 *Kelly* had been dispatched to Crete, with orders to bombard a German-held airfield just west of Suda Bay. However, with no air cover of her own, she was dangerously exposed, and after successfully accomplishing this mission in the early hours of 23 May, *Kelly* and its sister ship were sunk with all guns firing by a swarm of German dive-bombers.

Mountbatten had refused to abandon his position on the bridge, but was nonetheless rather miraculously among the 128 of *Kelly*'s crew who were rescued from the water – 136 more having perished – after using his tin helmet to make himself heavy enough to swim beneath the bridge screen after the ship turned turtle. After swallowing so much water that he felt his lungs would burst, he let go of his helmet and 'shot out of the water like a cork released', as he later told his daughter Patricia.[41]

The next day, when he arrived back at Alexandria, wearing a borrowed civilian suit but still smothered in fuel oil, he was surprised to be met, as he recalled, 'by the cheery grinning face' of his nephew Philip, who 'roared with laughter on seeing me' and said, 'You have no idea how funny you look. You look like a nigger minstrel!'*[42]

Philip's time in Alexandria did not offer much in the way of respite as the town was repeatedly bombed and parachute mines showered down on the inner harbour. But he was at least among friends, including his cousin David Milford Haven, who also happened to be on leave there at the same time. According to Alexandra, who was among the Greek royal evacuees, the three of them went to a swimming pool or the beach and 'splashed happily in the sun', and Philip also contrived to obtain 'an absurdly small car which streaked through the

---

* In a television programme in the 1970s, Mountbatten more tactfully recalled his nephew's exclamation as: 'Your face is absolutely brown and your eyes are bright red.'[43]

streets with the noise of a thousand demons'. 'For the first time,' wrote Alexandra, 'I found my two cousins handsome and attractive beaux, most useful at taking me around. I liked David's lazy smile and I liked Philip's broad grin.'[44]

Later, Philip tracked her down 'in his little wasp of a car' to the Shepheard Hotel in Cairo, from where they explored the old bazaars, botanical gardens and Gezira Sporting Club, which was still functioning with pre-war gaiety, before seeing his Greek cousins off at Port Said when they left for South Africa. A week or two later, he saw them briefly in Cape Town, too, en route for England where he was due to take his sub-lieutenant's courses and examination at Portsmouth.

His passage home was circuitous, his troopship being routed via Nova Scotia to pick up Canadian troops bound for Europe. But when it put in at Puerto Rico after crossing the South Atlantic, the Chinese stokers all jumped ship and so for the onward voyage to Virginia there was no alternative but for Philip and the four other midshipmen on board to take their place and shovel coal into her furnaces. When new stokers came aboard at Newport, the midshipmen were presented with certificates of qualification as boiler trimmers, and the ever-curious Philip grabbed the opportunity of hiring a car for a quick look at Washington.[45]

TWELVE

Osla and Lilibet

Given their very limited acquaintance and her young age, it seems unlikely that Philip spent a great deal of his time thinking about Elizabeth while he was away at sea, although they reportedly maintained a 'cousinly correspondence'[1] throughout the war, and in Cape Town in June 1941 Alexandra came across him writing a letter to 'Lilibet' which he insisted on finishing when she wanted to chat. Alexandra assumed that her cousin was fishing for invitations and, whether or not that was the case, several were forthcoming, with the result that Philip spent several of his rare leaves at Windsor. The first of these was in October 1941, when he regaled George VI with stories of his adventures in the Mediterranean,[2] and afterwards the king wrote to Victoria Milford Haven: 'Philip came here for a week end the other day. What a charming boy he is, & I am glad he is remaining on in my Navy.'[3]

Elizabeth, though, was still only fifteen at the time, and while she was undoubtedly going to be a catch before long, for the time being Philip was free to play the field. Even if he had been discarded by Cobina Wright, her place had soon been taken by Osla Benning, a beautiful Canadian-born debutante with 'dark hair, alabaster white skin, an exquisite figure and a gentle loving nature', as one friend described her.[4] They met in late 1939, when Osla was sharing a flat with Sarah Norton (later Baring), a god-daughter of Dickie

143

Mountbatten whom Philip had also known since childhood. Sarah Baring remembers: 'Osla didn't have a boyfriend at the time and Uncle Dickie said to me, "I don't think Philip's got a girlfriend at the moment, I wish you could find a nice girl for him because he doesn't know anyone", so I said "I know I'll get them together", and he said "Excellent!"'

So she did. 'I remember sitting in a nightclub – I think it was the Nut House [on Beak Street, Soho] – and telling Philip to come because I'd got a rather pretty girl I'd like to introduce him to, and anyway they became great friends, they had a lovely time together.'[5] Born in 1921, Osla was three months younger than Philip and had been brought over to Europe from Canada when she was a very young girl, following her mother's divorce from her American father. Her glamorous mother proceeded to go through three more husbands and Osla's childhood was, according to her daughter, Janie Spring, 'in many ways incredibly lonely, very isolated; she had a governess and had to speak French one day and German the next. Up until the age of about eight she had a foreign accent because she hardly ever spoke English.'[6] Osla was sent to various boarding schools, at least one of which she was asked to leave. Like Philip, she had a weakness for practical jokes and was 'always getting involved in escapades involving itching powder'. After finishing school in Austria, she came out in August 1939, and became one of the foremost debutantes of her year, much noticed.[7] Her only arguable defect, according to her daughter, was that she had 'quite thick legs'. One of her stepfathers, Geoffrey Courtney, had a string of polo ponies whose legs he used to bandage to stop them from swelling up and he tried doing the same with Osla's when she was young.

At the time she met Philip, Osla was working at the Hawker-Siddeley aircraft factory in Slough and living in a cottage nearby with Sarah Norton and her father, Lord Grantley, the monocled film-maker and raconteur – described by the *Evening Standard* as 'the last of the wits'[8] – who gallantly got up at 5.30 each morning to light the fire and make porridge for the girls before they left for work. In *Silver Spoon*, his book of 'random reminiscences', Grantley wrote that the girls were 'anxious to draw as sharp a contrast as they could between their days in the factory and evenings in the cottage' and that Philip was among the 'many interesting young men' who came for drinks. Grantley found the young prince 'the best of company' and was impressed by his 'forceful intellect'. 'He seemed to be interested in everything; and when asking me questions about films, for instance, he did not want to know about the stars but about the technicalities of how films were made.'[9]

As Osla and Philip became closer, her friend Sarah Norton saw less of them 'because they didn't want me around', although occasionally they all gathered at the 400 Club in Leicester Square, where there was a band for dancing, or the nearby Café de Paris, before it was bombed. Before long, Osla's girlfriends began to suspect that this was more than a passing fancy. Another friend, Esme Harmsworth (later Countess of Cromer), remembers not having seen Osla for some time and then having lunch with her at Claridge's. 'I noticed she was wearing a naval cipher as a brooch. They're jewelled and not the sort of thing you scatter around. "Oh," I said, "what's that? Who is it?" She blushed and ummed and ahhed and she eventually said "Well, he's called Philip." "Philip who?" "Well, he doesn't have another name … actually he's Philip of Greece." I'm sure it was a serious thing as far as Osla was concerned.'[10]

But although they were evidently keen on one another, according to Sarah Baring, 'it was very circumspect. I can tell you that right away. We just didn't think of *that* at all, we just weren't brought up to it. We were just brought up to what my mother used to call "behave nicely" … I mean the boys never even asked you to. You could kiss on the cheek, but not much more, we were allowed to hold hands in taxis, that was considered quite daring … there were those who went further and we always knew who they were – the word always gets round all the girls.'[11]

Osla was at least as innocent as most girls of her class and age. In her book *Debs at War*, Anne de Courcy pronounced her 'invincibly ignorant on sexual matters', citing the fact that she had once 'caused a mild sensation in a nightclub when she complained loudly that it was very inconsiderate of her boyfriend always to carry his torch in his pocket as it was so uncomfortable when dancing'. This was during the blackout, when torches were everyday items of equipment, but even so some of those within earshot suggested she 'grow up!' while telling her the more likely cause of her discomfort – although Osla apparently remained none the wiser.[12]

Philip was almost certainly more worldly, although he was evidently capable of restraint. The diarist James Lees-Milne was once told by June Hutchinson (the wife of the barrister Jeremy Hutchinson and daughter of Diana Lady Westmoreland) of a 'great friend' of hers – 'I forget the name' – who 'swore that when in her teens she used to lie in the same bed with Prince Philip, a bolster between them. They would talk for hours. She was much in love with him. He would not transgress the bolster ... When we said we did not believe it June said that only the young were capable of such restraint, such Tennysonian chivalric idealism. It is true.'[13]

When Philip was away at sea, 'Osla had no idea where he was half the time,' says Sarah Baring, 'but they kept in touch. I know because she used to show me the letters, very sweet nice letters about how much he was looking forward to seeing her when he got back, and all that sort of thing. But we didn't ask questions that were too personal, we just didn't. It was obvious that he was Osla's boyfriend in a simple nice way, so to speak. Every time his ship came back, it was Osla he would ring.'

By the time Philip returned to England in the summer of 1941, Osla had been recruited to work at Bletchley Park as a multilinguist in the naval section. One of her friends there, Lady Margaret Boyle, had Osla and Philip to stay at her family home, Kelburn Castle, in Ayrshire, around this time and remembers being particularly impressed by his clear voice when reading aloud to everyone from *Alice in Wonderland*, and how he calmly continued even after his entire audience had fallen asleep. She was also struck by the fact that he went out of his way to be kind and friendly to her young nephews, whose parents were away in the war.[14]

Back in London, when they went out dancing, Philip would take Osla in the early hours to Paddington Station so that she could catch the milk train to Bletchley. 'I do know that for her he was her first love,' says Osla's daughter.

> She always said to me that your first love is the most amazing thing. She never told me about him for years. She just said, 'I fell in love with a naval officer'. Then I found a wonderful picture of Philip, very young looking, with his hair all tousled, quite curly … I could see why they got on, they were both very much outsiders with no roots in the English milieu in which they moved. Neither of them, even by the standards of their time, had experienced much emotional warmth or security as children. Certainly my mother had only sporadic contact with her mother as she grew up, and did not have that proverbial nanny to act as an ersatz maternal influence. Although they were both very good looking, full of life and with a similar sense of fun, I think that, probably, unconsciously, they recognized this similarity in each other and this is what gave them a special bond.[15]

Whenever he was in London, Philip tended to stay on a camp bed in the dining room of the Mountbattens' house in Chester Street, which they had moved to at the start of the war. If not out with Osla, he might tour the nightclubs with David Milford Haven, who, being two years older, was by then already beginning to appear in the gossip columns. One evening in March 1942 almost ended in disaster after they borrowed the Mountbattens' Vauxhall and drove off for a night on the town. On their way home at 4.30 a.m. they crashed into a traffic island, wrote off the car and returned to Chester Street with their faces cut and bleeding. 'So, after facing death many times at sea,' Dickie told his daughter Patricia, 'they got their first wounds in a London blackout.'[16]

If Philip made the most of his leaves, he still managed to knuckle down to his naval studies, and in the sub-lieutenant's exam, which was divided into five sections – gunnery, torpedoes, navigation, signals and seamanship – he achieved the top 'one' grade in four of the subjects, and a 'two' in the other.[17] In June 1942 he was posted as a sub-lieutenant to the old Shakespeare-class destroyer *Wallace*, based at Rosyth on the Firth of Forth and escorting convoys of merchant vessels on the treacherous two-and-a-half-day passage between there and Sheerness – dubbed 'E-boat alley' because of the frequency of attacks on the lumbering convoys by nimbler German E-boats. These coastal convoys were also popular prey for German bombers and, bounded seaward by their own mine barrier, they had very limited room for evasive action whenever an attack occurred. Another potential hazard was the risk of collision in thick fog, and on one occasion, after a merchant ship leading one line of the convoy cut through into the forward boiler room of the *Wallace*, killing a leading stoker and badly scalding two others, Philip rushed down into the flooded boiler room to try to free the trapped men.

Despite such gallant and selfless acts, his tendency to yell at any crew member perceived to be guilty of sloppiness meant that, although he was by no means disliked, he never inspired quite the same level of affection as Mountbatten, who, for all his faults, was always immensely popular with his crew. Philip was undoubtedly a first-rate seaman, though, and was soon promoted to lieutenant. Then, in October, at his captain's request, he became first lieutenant, second-in-command of the ship, at the age of twenty-one one of the youngest in the Royal Navy to hold that position.[18]

Another young second-in-command in the same flotilla was Mike Parker, a bluff Australian a year older than Philip and a 'custom-made fellow spirit' destined to become his closest friend outside the family.[19] A breezy and apparently gregarious character, Parker was also, like Philip, to some extent a loner. In addition, he exhibited a 'typically Australian ambivalence about authority', it was later noted, 'and a strong streak of independence, not to say competitiveness, which was mirrored in the faintly mysterious Prince Philip'.[20] And while Parker's home was 12,000 miles away, the prince did not even have one, so Parker later admitted to having thought to himself: 'You're a poor bloody orphan, just like me!'[21] While other officers rushed off home at weekends, Parker recalled, 'we were the last blokes left on the quarter deck'.[22]

Both Philip and Parker were determined that their destroyer would be the best trimmed and most efficient in the flotilla. According to Parker's wife, Eileen, 'they tussled like mongrels over a bone if there was the faintest whiff of spare paint in the breeze ... They organised teams and challenged each other to cricket matches, and also to tourneys of bowls on the green outside the Fountain Hotel in Sheerness. Despite their rivalry, they had too much in common not to become friends. They were both young, both ambitious and both dedicated to the ideals of service that the Navy represented.'[23] Eileen Parker was yet another of those who was struck by how 'immensely handsome' Philip was: 'Tall, with piercing blue eyes and a shock of blond hair swept back from his forehead. I was not at all surprised to hear that every unmarried Wren on the base had her sights on him.'

Philip survived the hazards of the east coast convoys but that winter was to be overshadowed for him by news about his great childhood friend Alex Wernher, with whom he had spent so many of his holidays at Lubenham while he was growing up. In appearance, Alex was very like his mother, Zia, fair with slightly Slav eyes, although unlike her he was interested in the arts and music. He had conquered his early fear of horses to win the coveted 'Saddle' at Sandhurst for best rider, and in addition shot and played golf very well. According to the family biographer, he was 'a delightful, unspoilt boy' with 'all the charm in the world', and after joining the army he had become apt to exclaim: 'My God, life is good.'[24] By 1942, Alex was serving with the 17/21 Lancers out in Tunisia. On 2 December 1942, he wrote to his mother after ten days of fighting, describing his 'almost detached sensations' as he saw shells coming straight towards him. 'Well, Ma,' he concluded, 'so far all is well, and I hope my luck goes on. I feel it will somehow, as I seem to come out of all our engagements better than most. I think of you all a great deal ...' That night, as Alex's squadron headed back to harbour, he became trapped between his tank and another as it was being towed out of a gully, and his leg and hip were crushed. Despite his terrible injuries he remained amazingly cheerful, but with no penicillin or proper medical facilities, gangrene soon set in. The doctor gave him a pint of his own blood as he drifted in and out of consciousness. His last words were to send his family all his love. He died the morning after the accident.

At Christmas Philip sent the Wernhers a card as usual, but wrote in it simply 'Love Philip'. He had not heard the news of Alex's death, although Zia could not believe this and complained angrily to Dickie Mountbatten. Eventually, on 10 January, Philip wrote to her:

Ever since I got the telegram from Uncle Dickie, I have been in a daze. Alex filled a place in my life that was very important to me, he filled a place of a brother and for that alone I am eternally grateful to him. As the older boy he was the guide and the pillow and in a great many ways I tried to model myself on him. As I grew older I was able to find many of my shortcomings by just comparing myself to him and in some cases I managed to put them right … It is not easy for me to try and say what I thought of him, because there are no words which can describe a friendship between two boys, those things just are and one does not stop to think why. Dear Zia, I know you will never think very much of me. I am rude and unmannerly and I say many things out of turn which I realize afterwards must have hurt someone. Then I am filled with remorse and I try to get matters right …[25]

In June 1943 *Wallace* left its home station and joined an escort for a convoy across the Atlantic, and then on the return leg it made for the Mediterranean to assist in the Allied invasion of Sicily, a role reversal for Philip after his operations off Crete in 1941. While covering the Canadian landings, and quite possibly bombarding Philip's brother-in-law Christoph of Hesse on the German side, in the process,[26] *Wallace* was subjected to prolonged dive-bombing by Stukas and was continually at action stations, with Philip as first lieutenant coolly directing most of the operations from the bridge.[27]

On 8 July the night sky was especially bright and the ship's progress created a long, glowing trail of shining water, making it a particularly alluring quarry for the German bombers. After the first attack, which hit the side of the ship, the enemy aircraft disappeared, but everyone on board suspected that it would soon be back – most probably with reinforcements. 'It was obvious that we were the target for tonight,' recalled Harry Hargreaves, one of the yeomen aboard *Wallace* at the time, 'and they would not stop until we had suffered a fatal hit. It was for all the world like being blindfolded and trying to evade an enemy whose only problem was getting his aim right.'

After the initial onslaught, knowing that he had to come up with something fast, Philip 'went into hurried conversation with the captain, and the next thing a wooden raft was being put together on deck', remembered Hargreaves. Within five minutes they had launched the raft over the side, with a smoke float fastened to each end which, when activated, would make it look like the flaming debris of *Wallace* floating in the water. *Wallace* then steamed away from the raft at full speed for a good five minutes before cutting its engines. The telltale wake subsided and they lay there quietly in the darkness for some time until they heard an approaching aircraft. 'The sound of the aircraft grew louder until I thought it was directly overhead and I screwed up my shoulders in anticipation of the bombs,' Hargreaves recalled. 'The next thing was the scream of the bombs, but at some distance. The ruse had worked and the aircraft was bombing the raft. I suppose he was under the impression that he had hit us in his last attack and was now finishing the job.'

'Prince Philip saved our lives that night,' Hargreaves concluded. 'It had been marvellously quick thinking, conveyed to a willing team and put into action as if rehearsed. I suppose there might have been a few survivors, but certainly the ship would have been sunk. He was always very courageous and resourceful and thought very quickly. You would say to yourself "What the hell are we going to do now?" and Philip would come up with something.'[28]

Later *Wallace* took on fuel and ammunition at Malta, where a destroyer came alongside with some captured Italian generals and also Dickie Mountbatten, who as Chief of Combined Operations had helped to mastermind the successful invasion, and who came aboard to see Philip. Mountbatten was about to be appointed Supreme Allied Commander for South-East Asia, one of a meteoric series of promotions. 'What are they going to make you?' Philip wrote to his uncle in September,

Acting Admiral of the Fleet or something? You had better be careful … before you know what, you will have the prospect of 40 years without promotion in front of you. What a thought! As a string-puller, of course, you've practically lost all value, you're so big now that it might smell of nepotism (just to make sure I had the right word, I looked it up in the dictionary, and this is what it says: undue favour from holder of patronage to relatives, originally from Pope to illegitimate sons called nephews).[29]

That Christmas 1943, having, as he nonchalantly put it, 'nowhere particular to go', Philip went with David Milford Haven to stay at Windsor Castle. Before that he was to attend the annual royal pantomime, *Aladdin*, with the two princesses in the starring roles. However much, or little, twenty-two-year-old Philip had thought about his seventeen-year-old cousin in romantic terms before then, Elizabeth certainly seems to have thought a lot about him. According to her governess, Elizabeth had already let on to her that Philip was 'the one', and she now went pink with excitement at the prospect: 'Who *do* you think is coming to see us act, Crawfie?'[30] But shortly before the show, Philip came down with flu and was confined to bed in Claridge's. He recovered in time to attend the third performance, on Saturday 18 December, however, sitting in the front row alongside the king and queen and his cousin Marina Kent.[31] To Crawfie's eyes he appeared 'greatly changed' since the time she had seen him at Dartmouth before the war. 'It was a grave and charming man who sat there, with nothing of the rather bumptious boy ... He looked more than ever, I thought, like a Viking, weather-beaten and strained, and his manners left nothing to be desired.'[32] The pantomime went off well, with Philip entering into the fun and laughing loudly at all the bad jokes,[33] and Elizabeth 'more animated' than ever. 'There was a sparkle about her none of us had ever seen before,' recorded Crawfie. 'Many people remarked on it.'[34]

Afterwards he stayed the weekend of Christmas at Windsor, and, as Elizabeth told her governess, 'we had a very gay time, with a film, dinner parties and dancing to the gramophone'.[35] The highlight was Boxing Day evening, when dinner at the castle for the family and retainers was followed by charades, and afterwards, the king's private secretary, Sir Alan Lascelles, recorded, 'they rolled back the carpet in the crimson drawing-room, turned on the gramophone and frisked and capered away till near 1am'.[36] According to Margaret, Philip and David 'went mad and we danced and danced and danced … the best night of all'.[37]

The weekend proved to be a turning point. In his thank-you letter to the queen, Philip ventured to hope that his high-spirited behaviour 'did not get out of hand', yet also that she would not think it too presumptuous if he now added Windsor to Broadlands (where the Mountbattens were by now living) and Coppins (the Kents' house) as his favourite places; 'that may give you some small idea of how much I appreciated the few days you were kind enough to let me spend with you'.[38] After a subsequent visit to Windsor in July, he wrote to say how much he loved being with the royal family. 'It is the simple enjoyment of family pleasures and amusements and the feeling that I am welcome to share them. I am afraid I am not capable of putting all this into the right words and I am certainly incapable of showing you the gratitude that I feel'.[39] There is a sense in these letters that he at last saw a way of regaining what he had lost when his own family had disintegrated more than a decade previously.

Philip was still virtually unknown to the British public, but his presence that Christmas at Windsor, reported as it was in the press, nevertheless helped to fuel rumours of a possible future marriage. On 16 February 1944 Chips Channon was visited by his parents-in-law, Lord and Lady Iveagh, after they had been to tea with the king and queen at Buckingham Palace, and that evening he wrote in his diary: 'I do believe that a marriage may well be arranged one day between Princess Elizabeth and Prince Philip of Greece'.[40] The precise basis of Channon's prediction is unclear, although he may have heard that, shortly after the Windsor Christmas, Philip had informed his cousin George II of Greece of his intentions. The Greek king had then asked George VI and Queen Elizabeth whether they might consider his young cousin as a suitor for their daughter.[41]

While the king and queen pondered this unexpected request, Queen Mary wrote to say how suitable she thought Philip was.[42] She had long been an admirer, telling her lady-in-waiting Mabell Airlie that he was not only 'very handsome', but also intelligent with plenty of common sense. She had been knitting scarves and pullovers for him during the war and followed his 'brilliantly successful' career in the navy with keen interest.[43]

To begin with, the king and queen had misgivings about the match. According to Harold Nicolson, 'The family were at first horrified when they saw that Prince Philip was making up to Princess Elizabeth. They felt he was rough, ill mannered, uneducated and would probably not be faithful.'[44] But the more they got to know him, the more they found they liked him, especially George VI, whose biographer Sarah Bradford observes that Philip was 'very much the King's type of man' with his forthright manner, joshing humour and love of the outdoors.[45] Yet however highly he came to think of Philip, the king still found it hard to believe that his elder daughter had fallen in love with virtually the first young man she had met. In addition, he can hardly have relished the prospect of his happy family – 'Us Four', as he referred to them – being broken up so soon after the war, which had already greatly limited the amount of time he had been able to spend with them all at home together.[46]

The king eventually told his mother that, while both he and the queen liked Philip, who was 'intelligent, has a good sense of humour and thinks about things in the right way', they both thought Elizabeth 'too young for that now' and so were 'going to tell George [of Greece] that P had better not think any more about it at present'.[47] The king also told his mother that Elizabeth had not yet met 'any young men of her own age' – which was not quite accurate – probably also having in mind men who were British through and through, whom he thought might be more popular as a future consort than a foreign prince. In particular the king and the queen were known to favour

Hugh Euston, heir to the dukedom of Grafton, whose company Elizabeth had enjoyed while he was stationed at Windsor as a Grenadier Guardsman. Euston headed the list of handsome 'flirts' that she and her friends used to joke about,[48] although he later denied ever having thought of marrying her ('Good Lord, no!').[49] According to Sir Edward Ford, 'the Queen wanted to introduce her daughter to a wide range of possibles from the higher flights of the British aristocracy ... You'd often find three or four of them staying at Sandringham or Balmoral at the same time.'[50] Others who used to come to stay regularly included Johnny Dalkeith, heir to the Duke of Buccleuch, Sunny Blandford, heir to the Duke of Marlborough, and Lord Brabourne, who went on to marry Patricia Mountbatten.

THIRTEEN

Steady on, Dickie

During the spring of 1944, while others debated his marriage prospects, Philip was posted to a shipyard in Newcastle upon Tyne to help oversee the finishing touches to the new W-Class destroyer *Whelp*, which was commissioned for service in the 27th Destroyer Flotilla on its formation on 17 April 1944, and in which he was to serve for the remainder of the war.

While living quietly in a small hotel in Newcastle, he was tracked down by Olga Franklin, a journalist from the local paper, whose editor had told her breezily, 'There's some Greek prince in town.' Franklin duly went to interview him – his first press interview – and wrote it up as an article headlined 'Shipyard Stranger Is a Royal Prince'. Each day, the 'tall, ash-blond first-lieutenant' travelled to work by bus without anyone knowing who he was, she reported, but with the looks 'of a typical Prince in a Hans Andersen fairy tale', he would 'certainly have been noticed by many a girl worker in the shipyard'.[1]

Philip's grandmother, Victoria, had heard the marriage rumours but did her best to refrain from raising the subject with him, although in early April she admitted to Dickie Mountbatten that she had recently 'touched on' it, only to discover that he [Philip] was 'not inclined to confide in me, so I did not press him'. Victoria herself knew of 'no developments at present in the situation' but told Dickie that Philip was nonetheless 'fully aware that he must give it careful consideration'.[2]

It cannot have been easy for Philip to be continually made aware of his family's hopes and schemes for him. Even his mother, thousands of miles away in German-occupied Greece, seemed to be in on the intrigue, and in June 1944 she wrote to Philip (via her sister Louise in Sweden) mischievously letting slip that she had heard that while staying with Marina Kent at Coppins at Easter, Philip had paid 'an interesting visit', as well as lunching with 'a certain young lady & her parents before you left'.[3] Fifteen years Philip's senior, Marina was another of those who treated him as a protégé, and was later said to have done much to encourage the idea that he should marry Elizabeth. In August 1942 her husband George had been killed in an air accident en route for Iceland, and Marina had been left a widow at thirty-five with three young children. Thereafter she focused much of her surplus energy and ambition on her young cousin Philip. When Chips Channon went to stay at Coppins in the autumn he was struck by the fact that Philip's name appeared 'constantly' in the visitors' book.[4]

By now, the whispers were beginning to spread well beyond Philip's family. While staying near Coppins in July, the socialite Sir Michael Duff reported to his cousin Ettie Desborough:

The Duchess [of Kent] came to dinner, bringing Prince Philip of Greece, who is CHARMING, and I consider just right to perform the role of Consort for Princess Elizabeth. He has everything in his favour, he is good looking, intelligent, a good sailor, and he speaks ONLY English … I gather he goes to Windsor quite a lot. He is 24, and ripe for the job. But whether he likes P.E. or she him I can't say.[5]

While Philip was clearly now giving 'the job' serious consideration, he still saw Osla Benning from time to time, and for Christmas that year (the one he spent at Windsor) he had given her a large book, *Scraps and Sketches* by the caricaturist and illustrator George Cruikshank. Osla was by then sharing a flat with another friend, Sylvia Heywood, and Philip used to come for parties at which they ate Russian salad and dressing made from liquid paraffin and powdered eggs, and afterwards he would kip down for the night on the sofa. By the beginning of 1944, however, he and Osla had begun to drift apart and sometime that spring Osla became engaged to a young diplomat, Guy Millard, later ambassador to Italy. That came to nothing, but in 1946 she did get married to another diplomat, John Henniker-Major, whom she had met while she was working in the Conference Department at the Foreign Office, where he was assistant private secretary to Ernest Bevin, then foreign secretary. When Osla gave birth to their first son, Mark, in September 1947, Philip stood godfather – one of his last private engagements prior to his own marriage two months later. From then on, despite their very divergent lives, they remained friends until Osla's early death in 1974.[6]

Another of those Philip was reputed to have been in love with was his childhood friend Gina Wernher. But while Gina's mother, Zia, had been grooming her daughter to marry a Duke 'at least', to give her 'stability', she reasoned, Gina had told her that she had no intention of marrying anyone with a title and spending her life 'opening flower shows'. She nevertheless notched up eighteen proposals of marriage,[7] but later insisted that Philip had not been one of her suitors. Gina recalled that while Philip had been 'astronomically' good-looking and 'marvellously clever and amusing, and I loved being with him', the question of marriage never came up. 'We were friends, best friends, and we went out together and just had the best time, but nothing really serious happened. It wasn't like that … Philip knew lots of girls. We were just young people having fun.'[8] In any event, in the spring of 1944 she, too, became engaged – to the untitled Harold 'Bunnie' Phillips, Edwina Mountbatten's former lover.

* * *

In early June 1944, the news of Osla's and Gina's engagements prompted Dickie Mountbatten again to raise the subject of Philip's suitability as a future consort for Elizabeth with George VI. He now suggested that as a preliminary step Philip should give up his Greek nationality and become a British citizen. On his way to Karachi to resume his command in South-East Asia, Mountbatten was due to stop at Cairo on 23 August, and, so he told George VI, he intended to discuss his plan with the Greek king who was now living in exile in Egypt with assorted members of his family. But two weeks before he left George VI had second thoughts: 'I have been thinking the matter over since our talk,' he wrote to Dickie, 'and I have come to the conclusion that we are going too fast.'[9] The king wanted him to limit his conversation to Philip's application for British citizenship and not mention the potential marriage. 'I am sure this is the best way of doing this particular operation, don't you? Though I know you like to get things settled at once, once you have an idea in mind.'[10]

Four days before Mountbatten reached Cairo, Philip's destroyer *Whelp* – which had just finished escorting the battleship *Ramillies* to Algiers – put in at Alexandria en route via Suez for Ceylon, where it was to join the Eastern Fleet as part of the 27th Destroyer Flotilla. The British high commissioner Lord Killearn recorded going to an 'appalling' ball at the French Lycée, at which the only bright spot was being introduced to Prince Philip by the Greek crown prince and princess. Killearn found Philip 'a most attractive youth', and later in the evening the crown princess indiscreetly suggested that he 'would do very well for Princess Elizabeth!'[11]

When Mountbatten landed at Cairo four days later, Philip was there to meet him at the aerodrome. Mountbatten confided to Killearn that the purpose of his whistle-stop visit was to prepare the ground for Philip to apply for British nationality, with a view to his then becoming 'an additional asset' to the depleted British royal family. He explained that George VI had become concerned that, since the death of his younger brother, the Duke of Kent, in 1942, there was really only himself and the Duke of Gloucester, which often made it very difficult to carry on. A naturalized Philip might therefore be 'a great help to them in carrying out their royal functions'. He intended, he said, to sound Philip out about his proposition, which he duly did, 'with complete success', in the course of a stroll around the embassy garden, according to Killearn. Before flying on that afternoon, Mountbatten also had talks with George II and the crown prince of Greece, who were both also apparently in favour of the idea.

The high commissioner appeared to swallow Mountbatten's unlikely explanation at the time – at least, there is no hint of scepticism in his diary. However, as Ben Pimlott has argued, it seems implausible that George VI really wanted help in carrying out his official functions from such a young and distant cousin belonging to the discredited Greek royal family, 'just because he happened to be on the market'. It is more likely that Mountbatten saw that the only way Philip could possibly assist the Windsors was by marrying into them. Thus, suggests Pimlott, Mountbatten's mission was part of a 'considered plan, aimed at remoulding Philip for the requirements of the position both uncle and nephew wished him to hold', and to this end 'Philip needed to be not so much British, but non-Greek, in view of the unsavoury connections of his own dynasty'.[12]

In keeping with George VI's demand for discretion, however, Mountbatten maintained the pretence even with close family, writing to his mother afterwards that Philip 'entirely understood' that his proposed change of nationality was 'not connected with any question of marrying Lilibet', albeit adding 'there is no doubt that he would very much like to one of these days'.[13] The next February, 1945, he asked Alice not to say anything about it when she saw the king and queen on her arrival in Britain from Greece: 'The best hopes are to let it happen – if it will – without parents interfering. The young people appear genuinely devoted and I think after the war it is very likely to occur.'[14] Alice was shrewd enough to have worked this out for herself and Dickie's letter crossed with one from his mother Victoria reassuring him that she had had 'long talks' with Alice, and that she had found her to be 'most sensible about everything regarding Philip'. She knew all about 'the future plans etc' for her son, but felt that 'they lie in the hands of Providence & that she will not try to interfere in any way, which feeling I encourage'.[15]

Alice had stayed on in Greece for the past four years under the German occupation, a period of extreme hardship for the local population, not least since the Germans requisitioned all the food out of the shops and sent these supplies out of the country to Italy and Germany.[16] The Athenians were thus perpetually hungry and Alice spent much of her time running soup kitchens and orphanages, and organizing nursing sisters as district visitors. She was always clad in her grey nun's veil and gown, the habit of the religious order which she had founded.[17] She also sheltered a Jewish family in two rooms of her house, telling everyone, even her servants, that they were her former governess and her children. When the Gestapo called to interrogate her, she feigned simple-mindedness to save the family from the fate that had befallen the 60,000 Jews murdered in Salonika in 1941.*[18]

In December 1941, meanwhile, some eight months after the initial German invasion, she had written to Philip (once again via her sister Louise in neutral Sweden) of being full of hope 'even in these anxious times', and of walking around Athens looking at the houses 'to see if

---

* Shortly before she died in 1969, Alice asked to be buried in Jerusalem, near to her aunt Ella, brushing aside objections from her family that it was a long way away. 'Nonsense,' said Alice. 'There is a perfectly good bus service from Istanbul.' In 1993, she was posthumously awarded the title 'Righteous Among Nations', Israel's highest honour to a gentile and the same as that given to Oskar Schindler. The next year, Philip and his surviving sister Sophie attended the ceremony at Yad Vashem, the Holocaust memorial, to receive the honour on her behalf.

there is not a suitable one for us later on'. At the time she was living in Big George's house in the city centre, but it was

> very cold now as there is no means of working the central heating. Upstairs there is a room with a fireplace, so happily I have one warm room in which to dress and sit and eat. Aunt Ellen is well and lunches with me very often. We are the only ones and so we became very close friends … I am still busy with my charities but do most of my work here, as I have so little benzene … don't worry about me. I am really and truly in good heart.[19]

The German occupation at least made it easier for her to keep in contact with her daughters, and in spring 1942 Alice managed to obtain a visa from the occupying authorities to visit Louise in Sweden, stopping en route for three days in Berlin, where, she told Philip, she found Margarita and Theodora looking very well. 'Living in the country makes such a difference, where one can get butter, eggs, milk, etc. You can imagine what joy it was to see them for 3 days and to get news of their husbands and children. They were looking so pretty and chic.'[20]

When she eventually received a letter from Philip describing his part in the battle of Cape Matapan, she wrote back to him: 'Dear boy, you must know me by now and how absolutely I share all your ideas and principles. Papa and I have never been for shirking sacrifices and dangers and consequently we take it for granted that our son is the same.' However, she was puzzled by the fact that he was serving in a British ship as she had always assumed he was in a Greek one, especially given 'the dearth of Greek officers for them'.[21]

In January 1944 Alice again travelled to Germany, this time to comfort Sophie, whose husband Christoph had recently been killed in a plane crash while she was expecting their fifth child in thirteen years of marriage. Christoph had originally been viewed as a Nazi stalwart, although he was having second thoughts by the time of his death.[22] He had been an officer in the SS, head of the intelligence branch of the Air Ministry (the *Forschungsamt*), and won an Iron Cross for his part in planning the devastating bombing raids on Eindhoven and Rotterdam – notorious for their targeting of civilians – and served as a navigator in a Luftwaffe bomber squadron. He was at one time reputed to have been the navigator of the Messerschmitt 110 fighter-bomber that swooped down the Mall in September 1940 and tried to blow up the royal family while they were in residence. However, the American historian Jonathan Petropoulos has recently shown that at the time of the attack Christoph had been a staff officer and so the most he could have done would have been to help plan the raid – and even that possibility is highly speculative.[23]

After serving with his squadron in Tunisia and Sicily, and in actions against Malta, Christoph had been recalled to Germany in October 1943, when Hitler removed all German princes from active service. On 7 October, flying in thick fog, his aeroplane crashed in the Apennine foothills near Forlì. His body and that of his co-pilot were found two days later. The mysterious circumstances surrounding the crash – the plane was travelling at unusually low altitude in foggy weather and on an inexplicable south-westerly course – gave rise to the belief that his plane had been sabotaged on the orders of Hitler, possibly because the Führer questioned Christoph's loyalty and knew that if he returned to his job in intelligence in Berlin he would inevitably learn that his brother Philipp and sister-in-law Mafalda had been imprisoned in concentration camps.[24] 'Poor dear Tiny,' wrote Victoria, when she heard the news. 'She loved her husband & had been so anxious about him ever since he was in Sicily … This is now the 7th relation of mine who has lost his life flying.'[25]

Since leaving Berlin at the outbreak of the war, Sophie had been living with her mother-in-law, the Landgravine of Hesse, at Schloss Friedrichshof, on the wooded slopes of the Taunus foothills, north of

Frankfurt. She was not only looking after her children but also their cousins, the four children of Prince Philipp of Hesse, who had been interned at Flossenbürg concentration camp, Bavaria, in 1943, and his wife, Princess Mafalda, who had been kidnapped by the Gestapo and interned at Buchenwald after her father, the King of Italy, defected to the Allies. When one of Himmler's aides visited Sophie at Friedrichshof in November 1943, a month after Christoph's death, he was 'astonished by her terrible appearance, she has become thin and looks to be suffering a great deal'.[26] Alice arrived there at the end of January 1944, and she, too, was taken aback by how miserable her daughter seemed, later writing to Philip that Sophie was

> *so* brave when she is with her children and us, being her usual self and making jokes, but her hours in her room alone are hardly to be endured, and made all who love her suffer so much for her that I realize now how much easier it is to bear one's own suffering than to share another's. I never suffered after 'the accident' [the 1937 air crash that killed Cecile and her family] as I did those three weeks with Tiny and I certainly will never forget them as long as I live. Her children are perfectly adorable, you would love them, and the new baby [Clarissa, born on 4 February 1944] is too sweet for words.[27]

Alice returned to Greece in April 1944. Six months later, the country was liberated from German occupation, and soon afterwards Harold Macmillan visited Athens and found her 'living in humble, not to say somewhat squalid conditions' but 'obviously working very hard on relief, for children especially ...' When he asked her if she needed any food she admitted that she and her old lady-in-waiting had enough bread but had no 'stores' of any kind – sugar, tea, coffee, rice, or any tinned foods.[28]

According to her biographer, Alice had been out of touch with Andrea since she had last seen him in 1939, although she had received sporadic news of him from her sister Louise, and she knew of his continuing liaison with Andrée de La Bigne. Alice made no secret of having wanted to make a fresh start with Andrea, yet she was characteristically generous about the woman who had latterly taken her place, later describing the Comtesse to Philip as 'the friend who looked after Papa so touchingly to the end'[29] – even though Andrea's former Greek aide-de-camp had warned her that she was an 'adventuress, feathering her own nest'.[30] Adventuress or not, the Comtesse was an intriguing figure. As far as can be deduced she was the great-granddaughter of the nineteenth-century courtesan Valtesse de La Bigne, sometime mistress of Emperor Napoleon III and of the painters Edouard Manet, Gustave Courbet and Eugène Boudin. According to *My Blue Notebooks* by Liane de Pougy, Valtesse's fellow courtesan and occasional lover, Andrée's mother was Marguerite Roquet, née Godard, whose own mother was one of Valtesse's daughters.[31] Evidently, Andrée had quite a Bohemian upbringing. Liane de Pougy described in her journal an occasion in the summer of 1920 when she had several guests to her house, including the artist Max Jacob, and 'last but not least we opened our big gates to a ravishing grey motorcar from which Andrée de La Bigne emerged, all golden in a dress of blue Japanese silk – really stunning that girl – and loaded with chocolate caramels'. Andrée had been followed out of the car by André Germain, who then proceeded to read aloud his articles on Dadaism while Liane exchanged 'delicate touches, caresses, kisses, nips and scratches' with another girl who had arrived with Andrée.[32]

It is not absolutely clear how old Andrée was at this time, although there was an actress recorded as having been born in Normandy in 1903 by the name of Andrée Rose Godard (the maiden name of the mother of Andrea's Andrée) de La Bigne.[33] If this was the same Andrée, she was apparently a 'hauntingly beautiful blonde' who, under the stage name Andrée Lafayette, played opposite John Barrymore's Svengali in the 1923 film *Trilby*, and appeared in a further twelve films until 1934, and then two more in the 1950s. Her title Comtesse seems to have been *soi-disant* – at least there is no mention of her in the *Annuaire de la noblesse de France* and the present Marquis de La Bigne is aware of no one by that name amid the branches of his family tree. Equally, we do not know exactly when Andrea took up with her, although by some accounts it was as early as 1930.

By the beginning of the war, Andrea was still only fifty-seven; however, all the hours spent aboard Gilbert Beale's yacht, where the drinks arrived at eleven, had taken their toll on his health. His doctor diagnosed him as suffering from arteriosclerosis and an irregular heartbeat, and advised him to take things easy. In 1943 he wanted to visit Portugal but could not obtain a visa, and there is mention in the National Archives of an intended visit to Britain in 1944, but that, too, appears to have come to nothing. In August 1944, he attended a party with American friends in Nice to celebrate the liberation, after the Allies had landed in southern France, captured Marseilles and begun an offensive up the Rhône valley.[34] By that autumn, he and the Comtesse were living at a villa belonging to the Hotel Metropole in Monte Carlo. On 3 December 1944, after returning from a party in Marseilles, he woke up in the early hours of the morning sweating and later complained of a pain in his chest. A minute later his heart stopped, so the Comtesse later told Alice.[35] He was sixty-two.

When Alice received a telegram saying that Andrea had died, the fierce street fighting in the quarter in which she was living prevented her from passing the sad news on to her daughters. However, she did manage to get Dickie to send a naval message to Philip in *Whelp*, which had to be deciphered on board: 'So shocked and grieved to hear of the death of your father, and send you all my heartfelt sympathy. Following has been received from your mother: "Embrace you tenderly in our joint sorrow."'[36]

For Philip this came as yet another harsh blow. His father had become a slightly distant figure during the latter part of his childhood, and five years had passed since he had last seen him. Nevertheless, he had always retained a deep affection and sympathy for him. 'He really loved his father,' said his friend Mike Parker, who was serving in the same flotilla as Philip when Andrea died. 'He had a big image of him which persisted, and his death was a great shock to him.'[37] When Philip wrote to his mother, she replied that she took comfort from 'how wonderfully you took this great loss, for naturally I was sad for you being so far away & separated from us all at such a moment'. She also drew solace from the fact 'that I, like you, can feel him closer to me now' and from seeing 'with what veneration & love, all classes speak to me of Papa & how they rejoice that he has left a son to follow in his footsteps'.[38]

In December 1944, however, as first lieutenant aboard *Whelp* in the Indian Ocean, there was no prospect of Philip being able to get to the Riviera for his father's funeral, which took place at a chapel behind the Russian cathedral in Nice (after the war his coffin was transported to Greece for burial in the family ground at Tatoï). Instead, when his ship stopped at Colombo, Philip travelled up into the hills to spend Christmas with the Mountbattens at the King's Pavilion in Kandy. Some respite from his sadness was provided by a farcical Christmas Eve, when, by Philip Ziegler's account, 'the Sinhalese cook, overawed by the occasion, took refuge in drink and served dinner cold, late, and back to front: Christmas pudding at midnight, turkey at 1 am. Nobody minded, least of all Mountbatten.'[39]

Afterwards, Philip returned to *Whelp*, now deployed as part of the destroyer screen for the bombing raids on Japanese oil refineries on Sumatra. In late January, they picked up a Mayday signal from a stricken Allied bomber, which had been hit by a Japanese fighter near Palembang and had flown back across the shark-infested Java Sea in the hope of ditching near its own ships. Philip immediately sprang into action, activating *Whelp*'s search and rescue system, and directing the vessel at full speed towards the spot where the bomber had gone down. The plane had quickly sunk after ditching and its two-man crew struggled in vain to inflate their life raft. So after spending twenty minutes in the sea they were greatly relieved to see *Whelp* approaching. As they clambered up the scrambling nets, Philip peered anxiously over the side, having already alerted the sick bay and ordered hot food and dry clothes for the men. He later gave them dinner in the officers' mess, procured new uniforms from the purser, and, when they reached Fremantle in Western Australia a week later, suggested a run ashore, which turned into a 'memorable bender' in the port's bars, as the airmen later recalled. Both men were later reunited with their fellow pilots aboard *Victorious*. Nine of their comrades who had been shot down during the same raid were considerably less fortunate. Captured and imprisoned by the Japanese, they were beheaded in Changi three days after V-J Day.*[40]

From Fremantle, *Whelp* proceeded round to Sydney and then on to Manus in Papua New Guinea with the British Pacific Fleet. From there they continued northward to the Japanese Sakishima Gunto group of islands to the east of Taiwan, where *Whelp* had several exchanges with the enemy, and Philip performed more acts of gallantry, taking out one of the ship's whalers to rescue a pilot shot down and helping to save a drowning crew member clinging to a buoy.[41] In early May, *Whelp* took passage to Melbourne to be refitted, affording Philip the best part of three months of shore leave in Australia.

According to his cousin Alexandra, with his golden beard Philip 'hit feminine hearts, first in Melbourne and then in Sydney, with terrific impact', and yet he 'fought a series of delaying actions all aimed at one objective: non-involvement'.[42] Philip's friend Mike Parker, too, who had coincided with him in Sydney, was later at pains

---

* Some sixty years later the two airmen, twenty-one-year-old pilot Roy 'Gus' Halliday (later Vice Admiral Sir Roy Halliday) and air gunner Norman 'Dickie' Richardson, were reunited with Prince Philip on a BBC Radio 4 programme entitled *A Right Royal Rescue*.

to stress that although there were 'always armfuls of girls, nothing happened – nothing serious. What I mean was this: we were young, we had fun, we had a few drinks, we might have gone dancing and that was it.'[43]

Not everyone in Australia at that time was so chaste. Due to the circumstances of the war, society girls there seem to have been more generous with their favours than their counterparts in London. Robin Dalton, who had fallen in love with Philip's cousin David Milford Haven shortly before Philip arrived, recalled in her memoir that

> the men with whom we spent our time were, for the most part, on a few days leave … and we never knew when they left if they would be alive to return. What would seem like shocking promiscuity, not only physical but emotional – in peacetime, was felt as a beneficence of the heart. The fact that it was also rarely that one was caught out in one's perfidious spread of affection blinded one to the dangers … We did not consider ourselves promiscuous, we were in love.[44]

Robin Dalton met Philip at one of the open-house parties thrown by the rakish society photographer Jo Fallon at his home in the smart Sydney suburb of Bellevue Hill. Philip was a regular fixture at these gatherings and seemed to have 'two particular girlfriends', she recalls. 'One was Sue Other-Gee, from Melbourne. I don't know how serious that was. I remember thinking of her as an older woman but she was probably only 26 or 27. The other one was a society girl called Sandra Jacques. She was beautiful and modelled and sang in nightclubs. I know that they kept in touch.' According to Robin Dalton, Philip at the time was 'always jolly, but at the same time always cautious, emotionally tight …' According to Parker, he was 'quite reserved, quite restrained … always good company but self-disciplined … self-contained … careful. He didn't encourage gossip … There have been books and articles galore saying he played the field. I don't believe it. People say we were screwing around like nobody's business. Well, we weren't. You didn't. We didn't. That's the truth of it ...'[45]

Whatever happened ashore in Australia, as far as the crew members of *Whelp* were concerned, their first lieutenant was courting Princess Elizabeth. It was common knowledge aboard ship that their letters came and went from the ship's mailroom, and that he displayed a photograph of her in his cabin.[46] Back in Britain, Marion Crawford also professed to have been aware at the time that they wrote to each other. And she, too, recalled seeing a photograph of Philip on Elizabeth's mantelpiece and warning the princess that it might lead to gossip. The next time Crawfie went in to Elizabeth's room, it had been replaced by another one of Philip disguised behind the beard he had grown while at sea. 'There you are, Crawfie,' said the princess, 'I defy anyone to recognize who that is.'[47]

By March 1945, just short of her nineteenth birthday, Elizabeth had her own suite of rooms in Buckingham Palace, her own footman and housemaid and two ladies-in-waiting. That spring, she was at last allowed to join the Auxiliary Territorial Service, enrolling on a six-week course at Aldershot that aimed to make her not only an expert driver and map reader but also capable of stripping and servicing an engine. It is often cited as her first foray into 'ordinary' life. By the time she completed her training in mid-April, the war in Europe was virtually over, although pictures of the princess in overalls earnestly dismantling engines and changing tyres briefly became part of British propaganda. She also proudly wore her ATS uniform on V-E Day on 8 May, which she celebrated by slipping out of the Palace with Margaret and several young Guards officers and joining in with the singing in the streets. Virtually no one recognized the two princesses in the crowd. 'Poor darlings,' wrote the king in his diary later that evening. 'They have never had any fun yet.'[48]

By the time the princesses next took to the streets on 15 August, V-J Day, Philip was back at sea, having finally left Sydney in late July to escort the flotilla's flagship, *Duke of York*. They were on their way to assist in the intended invasion of Japan when the atom bomb was dropped on Hiroshima. Three days later, on 9 August, just as they reached the American-held island of Guam, east of the Philippines, another bomb devastated Nagasaki. When *Whelp* became one of the first Allied ships to enter Japanese waters, escorting the US flagship *Missouri* into Tokyo Bay on 2 September, it was to attend the formal Japanese surrender, the signing of which Philip witnessed aboard the American flagship.

FOURTEEN

Nothing Ventured …

After the end of the war, Prince Philip remained in the Far East with *Whelp* to collect and bring home prisoners of war, and did not arrive back at Portsmouth until 17 January 1946, whereupon he was given a notably anti-climactic first command, overseeing the ship's decommissioning. When that process was finished, he received an equally unexciting posting to HMS *Glendower*, a naval training establishment at Pwllheli in North Wales, moving in the autumn of 1946 to HMS *Royal Arthur*, at Corsham, near Bath, lecturing petty officers on 'sea warfare, morale and current affairs'.

Privately he gloomily conceded that these jobs could never compete with the buzz of the past five years. In a letter to Queen Elizabeth, he admitted that he had arrived home 'still not accustomed to the idea of peace, rather fed up with everything and feeling that there was not much to look forward to and rather grudgingly accepting the idea of going on in the peacetime navy'.[1]

His home postings did at least allow for more frequent trips to London, where Marion Crawford recalled Philip's MG sports car roaring into the forecourt of Buckingham Palace and the prince getting out 'hatless' and 'always in a hurry to see Lilibet'. According to Crawfie, all of a sudden Elizabeth began to take more trouble with her appearance and to play the tune 'People Will Say We're In Love' from the musical *Oklahoma!*[2]

Around this time, according to his friend Hélène Cordet (née Foufounis), Philip also travelled to Paris and took her for tea at the Ritz, arriving on a woman's bicycle that was far too small for him, having refused to avail himself of the car offered by the Greek embassy. They met on several subsequent occasions while he was there, renewing a bond that stretched back to childhood. In 1938, seventeen-year-old Philip had acted as best man and given Hélène away at her first marriage to an Englishman, William Kirby, in London, but that union did not last. During the war, while living in England, she had fallen deeply in love with a Free French airman named Marcel Boisot; the intensity of their relationship is convincingly portrayed in her memoir, *Born Bewildered*. However, their first child, Max, was born out of wedlock, in December 1943, and gossips, led by Philip's supposed friend Larry Adler, later raised questions about his and his sister's paternity, questions that were fuelled by the fact that Hélène disguised Marcel as 'Jacques' in her book. Because of who he was, and because he had stood as Max's godfather and was later said to have contributed towards his schooling at Gordonstoun, and because he happened to have been on leave at the time when both Max and his sister were conceived, the gossips pointed the finger at Prince Philip. However, Max Boisot, now a professor at ESADE business school in Barcelona, has always been adamant that the rumour is nonsense and says that he never saw anything to suggest that his mother and Philip had ever been romantically involved. Hélène's disguise of Marcel, he says, was simply due to her wish to protect his anonymity in view of the fact that he had deserted her at the end of the war, and Philip's help with the school fees was purely a means of recompensing the Foufounis family for all the help that they had given him when he was a child. Max Boisot, meanwhile, was given Marcel as his middle name, and he and his younger sister Louise, a former actress and singer dubbed 'France's Queen of Twist', saw their father regularly over the years until his death in 2002. When Louise

Boisot married in Greece in 1969, it was Marcel Boisot who gave her away.[3] For her own part, Hélène always denied the suggestion that her friendship with Philip was anything other than innocent, saying that he wasn't her type and that she preferred 'tall dark handsome men' – like Marcel Boisot.

Meanwhile, back in London, Philip stayed either with his grandmother at Kensington Palace or on a camp bed at the Mountbattens' house at 16 Chester Street. In visitors' books he wrote 'of no fixed abode'.[4] The Mountbattens' butler, John Dean (later Philip's valet), was struck by the fact that the prince's civilian wardrobe seemed to be 'scantier than that of many a bank clerk' and that often all he brought with him to London was a razor. When he had gone to bed Dean would wash and iron his shirt and darn his socks and have them ready for him in the morning. 'He was very easy to look after, and never asked for things like that to be done for him, but I liked him so much that I did it anyway.' Whenever Philip did bring a weekend bag, Dean noticed, when he unpacked it, that there was always a photograph of Princess Elizabeth in a battered leather frame.[5]

By now, according to Marion Crawford, Philip was coming 'as a matter of course' to dine informally in the old nursery at the Palace, which Margaret had taken to using as her sitting room. 'The food was of the simplest,' recalled Crawfie. 'Fish, some sort of sweet, and orangeade.' Just as Dean remembered that the prince was 'never immoderate in his pleasures', Crawfie noted that he 'drinks very little'. However, she also maintained that he did not smoke, whereas in fact he had acquired quite a heavy smoking habit in the navy during the war, often getting through a case of cigarettes a day, which he only gave up on his marriage.

After dinner there would be 'high jinks' in the corridors, as they played ball and raced around 'like a bunch of high-spirited children'. But although it was almost always the three of them together, according to Crawfie, 'everyone in the household was by now aware of what was in the air'. 'One could not see the young people together without realizing what they felt for each other.'[6]

Yet for Elizabeth it was still an anxious time, according to Crawfie, as Philip had not yet spoken to her about his feelings and at the same time she had to put up with people shouting 'Where's Philip?' while she was carrying out her public engagements. 'Poor Lilibet,' remarked her sister Margaret. 'Nothing of your own. Not even your own love affair.'

In April 1946, after being spotted with Elizabeth and a party at the Aldwych Theatre,[7] Philip travelled again to the Continent and across war-ravaged Germany in a Canadian army truck to turn up unexpectedly at Salem for the wedding of his widowed sister Sophie. The effort was characteristic of his loyalty to close family and friends, and would have been especially appreciated by Sophie, who had had a wretched time since the death of her first husband in 1943. In late 1944 she had heard reports that Princess Mafalda, whose children she was looking after, had died at Büchenwald after an American bombing raid on a nearby industrial site, but she did not know for sure until the Allies liberated the camp in April 1945. Mafalda's second son, Heinrich, who was eighteen at the time, first heard of his mother's fate on an Allied radio broadcast and wanted to believe that it was propaganda.[8] When the Americans arrived at Friedrichshof shortly afterwards, Sophie and her extended brood were required to leave within hours, being unceremoniously evacuated to a town house in the shadow of the old Kronberg castle, which then became a GI rest camp.[9] They later took refuge with Lu and Peg at Wolfsgarten, just north of Darmstadt, travelling there by cart with the children hidden under straw.[10] Just prior to the wedding, they went to retrieve the Hesse family jewels from Friedrichshof for Sophie to wear, only to discover that they had been stolen. The culprits turned out to be two US Army officers, soon to become man and wife, who had perpetrated what the *New York*

Times called 'the greatest gem theft in modern times'. The hoard was reported to be worth $3 million.[11]

Sophie's bridegroom was Prince George of Hanover, brother of Queen Frederika of Greece, who would soon become headmaster of Salem when the school was restarted, having been closed during the war. She had not seen Philip for nine years; when she had last seen him in 1937 he had been sixteen, 'not really grown up at all'. This time she was shocked by how closely he resembled their late father, with 'the same mannerisms, movements, ways of standing, walking, laughing … The colossal sense of humour, really seeing the funny side of things always …'[12] Philip apparently told her that he was thinking about getting engaged and that Uncle Dickie was being 'very helpful'.[13]

Afterwards, Philip travelled with Mike Parker to Monte Carlo to collect his father's effects from the Comtesse Andrée de La Bigne. They had arranged to meet at the *belle époque* Café de Paris, a regular haunt of hers. They got there first, ordered cocktails and waited for the Comtesse's arrival, which Parker later described as 'like a scene from a film'. Elegantly dressed and wearing blue glasses, she was 'very striking' and 'seemed totally at home. She and Philip hit it off at once.'[14] Andrea's few remaining possessions included books, pictures, clothes – many of them moth-eaten and darned, which Philip nevertheless had adapted to fit him – an ivory shaving brush which he also took to using, and a heavy gold signet ring which he wore from that day on.[15] In his will he had left seven-tenths of his estate to Philip and a tenth to each of his surviving daughters. However, it soon transpired that he had had debts of at least £17,500, and when the extent of his ultimate impoverishment became known, Victoria Milford Haven deduced that the Comtesse had 'sucked him dry etc. as such women generally do'.[16]

On 29 May 1946, back in London, Philip was photographed next to Elizabeth at the wedding of her new lady-in-waiting, Jean Gibbs, to

Andrew Elphinstone (Elizabeth's cousin) and was described in one newspaper merely as 'a figure still largely unknown to the British public'.[17] The speculation surrounding the couple was not always so tactfully inexplicit, so they generally tried not to be seen together, and if they were at the same party in concert they took the precaution of not dancing with each other.

Behind the scenes, however, the courtship was entering a new and bolder phase. In June 1946 Philip wrote to the queen apologizing for the 'monumental cheek' of having invited himself to the Palace. Yet 'however contrite I feel,' he wrote, 'there is always a small voice that keeps saying "nothing ventured, nothing gained" – well I did venture and I gained a wonderful time'.[18] Later that summer, the queen asked him to Balmoral for three weeks to shoot grouse and stalk. Philip was later hazy about what had happened there, admitting only, 'It was probably then that we, that it became, you know, that we began to think about it seriously, and even talk about it …'[19] The indications are that it was during this holiday that he proposed, Elizabeth accepted and they told her parents.[20]

Philip's thank-you letter this time bordered on the euphoric. 'I am sure I do not deserve all the good things which have happened to me,' he wrote to the queen. 'To have been spared in the war and seen victory, to have been given the chance to rest and re-adjust myself, to have fallen in love completely and unreservedly, makes all one's personal and even the world's troubles seem small and petty.' At last, he said, life had a purpose. 'I only realize now what a difference those few weeks, which seemed to flash past, have made to me.' The holiday had helped to dispel the depressed and uninspired feelings he had had about his future career in the navy since returning home. 'The generous hospitality and the warm friendliness did much to restore my faith in permanent values and brighten up a rather warped view of life. Naturally there is one circumstance which has done more for me than anything else in my life.'[21]

The king agreed in principle to let them marry,* but wanted no final decision to be taken until the next year when the family had completed their first – and, as it happened, last – overseas royal tour together to South Africa, by which time Elizabeth would be twenty-one.[22] Mabell Airlie attributed the king's foot-dragging to his 'secret dread' of an early marriage for his eldest daughter, whereby he would lose 'his constant companion in shooting, walking, riding – in fact in everything'.[23] It may equally have reflected his concerns that Elizabeth was still too young and had had scant opportunity to meet anyone else – the trip would give her more time to think after which she could then decide. But he was also aware that several senior courtiers were opposed to the match, notably his old friends Lord Eldon and 'Bobbety' Cranborne (who succeeded as Marquess of Salisbury in 1947), both of whom had been staying at Balmoral in August 1946 at the time that Philip is supposed to have proposed. Another guest in the same house party, the queen's younger brother, David Bowes-Lyon, was a 'vicious little fellow' who 'had it in for Philip right from the start', according to Gina Wernher.[24] Bowes-Lyon was notorious for his capacity for intrigue and untruthfulness, not to mention his extreme right-wing views and all-male fancy-dress weekends; though married, he seems to have been predominantly homosexual. He was nonetheless also the queen's closest sibling in age and rapport and did his best to turn his sister against the match.[25,26]

These guests at Balmoral reportedly found Philip 'rather unpolished',[27] an impression that may have had to do with reports that he had no plus fours and instead blithely went shooting in his flannel trousers and with a borrowed gun. An indiscreet footman let on that his 'solitary naval valise' contained no spare shoes, pyjamas or slippers, and that his only walking shoes had to be taken off to the local cobbler to be repaired.[28] The gamekeepers, meanwhile, muttered

---

* While Elizabeth was under the age of twenty-five his consent was required under the Royal Marriages Act of 1772.

about his 'rather erratic' shooting.[29] In the last respect, at least, he was very quick to improve. George VI's great passion for shooting and prowess as a shot had from their first acquaintance fired the enthusiasm of his prospective son-in-law. The king soon taught him all the finer methods of pursuit and, according to their friend and Norfolk neighbour Aubrey Buxton, thanks to his 'remarkable gift for learning anything new', within only a few seasons Philip 'acquired a degree of skill in the shooting field which many fail to show after a lifetime of sport'.[30]

More hostility towards Philip in other respects, meanwhile, was noted at Balmoral in 1947 by Jock Colville, the diplomat who had become Elizabeth's first official private secretary. 'Lords Salisbury, Eldon and Stanley think him no gentleman,' Colville confided to his diary, 'and in a sense they are right.'[31] He had not been to the right school for a start. Virtually every courtier was an Old Etonian – with the notable exception of the king's private secretary Tommy Lascelles, who had been to Marlborough but later bemoaned its unaristocratic ethos.[32] By having gone to such an unusual and remote alternative, Philip was seen to have missed out on the opportunity to make appropriate friendships and to steep himself in the habits and assumptions of the British ruling class. It made him seem even more of an outsider than he already was. Gordonstoun was seen as suspiciously German and dangerously progressive, although when a member of the royal family described it to Queen Mary as 'a crank school with theories of complete social equality where the boys were taught to mix with all and sundry', she was adamant that such a training would be 'useful' to the king's son-in-law.[33]

The jibe that he was 'no gentleman' also referred to what opponents perceived to be Philip's rude and overbearing manner. The self-reliance bred in him by his difficult upbringing could come across as cockiness, and he could appear arrogant when brushing aside obstacles in order to get things done. However, his forthrightness and independence were precisely the traits that had won Elizabeth's heart, accustomed as she had been all her life to fawning deference. 'He was not all over her,' observed one courtier, 'and she found that very attractive.'[34] There was, as one biographer put it, 'something of the wild stallion about him' and his 'raw energy and uninhibited behaviour spoke to a side of Elizabeth which had seldom been allowed to express itself. This shy, reserved young woman, desperately needed bringing out of herself and Philip was just the man to do it.'[35]

Yet the same characteristics did not always endear him to the older courtiers, nor, apparently, to the queen, who was a far more emollient character, highly adept at avoiding confrontation, and seems to have found the briskness of her prospective son-in-law slightly unappealing. 'The queen had produced a cricket eleven of possibles,' remembered Sir Edward Ford, 'and it's hard to know whom she would have sent in first, but it certainly wouldn't have been Philip!'[36] According to one of her daughter's ladies-in-waiting, the queen feared that Philip could prove awkward and disruptive, and found him 'cold and lacking in our kind of sense of humour. He wasn't able to see the ridiculous side of things, and that is perhaps rather Germanic. And he certainly didn't set out to charm her.'[37] She was said to refer to him privately and not altogether affectionately as 'the Hun' and to complain that he ran the royal estates 'like a Junker'.[38]

Philip's close links to Germany were, of course, largely shared by the whole of the royal family, yet Colville noted in his diary that courtiers opposed to the young suitor whispered darkly about his 'Teutonic strain'.[39] Another ex-courtier later explained: 'The kind of people who didn't like Prince Philip, were the kind of people who didn't like Mountbatten. It was all bound up in a single word: "German".'[40]

The association with his glittering yet controversial uncle was always going to be double-edged. Close as Mountbatten was to George VI, he was also a transparent intriguer – 'an elephant trampling down the jungle rather than a snake in the grass'[41] – and pushy with it. 'His ambition remained consuming,' wrote his biographer Philip Ziegler, 'and his efforts to conceal it were unavailing.'[42] Mountbatten was also seen as politically unsound on account of his friendliness with Labour politicians such as Tom Driberg, and because his wife, Edwina, was notoriously left-wing. Some of the old courtiers suspected that he planned to use Philip as a Trojan horse to infiltrate the monarchy, enabling him then to set about reforming the institution along lines that he saw fit.[43]

The queen and Princess Elizabeth also viewed Mountbatten with suspicion, thinking him a little too inclined to take advantage of the fact that he was a cousin of the king. The king also, while ostensibly fond of Mountbatten, was said by Lascelles to be 'under no illusions whatever about dear cousin Dickie!'[44] and the queen later said that they 'always took what Dickie said with a pinch of salt'.[45] Since returning from South-East Asia in June 1946, Mountbatten had spent considerable time and energy on smoothing the path for his nephew to marry the heir to the British throne, but his own reputation meant that his influence was often counter-productive as far as Philip was concerned.

The question of Philip's naturalization, meanwhile, had still not been resolved. The delay had been due to a combination of his absence abroad, hesitation by George VI and concern within the British government about its wartime Balkan diplomacy. There was also now the additional worry that it might be interpreted as admitting that the future prospects of the Greek monarchy were bleak, so George VI had been advised by his ministers that it would be better to postpone the matter until after a plebiscite on the restoration of the Greek monarchy had been held.[46]

The restoration of King George II of Greece eventually took place on 28 September 1946; it was thought unhelpful, however, for Philip to renounce his Greek nationality just as the king regained his throne.[47] So the matter ostensibly hung fire again until the late autumn, although behind the scenes Mountbatten was busy heading off other potential obstacles, discreetly briefing his friends and foes in politics and the press.

One contact who usefully straddled both fields was Tom Driberg, the Labour MP and journalist, a relatively new acquaintance yet one with whom, so Driberg's biographer Francis Wheen writes, Mountbatten had 'hit it off at once and discovered that they had much in common, including a sexual preference for men'.[48] This latter assertion is contentious, since while Driberg was the first man to be outed as a homosexual in a *Times* obituary, published in 1973, rumours in *Private Eye* and elsewhere that Mountbatten shared this orientation have been refuted by his official biographer, Philip Ziegler, and others. Yet there were other attributes that they irrefutably shared such as the contradictions in their belief systems, the fact that Mountbatten was 'a royalist and snob who nevertheless held left-wing views' whereas Driberg was 'a left-winger who nevertheless loved the monarchy'.[49] Their shared heresies created a bond of trust and Mountbatten saw Driberg as a convenient channel through which he could pass 'guidance' about his nephew to newspapers and politicians.

In early August 1946, shortly before Philip's first stay at Balmoral, Mountbatten had persuaded Driberg to ask some of the younger Labour MPs to lunch with his nephew at the House of Commons in order to forestall any likely xenophobic or republican rhetoric against him. Afterwards, he wrote to thank Driberg for 'being so kind ... He was tremendously thrilled by his day in the House, and very favourably impressed by you. It is most kind of you to say that you will help to give the right line in the Press when the news about his naturalisation is announced.'[50] When Driberg then offered to help with newspaper articles, Mountbatten became anxious, warning him not to let 'any form of pre-publicity break, which I feel would be fatal'. He also supplied Driberg with detailed information to show that Philip 'really is more English than any other nationality', that he had spent only three months in Greece since the age of one, spoke no Greek and 'had had nothing whatever to do with the political set-up in Greece'.[51] In his briefing to the Press Association, Mountbatten was also at pains to stress that 'the Prince's desire to be British dated back several years before the rumours about the engagement' and had 'no possible connection with such rumours'.[52]

The prime minister, Clement Attlee, meanwhile, took his own soundings and in early November he was assured by the Admiralty that Philip was 'in every way above average. In short, he is the type of officer we should not like to lose.'[53] Thus, when Mountbatten saw the prime minister and the home secretary in mid-November 1946, he obtained their agreement not only to his naturalization plan, but also to his nephew becoming known as 'HRH Prince Philip'. The next day he sent Philip a naturalization form to fill in, and told him what to put in it.[54] On 5 December, replying to a question in the Commons, the home secretary James Chuter Ede confirmed that Prince Philip of Greece had submitted an application through his commanding officer in accordance with the arrangements made to give early consideration to applications for naturalization from foreigners who had served during the war in HM Forces.[55]

There had been a certain amount of press speculation about an engagement prior to this – including a story in the *Star* newspaper on 7 September 1946 which had prompted Sir Alan Lascelles to take the unusual step of refuting it – but the announcement of the naturalization inevitably prompted a renewed bout of interest, and the ensuing coverage was a tribute to Mountbatten's genius at public relations and press manipulation. The *Sunday Pictorial* ran a full-page article obligingly hailing the potential consort as a paragon of all the virtues and 'a blond Greek Apollo ... as handsome as any film star'. Driberg, writing in *Reynolds News*, drew attention to Philip's success on the sub-lieutenant's course 'thus gaining nine months seniority out of a possible ten', and wrote that he was 'intelligent and broadminded, fair and good-looking'. He added helpfully that he could not, in truth, 'even speak Greek' having left the country as an infant, and that whatever his views on Greek politics might be, 'it seems fair to interpret his request for British citizenship as, in part, a desire to be disentangled from them permanently'.[56]

On 10 December the *News Chronicle* primly declared that 'the rational comment on all this Press build-up seems to be that the moment is approaching when the public should be given some explicit information ... This is not a trivial issue. The British throne has never been held in such good esteem as it is today. It is of the utmost importance that the strong links of mutual confidence should be preserved'.[57]

Yet for all the praise heaped on Philip, Elizabeth's rumoured choice of husband was controversial. A poll in the *Sunday Pictorial* on 12 January 1947 found that although 55 per cent were in favour of a marriage between her and Philip (providing they really were in love) 40 per cent were against. Many would have preferred her to choose a commoner, one reader observing that 'the days of intermarriage of royalty have passed'. To others the intended match was transparently 'a political move', and there was broad support for the xenophobic sentiments of one household: 'We, the Russell family – a father and two sons who have served in both wars – say, "Definitely no!" to a marriage with a foreign prince'.[58]

It was to counter this kind of reaction that Mountbatten kept up his press briefing campaign. The newspaper group that worried him most of all in the long term was the Express Group, whose owner, Lord Beaverbrook, had been pursuing a vendetta against Mountbatten for years. Mountbatten himself attributed the feud to a shot in the film *In Which We Serve*, inspired by his misadventures in the *Kelly*, in which a copy of the *Daily Express* from 1939 and bearing the unprophetic headline 'No War This Year' was pictured sinking in the sea.

But according to Mountbatten's god-daughter, Sarah Baring, the cause was more personal, having to do with Beaverbrook's suspicions that Mountbatten had been carrying on with Beaverbrook's mistress, Jean Norton (Sarah Baring's mother), later Lady Grantley.[59] This was apparently confirmed to Beaverbrook when he went through Jean's papers after her death in 1945.[60]

But whatever the cause of Beaverbrook's animosity, in early 1947 Mountbatten pulled off a masterstroke by inviting the two *Express* editors and their chairman to his house and asking the likely public reaction to his nephew taking out naturalization papers, and about the acceptability of Prince Philip as a British subject. Philip was there, too, although, according to the *Daily Express* editor Arthur Christiansen, he stayed in the corner of the room throughout the meeting, 'grinned cheerfully from time to time and said nothing. He was so little part of the gathering that when the whiskies and sodas were served he was not included in that round.'[61] In the intimacy of Mountbatten's drawing room, the newspapermen could not bring themselves to come up with any conceivable reasons why anyone should oppose Philip's change of nationality, and when the news was made public a month or so later they were hardly in a position to manufacture any of their own. Beaverbrook was later said to have been 'more amazed than enraged' when he learned how his editors had allowed themselves to be muzzled.[62]

Mountbatten, meanwhile, had been asked by Clement Attlee in December 1946 to become the last Viceroy of India. He was initially reluctant to take up this offer, mainly because he longed to return to the navy although he may also have been hesitant about leaving the country just as his plans for Philip seemed on the point of coming to fruition.

FIFTEEN

True Brit

Edwina recorded that she and Philip discussed Dickie's latest job offer 'till all hours'.[1] There were certainly advantages for Philip in having his uncle disappear off abroad at this time, given the discomfort he had often felt at the blatant orchestration of his courtship. 'Please, I beg of you,' he wrote to Dickie at one point, 'not too much advice in an affair of the heart, or I shall be forced to do the wooing by proxy.'[2] Whether or not Philip encouraged him to accept the appointment, Mountbatten eventually succumbed to the pressure to accept the viceroyalty.

On 18 March 1947, two days before they left for India, he and Edwina hosted a farewell reception for seven hundred guests at the Royal Automobile Club on Pall Mall. The party turned into a joint celebration: among more than eight hundred newly adopted British citizens listed that morning in the *London Gazette* was one 'Mountbatten, Philip; Greece; Serving Officer in His Majesty's Forces'; his address was given as 16 Chester Street, London SW1 – the Mountbattens' town house.[3] On taking the oath of allegiance, Philip had in the process elected to become a commoner, turning down the offer of HRH, and he also relinquished his right of succession to the Greek throne, to which he was then sixth in line.[4] The culmination of his hard-fought campaign for his nephew's naturalization was deeply satisfying for Dickie Mountbatten. However, no one at the time seems to have realized that the whole complicated exercise had been, in legal terms, both pointless and ineffective.

What Mountbatten and all the courtiers and politicians whom he had lobbied seem to have overlooked was that by virtue of the 1705 Act of Naturalization of the Most Excellent Princess Sophia, Electress of Hanover, and the Issue of her Body, as a descendant of Sophia, Philip had been *ipso facto* a British subject since birth. The point was to be tested in a case in 1956 involving Philip's distant cousin Prince Ernst August of Hanover, and was confirmed to Mountbatten in a letter he received in 1972 from the former Lord Chancellor, Lord Dilhorne, who concluded that 'the naturalization of Prince Philip was quite unnecessary and of no effect for you cannot naturalize someone who is already a British subject'.[5] Given his obsession with all things genealogical, it had been a surprising oversight by Mountbatten. In 1947, however, he basked in the mistaken belief that he had pulled off a tremendous coup, doubly gratifying given that Philip had now adopted his surname.

Philip might have been expected to take his paternal dynastic name of Schleswig-Holstein-Sonderburg-Glücksburg. This, though, would have looked incongruous on a British passport, and by drawing attention to his German ancestry with the trials at Nuremberg only recently concluded it would have been distinctly unhelpful to his cause. Genealogists at the College of Arms had come up with the snappier alternative of Oldcastle, an anglicized version of Oldenburg, the German duchy where the royal house of Greece and Denmark had originated, but this did not find favour either; as much as anything because it was thought to sound slightly plebeian. The home secretary, Chuter Ede, told George VI that he was sure 'something grander and more glittering could be found',[6] and eventually it was suggested that Philip resort to his mother's name, which had, of course, been anglicized during the previous era of anti-German hysteria. According to official documents, Philip's choice of name was agreed by the king on the advice of the home secretary,[7] but there was little doubt as to where Chuter Ede's inspiration had come from. Dickie Mountbatten was later said to have been 'delighted' by the news; however, he was perhaps not so surprised as he implied.[8] In any event, the prospect of installing the House of Mountbatten on the British throne had never seemed more realistic. Philip, meanwhile, by his own account, 'wasn't madly in favour [of taking the name Mountbatten] … but in the end I was persuaded, and anyway I couldn't think of a reasonable alternative'.[9] His ambivalence persisted, not least because the surname resulted in lingering confusion about the identity of his father.

By the time of Philip's naturalization, the royal family had been away for almost six weeks on their tour of South Africa, which was Elizabeth's first journey outside the British Isles and afforded an opportunity for the whole family to recuperate after the traumas of war.[10] Shortly before they had left for Cape Town, on 1 February, Elizabeth and her parents had attended a small dinner party given by the Mountbattens at 16 Chester Street.[11] Philip had been there to say goodbye and he later wrote to thank the queen for 'the heartening thing' she had said to him, which helped to 'keep my spirits up' while they were away.[12] He was still well aware that things could yet go wrong, however, especially if his uncle meddled too conspicuously in his marriage plans. The day after his thank-you letter to the queen, he wrote to Dickie: 'I am not being rude, but it is apparent that you like the idea of being General Manager of this little show, and I am rather afraid that she might not take to the idea quite as docilely as I do. It is true that I know what is good for me, but don't forget that she has not had you as Uncle loco parentis, counsellor and friend as long as I have.'[13]

With the engagement still not yet official before the royal family left for South Africa, Philip had not been asked to attend the farewell luncheon or come to Waterloo to see them off, and he was not at the

pier to welcome them home on 11 May either – giving rise to speculation that the relationship had been broken off. But after their return
Philip wrote to the queen to say that he was sure the delay had been
the right thing but that he and Elizabeth now wanted to start their
new life together.[14] Soon, according to Crawfie, his sports car began to
appear with its old regularity at the side entrance to Buckingham
Palace;[15] however, it was not until 7 July that the queen wrote to tell
her sister May Elphinstone '*very secretly*' (underlined in black and red)
that Elizabeth had 'made up her mind' to become engaged to Philip
Mountbatten, whom she had known 'ever since she was 12, & I think
she is really fond of him, & I do pray that she will be very happy'.[16]

On the evening of 9 July 1947 a Court Circular was issued from
Buckingham Palace: 'It is with the greatest pleasure that the King and
Queen announce the betrothal of their dearly beloved daughter The
Princess Elizabeth to Lieutenant Philip Mountbatten, R.N., son of the
late Prince Andrew of Greece and Princess Andrew (Princess Alice of
Battenberg), to which union the King has gladly given his consent.'

That evening Philip drove from Corsham to Buckingham Palace to
dine with the king, while Elizabeth went to a dinner party at the
Dorchester and then on to a dance a short distance down Park Lane
at Apsley House.[17] She wore her platinum engagement ring comprising jewels that had belonged to Alice and had been deposited by
Andrea in a bank in Paris in 1930 after she was taken off to the clinic
at Kreuzlingen. Also in the bank was Andrea's Star of the Order of the
Redeemer, which Philip had planned to wear at the wedding, but
which turned out to have paste diamonds, Andrea having apparently
sold the originals when he was hard up.[18]

The next day, the engaged couple made their first public appearance at a garden party held at Buckingham Palace.[19] In the drizzle that
fell between short spells of sunshine, Harold Nicolson watched everybody 'irreverently and shamelessly' straining to see the bridal pair.[20]
Lady Airlie thought Elizabeth looked 'flushed and radiant with

happiness', although Philip 'shook hands rather shyly'. She liked the fact that he was wearing his 'shabby' uniform with 'the usual after-the-war look', having not bought a new one for the occasion 'as many men would have done, to make an impression'. 'Observing him I thought that he had far more character than most people would imagine. I wondered whether he would be capable of helping Princess Elizabeth some day as the Prince Consort had helped Queen Victoria. I felt that he would, although I should not live to see it.'[21]

For Philip, the shyness was perhaps a result of realizing that there was no going back now. In the immediate aftermath of the announcement, others noticed that he appeared withdrawn and reflective. As the extent of what he was taking on finally dawned on him, he may well have wondered how well suited he would be to his new role, temperamentally and otherwise. Four days after the garden party, the newly betrothed went to Sunday lunch with the Duchess of Kent, where one of the other guests, Sir Michael 'Mikie' Duff, observed (in a letter to his friend Ettie Desborough) that 'Princess E looked radiant, & he not quite so much'. Duff had known Philip for several years but was now inclined to downgrade his original assessment of him (in 1944) to 'charming in a rather dull way'. 'I don't think he has very endearing qualities,' wrote Duff to Ettie,

> but they may grow, he's a bit 'Naval', if you know what I mean, & none of the gaiety of Dickie Mountbatten (or what we all thought gay) and his manners are a trifle rough ... Philip of Greece gives me the impression of taking all the wrong & trivial things to heart, & not the things that really matter ... He scowls a bit as though a fly were a permanent guest on his nose! I think all Royalty scowl, the male members especially. I suppose it's done in self-defence![22]

* * *

The press reaction to the engagement was on the whole far more favourable. The *Daily Telegraph* pronounced it 'completely a love match'[23] while Beaverbrook's *Daily Express* declared: 'Today the British people, turning aside from the anxieties of a time of troubles, find hope as well as joy in the royal romance.'[24] Almost all papers – except the *Daily Worker*, for whom the engagement was, of course, 'not to our liking' – struck a similar note. However, they recommended that the ceremony be an austere affair, given that food rationing and controls on imports of petrol, tobacco and paper were still in force.

The unusually hard winter of 1946–7 – the worst for decades, during which ice floes were seen off the coast of Kent and the Thames froze over at Windsor – had brought about a fuel crisis and an economic standstill, with rising unemployment and falling production. At his naval training base Philip had had to lecture his students by candlelight and wearing his naval greatcoat.[25] 'Any banqueting and display of wealth at your daughter's wedding will be an insult to the British people at the present time,' the Camden Town branch of the Amalgamated Society of Woodworkers warned the king, 'and we would consider that you would be well advised to order a very quiet wedding in keeping with the times.'[26] However, the *Express* countered the killjoys by declaring that 'Life is too drab to pass up this chance for having fun' and Churchill welcomed the wedding as 'a flash of colour on the hard road we have to travel'.[27]

Ordinary people, too, reacted well to the news. 'Princess Elizabeth is engaged (official),' noted one fifty-year-old spinster in her diary, '& judging from the laughing photographs of her taken at a dance at Apsley House it is the "love match" it is claimed to be & we are all glad about it.' As for Philip, she added he was 'the type "easy on the eye", which any young girl would fall in love with'.[28] Newspaper reports that as a schoolboy Philip had fared unspectacularly in the classroom and 'preferred sports' gave rise to the misleading impression that he was amiable but dim; 'a nice enough man even if not over bright', as one housewife put it. An American correspondent who claimed to have canvassed 'dozens of Philip's friends' concluded that he 'would be considered "a good all-round man" at an American university and would make the best fraternity on the campus, but some of his frat brothers would undoubtedly find him painfully exuberant at times. He gives the impression of being "a man's man".'[29] Boisterousness and machismo did form part of Philip's make-up, however those who knew him better also perceived an even sharper brain than that of his uncle, Dickie Mountbatten.[30]

To Mountbatten's satisfaction, the newspapers at home made much of Philip's British connections, his education at Cheam and Gordonstoun and his wartime service in the Royal Navy. 'An effort had obviously been made,' noted Jock Colville in his diary, 'to build him up as the nephew of Lord Louis Mountbatten rather than a Greek Prince.'[31] One contemporary account depicted Philip as 'thoroughly English by upbringing' and said that he had 'that intense love of England and the British way of life, that deep devotion to the ideals of peace and liberty for which Britain stands, that are characteristic of so many naval men'.[32]

Little was made of his disrupted family life or the fact that his brothers-in-law had all fought on the wrong side in the war. What references there were tended to be misinformed: in March, when Philip's naturalization had been announced, the *News Chronicle* told its readers that his brother-in-law, Christoph of Hesse, was 'unlikely to be invited as a guest to any British wedding'.[33] Indeed, he was an unlikely invitee, if only because he had died three years earlier.

The friendly attitude adopted by certain sections of the press towards Philip owed something to the efforts of Tom Driberg, who obliged Mountbatten by telling his friends on the left that they should not object to the engagement because the prince was 'something of a socialist himself'.[34] The claim was not as spurious as it sounds.

Influenced by his uncle, whom the Establishment had long regarded as 'rather pink', Philip had become relatively progressive in his views on politics, and in 1945 he had told Dickie that he was not in the least 'antagonistic to principles of Socialism'.[35] His opinions were certainly well to the left of the instinctive conservatism of the king and queen, and he was not shy about airing them. In December 1946 he had written to the queen apologizing (again) for getting carried away and starting 'a rather heated discussion'. He hoped she did not think him 'violently argumentative and an exponent of socialism' and would forgive him 'if I did say anything I ought not to have said'.[36]

In this respect, Philip's views were more in tune with the changing mood of the country immediately after the war, the British people having turned dramatically against Churchill and the traditional ruling class of the landed aristocracy which he was seen to represent. The 1945 general election had brought about a landslide victory for the Labour party under Clement Attlee, which in turn led to the establishment of the welfare state. 'Everything is going now,' George VI told Vita Sackville-West in 1948. 'Before long I shall also have to go.'[37]

After the announcement of the engagement, Mountbatten told Driberg he was

agreeably surprised to find that only the *Daily Worker* appeared to condemn my nephew's engagement on political grounds. Even if they knew the truth about him, I feel it would be too good a propaganda point for them to pass up altogether. I am so grateful to you for telling people the truth about him. As you know, I am an ardent believer in constitutional monarchy as a means of producing rapid evolution without actual revolution, but only if monarchy is wisely handled. I am sure Philip will not let the side down in this respect.[38]

On 3 August 1947, less than a fortnight before India gained independence, Mountbatten again wrote to Driberg from New Delhi thanking him for 'sticking up for my nephew Philip against the infantile Leftist readers of *Reynold's News*' and offering guidance on how best to tackle those cavilling at the cost of the royal wedding and the suggestion that Philip be paid an allowance.

Mountbatten had, he wrote, passed on Driberg's remarks about the 'substantial minority feeling against lavish allowances' to him on marriage and 'the expensive use of scarce resources' for the wedding.

You can rest assured that he thoroughly understands this problem, and indeed he spoke to me about it when I was home in May. I am sure he is entirely on the side of cutting down the display of the wedding, and his own personal feelings are against receiving any civil list for the very reasons which you give. I, however, have persuaded him that he should take something for reasons which I will now explain.

As you know the present dynasty in Greece was founded by King George I, brother of Queen Alexandra and younger son of the King of Denmark. The Danish Royal Family was by no means rich enough to endow a younger son with personal riches and wealth on taking up the Crown of Greece. Any small property the family were able to acquire in Greece from personal means was largely destroyed and swallowed up in the many revolutions and periods of exile. The Civil List salary of a Prince of Greece was never very big, and any rights that Philip may have had to a Greek Civil List, he renounced together with his rights of succession in 1944. To my certain knowledge his private means are very small and he is almost entirely dependent on his Naval pay which is slightly under £1 a day and after tax is paid I do not suppose amounts to as much as £300 a year.

His tiny little two-seater made a big hole in his private fortune, and except when travelling on an officer's warrant he usually goes Third-class by train. He has no complaints; he is very happy on his present

Naval pay and could quite well manage as a bachelor with no official standing. As a future Prince Consort, however, I think you will agree that Third-class travel would be regarded as a stunt and a sixpenny tip to a porter as stingy. If he is to devote much of his time to public duties, I submit the public must at least find the means to enable him to carry these duties out. He cannot and should not spend his entire time merely accompanying his wife. I know he intends to go on serving in the Navy, and he is still bound on many occasions to be separated from her and still carrying out public duties. What is he to do? Borrow money from his wife to pay for the hire of a car to go and open a War Memorial at Plymouth?

Be reasonable Tom, he cannot possibly uphold the dignity of this nation on £300 a year any more than the Prime Minister was able to uphold the dignity of his office on £10,000 a year! Mr Attlee had to have a very large tax-free allowance for expenses; and what I know is in Philip's mind is to ask for his expenses and either no Civil List salary or a comparatively small one.

It really amounts to this: you have either got to give up the Monarchy or give the wretched people who have to carry out the functions of the Crown enough money to be able to do it with the same dignity at least as the Prime Minister or Lord Mayor of London is afforded ... I simply cannot advise him to try and do the job on the pay of a Naval officer. He would be letting down his future wife and the whole institution of the monarchy.[39]

Overall, though, Mountbatten was euphoric about the engagement. 'She couldn't have picked a better man,' he wrote to Attlee. Edwina, meanwhile, assured her friend Lady Reading that Philip was 'extremely cultured, well-read, of a progressive mind ... In fact he will I think be a breath of fresh air into the Royal circle.'[40]

SIXTEEN

Royal Wedding

The announcement of the engagement brought about a dramatic change in Philip's life. He was given a secretary to organize his social diary, a detective to follow him around and a valet – the Mountbattens' former butler, John Dean – to keep his wardrobe in good order. The 'shipyard stranger' of 1944 was suddenly one of the most talked-about people in the country. Everyone knew all about him. They knew, for example, that he drove a black, green-upholstered MG sports car bearing the number plate HDK 99, and that in late October, while returning alone to Corsham one night, the car skidded on a corner, left the road and came to rest in a hedge. Though his car was 'fairly badly damaged', Philip was reported only 'slightly bruised', with a twisted knee but otherwise unhurt, and he was able to carry out his full naval duties the next day.[1]

During the engagement he remained in his teaching post at Corsham and when in London stayed at his grandmother Victoria's apartment in Kensington Palace, where his mother Alice was now also living. Shortly before the wedding, David Milford Haven, whom he had chosen as his best man, also moved in from the flat in Chelsea that he had been sharing with his girlfriend, Robin Dalton. Dean – who subsequently 'did a Crawfie' by writing a book about Philip – valeted them both and was astonished at first by their 'humble' rooms in the palace attic, with bare floorboards and worn rugs. They behaved at times 'like schoolboys', recorded Dean, and if arriving back late at night they would climb over the roof and in through their bedroom windows to bypass the creaking staircase past their grandmother's rooms – especially in David Milford Haven's case when he had his girlfriend in tow.

In the mornings, Dean took them tea at eight o'clock, drew their curtains, saw to their clothes and cleaned their shoes. Philip was generally 'a cheerful riser, leaping out of bed to take a hurried tub', but on some days he would grunt and turn over and not want to be disturbed. Dean found Philip easier to work for than his cousin, who was 'inclined to be indifferent, even abrupt'.[2] But he had a job trying to make him look smart, with his heavily repaired suits, well-worn shoes and his habit – which persisted despite Dean's admonishments – of putting his hands in his jacket pockets, causing it to lose its shape. When Philip first wore a kilt at Balmoral that August, according to one of the pages, he attempted to make light of his embarrassment by performing a mock curtsey to the king, which did not go down as well as he'd hoped.[3]

Staying at Balmoral that summer, Philip again found himself among his detractors, Lord Eldon, the Marquess of Salisbury and David Bowes-Lyon, although his position was far more secure now that the king and Privy Council had formally approved his betrothal. Jock Colville, while noticing the hostility towards the future consort, found him intelligent and progressive, although he also sensed a slight imbalance in the feelings of the engaged couple, recording that, while the princess was clearly in love, Philip appeared more 'dutiful'.[4] By the time of the wedding, however, Colville had come round to the conclusion that the pair 'really are in love'.[5]

Philip's letters to the queen support this, whereas the previous impression was possibly due to the fact that Philip was never one for great displays of emotion, and Elizabeth's position as heir to the throne was hardly going to make him any more demonstrative. 'He's not a person who shows love,' said one of the guests who had been present at Balmoral with Philip in 1946. 'Given the sort of experience he'd had [as a child], you probably would shut yourself away a bit to avoid being hurt. Affection is not his natural currency.'[6] Mike Parker added: 'He doesn't wear his heart on his sleeve. I always wanted to see him put his arms around the Queen, and show her how much he adored her. What you'd do for any wife. But he always sort of stood to attention. I mentioned it a couple of times, but he just gave me a hell of a look.'

Nevertheless, Lady Mountbatten, who, with her husband Lord Brabourne, often had them to stay at their cottage on his family's estate, recalls them being 'very cosy and natural together',[7] and Sir Edward Ford was reassured by the telling fact that in games of Murder in the Dark at Balmoral, they always seemed to find each other when the lights went out.[8]

The wedding was due to take place on Thursday 20 November, and, as part of the build-up, at the beginning of October Philip took a further step towards being anglicized when he was received into the Church of England in a private service before the Archbishop of Canterbury at Lambeth Palace.[9] A month later George VI gave him the Order of the Garter (a week after Elizabeth received hers so that she had precedence) and arranged for him to be created Duke of Edinburgh, Earl of Merioneth and Baron Greenwich – compliments to Scotland and Wales as well as recognition of his naval back-ground. He was also made a Royal Highness, which he had turned down before the engagement but which his marriage to the princess was now thought to justify. 'It is a great deal to give a man all at once,' the king wrote to Queen Mary, 'but I know Philip understands his new responsibilities on his marriage to Lilibet.'[10] The peerages were not announced until the eve of the wedding, too late for the printers of the order of service sheets, which billed him as Philip Mountbatten, RN, although in sufficient time to forestall the possibility of the future queen ever being known as plain Mrs Mountbatten.[11]

Fifteen hundred of their wedding presents went on show to the public at St James's Palace, although for obvious reasons not the chestnut thoroughbred filly, Astrakhan, which had been given by the Aga Khan and was to become Elizabeth's first flat-race winner in 1950, or the turkey sent by a lady from Brooklyn 'because she [the princess] lives in England and they have nothing to eat in England'.[12] Many Londoners had posted nylon stockings and hand-knitted tea cosies. Gandhi gave what was described in the exhibition catalogue as a 'fringed lacework cloth made out of yarn spun by the donor on his own spinning wheel'.[13] Intended as a tray cloth, this had been made at the suggestion of Dickie Mountbatten as an appropriate gift from one who had renounced all worldly possessions. However, as the royal family viewed the presents, Queen Mary mistook it for Gandhi's loin-cloth and muttered to her lady-in-waiting: 'Such an indelicate gift! What a horrible thing.' Philip overheard her and bravely sprang to the Mahatma's defence. 'I don't think it's horrible,' he ventured. 'Gandhi is a wonderful man; a very great man …' Queen Mary moved on in stony silence.[14]

Vying for public attention with the presents was the four-tier cake, of peculiar fascination to the nation after years of sugar rationing. Its elaborate decorations included renditions of Philip's finest hour, a scene from the night battle of Cape Matapan in 1941 and a depiction of *Valiant* whose searchlights he had so efficiently directed. The cake had been considerably reduced in size and weight from the original design, in keeping with the prevailing austerity,[15] and similar considerations affected the production of Elizabeth's dress, although the designer Norman Hartnell told how, when his assistant returned from a components' gathering trip to America and was asked by customs whether he had anything to declare, he answered in a lowered tone: 'Yes, ten thousand pearls, for the wedding dress of Princess Elizabeth.'[16]

Philip as a schoolboy at Gordonstoun, honing his sailing skills on the
Moray Firth, and (below) in the harbour at Hopeman.

LIFE

HOLLYWOOD PARTY

FEBRUARY 17, 1941 **10** CENTS
YEARLY SUBSCRIPTION $4.50

Cobina Wright, whom Philip fell for in Venice in 1938, and (below) Osla Benning, in the fur hood, the beautiful Canadian-born debutante who was his most serious girlfriend before Princess Elizabeth, seen here at the Whaddon Chase point-to-point in 1939, the year that she met Philip; with her is Babette Talbot Baines.

Philip acting as best man at the wedding of his close friend Hélène Foufounis (later Cordet) to William Kirby in 1938. She denied rumours of a romance with Philip.

The first significant meeting, at Dartmouth Naval College in July 1939, between the cadet Philip (in uniform towards the back right of the picture, next to Dickie Mountbatten) and Princess Elizabeth, third from left, looking over the railing.

A bearded Philip during the war; Elizabeth kept this photograph on her mantelpiece.

The look of love: Philip and Elizabeth at the wedding of Patricia Mountbatten and John Brabourne in 1946.

Us Five: Philip walks
alongside the compact
family unit on the way
to the Brabourne
wedding in 1946.

Philip and Elizabeth on
their wedding day, 20
November 1947, in the
Throne Room at
Buckingham Palace.

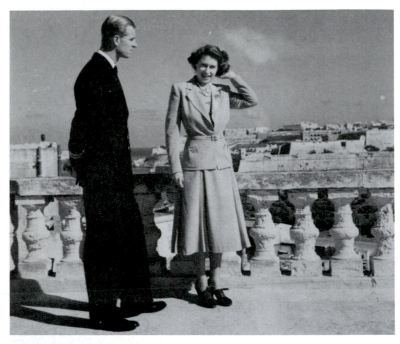

Their happiest time: Malta 1949.

Philip waterskiing while in command of the frigate
Magpie in the Mediterranean, 1951.

Philip's best man, David Milford
Haven, with his girlfriend Robin
Dalton, on holiday in France in 1946.

The showgirl Pat Kirkwood, whose legs Kenneth Tynan pronounced 'the seventh wonder of the world'. She too refuted rumours of an affair with Philip.

The Thursday Club cricket team. Philip is in the middle row, third from right, between Baron, in striped blazer, and Baron's twin brother Jack Nahum, Mike Parker is on the far left in the deerstalker. James Robertson Justice is behind him with a tankard. David Milford Haven is at Baron's feet.

Philip's mother Alice, in her new nun's robe made specially for the occasion, leads his relations out of Westminster Abbey after the coronation in 1953. After her come Theodora and Berthold of Baden and their son Max; Margarita and Friedel Hohenlohe and their daughter Beatrix; Sophie and George of Hanover, and Sophie's daughter Christa of Hesse; and 'Big' George and Marie Bonaparte.

Given the pressure to buy British, questions were also raised about the nationality of the silkworms that had provided the satin from which the dress was made. In answer to an enquiry from Downing Street, the Palace replied that the silk for the dress came from Chinese silkworms ('from Nationalist China, of course,' added Hartnell)[17] but woven in Scotland and Kent; the train contained silk produced by Kentish silkworms and woven in London; and the going-away dress contained several yards of Lyons silk which Hartnell happened to have in stock from 'a consignment held under permit'.[18]

As the wedding day drew nearer, Philip's stock continued to rise with the general public. Accompanying his fiancée to Clydebank to name the new Cunard liner *Caronia*, he received a great burst of applause from the crowd of 40,000 thronging the shipyard when Elizabeth mentioned his love of the sea and ships in her speech.[19] Within court circles, however, he was still looked upon with suspicion. On the way back south from Clydebank the royal train was held up in a siding and the princess's secretary Jock Colville went with Philip down the track to the signal box. 'I watched P narrowly,' Colville recorded in his diary. 'He is a strong believer in the hail-fellow-well-met as opposed to the semi-divine interpretation of Monarchy.' Colville also noted what he interpreted as one 'appalling gaffe', when a signalman joked that he was waiting for someone to die in order to be promoted, to which Philip responded: 'Like me!' 'No doubt he meant in the Navy,' wrote Colville, 'but another interpretation was obvious.' Colville thought it likely that Philip would be popular with the public but took the view that he could also be 'vulgar' and was at times 'quite off-hand' with his fiancée.[20]

A few days before the wedding, royal relations began to arrive in London. Some of the less well off had been helped with their travel expenses by the Windsors and they were all put up at Claridge's, with the exception of Philip's mother Alice and Queen Frederika of Greece, who stayed at Buckingham Palace. Philip's cousin Alexandra, whose husband Peter had been deposed as King of Yugoslavia in 1945, recalled that with the wedding invitation came additional ones to a dinner and ball at Buckingham Palace and other receptions, along with instructions as to which boat train they should catch from Paris. It was a convivial journey. On board the same train she found Queen 'Freddie' of Greece, the plump and bejewelled Queen 'Ena' of Spain, the Comte de Paris, the Count of Barcelona, pretender to the Spanish throne, and King Michael of Romania, Philip's cousin and childhood playmate who, on his return, would be forced (at gunpoint) to relinquish his throne.[21] At Claridge's they were joined by the King and Queen of Denmark, the kings of Norway and Iraq, the Queen Mother (Helen) of Romania, the Princess Regent and Prince Bernhard of the Netherlands, the Prince Regent of Belgium, the Crown Prince and Princess of Sweden, Prince Jean and Princess Elizabeth of Luxembourg, and the Duchess of Aosta. At dinner all of them sat around a single large table. It was one of the biggest gatherings of royalty that century, although none of these guests quite measured up to the family that Philip was marrying into, and their individual circumstances varied considerably. 'When I am back behind the Iron Curtain,' Queen Helen of Romania said to Chips Channon, 'I shall wonder whether all this was a dream.'[22]

Notable absentees included the bride's uncle, the Duke of Windsor, who was not invited, and her aunt, the Princess Royal, who was rumoured to have boycotted the occasion in protest at the continued ostracism of her brother eleven years after his abdication.[23] And although the *Daily Telegraph* confidently reported that Philip's three surviving sisters would be invited to the wedding,[24] sensitivity to the depth of the anti-German feeling in Britain eventually meant that none of them was. The sisters found it hard to come to terms with this decision, especially since several of those who did receive invitations had had associations with Hitler's allies during the war. Shortly before the wedding, Sophie wrote to Dickie Mountbatten from Wolfsgarten: 'It is not very easy, I assure you, to make the press (who interview us continually) understand & they keep insisting that we must be estranged, which only makes a difficult and humiliating position even more unpleasant.'[25] In a bid to console them, after the wedding Alice later sent them a twenty-two-page description of the ceremony, in which they learned, among other things, that Philip had signed the register with the gold fountain pen engraved with their names which they had given to him as a joint wedding present.*[26]

Although the decision to exclude his sisters was designed to protect Philip from adverse press comment, their absence deprived him of much-needed family support in the lead-up to the big day, when he was understandably rather on edge. A few days before the wedding, the photographer Baron Nahum, whom Philip had befriended through the Mountbattens, organized an unofficial stag dinner party, at which earthy jokes were cracked at the prospective groom's expense. One of the guests, Larry Adler, later recalled feeling reluctant to join in when he saw how uncomfortable Philip looked. 'He was getting married and he was scared. His face was white. He was beginning to realise what he had let himself in for. He said "I suppose I won't be having any fun any more."'[27]

Philip's official stag party took place at the Dorchester on the eve of the wedding, with comrades from the 27th Destroyer Flotilla and Dickie Mountbatten, briefly back from India in the midst of the problems over Kashmir, as the senior guest. Around midnight a few press photographers were invited in to take pictures of the guests. Mountbatten was heard to holler 'I'm being outflanked!' as he saw a photographer move round to get a side shot. Eventually a few of the

---

* More normal family relations were re-established quietly the next year, when Sophie and her second husband, Prince George of Hanover, who had by now become headmaster of Salem, came over to visit Gordonstoun at Philip's expense and Philip and Elizabeth took the opportunity of inviting them to stay at Birkhall on the Balmoral estate.

guests persuaded the photographers to part with their flash bulbs, which they then hurled against the walls, 'uttering bloodcurdling war whoops as they exploded'. Philip left at 12.15, reportedly one of the few guests who was still quite steady.[28]

When John Dean woke him with his tea at seven the next morning at Kensington Palace, he found him 'plainly in good form, extremely cheerful and in no way nervous'.[29] Yet after breakfast of toast and coffee, when his cousin Patricia Mountbatten said something about what an exciting day it was for him, Philip responded: 'I'm either being very brave or very stupid.' 'I imagine every bridegroom must to some extent think I hope to God I'm doing the right thing,' she says now, 'but for him, can you imagine? Everything was going to change for him, he was giving up his freedom. He is quite intelligent enough to have foreseen a lot of the problems from his point of view, but thank God he did marry her.'[30]

One of the changes Philip had committed to at Elizabeth's request was to give up smoking, so when David Milford Haven arrived they steadied their nerves with a gin and tonic before setting off to Westminster Abbey, where they were due to arrive at 11.15. Philip wore his ordinary naval uniform, now decorated with the insignia of Knight Companion of the Order of the Garter, and the ceremonial sword that had belonged to his grandfather, Louis of Battenberg. Before leaving, he shook hands with the palace retainers who had lined up to see him off and ordered coffee for the waiting members of the press.[31]

Over at Buckingham Palace, the atmosphere was equally tense, not least because a footman had contrived to misplace Elizabeth's bouquet and at the last moment the pearl necklace that the king had given her was found to have been left with the other presents on display at St James's Palace, a few hundred yards away down the Mall. The princess was almost due to leave for the Abbey, but she was determined to wear her father's present for her wedding. She asked Jock Colville if he could possibly retrieve it. 'I looked at my watch,' recalled Colville, 'I rushed along the corridor. I galloped down the Grand Staircase and into the main quadrangle of Buckingham Palace. Take any car, the Princess had called after me. So I ran towards a large Royal Daimler. "To St James's Palace" I cried to the chauffeur, and I flung open the door of the car. Before I could leap in a tall elderly man, ablaze with Orders and Decorations, began to emerge. It was King Haakon VII of Norway. "You seem in a hurry, young man," he said. "By all means have my car, but do let me get out first."' Amazingly, the police officers guarding the presents at St James's Palace believed Colville's improbable story and he made it back just in time for the princess to wear her pearls.[32]

At the Abbey, the only one of Philip's immediate family in the congregation was his mother, Alice, who sat on the north side of the Abbey, opposite the king and queen, and alongside her mother Victoria and other Mountbatten relations – her sister Louise and brother Dickie and their spouses. Alice would later write to Philip to say 'how wonderfully everything went off & I was so comforted to see the truly happy expression on your face and to feel your decision was right from every point of view'.[33] From Andrea's side of the family, there was only Big George, the sole survivor of Andrea's eight siblings, and his estranged wife, Marie Bonaparte.

In his address, the Archbishop of York maintained that the royal wedding was 'in all essentials exactly the same as it would have been for any cottager who might be married this afternoon in some small country church in a remote village in the Dales',[34] yet most cottagers would surely have been taken aback by the magnificence of the occasion. Such was the quantity of royalty present that British MPs had had to ballot for places in the congregation and many were affronted to miss out, not least Rab Butler who was seen disconsolately wandering about in the crowd outside. Chips Channon, the Conservative MP for Southend-on-Sea, was also excluded, but from his vantage point in the parliamentary enclosure he could at least see that Elizabeth looked 'well, shy and attractive, and Prince Philip as if he was thoroughly enjoying himself'. There were cheers and shouts from the crowd for the various illustrious guests as they arrived, Channon noted, but the warmest reception was reserved for Winston Churchill, by now Leader of the Opposition. When he entered the Abbey, a little late, Channon recorded, 'everyone stood up, all the Kings and Queens'.[35]

With the economy weak and London still full of gaping holes where the bombs had fallen, the government had decided that it would be inappropriate to declare a national holiday, and, in keeping with the prevailing austerity, afterwards there was a relatively modest three-course wedding breakfast for a hundred and fifty, in contrast to the ten-course banquet that the Duke and Duchess of Kent had sat down to in 1934.[36] Overall, though, it was still a spectacular event. Trafalgar Square was so crowded that 'not a pigeon could find foothold', one newspaper reported. Londoners brought out their Blitz mattresses and blankets and slept on the kerbstone route to be sure of a good view, and in the morning women could be seen washing in hot water from vacuum flasks before putting on their make-up.[37] At long last, 'a little colour and pageantry were restored to the country,' noted Jock Colville. 'The Blues and Life Guards put on full dress uniform for the first time since 1939; magnificent carriages emerged from the Royal Mews, the horses glistening and the coachmen and postilions resplendent in State Livery. The war, it seemed, really was over.'[38] It was estimated that two hundred million people throughout the Empire listened to the service on the wireless.[39]

It was an emotional occasion for the royal family, particularly the king. 'I was so proud of you & thrilled at having you so close to me on your long walk in Westminster Abbey,' he wrote afterwards to his daughter, 'but when I handed your hand to the Archbishop I felt that I had lost something very precious.' Elizabeth was 'so calm &

composed during the Service,' he went on, '& said your words with such conviction, that I knew everything was all right.'[40] Yet during the signing of the register the king came close to tears and told the Archbishop of Canterbury: 'It is a far more moving thing to give away your daughter than be married yourself.'[41] When the time came for them to go away, the king made a courageous stab at being cheerful, grabbing the queen's hand and running after the carriage, throwing rose petals at his daughter and son-in-law as the landau sped off towards Waterloo. Ultimately, though, for him this was as much an end as it was a beginning.[42] With the marriage, he became yesterday's man. 'In a curious way he was written off,' wrote Philip Ziegler in his study of people's feelings towards the monarchy. 'Elizabeth was the future.'[43] As the forward-looking husband at Elizabeth's side, Philip was very much part of that future.

SEVENTEEN

Duke of Hazards

It had been reported that Philip and Elizabeth intended to spend their honeymoon with the Mountbattens in India,[1] but with modesty in mind they eventually opted to remain in Britain. The first week was spent at Broadlands, the Mountbattens' sumptuous Palladian house by the River Test in the New Forest, and the unrelaxing time they had there served to underline the least appealing features of the new life Philip had taken on. Their supposed haven was besieged by incessant telephone calls and, whenever he and Elizabeth ventured out for a walk or a ride, they had to evade sightseers and reporters who hung like monkeys in the trees or hid in the long grass to spy on them. When they went to Romsey Abbey for the Sunday morning service, people clambered over the tombstones and up ladders to peer at them through the windows.[2]

But at least they seemed to be happy with each other. Two days after arriving, Elizabeth wrote to her mother to say that they felt entirely at ease together and behaved 'as though we had belonged to each other for years! Philip is an angel – he is so kind and thoughtful, and living with him and having him around all the time is just perfect.'[3] The queen replied that she was 'so happy in your happiness'. She had always hoped that her daughter would be able to make a marriage that satisfied her heart as well as her head, and she told Elizabeth that she and the king 'both love Philip already as a son'. She looked forward to having just as much fun as before, now that 'us four' had become 'us five'. 'Darling Lilibet, no parents ever had a better daughter, you are always such an unselfish & thoughtful angel to Papa & me ... That you & Philip should be blissfully happy & love each other through good days and bad or depressing days is my one wish – a thousand blessings to you both from your very very loving Mummy.'⁴

The second part of their honeymoon was a great deal more restful, two weeks spent staying at Birkhall, a manor house on the Balmoral estate, nine miles from the castle, where it snowed heavily and they spent much of their time huddled around log fires. They were still 'blissfully happy', Elizabeth told her mother, but she now wanted the queen's advice on how best to ease her husband's introduction to court life. 'Philip is terribly independent and I quite understand the poor darling wanting to start off properly, without everything being *done* for us,' she wrote. She ended this letter by again extolling the joys of her newly married life: 'It is so lovely and peaceful just now – Philip is reading full length on the sofa, Susan [her favourite corgi] is stretched out before the fire, Rummy is fast asleep in his box beside the fire, and I am busy writing this in one of the arm chairs near the fire (you see how important the fire is!). It's heaven up here!'⁵

The queen was delighted by her daughter's letters, which she read over and again, and she would have been doubly reassured by those she received from her new son-in-law, who was uninhibited in describing his love for her daughter while also casting a watchful eye towards their future: 'Lilibet is the only "thing" in this world which is absolutely real to me,' wrote Philip,

> and my ambition is to weld the two of us into a new combined exist-
> ence that will not only be able to withstand the shocks directed at us
> but will also have a positive existence for the good ... Cherish Lilibet?
> I wonder if that word is enough to express what is in me. Does one

cherish one's sense of humour or one's musical ear or one's eyes? I am not sure, but I know that I thank God for them and so, very humbly, I thank God for Lilibet and for us.[6]

When they returned to London, Jock Colville found the heir to the throne looking 'very happy, and, as a result of three weeks' matrimony, suddenly a woman instead of a girl'. Philip, too, seemed happy, 'but a shade querulous, which is, I think, in his character'.[7] Colville was not the only person to observe this trait, yet there were certain circumstances at the time that served to put Philip more on edge than he might otherwise have been. For a start, he and Elizabeth had no home of their own – a matter of particular importance to Philip having not had a bedroom of his own for much of his childhood. Their designated country house in Windsor Great Park – Sunninghill Park – had mysteriously burned down and their intended London residence, the bomb-damaged Clarence House, on the Mall next to St James's Palace, was in need of extensive renovation work which would take eighteen months to complete. In the meantime, Chips Channon was asked if he would lend or let his house for 'some months', but he declined: 'Too much of an upheaval,' he wrote in his diary.[8] Instead they resorted to borrowing Clock House at Kensington Palace from the Earl and Countess of Athlone, Elizabeth's great-aunt and -uncle, while they were away, but when the Athlones returned after three months they were obliged to move into Buckingham Palace, where Philip was given a bedroom in Elizabeth's former apartments, with a sitting room between his room and hers. Living under the same roof as his in-laws was far from the ideal start to married life. As Elizabeth had written to her mother while on honeymoon, she wanted to enable Philip to become 'boss in his own home', and she knew how hard this would be back in her old rooms at the Palace where they would be subject to endless protocol. As it turned out, there was indeed considerable friction between Philip and some of the courtiers, whom he viewed as excessively stuffy and conservative, while they found him brash and abrasive.

Another drawback of their living arrangement was that their all too rare moments of intimacy were regularly intruded upon by his valet or her lady's maid. Elizabeth's devoted dresser Bobo MacDonald would be in and out of her bathroom when the princess was bathing, making it difficult for Philip to share a bath with her.[9]

Buckingham Palace was at least convenient for his job at the Admiralty, to which he walked each day down the Mall, often unrecognized. However, for someone accustomed to seeing regular action on the high seas, his new role as an operations officer – 'shuffling ships around', as he described it[10] – was yet another source of frustration. His daughter Princess Anne later admitted that her father had been 'bored stiff' by the job. More absorbing was the staff course he attended from March to September at the Royal Naval College, Greenwich, where he stayed during the week, coming home to Elizabeth only at weekends.

At Buckingham Palace, meanwhile, life was 'very, very frustrating for him', recalled Lord Brabourne, who saw a lot of Philip and Elizabeth in the period just after their marriage. 'It was very stuffy. Lascelles was impossible. They were absolutely bloody to him. They patronised him. They treated him as an outsider. It wasn't much fun. He laughed it off, of course, but it must have hurt.'[11]

In this hostile environment Philip made sure he had an ally by asking his old friend Mike Parker to become his equerry[12] – although Parker's breezy demeanour did not go down well with some of the courtiers. In December 1947 Philip and Elizabeth gained a steadier and more influential support with the appointment of Lieutenant General Sir Frederick 'Boy' Browning as Comptroller and Treasurer of their joint household. Philip had first met Browning in Ceylon at Christmas 1944 while staying with his uncle Dickie Mountbatten, whose chief of staff Browning had just become. Married to the novelist Daphne du Maurier, Browning was a dashing war hero who had won a DSO and Croix de Guerre on the western front by the time he was twenty. During the Second World War, he had commanded the disastrous British 1st Airborne Division's landing at Arnhem, and was said (during his lifetime at least) to have warned Montgomery before-hand: 'We might be going a bridge too far.' In the film that took its name from Browning's supposed words, his fictionalized character was played by Dirk Bogarde.

Known for his handsome appearance – Baron said he was the best-looking man he had ever photographed – and physical prowess, Browning also had a reputation in military circles for being inclined to sulk when thwarted and was prone to occasional displays of bad temper.[13] Mountbatten, though, thought extremely highly of him and had recommended him to Philip in the autumn of 1947 in the warm-est terms:

> Boy has drive, energy, enthusiasm, efficiency and invokes the highest sense of loyalty and affection in his subordinates. His judgment in all matters that he understands is absolutely sound, and he would rather die than let his boss down … he is not a 'yes man' or even a courtier and never will be. He will fearlessly say what he thinks is right … Frankly, Philip, I do not think you can do better.[14]

The fact that Browning had been in the Guards certainly helped. The royal household was heavily populated by former Guards officers who were inclined to tell Philip and his wife what they should and should not do. Now Philip would have a Guards officer of his own who was prepared to stand up to them.[15] Colville later wrote to Browning's wife Daphne that they were all 'from Princess Elizabeth downwards, rather dreading the arrival of an awe-inspiring figure. But in no time at all awe turned into affection …'[16] According to Browning's biographer, Richard Mead, the erstwhile strict disciplinarian with an explosive temper had mellowed considerably while on Mountbatten's staff in the Far East, and while his feelings for the princess 'already amounted to little short of adoration ... he was to develop very quickly a considerable regard for her husband'.[17] Despite the twenty-five-year age gap and their different service backgrounds, they shared a passion for boats and yachting and it was in Browning's yacht *Fanny Rosa* that Philip stayed for his first visit to Cowes Regatta in 1948.[18] The next year, with his boss again aboard, Browning contrived to steer *Fanny Rosa* aground on Ryde Sands, to his acute embarrassment. Mead records:

> The vessel was left high and dry for ten hours, listing at 50 degrees, and became an object of interest to large numbers of holidaymakers who were able to walk out and inspect her before she was floated off again at the next high tide. The Duke was forced to remain on board instead of transferring to [his own yacht] *Bluebottle*, which was competing in the Dragon class championships.[19]

Meanwhile, one of Browning's first official tasks had been to find an alternative country house to the one that had burned down, and he soon located Windlesham Moor, near Sunningdale, a two-storey whitewashed house in fifty acres, famous for its rhododendrons. They rented it to use at weekends, with a housekeeper brought down from Balmoral and five other resident staff. If relatively modest by royal standards, it was hardly cramped – with a hall, dining room, 50-ft drawing room, study, 'Chinese room', games room, loggia, five main bedrooms and staff quarters.

Philip in particular enjoyed getting away from the formalities of the Palace. His valet John Dean recalled that 'the Duke enjoyed taking his coat off for such tasks as hanging pictures and moving chairs to wherever the Princess thought they would look best'. According to Dean, Philip was an avid homemaker, and whenever he attended the

Ideal Homes Exhibition or some such, he was liable to return with 'an electric mixer or some other gadget – quite possibly something intended to make life easier for a servantless couple in a small flat. Once he bought a washing machine. Another time he turned up with some tins of soup.'[20]

Back in London during the week, they both had engagements to carry out, and on top of this Colville sought to broaden their political education, although he noted that Elizabeth concentrated better on the details while Philip grew impatient if his interest was not immediately aroused.[21] Colville was often temperamentally at odds with Philip and he experienced more of his fractiousness when, in February 1948, he suggested that the young royal couple should visit Paris to bolster diplomatic ties with Britain's wartime ally. Philip complained that Colville should have checked with him first before airing his proposal with the foreign secretary and the king,[22] but eventually he agreed to go – albeit at a time that would not interfere with what *The Times* reported as 'the Duke's self-imposed resolution to spare himself no part of the routine of naval service'.[23]

The visit duly went ahead in mid-May over the hottest Whitsun weekend ever recorded in the French capital. Ostensibly, it was a great success and Colville recorded that 'in four hectic days the Princess had conquered Paris'.[24] Behind the scenes, however, one or two details went awry. For one thing, so Nancy Mitford later reported, the food at the British embassy had been so bad that 'poor Prince Philip was poisoned … & his visit was one long session to the loo'.[25] He had stoically insisted on going through with the packed programme,[26] although his discomfort probably rendered him more susceptible to the 'frightful rage' he flew into when he spotted a hidden photographer at a restaurant.[27]

Elizabeth, too, was tired and listless, and at the British embassy reception in her honour she had met only half the guests when Philip led her from the room to rest.[28] It was soon rumoured that she was pregnant, although at the end of May Chips Channon doubted this when he saw the royal couple at a dance at Coppins, and observed that the princess 'danced every dance until nearly 5am'. Philip, meanwhile, 'was wildly gay with his policeman's hat and hand-cuffs. He leapt about and jumped into the air as he greeted everyone … His charm is colossal, like all the Mountbattens.'[29]

The charm was at last beginning to work on some of crustier courtiers. In early June, after a coded announcement from the Palace that the princess would 'undertake no public engagements' from the end of that month (i.e. she was indeed expecting a baby), even the hitherto hostile Tommy Lascelles began to rhapsodize about her husband: 'Such a nice young man, such a sense of duty – not a fool in any way – so much in love poor boy – and after all put the heir to the throne in the family way all according to plan.'[30]

Philip was also beginning to get a favourable press for his speeches, for which it was observed he 'used no notes, was never at a loss for a phrase, revealed considerable wit [and] smiled as he talked'. 'The more I hear Prince Philip speak in public,' wrote one columnist on the *Evening Standard*, 'the more I am impressed by his ability … Royalty have not produced a speaker of such charm and friendliness since the days of the Prince of Wales.'[31]

Nevertheless, his refusal to have his speeches written for him and instead speak off the cuff did also cause unease. According to the *Sunday Pictorial*, some of the king's advisers felt the prince was treading a dangerous path, and breaking the rule that all royal speeches except very minor ones 'should be prepared in advance so that any phrases that might give rise to repercussions can be blue-pencilled'.[32]

There were reservations, too, about some of Philip's friends, notably the photographer Baron Nahum. The son of Italian immigrants from Tripoli, Baron (as he was always known) had first entered Philip's orbit in 1947 while spending the weekend at Broadlands with Dickie Mountbatten, who in turn knew the photographer through their shared infatuation with the beautiful Frenchwoman Yola Letellier.[33] Philip had subsequently asked Baron to take pictures at his wedding and Baron invited the prince to join his luncheon club.

Baron's Thursday Club convened each week in the second-floor dining room of Wheeler's fish restaurant on Old Compton Street, Soho, for what the press called 'rip-roaring stag parties' – and reputedly for other gatherings which were 'not always stag'.[34] Other members included Philip's best man David Milford Haven and his equerry Mike Parker, the editors of the *Daily Express* and the *Daily Mail*, artists Feliks Topolski and Vasco Lazzolo, actors James Robertson Justice, Peter Ustinov and David Niven, and the harmonica player Larry Adler – an indiscreet name-dropper who told a stream of lurid stories surrounding the club's activities, although others averred that these amounted to nothing more risqué than the telling of coarse jokes.[35]

More occasional guests included Kim Philby, yet to be unmasked as a spy, and Stephen Ward, the fashionable 'society osteopath' and portrait painter who was later embroiled in the Profumo affair, which culminated in John Profumo's resignation as Secretary of State for War after lying to the House of Commons about his affair with Christine Keeler, who was also the mistress of a Russian naval attaché. In the memoir that was found after he committed suicide in 1963, Ward claimed that Philip had attended at least one of his infamous parties at Cavendish Square, where he was seen with 'a very attractive girl called Mitzi Taylor'.[36] According to Lord Denning, who conducted the inquiry into the Profumo affair, Ward was a notoriously unreliable witness; nevertheless, his slight acquaintance with Philip gave rise to wild speculation that the prince might have been the mysterious 'Man in the Mask' who had served dinner to Ward's guests wearing only a small lace apron; *Private Eye* briefly took to calling him 'The Naked Waiter'. In 1963 it was also used by the *Daily Mirror* as a pretext to run the enticing front-page headline 'Prince Philip and the Profumo

Scandal', above an article which then explained that, although Philip had sat for a portrait by Ward, any suggestion that he was somehow embroiled in the affair constituted 'the foulest rumour' and was 'utterly unfounded'.[37]

But the rumours continued to surface. In 1987, Anthony Summers, a former *Panorama* reporter and author of a book on the Profumo affair, said in an interview on BBC Radio Ulster that among the photographs found in Ward's flat after he died was one in which two girls were shown with Prince Philip, Baron and another man. The girls were naked, the men were not, and Summers later stressed that he was not claiming that they were doing anything sexual. When the BBC subsequently apologized to Buckingham Palace for the reference, the Palace brushed it off as 'old hat'.[38]

Jack Profumo himself remained convinced that the prince had never forgiven him personally for the various unhelpful media associations. In 1995, Profumo – by then redeemed by his work for Toynbee Hall, the East End charity, and the dignity with which he had borne his humiliations – found himself, rather to his horror, placed on the right-hand side of the queen at Margaret Thatcher's seventieth birthday party at Claridge's. After dinner, in another room, Profumo walked past Philip's chair, and, as he later related to his son, David, he said, 'Look, Sir, I just want to take the opportunity of thanking you for letting me sit next to your wife tonight.' Philip replied: 'Nothing to do with me.' That may very well have been the case, however the manner in which he said it left Profumo with the distinct impression that the prince 'wanted to make it abundantly clear that it was not with his approval'.[39]

In the late 1940s, however, neither Ward nor Profumo was yet notorious and it was Philip's association with Baron that caused more brows to furrow at the Palace. Besides the gatherings at Wheeler's, the photographer was known to hold louche parties at his studio in Brick Street, Mayfair, and was said to be 'at the centre of a very disreputable world indeed', according to his friend Robin Dalton, who had been introduced to him by Philip. 'One heard lurid tales of orgies.'[40] Philip's friendship with Baron admitted him into a social circle a world away from the 'ghastly courtiers' who so blighted his dealings with the royal household. As Sarah Bradford notes, 'it was a world in which aristocrats met showgirls, a peculiarly 1950s London phenomenon',[41] and, as one former royal aide recalled, 'People wondered whether this was an appropriate milieu.'[42]

In October 1948, a month before Elizabeth was due to give birth, Baron was responsible for introducing Philip to the first of the showgirls with whom he was rumoured to have had an affair. Her name was Pat Kirkwood, a beautiful raven-haired musical comedy star whose legs Kenneth Tynan pronounced 'the eighth wonder of the world'. Baron had been smitten with her for the past year, and by her account they were 'sort of unofficially engaged' – although she seems to have strung him along and he certainly felt that his love was not requited. One Thursday evening while she was starring in the musical *Starlight Roof* at the Hippodrome, near Leicester Square, Baron brought Philip and an equerry along to meet her in her dressing room after the show. They dined at Les Ambassadeurs, the raffish club in Mayfair, and afterwards at Philip's request went on to the Milroy supper club, where he asked Kirkwood to dance. According to her recollection, they danced for about an hour, foxtrots, sambas, whatever the band played – 'he wouldn't let me sit down'. Others in the club looked on aghast. Philip's reaction to the onlookers was to mimic their shocked expressions. Baron later told Kirkwood that some of them were, improbably, courtiers, who then told the king, who was furious and gave his son-in-law a dressing down.

Gossip about an affair rumbled on until 1957, when, in the wake of Mike Parker's divorce and consequent resignation from Philip's service, the *Baltimore Sun*'s 'Mayfair Set' correspondent felt emboldened to report the 'troubling whispers' that the Duke of Edinburgh had 'more than a passing interest in an unnamed woman and was meeting her regularly in the apartment of the court photographer [i.e. Baron]'. The story was soon splashed across American newspaper front pages: 'Report Queen, Duke in Rift Over Party Girl'.[43]

However, when Philip was introduced to Kirkwood again several years later at a command performance, he appeared unfazed and told her: 'I *did* enjoy myself that evening at Les A.' It was a typically disarming remark that effectively demonstrated their innocence. According to Kirkwood, they hadn't even danced cheek to cheek and later they had all gone back to Baron's flat for scrambled eggs before Philip returned to Buckingham Palace. There was nothing more to it, she said.[44]

The same innocent interpretation was capable of being made of the story related nearly fifty years after the event in the *Daily Mirror* under the front-page headline 'Philip's 27 Trysts with Beauty'. The newspaper's informant was Norman Barson, a former Grenadier Guardsman who had served as a footman at Windlesham Moor during most of 1948. According to the footman, although Philip and Elizabeth generally came to the house for the weekend with friends and family, over a period of some eight months in 1948 Philip regularly came on a Tuesday or Wednesday as well, phoning ahead to give warning and then arriving in the early evening in his MG with an attractive, slim, fair-haired, chic and well-spoken female companion who was not his wife. 'I never knew the woman's name,' Barson recalled, 'but they seemed very close. She would look lovingly into his eyes.' With her beret and white mac she reminded Barson of a girl from the French Resistance, although he was later told that she was Greek.

Barson would serve them gin and orange and beef sandwiches by the open fire. 'He always poured the lady's drink,' the footman recalled. 'He hardly drank at all. I could later hear them laughing and joking, but I never once heard him refer to her by name.' They would stay for anything up to three hours, after which the staff would find cushions strewn about the floor, along with the daily newspapers and magazines. They never stayed overnight.

'We gossiped as staff do and jokingly referred to her as his "fancy woman" or "ladyfriend" – even though I never saw them kiss or canoodle. I remember thinking he acted exactly the same with her as with the Queen. He was charming to both of them. He stared into their eyes with his head on one side and made them laugh.' During these visits, according to Barson, Prince Philip would use the servants' entrance and as he left he would say: 'Don't forget Norman, you haven't seen me.'[45]

Barson's description of this mystery blonde could have fitted Philip's old friend Hélène Foufounis (later Cordet), however his story in other respects is uncorroborated and another of their footmen from the same era, John Gibson, was adamant that Philip was never unfaithful to his wife. 'I just don't believe all that stuff about him having other women,' he told the journalist Graham Turner. 'I've met many gentlemen – you do in private service – and I had a feeling about some of them. He never gave me any other feeling than that he was devoted to her.'[46]

Rumours about other women would continue to beset Philip, albeit never accompanied by much in the way of hard evidence – one theory was that he had, as Sarah Bradford wrote, 'learned to carry on his flirtations and relationships in circles rich and grand enough to provide protection from the paparazzi and tabloids'.[47] His friends and relations insist that all he ever indulged in were flirtations, pointing out that he only had to be seen putting his arm round a girl for people to jump to the conclusion that they were going to bed together. 'The fact is,' says one relation, 'if you're married to someone as vital as Prince Philip, who's really three men rolled into one, it's really quite restful in a way for the wife to have him satisfied with a lot of flirtation, rather than having him sitting around frustrated and shouting at you. So it works extremely well. But he has said that if the bloody papers think I've had these affairs, I almost wish I had because it's so unfair to be accused of having them when I haven't.'[48]

Even if he had strayed, however, Philip could plead in his defence an almost unique set of mitigating circumstances. He came from an era and a family background in which mistresses were the norm, where loyalty was expected of the husband, though not necessarily fidelity. And after marrying Princess Elizabeth, his personal freedom and privacy had been so curtailed that it would have been natural for him to feel the occasional urge to escape. In any event, the consensus among those in a position to know best is that his marriage to Elizabeth was a success, with a strong sense of mutual dependence, a visible fondness and a marked ease in each other's company.

In the lead-up to the birth of Philip and Elizabeth's first child, there was some confusion over whether the home secretary, James Chuter Ede, would need to attend the royal birth in accordance with previous custom. The king was initially in favour of his being there, but when it was pointed out to him that representatives of the Dominions might also like to come, and that there might be up to seven of them milling about in the passage while Elizabeth gave birth, the ritual was declared 'archaic' and abandoned.[49] The other matter to be settled prior to the birth was how the child would be titled. Under the royal warrant issued by George V in 1917 when he asked members of the royal family to give up their German names and titles, the style of Royal Highness was restricted to the offspring of the sovereign and his sons. No thought had been given to the offspring of the sovereign's daughters, and so as things stood Elizabeth's child would merely have the courtesy use of Philip's second title, Earl of Merioneth, if a boy; and be known as Lady X Mountbatten if a girl. Prompted by Tommy Lascelles, less than a week before the birth, the king thus issued new letters patent to ensure that any children of Philip and Elizabeth would have the title of Prince or Princess and the style of His or Her Royal Highness.[50] The child's surname was not established at this point, but it was to become the subject of hot controversy before long.[51]

Elizabeth went into labour on the afternoon of Saturday 13 November, but by early evening of the next day her ordeal was still not yet over and a restless Philip changed into flannels and took Mike Parker off for a game of squash on the Palace's recently renovated court. They broke off for a swim in the pool, and they were back on the court by 9.15 p.m. when Lascelles hurried in with the news that a boy had been born.[52] Philip rushed back and bounded up the stairs to the Buhl Room where his wife was still under anaesthetic. He opened bottles of champagne for the medical and household staff to toast the health of the infant prince, and when Elizabeth awoke he was at her bedside with a bouquet of carnations and roses.[53]

By the time the proclamation announcing the birth of a prince had been posted on the railings outside Buckingham Palace just before midnight, a crowd of some three thousand had gathered at the gates and serenaded a tall figure with 'For He's a Jolly Good Fellow' in the mistaken belief that he was Philip.[54] The subsequent announcement on the wireless was the signal for the firing of guns and lighting of bonfires. Four thousand congratulatory telegrams arrived at the Palace post office that night, and the fountains of Trafalgar Square flowed blue for a boy all the following week.

Among the telegrams that left the Palace that night was one from Philip to his mother, Alice, which reached her on the Greek island of Tinos, where she now dressed in the austere grey habit of the religious sisterhood of Martha and Mary which she had founded, along the lines of Aunt Ella's foundation in Moscow. As she had explained to Philip in March 1948: 'Now that the last of my children is married & has a home, I feel the need of a whole time job to keep me occupied.'[55] When she received the telegram about the birth of her grandson

Charles, she wrote to her son: 'I think of you so much with a sweet baby of your own, of your joy & the interest you will take in all his little doings. How fascinating nature is, but how one has to pay for it in the anxious trying hours of the confinement.'[56]

Alice also received a letter from her sister Louise to say that Elizabeth was recovering well after her thirty hours of labour and that the baby was 'sweet with a well-shaped head, an oval face & a little bit of fair fluff of hair'. 'I am so happy for Philip,' Alice wrote to Dickie, 'for he adores children & also small babies. He carries it about himself quite professionally to the nurse's amusement.'[57]

Even before he had been named, it was established that the 7lb 6oz prince was fifth in descent from Queen Victoria, thirty-second from William the Conqueror and thirty-ninth from Alfred the Great. Notwithstanding his 'foreign' father, genealogists hailed him the most English prince since Henry VIII, the most Scottish since Charles I, and the first potential Prince of Wales to be a direct descendant (via his maternal grandmother) of Owen Glendower.[58]

No announcement about what the prince was to be called was made until his christening on 15 December, when he was given the names Charles Philip Arthur George, the only slight surprise being the first, given the haplessness of previous English kings of that name. According to Dean, 'it was the Duke's suggestion ... because they wanted to break away from the more obvious family names'.[59] Of Charles's eight godparents (who included George VI and Queen Elizabeth), three were Philip's relations: his eighty-four-year-old grandmother, Victoria Milford Haven; his seventy-eight-year-old uncle, Big George of Greece; and his cousin Patricia Brabourne. Another, King Haakon of Norway, was equally related to both Philip and Elizabeth.

Dean recalled that in the immediate aftermath of Charles's birth, Philip was in a 'wonderful mood',[60] but his and his wife's happiness at the birth of their son was soon tempered with anxiety over the grave state of the king's health, beleaguered as he was by the stresses of war and too much smoking. That autumn he had become very unwell, suffering from severe cramp and restricted circulation in his legs, and two days before Prince Charles's birth he had been diagnosed with arteriosclerosis, with such a risk of gangrene in his right leg that his surgeon contemplated amputating it. Elizabeth had been shielded from the news during her confinement, but, two days after Charles was born, the king reluctantly gave in to the advice of his doctors to cancel his planned tour of Australia and New Zealand. The implications for Elizabeth and Philip – who had already opted to go on half-pay in the navy because of his increasing public duties – were obvious in terms of the extra responsibilities they would now have to shoulder. The king did briefly rally after an operation to restore the circulation to his legs in March 1949, but he would never be properly well again. From this time on, as Ben Pimlott wrote, Elizabeth and her healthy family became 'the present, as well as the future – her energy and composure linked in the public mind to the visible fatigue of the ailing King'.[61]

EIGHTEEN

Their Happiest Time

The young couple's heavier responsibility was at least accompanied by more independence, especially after they finally moved into Clarence House at the beginning of July 1949. This was Philip's first proper home since his father abandoned St Cloud when he was ten, and, after doing much to oversee its renovation, he was eager to play a full part in the running of the household.

Built in the 1820s for King William IV when he was Duke of Clarence, to designs by John Nash, the architect of Buckingham Palace, Clarence House had most recently been lived in by the Duke of Connaught, Queen Victoria's last surviving son, who had died in 1942, aged ninety-one. The old duke had neglected to carry out any modernization or install any bathing facilities to supplement the copper bathtub in a cupboard in one of the bedrooms, and the decoration was 'in very bad taste', according to the report putting the case to the Treasury for its refurbishment. Wartime bombing had contributed to the general air of dilapidation, causing the roof to leak in several places and the plaster ceilings to become unstable.[1] The £50,000 to pay for the necessary work was voted in by Parliament, amid protest from trades unions that the money ought to have been spent on public housing. There was thus concern lest news get out about the cinema 'and ancillary accommodation' that Philip had asked to be installed in the basement – even though he was prepared to pay for it himself – and in the end it was given as a wedding present by the Kinematograph Renters' Society, which included British and American film companies.[2] Despite all the precautions, the *Daily Express* eventually printed a news item about it, with the result that a resident of Teignmouth compared it unfavourably with the refusal to grant a licence for the reinstatement of a burnt-out cinema in that town.[3] Clarence House benefited from countless other gifts besides, both from individuals and from countries. Nations jostled to provide samples of their native timber – jarrow from Australia, maple from Canada, etc – for panelling rooms and building other items of fitted furniture. This presented further headaches for the architects as photographs of the finished rooms would inevitably be expected, and hurt feelings might arise where a donor country had envisaged its timber being used in a private room rather than a servant's quarters.[4]

To Philip's irritation, meanwhile, the interior decorator also let slip details about his bedroom – panelled in white Scottish sycamore, with 'a large single bed', bed coverings 'the colour of vin rosé', damask drapes and an oatmeal carpet.[5] His closet would eject any suit or uniform he wanted at the press of an electronic button.[6] Other time-saving devices were borrowed from the gadget-strewn penthouse of his uncle Dickie Mountbatten, whose desire for technical ingenuity in such matters knew no bounds. Mountbatten's devoted valet, Charles Smith, memorably recorded among other contrivances 'a "Simplex" shirt with built-in Y-fronts that he could slide into like a stretch suit … Then, while he dried his chest, I took another towel to dry his back.'[7]

Philip had his own bedroom next door to Elizabeth's, an arrangement common to a great many upper-class couples at that time. However, they both seem to have 'enjoyed the visitation rituals which that system involves', as Robert Lacey put it, citing the story told by the valet, James MacDonald, that when he entered Philip's door one morning, he was embarrassed to see the princess in her husband's bed.

While she was wearing her usual silk nightgown, Prince Philip appeared to be naked. 'He didn't care at all,' said MacDonald. He did not go in for pyjamas. When he visited the Brownings in Cornwall, his stand-in valet for the occasion, unacquainted with the duke's habits, fretted that whoever had packed his suitcase had failed to put in any pyjamas. But when Boy Browning offered to loan him a pair, Philip replied, 'Never wear the things.' Browning was a little more surprised, some years later, to see a naked Philip teaching his children to swim in the pool at Buckingham Palace.[8]

The dressing tables in each of their rooms were placed close enough to the communicating door to enable them to talk to each other while dressing. Dean recalled: 'Often while I was attending the Duke, and Bobo was helping the Princess to complete her preparations, they would joke happily through the half-open door.' Philip's blue bathroom was decorated with pictures of the ships in which he had served during the war. In his study, he installed a cabinet with a small fridge so that he could reach for cold drinks at any time without bothering the staff.

The renovation work took nearly eighteen months to complete, and both Philip and Elizabeth took a keen interest in all the plans, visiting the house sometimes twice a day to monitor progress, and in Elizabeth's case helping to mix the green paint for the dining-room walls. They consulted their staff about the design of the places where they were going to work. The result was that 'the staff quarters were as near ideal as could possibly be imagined',[9] according to Dean, who operated from a brushing room adjoining Philip's dressing room, fitted with the very latest in valeting equipment, the electric trouser press.[10]

The project eventually came in £28,000 over budget,[11] and again there were complaints about the cost, which would perhaps have been louder had it been known that even the staff were now going to be living, by their own account, in the lap of luxury. In his book, Dean went into raptures about their 'wonderful' accommodation: 'There was a radio in every bedroom, television and a radiogram in the servants' sitting-room, and all sorts of games in the recreation room.' Dean's bedroom on the second floor was attached to 'a large and luxurious bathroom' and furnished with wedding presents from the people of South Africa. John Gibson, the nursery footman whose principal responsibility was to polish and push Prince Charles's pram, recalled 'living at a level of luxury I could never before have dreamed of'.[12] At the top of the house there was a staff sitting room and the junior staff bedrooms, each one carpeted wall-to-wall in Edinburgh green, with curtains to match and patterned wallpaper, and furnished with armchairs and other items that had been given to the royal couple as wedding presents. Each room had a writing desk, with blotter, pens and headed notepaper. Philip had even arranged for music to be piped to a speaker on each bedside table. In the servants' hall in the basement, he installed a 'sleek, white, very futuristic television set' – a wedding present from the Mountbattens.[13]

Despite the luxuries, there were still 'an alarming number of changes among the indoor staff', according to Dean. Partly this had to do with their having little time off – a half-day a week and every other Sunday – and regularly working nights. Additional free time was possible during the day and whenever Philip and Elizabeth were not in residence, but for some the restrictions or sheer drudgery became too much. One bored girl was caught hanging out of an upstairs window trying to attract the attention of a guardsman on duty below and was promptly dismissed, 'quite properly I think', recorded prim Mr Dean.[14]

Philip and Elizabeth, though, were thought of as highly considerate employers, always interested in the welfare of their staff. To the footman Gibson, they were 'just ordinary people … a lot less formal than some people I came across – people much further down the social scale'.[15] Most mornings it was Elizabeth who took the corgis for a walk in St James's Park, wearing an old raincoat and headscarf, her detective following a discreet distance behind. For breakfast she ate eggs and bacon and scones (served by a footman in navy-blue battle-dress livery, with epaulettes in Edinburgh green), while Philip made do with coffee and toast, and would often have left for work before the princess came down.[16] They never dressed for dinner when they were alone, and both liked plain food, according to Gibson, who gathered his intelligence from his wife Betty, one of the kitchen maids. Dinner would often consist of no more than cold meat and salad, or sausages and mash. The staff, on the other hand, would sit down most nights to a three-course 'high tea'.[17] According to Dean, Philip took a more active interest than his wife in the way the house was run, and it was he who made any alterations or suggestions in the menu book.[18]

The staff referred to Philip as 'the Duke', and were impressed by his down-to-earth manner: 'There was no pomp and ceremony,' wrote Gibson. 'He was very rough and ready.'[19] However, few if any of Philip's hosts made that assumption whenever he went to stay elsewhere. When, in April 1950, he visited Boy Browning and Daphne du Maurier at their Cornish home, Menabilly, their daughter Flavia recalled that it 'really set the house about its ears; everything was spring cleaned that could be spring cleaned; new glasses were bought as so many of the wine ones had tiny nicks in them; the silver was polished until you could see your face in it'.

In advance of the royal visit the children were told to tidy everything in sight and were made to have their hair cut and washed and their clothes were sent to be cleaned. The governess, though, wasn't 'much struck', according to Flavia, and kept saying 'What a fuss', while their daily went about muttering, 'Well, *they* are no better than us.' For some reason the governess also took against the man who had been brought in to act as Philip's valet, even before they had arrived, refusing to make his bed, declaring, 'He can do it himself.'

Boy Browning, meanwhile, fretted over laying the table, and was eventually observed to hurl the cutlery on to the floor, screaming, 'Christ, the bloody things, why haven't we got a butler? Why is everybody so bloody hopeless in this house?'

When Philip eventually arrived at about tea time, they all met him out on the gravel, Daphne and Flavia doing a curtsey, and Browning and their son Kits giving a slight nod of the head. The valet appeared surprised that there were no staff to carry the luggage. 'Wait until you see your unmade bed,' thought Flavia. 'It was the detective,' she wrote, 'who eventually heaved and sweated with the suitcases while the valet cast his eye about him, soon making demands for an iron and so forth.' After tea, the children were allowed into the drawing room, where 'HRH paced the floor in a restless manner, suddenly throwing himself down in a chair and picking up a *Country Life* or yachting paper, leafing through it and then snatching up another'. Daphne was in good form, according to her daughter, 'chatting away and laughing, much more relaxed than the two men'. The next morning, Browning was up at the crack of dawn to lay the breakfast table – he would trust no one else. When they had gone, Philip giving them 'a huge grin as the car swept through and waving his hand out of the window', they discovered that the valet had left all the rooms immaculate, the sheets neatly folded; 'it looked as if no one had ever been there'.[20]

There were similar flutterings in grander houses, for example whenever Philip took Elizabeth to stay with the Wernhers at Luton Hoo, where they first went together in April 1949 and thereafter spent a shooting weekend each November. These occasions were supposedly 'quite informal', although, as the Wernhers' butler remarked, 'Heaven knows what we would have had to do if they had been formal.' The cook got herself into such a frenzy that Harold Wernher had to tell the watchman to ensure that she went to bed at a reasonable time – although even then she was up again at four in the morning, labouring over such creations as meringue swan on mango ice cream, strawberry trees and boned and walnut-stuffed poussin. Zia Wernher, though, maintained her customary air of authority. On one occasion, her granddaughter Sacha (later Duchess of Abercorn) was horrified to be told by Zia to go upstairs and hurry the queen (as Princess Elizabeth had by then become) along for dinner, and was greatly relieved to see her running towards her down the corridor, holding up her skirts.[21]

Whenever Philip returned home from trips away, Gibson recalled that 'he'd go right round the house to speak to everybody, just like a naval officer getting back to his ship'.[22] He still yearned to be back on a real ship, though, and in the autumn of 1949, with the blessing of the now slightly fitter King George, Philip finally returned to active service in the navy as second-in-command of *Chequers*, leader of the first destroyer flotilla of the Mediterranean Fleet based in Malta.*

Philip flew out to Malta that October. With *Chequers* undergoing a refit, to begin with he stayed at the hilltop Villa Guardamangia as a guest of the Mountbattens, Dickie having recently taken command of the First Cruiser Squadron. Mountbatten ranked only third in the naval hierarchy in Malta, quite a comedown from being wartime Supreme Allied Commander in South-East Asia and then Viceroy of India – 'very levelling and educative' so Edwina told her friend Nehru, to whom she had become strongly attached while in India.[23] The comforts available at the villa did not quite match those of the Viceregal Palace in New Delhi, but they were waited on by a staff of nineteen. Mountbatten was delighted to have his nephew there, although he told his daughter Patricia that at first Philip was 'very busy showing his independence', sometimes rather brusquely. 'The

---

* His commanding officer was Group Captain Peter Townsend's brother.

trouble,' he wrote, 'with not having a real son of one's own but only a couple of nephews and a son-in-law is that however much one may like them they will never feel the same way about the older generation if one isn't their real father, not that I blame them tho' it makes me feel a bit sad at times.'[24] A few weeks later he was relieved to report that 'Philip is right back on 1946 terms with us and we've had a heart-to-heart in which he admitted he was fighting shy of coming under my dominating influence and patronage!'[25]

Elizabeth had stayed behind in London, but she flew out to join her husband for their second wedding anniversary, on 20 November, accompanied by her maid, Bobo MacDonald, a footman, a detective (a strict teetotaller who was horrified to discover that the princess had given him a chocolate liqueur during their journey out), and Philip's valet, John Dean.[26] The infant Charles, who had just celebrated his first birthday, was left at home in the care of the nursery staff and his grandparents.

For the Mountbattens, Elizabeth's arrival at their house caused a certain amount of upheaval, with Edwina giving up her own quarters to the royal couple, moving into Dickie's bedroom while he was banished to another – an inconvenience he was only too happy to tolerate so long as it meant having the heir to the throne under his roof. He would have been happier still to have known that their second child was conceived there, shortly after Elizabeth's arrival. If he had been made aware that Elizabeth was a little suspicious of him, Dickie was determined to put that right. 'I don't think I need tell you how fond I've become of her,' he wrote to his daughter Patricia in December. 'Lilibet is quite enchanting and I've lost whatever of my heart is left to spare entirely to her. She dances quite divinely and always wants a Samba when we dance together and has said some very nice things about my dancing.'[27]

Elizabeth carried out a handful of public engagements in Valletta, visiting hospitals and naval ships, and occasionally unveiling plaques.

But otherwise her life there was remarkable for its ordinariness, driving her own Daimler about the island, often alone, enjoying such novelties as shopping and visiting the hairdresser and generally 'mucking in' with the other service wives. The Maltese knew perfectly well who she was but they respected her privacy. There were never sightseers loitering outside the villa.[28] 'It's lovely seeing her so radiant and leading a more or less human existence for once,' Edwina wrote to Nehru. Dean agreed: 'They were so relaxed and free, coming and going as they pleased like an ordinary young married couple. I think it was their happiest time.'[29]

Whenever Philip was off duty they would dine and dance together in the local restaurants and hotels, and go on boating expeditions with the Mountbattens to nearby creeks and bays to picnic and swim, sometimes spending the night on board. While their wives sunbathed, Philip and his uncle would go water-skiing or spearfishing – the latter a favourite pursuit of Dickie, an expert underwater fisherman who kept a large arsenal of harpoon guns and descended as deep as 150ft.[30] When someone once asked him which he preferred, polo or diving, he paused for a moment before replying: 'Well, polo, after all, is only a game.'[31]

Determined to be his own man, Philip initially shunned Dickie's suggestion that he also take up polo, saying that he wasn't going to 'ponce around on a horse', that it was a 'snob sport' and that he preferred to play hockey with his ship. But Elizabeth far preferred to watch the polo than hockey and she sensibly advised Dickie to stop nagging Philip to play, predicting that in his own time he would come round to the idea of it, which he did. His horsemanship, eye for the ball and wiry physique combined to make him a natural, and the game was to become one of the great passions of his young life.[32]

Elizabeth enjoyed herself so much on this first visit to Malta – she returned for another six weeks in the spring – that she asked Edwina if she could prolong her stay and remain with the Mountbattens over

Christmas, after which Philip was dispatched with *Chequers* to patrol the Red Sea with six other warships following the outbreak of disturbances in Eritrea. When Elizabeth eventually left for home on 28 December, she did so 'with a tear in her eye and a lump in her throat', wrote Edwina. It was, she added, 'like putting a bird back into a very small cage'.[33]

On arriving back in England, however, she appeared to be in no great hurry to see her one-year-old son Charles, spending four days at Clarence House, attending to engagements and a backlog of correspondence, and then going racing at Hurst Park, where she saw her horse Monaveen win at 10-1, before eventually being reunited with Charles at Sandringham, where he had been looked after by his grandparents.[34] While she was away Elizabeth had missed out on seeing her son's first steps and his first teeth. His first word was apparently 'Nana', addressed to his nanny, whom he saw more of than any other person.[35] Similar observations might have been made about countless other upper-class children at that time, yet even friends acknowledged that Elizabeth was a somewhat unsentimental mother. She was not good at showing affection, and did not go in for hugging and kissing her boy as much as some mothers might.[36] Added to that, she was busy learning how to discharge her various duties as heiress presumptive, which meant spending far less time with her son than she would have liked – normally an hour in the morning and another between tea and bathtime.

With all the demands on her time, Elizabeth was inclined to leave much of the responsibility for bringing up their children to Philip, who was, according to friends, a 'marvellous father' and much more playful than Elizabeth with the children when they were young.[37] However, he had very definite views on how he wanted his son to turn out, and by Charles's first birthday he had already bought him a cricket bat and been reportedly heard to declare on more than one occasion: 'I want him to be a man's man.'[38] He saw it as his responsibility to prepare him for the rigours of being king one day. According to a close friend,

> Prince Philip could see that Charles was a terribly sensitive boy who was going to come up against a lot of problems, and he thought he should help him not to take to heart a lot of the things that children take to heart, and not rush to pick him up every time he fell over and say 'Oh dear, dear have you hurt yourself' but rather, 'Oh come on that's not so bad'. I'm sure he just wanted to help make his character more robust ... but in retrospect I think he overdid it sometimes and perhaps he was a bit untactful.[39]

In the early years of Charles's life, Philip was also often away. When he did eventually return home on leave in July 1950, it was to await the birth of their second child, Anne, on 15 August, after which Charles would cease to be the sole focus of his parents' already sporadic attention. During this leave, Philip was reunited with his mother, Alice, who, having missed the birth of Charles, came over from Tinos for Anne's. The *Daily Mail* had tracked her down there the previous year and announced to its readers: 'Philip's Mother – Living as a Nun'. But she had declined to be interviewed about her work, explaining: 'Duty is its own reward. I am not a politician or a film star. Taking pictures of me at work would be posing.'[40]

Philip's long absences were set to continue. Before his leave, and just short of his twenty-ninth birthday, he had been appointed to his first proper command, the frigate *Magpie*. In early September 1950 he returned to Malta and was piped aboard *Magpie*, which he now determined to make one of the finest in the fleet. Under intense scrutiny, he wanted his crew to excel not just in naval exercises but also in the annual regatta, and to this end he practised the rowing crews so hard that their hands blistered. They duly carried off six out of the ten first prizes in the regatta, their new commander – or 'Dukey' as the crew nicknamed him – rowing stroke in the officers' whaler race, stripped to the waist and wearing sunglasses, which were regular items of attire for him in those days. Reactions to Philip's style of command varied. 'He made us work like dogs,' one of his ratings recalled, 'but treated us like gentlemen.' Another said that he 'stamped about like a ——ing tiger', and another that he'd rather die than serve in that ship again.[41] All his life Philip would remain fiercely demanding of his staff and scorching in his criticism. But even if *Magpie* was not the happiest ship in the fleet, it was certainly one of the most efficient, and proudly sported a large red plywood cockerel at the masthead on the day she became cock ship of the flotilla.

The difficulty for Philip of juggling his responsibilities was brought home at the end of September 1950, when his grandmother Victoria Milford Haven died, aged eighty-seven. She had done as much as anyone to bring him up, yet Philip, who had only recently taken command of *Magpie*, was unable to return for the funeral and his attendance at the memorial service would depend on the movements of his ship – which did at least permit him to return briefly for the christening of Anne in October.[42] His mother Alice had been with Victoria at Kensington Palace when she died and afterwards described her mother's final moments to Philip: 'She was practically sitting up to ease the breathing & so we had a good view of her with such a calm & peaceful expression, as one who is having a good sleep & the breast rising & falling so evenly and gently, until it quietly stopped at 8 am, a beautiful end.'[43]

During his command of *Magpie*, he visited the kings of Jordan and Iran and dined with the presidents of Turkey and Iran, and in November 1950 he stood in for the king opening Gibraltar's new Legislative Council. Other ports of call included Alexandria, where he revisited his wartime haunts and used what seemed to his shipmates to be flawless demotic Greek to cajole the owner of a cinema into reserving the best seats in the house for the gunroom officers,[44] and

Monte Carlo, where he impressed observers by skilfully negotiating the difficult shallows of its harbour in such squally conditions that other ships weren't putting to sea[45] – further evidence that he was almost certainly a more accomplished seaman than his uncle Dickie, who invariably travelled too fast and sometimes in the wrong direction, even if he did not quite share his flair for man management.

On 25 November 1950, shortly after Charles's second birthday and when Elizabeth had recovered from giving birth to Anne, she flew out to Malta to join Philip, again leaving the children with their grandparents in England. For the first ten days, with *Magpie* in port, they again stayed at the Villa Guardamangia, having taken on the lease from the Mountbattens after they returned to London in May. Each morning Philip rose at 6.30 for a quick breakfast before rowing himself across the creek to his ship, returning in the afternoon in time to drive Elizabeth out to a polo game at the Marsa Club. On 5 December they sailed for Greece for an unofficial visit to Philip's cousin King Paul and Queen Frederika. It was Elizabeth's first visit to her husband's homeland and they received a warm welcome from the Greek people, and stayed with the royal family at Tatoï. According to Alexandra, when Philip took King Paul aboard *Magpie*, the king was 'astonished that Philip was still simultaneously carrying on a lot of his English office work, including the preparations for the Festival of Britain and complicated plans for an overseas tour' and that he 'spent hours drafting his own letters and memos in pencil'.[46]

They also made a surprise call on the British ambassador, Sir Clifford Norton, whose wife had given the royal couple the key to their beach hut without telling her husband, who then answered the door in his pyjamas when they turned up one evening brandishing saucepans in the hope of a late-night cook-up.[47] They later stayed with the Nortons at the embassy in Athens, and Sir Clifford and his wife formed the impression that the princess was 'very shy and rather withdrawn, a bit of a shrinking violet in fact, and he [Philip] was young and vigorous and jollied her along. He didn't actually say, "Come on, old girl!" but it was that sort of thing.'[48]

These happy and relatively carefree days were soon to draw to a premature end. Back in England, the king tired easily, even with a lighter workload. His frail appearance did not go unnoticed by the public, especially when he opened the great Festival of Britain in May 1951, designed to celebrate the centenary of Prince Albert's Great Exhibition. At the end of that month he retired to bed with what he took to be flu, but he was unable to 'chuck out the bug', as he put it, and so he was ordered by his doctors to undertake no public engagements. This meant that he would need to call on Elizabeth and Philip to help him carry out his duties. Thus, in mid-July 1951 they returned from Malta for good. Plans were already afoot for a tour of their own of Canada in September and it was looking increasingly inevitable that they would also have to take the place of Elizabeth's parents on their projected tour of Australia and New Zealand the next year.

For his part, Philip understood that he could no longer pursue an active naval career and support his wife in carrying out her increasingly demanding duties as heiress to the throne. He left the navy on 'indefinite leave', never to return. It was just about the only regret he would admit to in later life. 'It was not my ambition to be president of the Mint Advisory Committee,' he told one interviewer years later. 'I didn't want to be president of the World Wildlife Fund. I was asked to do it. I'd much rather have stayed in the Navy, frankly.'[49] He had only just turned thirty and had shown great promise as an officer. While his brusque and rebellious temperament may ultimately have counted against him,[50] it was more than conceivable that he would have gone on to emulate his grandfather and uncle. 'Prince Philip was a highly talented seaman,' said Lord Lewin. 'No doubt about it. If he hadn't become what he did, he would have been First Sea Lord and not me.'[51]

NINETEEN

Second Fiddle

Philip and Mike Parker made the most of their last days in Malta, swimming each night after dinner and boating out to the islands for underwater fishing and barbecues. On 20 July 1951 Philip captained his polo side to win a tournament, scoring the third of their four goals,[1] before flying to London the next day, attended by Parker and John Dean. Back at Clarence House, he looked sadly at his white naval uniforms and said to his valet: 'It will be a long time before I want those again.'[2] The plan had been for him to take up another naval appointment after the return of the king and queen from their planned tour of Australia and New Zealand in the middle of the next year,[3] but the king's declining health soon put paid to that.

For a time after Philip's return, the king had appeared to be getting better and in August he wrote to a friend from Balmoral to say he was 'stronger every day'. He was fit enough to enjoy a whole day's grouse shooting and one of the guns, Aubrey Buxton, observed that he was 'still the same laird, alert to every detail, eager for sporting news, pertinacious and critical'. Even after reluctantly flying south for a day to London for more tests, when he got back to Balmoral that evening he went straight to the sand-table model of the moors and forest 'to hear explained in every detail the experiences of the shooting party which he had been obliged to despatch that day without himself'.[4]

Eventually, after the king returned south from Balmoral, a bronchoscopy confirmed that he was suffering from lung cancer, as many had long feared, in all probability caused by a lifetime of heavy smoking, even if medical science did not make that connection at the time.[5] The king was informed of the need to remove his left lung, although the true diagnosis was withheld from him and the general public. The operation was performed on 23 September and by early October he was able to sit up in bed. When he first rose from his sickbed after his lung operation he was keen to discover if his arms would lift easily above the shoulder, and playfully he raised them two or three times as if bringing a gun to his shoulder.

All had gone according to plan, but the long-term prognosis was bleak, and Elizabeth had already intimated to her dress designer, Hardy Amies, that she and Philip might be going to Australia and New Zealand in his place.[6] On 9 October the king's Antipodean tour, which was to have been the first by a reigning sovereign to those Dominions, was cancelled.

During the summer, Elizabeth continued her apprenticeship by standing in for her father on many of his public engagements, reading the king's speech at the state banquet given for King Haakon of Norway, and taking her father's place at the ceremony of Trooping the Colour. Philip had to readjust to the prospect of playing second fiddle to his wife. Eager to carve out a distinct role for himself, he took his first step towards becoming, as the historian Richard Weight put it, 'a Prince Albert for the jet age'.[7]

Philip had long evinced an interest in science and technology, and in 1951 he accepted the presidency of the British Association for the Advancement of Science. He made a considerable impact with his inaugural address to the Association in August 1951, ambitiously titled 'The British Contribution to Science and Technology in the Past Hundred Years'. His starting point was the Great Exhibition of 1851 that had been masterminded by Prince Albert, his great-great-grand-father and predecessor as prince consort.

Philip had been preparing the speech for months in his cabin aboard *Magpie*, which to his steward's exasperation became strewn with books and papers supplied by Sir Harold Hartley, secretary of the Association, who was to become his scientific mentor. 'The more I read the material you have been sending me the more confused I get,' he admitted to Hartley in January.[8] The press gave Philip's lecture a highly enthusiastic reception, relieved, as Weight expressed it, 'that after fourteen years of being saddled with a shy and unhealthy king they had a consort with some charisma and brain'.[9] Some months later, following the death of the king, *The Times* recalled how 'old courtiers marvelled at his [Philip's] unprecedented action in compos-ing his own address' and declared that 'the British public can be profoundly thankful that the Queen should be supported by a person-ality of outstanding vitality who is in step with the march of the modern world'.[10]

Not everyone was so appreciative. Harold Macmillan noted causti-cally that the lecture seemed to

please the 'Left' very much. I fear this young man is going to be as big a bore as Prince Albert and as great a trouble. Let us hope that the King may live to be a great age and the power of the Mountbattens (the Orléanists of Britain) be cashed accordingly. Lord and Lady Mount-batten have done enough harm by their conduct in India to last a long time. But I feel sure that they hope to exercise great influence in Britain through the Duke. What does the Duke know about patent law? ... I suppose he will speak about the 'net book agreement' at his next effort. It was really much better when royalty were just pleasant and polite, with the appropriate courtesies or the simple truths which both George V and VI have done so well.[11]

However, others credited Philip with helping the British to see themselves as a modern and innovative people. In Weight's analysis, by travelling about the country over the course of the next decade and visiting research centres and factories and making speeches he 'turned statistics into patriotism'.[12] The press was impressed by the intensity of the young prince's interest. When, in June 1952, he visited de Havillands and flew in a Comet, the world's first passenger jet aeroplane and a potent symbol of Britain's technological advancement, *Picture Post* commented: 'This was no royal chore, no concession to the spit and polish brigade. He wants to see for himself how Britain goes to it.'[13] Philip was applauded for galvanizing British industry and helping to put the country back on her feet, and Richard Dimbleby went so far as to suggest that he had inspired miners to break all production records in the weeks after his visit to a colliery in the north of England.[14]

On the evening of 7 October 1951, barely two weeks after the king's operation, Philip and Elizabeth flew to Canada for their slightly postponed visit. Going by air rather than by sea as originally planned was the only way they could catch up with the programme, yet it was still controversial given that none of the immediate royal family had yet flown the Atlantic. Winston Churchill, Leader of the Opposition, was deeply opposed to the heir of the throne taking such a risk and only relented after Philip reminded him of the flights he had taken across the Atlantic during the war while he was in the rather more responsible position of prime minister.[15]

Notwithstanding the disaster that had befallen his sister Cecile and her family, Philip had long been a great advocate of flying, and he spent much of the journey over to Newfoundland on the flight deck of the BOAC stratocruiser, grilling the pilot about the controls – which he was soon to learn to use himself.

On their arrival at Montreal to a twenty-one-gun salute, they were met by the Canadian prime minister Louis St Laurent and the governor-general, Field Marshal Viscount Alexander of Tunis. Alexander accompanied the royal couple on to Quebec and the capital, Ottawa, and enjoyed their visit far more than the recent one of his old friend Churchill, whom he found to be 'increasingly indifferent to social courtesies' in his old age; one evening Churchill had sent down a message shortly before dinner to say that he felt disinclined that night to sit between two women and wished his neighbours at the table to be Alexander and the prime minister.[16]

Since arriving in Canada in 1946, Alexander had enthusiastically taken to the local way of life, and accordingly he held a square dance party for Elizabeth and Philip and invited along eighty other young people. A hurried shopping trip by John Dean enabled them to look the part, Elizabeth in a brown checkered blouse, Philip in blue jeans with wide turn-ups, bold-check shirt, red choker, cowboy belt and loafers. Their sixty-year-old host wore an equally vivid check shirt and buckskin jacket.[17]

Canada presented the couple with their sternest test yet, particularly as the tour was constantly overshadowed by the king's illness. Elizabeth's private secretary Martin Charteris accompanied them and slept with the accession documents beneath his bed, just in case. Overall it was a success, although the Canadian press, insensitive or oblivious to the princess's anxiety about her father's health, wondered why she didn't smile more, and Philip offended some of his hosts when he referred to Canada as 'a good investment'. As usual he had written the speech himself and, as Sarah Bradford later noted, it was 'not the last time he was to fall into a verbal trap of his own making which a trained courtier would have avoided'.[18]

There was the occasional off-the-cuff lapse as well, as when he enquired of some importunate photographers at Niagara, 'What are you belly-aching about now?' Overall, though, Philip was more of a hit with the Canadian crowds than Elizabeth, who reported in a letter to her mother that young women screamed when he waved, and men shouted, 'Good old Phil!'[19] But despite her own awkwardness, Elizabeth pronounced herself pleased by Philip's 'succès fou' and the way his 'legend' got around.[20]

One of the reporters covering the tour wrote that 'He [Philip] smiled more, waved more, unbent more'.[21] A 'reassuring step or two behind' he was 'ready to smooth occasional embarrassments which intrude themselves between the subject and a shy and fabled Princess, relieving the tension of tradition with an impromptu remark, an unexpected smile, and the natural – yet somehow unorthodox – action'.[22] He also pleased Canadians by making various small diplomatic gestures, such as donning a ten-gallon Stetson to watch a rodeo in the snow at Calgary.[23]

Philip was observed by the press to be a 'man of action', of 'limitless' energy and curiosity, prepared to try anything, whether it be driving the royal train, on the bridge of the Canadian destroyer *Crusader*, at the wheel of the royal barge on the Ottawa River, driving the royal cars on Vancouver Island and in the co-pilot's seat of the Royal Canadian Air Force aircraft which they used frequently during the tour. Impressed by the zip fasteners on the jumpers worn by Canadian ratings, he made sketches for a more up-to-date British naval uniform including zips. He also suggested the Plexiglas top to the royal car, which was duly made by an aircraft plant so that the princess could be seen in all weathers.[24]

To reach all seven of the Canadian provinces meant travelling 10,000 miles in just over a month, from the Atlantic to the Pacific and back again. Much of the time was spent on the governor-general's train and, as they covered the vast expanses, crowds of people came huge distances from their homes and waited at remote stops along the way to see them. Dean vividly recalled them coming to a halt late one night in a snowstorm at a tiny station in the Rockies: the train was immediately lit up by arc lights, a band began playing and the crowd sang 'The Loveliest Night of the Year' as Elizabeth and Philip stepped on to the platform. They departed later to the sound of 'Will Ye No Come Back Again?'[25]

Aboard the train, Philip sought to relieve the boredom with practical jokes – leaving an imitation tin of mixed nuts (acquired from a Canadian joke shop by his valet) on Elizabeth's table from which a toy snake sprang out, and chasing her down the corridor of the royal car flashing a set of false teeth.[26] He was not invariably cheerful, however, and one morning at breakfast he was overheard by one of the entourage calling his wife 'a bloody fool!' Charteris, who was there at the time, excused Philip's occasional 'naval turn of phrase' on the grounds that he was restless and frustrated. As Charteris pointed out, the prince had been obliged to give up a promising career in the navy

to do – what? He hadn't yet defined his role, found his feet as consort. He was certainly very impatient with the old style courtiers and sometimes, I think, felt that the Princess paid more attention to them than to him. He didn't like that. If he called her 'a bloody fool' now and again, it was just his way. I think others would have found it more shocking than she did. Although she was very young, she had a wise head on her shoulders. She always understood him – and his ways. And valued his contribution – which has been immense and is underestimated. I believe history will come to judge him well.[27]

Those close to the royal couple saw that Philip's unobtrusive yet firm support for his wife on this tour did much to help Elizabeth to overcome her diffidence, to the extent that at the end of the tour a Canadian observer was able to say 'We're sending you back a new Princess'.[28]

If Philip had to some extent outshone his wife in Canada, the balance was restored during their subsequent short stopover in the United States, where they stayed with President Harry Truman. The president appeared to fall in love with the princess and in public behaved, as the British ambassador described it, like 'a very proud uncle presenting his favourite niece to his friends'. To help ensure the royal couple the warmest of welcomes, Truman had given all federal employees time off work, and they obligingly lined the streets of Washington to cheer. 'When I was a little boy,' said Truman, 'I read about a fairy princess, and here she is.' In a speech in the Rose Garden of the White House, he declared: 'We have many distinguished visitors here in this city, but never have we had such a wonderful couple, that so completely captured the hearts of us all.'[29]

The *Washington Star* agreed that the princess 'ought to be told the simple truth by somebody … that she had charmed and captivated this city to such an extent that our oldest inhabitants, searching around among their memories, are hard put to recall the name of any past visitor quite comparable to her in terms of good looks and sweetness of personality'.[30] The extraordinary reception given to Elizabeth and Philip by the American crowds prompted the seasoned royal watcher Dermot Morrah to conclude that 'no people can derive more passionate excitement from the contemplation of royal personages than those who are constitutionally vowed to repudiate the monarchical idea'.[31]

Before they left, Truman insisted on the royal couple going to see his mother-in-law, deaf and bedridden on the top floor. 'Mother!' the president bellowed as they entered her room. 'I've brought Princess Elizabeth to see you!' While they were away there had been a general election which returned seventy-seven-year-old Winston Churchill to 10 Downing Street at the head of a new purely Conservative administration. The old lady had evidently heard something of this and in her befuddlement she said to Elizabeth: 'I'm so glad your father's been re-elected.'[32]

Philip and Elizabeth eventually made their way home in the liner *Empress of Scotland*, thereby missing their son's third birthday on 14 November. In the absence of his parents, Prince Charles had celebrated with a small tea party at Buckingham Palace after being 'taken in his perambulator into St James's Park', so *The Times* reported, 'where he waved and smiled to the many people who wished him a happy birthday'.[33] Philip and Elizabeth arrived home three days later, completing the last leg by train from Liverpool to Euston. According to *The Times*, Prince Charles 'began to skip joyfully' as he caught sight of them on the platform and Elizabeth 'knelt down and hugged Prince Charles affectionately'.[34] However, the Pathé film footage of the occasion shows that in fact, when they stepped off the train, neither Elizabeth nor Philip gave Charles a glance until they had both greeted the queen and Princess Margaret, and only then did Elizabeth bend down and give him what looked to be at most a peck on the cheek – it could scarcely be described as an affectionate hug. A few moments later, Philip cast his first glance down at his son and patted him on the head.[35] Such greetings were rendered more awkward by virtue of being made under the gaze of the public, and the demeanour of Philip and Elizabeth towards their son was perhaps no different from that of a great many parents in those days. But even so, the lack of warmth affected the sensitive and timid Charles – he later said as much to his biographer Jonathan Dimbleby. In any event, in this instance he had little time to enjoy his parents' company before it was announced that they would be off again, this time on the Commonwealth tour scheduled to begin at the end of January.

Churchill had welcomed the royal couple home from Canada with his usual barrage of flattery: 'Madam,' he said, 'the whole nation is grateful to you for what you have done for us and to Providence for having endowed you with the gifts and personality which are not only precious to the British Commonwealth and Empire and its island home, but will play their part in cheering and in mellowing the forward march of human society the world over.'[36] The king marked the success of their tour by making both Elizabeth and Philip Privy Counsellors.[37]

In preparation for their next tour, Philip devoted his spare hours to studying Australian affairs and visiting the London Wool Exchange to bone up on sheep farming and its attendant vocabulary. He relished being back at Clarence House, and the renewed optimism about the king's health even allowed him to entertain thoughts of a possible reprieve for his naval career. Within a few months his term of service would qualify him for promotion to commander, in which case he could realistically expect to go to sea again in 1953 in command of his own destroyer.[38] But, again, such hopes depended on the king getting better.

For Christmas the family gathered, as usual, at Sandringham. Having prerecorded his dreaded Christmas Day broadcast, the king was 'especially gay and carefree' and, though still gaunt in appearance he was 'more contented in mind and confident in health than he had been at any time since the war'.[39] On several days he went out shooting, moving between stands by car and taking the occasional shot with a light gun; he was 'delighted to find that he achieved his normally high standard'.[40]

He and the queen looked forward to a trip to South Africa in March which he hoped would complete his convalescence. By the end of January his doctors pronounced themselves 'very well satisfied' with his progress and on 30 January the whole royal family, including the king, queen, Elizabeth, Philip and Margaret, attended by the king's equerry, Peter Townsend, went to watch the musical *South Pacific* at the Drury Lane Theatre. The evening culminated in the whole company lining the stage facing the royal box and singing the National Anthem, after which there was prolonged cheering from the audience.[41] The next morning the king accompanied Elizabeth and Philip to London airport and stood on the tarmac in the bitter wind, holding his hat and waving goodbye as they departed for Nairobi on the first leg of their Commonwealth tour.

* * *

After arriving in Kenya, accompanied by their attendants, Mike Parker and Lady Pamela Mountbatten (later Hicks), two days of engagements were followed by the ninety-mile drive upcountry to Sagana Lodge, a cedarwood lodge in the Aberdares which had been given to Elizabeth and Philip by the people of Kenya as a wedding present. They passed a happy couple of days trout fishing and riding there before, in the late afternoon of 5 February, making the short onward journey to Treetops, a renowned observation lodge in the branches of a giant fig tree whose platform afforded an excellent view of the big game that came to the waterhole and salt lick beneath the tree. The famous 'white hunter' Jim Corbett had agreed to stand guard at the foot of the tree. Elizabeth and Philip were told that he was there to protect them against the threat of wild animals, whereas in fact he was also on the lookout for Mau Mau guerrillas, who were already active in the vicinity.

The royal party was required to walk the last quarter of a mile from the drop-off point to the lodge, which, as Lady Pamela remembers, turned into a nerve-racking ordeal for their host, Sherbrooke Walker. Four hundred yards from Treetops, they saw a white pillowcase fluttering from one of the windows, an agreed signal that there was danger up ahead, and Walker soon spotted a herd of cow elephant and their young at the waterhole. Nearby were some young bulls, angrily trumpeting in the evening air. He stopped, unsure of what to do next, feeling the full weight of his responsibility for the safety of the heir to the throne and her husband. Philip and Elizabeth could see the elephant, too, but neither of them apprehended the full extent of the danger. After a while, Philip became impatient. 'Well,' he said, 'is this it? Should we go on?'[42] Walker hesitated before eventually cocking his rifle and going on. To his great relief, they all climbed the ladder to the viewing platform in safety.

When they got up there, Elizabeth began excitedly filming, capturing a cow elephant suckling her young and afterwards giving one of them a swimming lesson. After dinner and a two-hour lie down, they got up again. 'All night we were up filming and watching,' recalls Lady Pamela, 'it was so exciting, really wonderful … But of course what we didn't know was that while she had climbed up that ladder as a Princess she was going to have to climb down again as Queen.'

After seeing them off at London airport, the king and queen had returned with their grandchildren to Sandringham. On 5 February the king went out shooting. It was a hare day, the pheasant season having just ended, and there were some twenty guns in the party, including tenants, local policemen and visiting gamekeepers. The king's servant James Macdonald later recalled that his master was as 'gay and happy' as he had ever seen him. The king's personal tally for the day was nine hares, three of which he killed with the last three shots that he fired.[43] At the end of the day, after thanking the keepers, he said to his servant: 'Well, Macdonald, we'll go after the hares again tomorrow.'[44] That evening, the queen found him 'in tremendous form & looking so well and happy'. He retired to bed at 10.30 p.m. and around midnight a watchman saw him adjusting his window latch to allow more air into his room.[45]

The next morning at 7.30, when Macdonald went in with his early morning tea, he found the king dead, from a coronary thrombosis in the early hours. As he was carried from his house to the little church, where his gamekeepers were to watch over him, a cock pheasant called in the parkland.

In his broadcast to the nation two days later, Churchill said that during these last few months, 'the King walked with death, as if death were a companion, an acquaintance, whom he recognized and did not fear'.[46] But to those closest to him, his death came, if not out of the blue, certainly as a profound shock. As Princess Margaret saw it: 'He died as he was getting better.'[47] Although the photograph of the gaunt king seeing Elizabeth and Philip off at London airport came to look prophetic with hindsight, there was no premonition at the time of what was to happen. 'They knew the King was ill,' remembers Lady Pamela, 'but I don't think for a moment they would have gone if they'd thought that he was about to die. They thought he was recovering.'[48]

Kenya is three hours ahead of Britain, but since nobody knows exactly when the king died, nobody knows at what time Elizabeth succeeded. Mike Parker later recalled that he had taken the princess up to a lookout point at the top of the tree to see the dawn coming up. An eagle came and hovered above their heads and Parker was momentarily frightened that it would dive on them. 'I never thought about it until later,' he told Ben Pimlott, 'but that was roughly the time when the King died.'[49] Equally possibly, at the time of her father's death, the princess may have been watching baboons, or resting, or having breakfast. In any event, she and Philip had no inkling of what had happened. 'Because of where we were at the time,' recalls Lady Pamela, 'we were almost the last people in the world to know.'

After breakfast, the party returned to Sagana Lodge, exhausted, to spend the rest of the morning resting and trout fishing. A few hours later Martin Charteris was at the Outspan Hotel in nearby Nyeri, when, after 'a rather good' lunch, he bumped into a journalist emerging ashen-faced from a phone booth in the lobby. 'Is anything wrong?' Charteris asked. The journalist told him, shaking, that there had been a Reuters flash to say that the king had died.

Charteris could not get through to Buckingham Palace on the phone so he called Mike Parker at Sagana with the unconfirmed news. Parker crept into the sitting room where Elizabeth sat at her desk with her back to him, writing letters, and crept out again with the portable wireless. He twiddled the dial to find the overseas wavelength of the BBC on which he heard confirmation of the king's death.

By then it was 2.45 p.m. local time and Philip was having a siesta, after having been up for most of the previous night. Parker woke him with the news. 'He looked absolutely flattened,' Parker later recalled, 'as if the world had collapsed on him. He saw immediately that the idyll of his life and their life together had come to an end. I never felt so sorry for anyone in my life.'[50] Philip said nothing to Parker, but breathed in twice very deeply as if in shock.[51] Then he composed himself and went to find Elizabeth. 'He said something like let's go for a little walk in the garden and look at the fish,' remembers Pamela Hicks, 'and so Mike and I watch and they're doing the naval quarter-deck thing of pacing up and turning back, pacing up, turning back, for a few minutes, and then, you know, they come back in and I, thinking that she had lost her father whom she loved, rushed up and gave her a hug and thought how awful for you, and then I suddenly thought, my God, she's queen, remember to curtsey. She was always so considerate and she just said, "I'm so sorry, it means we're all going to have to go back home".'

Soon afterwards, Martin Charteris arrived, having hurried over from his hotel, and found Elizabeth 'very composed, absolute master of her fate', at her desk drafting telegrams of apology for the curtail-ment of their tour. Philip was lying back on a sofa, his arms spread out, an open copy of *The Times* covering his face.

TWENTY

Oh, the Future!

When Philip married Elizabeth, George VI might have been expected to reign for at least another twenty years. The king was fifty-one at the time and his father George V had died aged seventy, his grandfather Edward VII at sixty-eight, his great-grandmother Queen Victoria at eighty-one, William IV at seventy-one and George III at eighty-one.

In the meantime, Philip would have hoped to forge ahead towards high command in the navy, while also enjoying a relatively carefree life ashore. The premature death of his father-in-law precluded all this. The change in Philip's life was always going to come sooner or later, but barely five years after his marriage, at the age of just thirty-one, was too soon for such a vigorous and headstrong young man to slip happily into his new role of walking a yard behind his wife at public functions.

His mother Alice was quick to appreciate his predicament. She had seen Philip in January shortly before he left for Kenya, when she stayed at Sandringham on her way to New York to raise funds for her sisterhood, and was teased by the queen for her 'very fetching' grey habit.[1] Alice was still in America when she heard that the king had died. 'All my thoughts are with you in this sad loss,' she wrote to Philip.

I know how fond you were of your father-in-law & how you will miss him. I think much of the change in your life this means. It means much more personal self-sacrifice, as I am fully aware, but every sacrifice brings its reward in a manner we cannot foresee. Such has been my experience in my own life with its many ups and downs. Remember that Papa with his brilliant brains & sportsman like outlook (such as you were alas! too young to know) will be with you in spirit. Commune with him & you will feel help & comfort in the responsible years to come as friend & adviser to your dear wife in her new position, who I also love as a daughter.[2]

Whether or not Philip took his mother's advice, he seemed to spend the first few months of his wife's reign in profoundly low spirits. On the day of the king's funeral, he was observed by his aunt Nada Milford Haven to be very thin, and he told her that 'his one idea was to get to Coustalado [her villa at Cannes] as soon as possible'.[3] His sister Margarita later noticed that he could hardly be persuaded to stir from his room at Clarence House.[4] 'You can imagine what's going to happen now,' he said to her, referring to the depressing prospect of moving to Buckingham Palace. His mood echoed Prince Albert's despairing entry in his diary soon after marrying Queen Victoria: 'Oh, the future!'

An assertive character, Philip had until that time been head of the family. 'I suppose I naturally filled the principal role,' he later recalled. 'People used to come to me and ask me what to do. In 1952 the whole thing changed, *very very* considerably.'[5] Elizabeth was now not only queen but also head of the family, and Philip was her subject, required in public to address her as 'Ma'am' and to bow when she entered the room. She had a definite position in the country; he did not. She possessed an abundance of qualities that would make her an excellent queen. His restless energy and strident opinions made him rather less obviously cut out to play the supporting role. Within a year of her accession, Churchill remarked of Elizabeth: 'All the film people in the world, if they had scoured the globe, could not have found anyone so suited for the part.'[6] Of her husband, the prime minister confided to an aide in June 1952 that, although he wished him no ill, he 'neither liked nor trusted him and only hoped he would not do the country any harm'.[7]

Elizabeth's accession had brought about a remarkable transformation in her previously diffident character. Soon after the death of her father, an old court favourite asked her whether Churchill was treating her as Melbourne had treated young Queen Victoria. 'Not at all,' she replied, 'I find him very obstinate.'[8] Around the same time, she told a friend: 'I no longer feel anxious or worried. I don't know what it is – but I have lost all my timidity somehow becoming the Sovereign and having to receive the Prime Minister.'[9] As Martin Charteris observed, while 'for the rest of us [courtiers], it was wonderful to behold … I can see that he [Philip] might have found it somewhat disconcerting'.[10]

Elizabeth's sudden pre-eminence had become apparent immediately on landing at London airport at dusk on 7 February 1952, after their sad flight home from Kenya. While the slight figure of the new queen descended the aircraft steps alone to be greeted by a tearful Churchill and a line of ministers dressed in black, Philip stayed out of sight aboard the plane until she was halfway down, and only then did he emerge to follow her.[11]

Next morning, the faithful consort offered Elizabeth his arm for the walk across the snowy courtyard from Clarence House to St James's Palace for the meeting of the Accession Council, which Harold Wilson later described as 'the most moving ceremonial I can recall'.[12] To the assembled privy counsellors, looking a little scruffy in their ration-book mourning clothes,[13] Elizabeth read out her formal declaration of sovereignty and ended by saying, 'My heart is too full for me to say more to you today than that I shall always work as my father did throughout his reign, to uphold the constitutional government and to advance the happiness and prosperity of my peoples … I pray that God will help me to discharge worthily this heavy task that has been laid on me so early in my life.' With that, Philip stepped forward and silently led her out to her car, where she broke down and wept.

While Elizabeth mourned her father, Philip mourned the end of his free life, and the year ahead was to be a bruising one for him as he struggled to find a new sense of purpose. As he recalled, 'there were plenty of people telling me what *not* to do. "You mustn't interfere with this." "Keep out." I had to try to support the queen as best I could without getting in the way. The difficulty was to find things that might be useful.'[14]

The comparison was continually made between his position and that of Prince Albert, his great-great-grandfather and immediate predecessor as prince consort, also an instinctive modernizer with a keen interest in science and industry. Yet the differences between them were far greater than any resemblances. While Albert had much to do as Queen Victoria's secretary and adviser, Elizabeth inherited an effective department of state in which her husband had no entitlement to lighten her burden, and he was continually warned by courtiers against straying into affairs that were not his concern.[15] Albert had become virtual ruler of England, so Disraeli once remarked, interviewing Queen Victoria's ministers, criticizing their submissions and drafting the queen's official letters and memoranda. Yet Philip was from the outset forbidden by the constitution from participating in politics and he neither desired nor was given the title of 'Prince Consort' which Victoria had conferred on Albert.

The Queen Mother was among those who were concerned by Philip's want of an official role, and soon after her husband's death she wrote to Sir Alan Lascelles suggesting that her son-in-law should play a part in organizing her daughter's crowning. Lascelles, mindful that Philip was 'insupportable when idle',[16] proposed to Churchill that he be made chairman of the Coronation Commission,[17] an august body that included the Archbishop of Canterbury and prime minister among others. The commission met for the first time on 5 May 1952, and quickly decided that the coronation would have to wait until the next year in view of the ongoing restoration of Westminster Abbey and the continuing economic crisis. 'Can't have coronations with bailiffs in the house,' said Churchill.[18]

In the meantime, Philip determined to act as Elizabeth's 'eyes and ears', taking advantage of his greater freedom to get around the country, visiting factories and coal mines, broadening her experience by proxy and keeping her informed about the state of public opinion. However, even on such forays, he ran the risk of causing offence. In late February, barely three weeks after Elizabeth's accession, the Conservative MP Enoch Powell complained to Churchill that Philip had visited the House of Commons to listen to a debate – something a royal consort had not done since 1846, according to Powell – and been seen to express his own opinions about what he heard in defiance of his constitutional position. The government chief whip agreed that Philip had not been 'exactly poker-faced', and the prince was quietly ticked off.[19]

Far more upsetting than this for Philip was the dispute over the royal family name. Two days after the king's death, Mountbatten had held a dinner party at Broadlands and triumphantly toasted the fact that the House of Mountbatten now reigned.* One of his guests, Prince Ernst August of Hanover, reported this to Queen Mary, who spent a sleepless night before summoning the prime minister's secretary, Jock Colville.

---

* Precedent was partially on Mountbatten's side: Victoria of Hanover and Albert of Saxe-Coburg-Gotha's son, Edward VII, reigned as a member of the House of Saxe-Coburg-Gotha. On the other hand, George V had demonstrated during the First World War that it was possible for a monarch to change the name of the royal house at will.

However supportive Queen Mary had once been of Philip, their disagreement over Gandhi's homespun wedding present had demonstrated that there were limits to her indulgence. In this instance she was adamant that her husband George V had founded the House of Windsor in perpetuity and that no 'Battenberg' marriage, however solemn and effective in English law, could change it.[20] 'What the devil does that damned fool Edinburgh think that the family name has to do with him,' she muttered.[21]

When Colville told Churchill about Mountbatten's presumption, the prime minister reportedly 'went through the roof'[22] and determined to reassure the dowager queen that there would be no change to the name and style of the ruling dynasty. The same day he consulted his cabinet which agreed 'strongly' that 'the Family name of Windsor should be retained' and invited the prime minister 'to take a suitable opportunity for making their views known to Her Majesty'.[23]

Philip, in fact, was not in favour of the name Mountbatten either, and instead he proposed as a compromise that his children should take the name of Edinburgh and that the royal house should be known as Windsor and Edinburgh. But Churchill was unsympathetic even to this proposal and gave 'a firm, negative answer'.[24] Thus, in early April Elizabeth formally announced that her royal house would be that of Windsor and that her descendants should bear that surname.[25] 'I hereby declare My Will and Pleasure that I and My children shall be styled and known as the House and Family of Windsor, and that my descendants who marry and their descendants, shall bear the name of Windsor.'[26] Harold Macmillan was not alone in deeming it 'a very good thing that the influence of the Consort and his family have had an early rebuff'.[27]

For the consort and his family, however, the rebuff was little short of an outrage. 'I am the only man in the country not allowed to give his name to his children,' said Philip.[28] 'I'm nothing but a bloody amoeba.' This latter assertion has often been misinterpreted as meaning that he felt reduced to the status of sperm factory, whereas, on the contrary, he was bemoaning the lack of recognition being given to his role in the reproductive process. 'He was deeply wounded,' remembered Mike Parker.[29] According to a relation, not being allowed to pass his name down to his children was 'the thing that hurt him most ... He had given up everything – and now this, the final insult. It was a terrible blow. It upset him very deeply and left him feeling unsettled and unhappy for a long while.'[30] It was not until eight years later, just before the birth of Prince Andrew, that a compromise was agreed whereby the name Mountbatten-Windsor was to be used in future for those of the queen's descendants who were not entitled to be called Royal Highness. But as far as Philip was concerned this was almost certainly too little, too late. The indomitable Mountbatten, meanwhile, continued to maintain that, although 'the House of Mountbatten only reigned for two months, from 8th February to 9th April 1952 ... historically it takes its place among the reigning houses of the United Kingdom'.[31]

Mountbatten later told Elizabeth Longford that he suspected the rejection of his name had to do with 'Beaverbrook's hatred of me coupled with Winston's disenchantment with what I did in India'.[32] There was some truth in this: as we have seen, Beaverbrook greatly disliked Mountbatten, and Churchill bore a grudge against him for, as he saw it, 'giving away' the Indian subcontinent in 1947.[33] However, the reservations about Mountbatten went considerably further than the prime minister and the *Express* newspaper proprietor. Senior courtiers had long feared that he would become a pernicious power behind the throne – there was talk that he was plotting to get Philip made king or king consort.[34] When the Duke of Windsor came over from America for his brother's funeral (having first learned of his death from newspaper reporters who flocked to the Waldorf Towers where he and the duchess were staying) he noted of Mountbatten that 'one can't pin much on him but he's very bossy & never stops talking. All are suspicious & watching his influence on Philip.'[35]

Mountbatten's daughter Patricia remembers that 'at that time there were a lot of people in the Establishment who persisted in regarding my father as rather pink – rather understandably. He was very progressive and it was thought that he could be quite dangerous by the old established courtiers and naughty old Churchill who never forgave my father for "giving away" India – can you imagine?'

Given the strength of her feelings for Philip, perhaps the most puzzling aspect of the whole episode is that Elizabeth should have gone along with this snub to her husband. She would doubtless have been influenced by the views of her mother and grandmother, both of whom strongly favoured the retention of the Windsor name, and by the assumption that any change would go against the wishes of her father – as expressed by the Lord Chancellor in his memorandum of 7 April:

> It may be assumed that He [George VI] expected to be succeeded by a daughter, but it is certain that it was His wish that the name of the Royal House should in that event continue to be Windsor. When he conferred a dukedom on HRH the Duke of Edinburgh he did not intend that the name of Edinburgh should supersede that of Windsor as the name of the Royal House ... Permanence and continuity are valuable factors in the maintenance of a constitutional monarchy and the name of the Royal House should not be changed if change can be avoided.[36]

But perhaps the decisive factor was that the issue came so early in the queen's reign, and if it hadn't been for the fact that Churchill was her first prime minister and he was giving her advice as to what was the best thing to do she would have stood up to it. 'I think if it had happened ten years later,' says one of Philip's relations, 'she would have said, "Oh, for goodness sake don't be silly ..." I think perhaps it *may* have spoiled things for a bit between them [Elizabeth and Philip].'[37]

The issue evidently troubled Elizabeth: the Conservative politician Rab Butler recalled that the only time he ever saw the normally composed queen close to tears was when she was discussing it.[38] In her marriage vows, she had managed to alienate both progressives and some traditionalists by promising to obey Philip, having 'always believed', so one authorized account had it, 'that the principle of the husband being head of the family is the only guarantee of happiness in the home'.[39]

As if to heighten Philip's sense of persecution, while the name of the royal house was being debated, the consort's throne was removed from the House of Lords in the mistaken belief that only a queen consort could sit on a throne and share the monarch's canopy at the State Opening of Parliament in November 1952. As a prince consort he would have to make do with a mere chair.[40] Reputedly seething at this injustice, the relegated Philip struck Cecil Beaton as 'nothing more than an adequate consort' when the photographer attended the State Opening, and furthermore appeared to be 'extremely ill, his eyes hollow and his pale hair already beginning to thin. I doubt if he will live long.'[41]

At every turn, there seemed to be an attempt to undermine Philip. Elizabeth sought to counterbalance the various slights by ensuring that he took 'Place, Pre-eminence and Precedence next to Her Majesty' and by having the 1937 Regency Act amended so that, when she was away, Philip and the Queen Mother would act as Counsellors of State, and he would become Regent (in place of Princess Margaret) in case Prince Charles should become king before the age of eighteen. Yet the latter was of almost no practical significance since the queen scarcely ever went abroad without her husband, and Charles was not destined to succeed as a minor.

When Elizabeth attempted to confer the cherished appointment of Colonel of the Grenadier Guards on Philip, the regiment's officers made it clear that, while they could not refuse to accept the prince as their new Colonel, they would not welcome him – presumably on account of his German ancestry. Rather than challenge this prejudice, the queen elected to ask a retired general to fill the post.[42]

There was further disappointment for Philip over where he and Elizabeth were to live. Reluctant to leave Clarence House, his first proper home since he was ten, and knowing that the Queen Mother did not want to move from Buckingham Palace either, he suggested that they all stay put, while the business of monarchy continued to be conducted from the Palace. However, the old guard of courtiers, led by Sir Alan Lascelles, who had automatically become Elizabeth's private secretary when she became queen, were adamant that the sovereign had to live at the Palace, which had been the principal state residence of the monarchy ever since the accession of Queen Victoria. Churchill, too, would not hear of the queen living elsewhere.

So, after spending Easter of 1952 at Windsor, Philip and Elizabeth moved into rooms on the ground floor of the north-west corner of Buckingham Palace, the so-called Belgian Suite which the king and queen had occupied during the war. The Queen Mother suggested that this arrangement would afford her the time to move out of her own suite on the first floor 'without any ghastly hurry'. She assured her daughter that she 'could be quite self contained upstairs, meals etc, and you would hardly know I was there … It is so angelic of you both to tell me I can stay on for a bit at B. P. and I am most grateful for your thoughtfulness. I know that it took Granny [Queen Mary] some months to pack up everything & I fear that I shall need some time too. But what is a few months in a lifetime anyway! Thank you darling for being such an angelic daughter.'[43] Philip, though, did not seem to respond well to their new quarters, and in June 1952 spent three weeks in bed with jaundice, a condition often associated with stress and depression.

Eventually, Philip and Elizabeth took over the first- and second-floor apartments on the north side of the central quadrangle. Above them on the top floor was the nursery, where the routine for Charles and Anne remained much the same as at Clarence House, although their parents jointly decided to put an end to the tradition that royal children should bow and curtsey on entering the presence of the sovereign.[44] The formalities persisted for the grown-ups, however, so that Queen Mary, the Queen Mother and Princess Margaret all curtseyed to the queen when they met in public.[45]

After the move to Buckingham Palace, Philip found that he was no longer master of his own house. The Palace was the sovereign's domain, and he was not the sovereign. The same went for Windsor.

At Clarence House, Philip had run what Mike Parker liked to call 'a tight ship', although, when the Duke of Windsor visited in February 1952, he found the atmosphere 'informal and friendly. Brave New World. Full of self-confidence and seem to take the job in their stride.'[46] Philip now decided to modernize things at the Palace. In the manner of a naval officer taking up a new command, within a few days of arriving at his new home he began an Organization and Methods Review, visiting every one of the six hundred-odd rooms in the Palace and asking everyone on the staff exactly what he or she was doing, and why.

The initiative did not go down well with some of the starchier courtiers, who distrusted Philip's reforming instincts and felt that the inner workings of the Palace were no legitimate concern of the consort. However, the deputy comptroller of supply and a veteran of three reigns later admitted that the questions Philip asked were 'exactly those which lots of us had wanted to ask for years',[47] and one of the younger courtiers, Edward Ford, recalled that the prince's arrival at the Palace was like 'a breath of fresh air'.[48]

Philip broke new ground by walking through the basement passages, carrying his own luggage and calling for any help he required rather than ringing a bell. Infuriated by any sort of time-wasting, he began ordering his sandwiches direct via a scribbled note, or telephoned the chefs' office himself – rather to their surprise – to explain his requirements. When electric frying pans came on the market, he took to cooking his own eggs and bacon in the morning in their private dining room – until Elizabeth complained that the smell lingered until lunchtime.

Perhaps because of the premature loss of his cherished professional career, Philip seemed determined to show that he was nonetheless still a man. 'I don't like to be "Highnessed",' he rebuked an obsequious woman. 'Just call me "Sir". This is the 20th century. You're not at King Arthur's court, you know!'[49] On another occasion he rounded on a footman who opened a door for his young son: 'He's not helpless. He's got hands, hasn't he?'[50] Such brusqueness was in part symptomatic of the frustrations Philip felt in acclimatizing to his new life, but there was also a sense in which, inspired by his uncle Dickie's radicalism, he envisaged a less stuffy and more popular monarchy, relevant to the lives of ordinary people.[51]

The move to Buckingham Palace had also entailed Philip acquiring his own office, which included five secretaries, two pages, two valets, a chauffeur, chief clerk, sergeant orderly and a police officer.[52] The secretaries, in particular, highlighted the gulf between Philip's office and the old guard of courtiers who presided over the queen's household, led by the antagonistic Tommy Lascelles. The girls in Philip's office tended to be considerably younger and prettier than those working with the queen's private secretary, and, according to one of them, the 'terrifying' Lascelles used to 'stare at them as if they were in the Folies Bergère'.[53]

Philip's office was run by Boy Browning, who, as Treasurer, not only oversaw his financial affairs, including the allocation of his Civil List allowance – then a relatively paltry £40,000 – but also acted as the main point of contact for Philip's numerous honorary appointments in the armed forces and his burgeoning portfolio of patronages. In the years before Elizabeth's accession, Philip had become involved with a number of organizations where he felt he could make a worthwhile contribution and the number of these now grew substantially, tending to be of a sporting, maritime, educational or scientific nature. He was rarely content to act merely as figurehead, although, because his time was limited, much of the work inevitably landed on Browning's desk – a load that eventually became too great for Browning, who, already experiencing tensions in his marriage to Daphne du Maurier, began drinking too much and eventually suffered a nervous breakdown.

Before that, on Philip's behalf, Browning had become deeply involved in the work of the National Playing Fields Association, the successful campaign to preserve the *Cutty Sark* (which was moved to its permanent berth at Greenwich in 1954 and opened by the queen in 1957), and the Duke of Edinburgh's Award Scheme. The latter was based on the ideas of Philip's old headmaster, Kurt Hahn, although when Philip first suggested it shortly after the coronation to the then education secretary, Sir David Eccles, it drew the supremely tactless response: 'I hear you're trying to invent something like the Hitler Youth!' As one senior courtier later observed: 'The insult to a man who had risked his life for Britain during the war was unforgivable and unforgettable.'[54]

Next to Browning in seniority was Mike Parker, who now became Philip's private secretary, followed by Squadron Leader Peter Horsley, an almost exact contemporary of Philip's, who joined the team as a full-time equerry-in-waiting. Despite the apparent respectability of his air force career – which he ended as Deputy Commander in Chief, Strike Command – Horsley was by some distance the least conventional member of the prince's entourage. As a wartime pilot in Mosquito night intruder operations, he had been shot down and his plane fell burning into the sea off Cherbourg. He spent three days in a tiny, storm-tossed rubber dinghy, which twice capsized before eventually he was rescued. During his subsequent rehabilitation at

Loughborough he fondly remembered a Belgian nurse who treated his severe state of the shivers by undressing, joining him in bed and warming him with her body.

As he recovered, Horsley became convinced that he had hovered between this world and the next, and that he had received messages from three fellow officers, including his navigator, whom he knew to be dead. His experiences engendered a fascination with the paranormal, one of several interests he was to share with Prince Philip.

Philip's interest in UFOs and related phenomena had been stimulated by discussions with his uncle, Dickie Mountbatten, who wrote in 1950 that flying saucers were 'not "aeroplanes" with silly little almost human pilots but themselves the actual inhabitants: Martians, Venusians, Jupiterians or what have you ... If they really come over in a big way that may settle the capitalist–communist war.' [55] Philip himself subscribed to the *Flying Saucer Review* and corresponded with the ufologist Timothy Good, self-proclaimed 'leading authority on UFOs and the alien presence – the most highly classified subject on Earth'. 'There are many reasons to believe that they exist,' the prince wrote to Good. 'There is so much evidence from reliable witnesses.' [56] In the period just after the coronation, he authorized Horsley to follow up any credible reports of sightings, and several witnesses were invited to Buckingham Palace to give their accounts to the prince and his equerry. In his eccentric memoir *Sounds from Another Room* (1997), Horsley later recalled having met during this time an extra-terrestrial creature called Janus, who observed that Prince Philip 'is a man of great vision, a person of world renown and a leader in the realm of wildlife and the environment. He is a man who believes strongly in the proper relationship between man and nature, which will prove of great importance in future galactic harmony.' [57]

Horsley conceded that he had never got as far as mentioning the encounter to Philip – or anyone else for that matter – at the time, explaining later that he was 'very busy and had to get on with my job'. He also admitted that he could not describe Janus, pleading that 'the room was poorly lit by two standard lamps and for the most part he sat in a deep chair by the side of a not very generous fire. In fact I never really got any physical impression of him.'[58]

While it was Parker who dealt with requests for Philip's engagements and handled the general correspondence, Horsley saw to the details of the engagements once they had been accepted, agreed the programmes and made the travel arrangements. In his memoirs he admitted to the occasional cock-up, such as when he muddled up places for a luncheon in Quebec, but Philip was admirably unfazed and seemed amused and told everyone to 'just sit anywhere'. The lunch was apparently a great success.

Horsley's other role was to push through arrangements for Philip to learn to fly, a long-held ambition of the prince's, although many, including Churchill, were very jumpy at the prospect. The dangers were underlined in the summer of 1952 at the Farnborough Air Display, where Philip met the celebrated test pilot John Derry the day before his plane broke up and fell to the ground, killing thirty-one people in the crowd as well as Derry himself. Philip was undeterred, however, and his determination eventually prevailed. The anxious brass hats were eventually persuaded of the likely advantages in saving time on one-day engagements and of the prince being able to take the controls in an emergency – not to mention saving him from the indignity of having to wear the uniform of a Marshal of the RAF (having sprung to the top rank in all services) without wings.

In November 1952 Philip went for his first lesson at White Waltham airfield, his instructor, Flight Lieutenant Caryl Gordon, having been made aware in blunt terms of the weight of his responsibility. 'If you kill him,' said his CO, 'you realise what it will do to the queen?'[59]

Despite this burden, Gordon established a good rapport with his novice. He was far from obsequious – which would not have endeared him – and on at least one occasion had a stern word with Philip about the dangers of overconfidence, which was apparently taken with good grace. When Philip completed his first solo flight in a Chipmunk just before Christmas, after only ten hours of flying, Gordon recorded, however, that 'His take-off, circuit and landing were beyond reproach'. A month later, Gordon watched anxiously as Philip completed his first solo spin, and admitted to being 'perturbed at the number of turns he completed before recovering'.[60]

Philip eventually received his wings on 4 May 1953, a month before the coronation and a few weeks before his thirty-second birthday. Determined to log as many hours as possible, he went on to become a highly skilled pilot, frequently flying his family up to Balmoral, and later taking Charles back for the start of the new term at Gordonstoun. Besides its technical attractions, flying had the benefit for Philip of taking his mind off the drawbacks of his life as consort, as there was no time to think about anything else once he was at the controls.[61]

Other welcome distractions for Philip during this time included racing his 20-ft Flying Fifteen keelboat *Coweslip* on the Solent with its designer Uffa Fox, who became a good friend; and punt-gunning – stalking wildfowl in a punt with a large mounted shotgun – around the Wash with the actor James Robertson Justice, one of his cronies from the Thursday Club whom Elizabeth collectively referred to as 'Philip's funny friends'. Fourteen years Philip's senior, Robertson Justice was a Falstaffian figure whose eventful career had included spells with the Canadian Mounties and with the International Brigade during the Spanish Civil War, when he was said to have halted a charge by pointing to the sky and exclaiming: 'Look! Greylag geese!' His rumbustious nature made Elizabeth rather uneasy about their punt-gunning expeditions, particularly since she knew that the high-calibre charges they used had already caused several accidents.[62]

Accompanying them on some of these expeditions was Peter Scott, an equally vibrant character, the only child of Captain Robert Falcon Scott, who had perished in the Antarctic in 1912 when Peter was three. Captain Scott's last message to his wife had been to encourage his son to develop an interest in natural history – better than games, he said – but Scott junior excelled at both, winning a bronze medal at the 1936 Olympics as a single-handed yachtsman and founding the famous wildfowl and wetlands reserve at Slimbridge in 1946. A talented artist to boot, he had sketched the young Princesses Elizabeth and Margaret, and further supplemented his income as part of the BBC commentary team for the marriage of Philip and Elizabeth.

After the wedding, Scott had become another of Philip's regular sailing companions, and he also looked after the five young Trumpeter swans which had been given to Philip and Elizabeth on their tour of Canada. In April 1952 they visited Slimbridge to inspect them, prompting Scott to write earnestly in his annual report: 'Her Majesty's gracious interest in the Trust's progress is, of course, a source of great gratification to all those who have our cause at heart.' Scott's biographer Elspeth Huxley charged him with having an 'excessive regard for royalty', yet, whatever his motivation, it was Scott who first interested Philip in birdwatching, and their burgeoning friendship would lead to the prince's eventual involvement in the World Wildlife Fund in the 1960s.

Men such as Uffa Fox, James Robertson Justice and Peter Scott were especially important to Philip during this period in view of the fact that, of his two closest childhood friends, Alex Wernher had been killed in the war and David Milford Haven had blotted his copybook by trading on having been Philip's best man to advance his business career. 'On the day he [Milford Haven] looked handsome and the bridesmaids all thought he was very good news,' recalls Lady Pamela Hicks, 'but as best man in retrospect he put his foot in it. It was so embarrassing for Prince Philip, because he was up against those hostile courtiers, everybody was against him, and all he could do was to produce his best friend and first cousin, who then as his only contribution to the wedding, did what all the courtiers expected … it was bad, bad, bad, bad – to such an extent that it was a long time before he was invited back to the Palace.'[63] Milford Haven went on to lead a rather rackety life, his name romantically linked to a string of beautiful women, including Princess Margaret and Eva Bartok, the Hungarian-born actress, whom he introduced to the teachings of the Indonesian guru Pak Subuh. Twice married, he died in 1970, aged fifty, leaving a widow and two young sons.

TWENTY-ONE

Her Liege Man

Despite the ructions behind Palace doors, by the autumn of 1952 Philip gave the impression at least of adjusting well to his new role. In November, Marina Kent told Dickie Mountbatten that she thought her cousin was 'coping with it in the right way. He has a charming "approach" with people & an easy manner & speaks (it seems) very well in public. Never too much in the background & yet not too much in front. Has his own opinions & plays an intelligent part in things. I think & pray "They" are very happy.'[1]

The following spring, when Violet Bonham Carter attended the coronation production of *Henry VIII* at the Old Vic, in the interval she had a long talk with Philip whom she found 'very easy'. 'He has a touch of German "thoroughness" – talking of a survey of a town in which boys' and girls' games had been analysed – the boys always playing in teams & the girls specializing in individual performance, like skipping. But I thought him lively, natural and agreeable. There is no doubt that the longer "royalties" have had out of the compound the better they are at their job.'[2]

His star was also now standing higher with the wider public, who appreciated his ability to connect with the man in the street and to talk bluff common sense to factory owners. When the *Daily Mirror* polled its readers in February 1953, 42,680 thought that Philip should be at his wife's side during the coronation ceremony in the Abbey, while just 432 thought that the ceremony should centre entirely on the queen. 'These figures show overwhelmingly Britain's affection and high regard for Philip,' declared the paper's editorial. 'The people think he is a fine man doing a fine job. The *Daily Mirror* agrees.'[3]

In the *Sunday Dispatch* in April, the editor of *Burke's Peerage*, Leslie Pine, went further: 'The Duke of Edinburgh has a prestige (apart from his great popularity) at the beginning of his career equal to that of his great-great grandfather [Albert] at the end of his life. The Queen has at her side a man of character and ability, proven in war and in peace, to assist her in the heavy responsibilities ahead.'[4]

By this time the country was reaching fever pitch in anticipation of the coronation, the preparations for which Philip had been overseeing as chairman of the Coronation Commission. The appointed day was 2 June 1953, a Tuesday, the day before Derby Day, and held by meteorologists to be the sunniest in the calendar.

The efficient organization of the occasion owed something to Philip's youthful and energetic chairmanship, but the principal choreographer was the commission's vice-chairman, the Duke of Norfolk, hereditary Earl Marshal of England, a robust and occasionally crotchety former army officer with a near religious devotion to the turf. In the run-up to the event, Norfolk was approached by a peer who was worried he might not be invited on account of his divorce. 'Good God, man,' said the duke. 'This is a coronation, not Royal Ascot.'[5] He was no highbrow and, as a young man, he had, as Kenneth Rose put it, 'failed to pass what in those days was an undemanding entrance examination to Christ Church, Oxford, particularly when the candidate was a duke'.[6] But no one disputed his expertise in organizing state ceremonials: he had previously masterminded both the funeral of George V and the coronation of George VI. Shortly before the coronation, he calmly told Mike Parker that the crown would go on Elizabeth's head at '12.34, give or take a few seconds',[7] and he left no one in any doubt as to who was in charge. 'If the bishops don't learn to walk in step, we'll be here all night,' he barked during the rehearsals in the Abbey.[8]

In the weeks before the event, newspapers seemed to carry virtually no stories that were not in some way related to the coronation. Houses were decorated in red, white and blue, car aerials fluttered with Union Jacks, and streets were made ready for parties. It was to be the victory celebration that austerity had postponed.[9] 'Never has there been such excitement,' wrote Jock Colville, 'never has a monarch received such adulation.'[10] The adulation was particularly important at this time because, as Churchill expressed it, the crown had come to be 'far more broadly and securely based on the people's love and the nation's will than in the sedate days … when rank and privilege ruled society'.[11]

On coronation eve, the route to the Abbey was lined with half a million people, stoically camping out for a night of incessant rain. Their 'extraordinary stillness and tranquillity' was noticed, as was the fact that many people went to church to pray, take communion, and to meditate.[12]

Coronation day also began dull and drizzly, despite the assurances of the weathermen. However, morning newspapers carried the uplifting headlines that Mount Everest had been conquered for the first time by a British-led team, of which Philip happened to be patron. Although it was a beekeeper from New Zealand, Edmund Hillary, and a Nepalese sherpa, Tenzing Norgay, who had actually reached the summit, the news was broadcast through loudspeakers to the crowds along the coronation route as if it were very much a British achievement, an auspicious symbol of the New Elizabethan Age. The expedition leader, John Hunt, became the first director of the Duke of Edinburgh's Award scheme.

The horse-drawn processions to Westminster Abbey began at eight o'clock in the morning, with the elaborate coach of the Lord Mayor of London, followed later by various senior members of the royal family, colonial rulers and prime ministers and heads of state of the

Commonwealth. The star of the parade was the great big Queen Salote of Tonga, 'the tallest Queen of the smallest kingdom', waving merrily at the crowd from her open carriage, impervious to the cold and rain. With her travelled the frail little figure of the Sultan of Kelantan. 'Who's that?' someone supposedly asked Noël Coward as he watched the procession on television. 'Her lunch,' replied Coward.[13]

Junior members of the royal family were driven to the Abbey in cars. They included the Mountbatten family, among them Philip's mother, Alice, wearing her long, grey nun's robe which she had had newly made for the occasion, and in which she presented a striking image as she made her stately progress up the aisle of the Abbey. With her were Philip's three surviving sisters, Theodora, Margarita and Sophie, and their German husbands. They were all seated in the royal box behind the Queen Mother, the royal princesses and four-year-old Prince Charles, in white satin suit and Brilliantined hair, making his first ceremonial appearance.[14] After having been excluded from the wedding, Philip's sisters had been all the more determined to be there this time and had 'fixed that in Philip's mind!!!' shortly after Elizabeth's accession, so Margarita told Dickie Mountbatten.[15] After some discussion, it was judged that enough time had elapsed since the war for their presence not to raise a furore, although they were strictly rationed to two children each, and other German relations were 'firmly put off'[16] – as was the Duke of Windsor.

Philip's aunt Louise was also excluded, much to her annoyance, as was Queen Frederika. Another notable absentee was Queen Mary, who had died a little over two months earlier, having thoughtfully left instructions that court mourning was not to interfere with her granddaughter's coronation.

Philip and Elizabeth had spent the preceding days attending various celebratory parties, including the Household Brigade's Coronation Ball at Hampton Court on 29 May, and a prime ministers' lunch for Commonwealth leaders at Buckingham Palace. Much of their spare time was devoted to rehearsing their coronation routines in the Palace ballroom, tying bed sheets together to imitate the movements of Elizabeth's 60-ft coronation train. Philip, as usual, could not resist making light of some of the proceedings. 'Don't be silly,' Elizabeth rebuked him on at least one occasion. 'Come back here and do it again properly.'[17] She reportedly also begged the Bishop of Durham, Michael Ramsey – whose job was to stand at her right-hand side as her chief supporter – to keep his expressive eyebrows still 'because they made her smile and she did not wish to smile in the wrong place'.[18]

On the actual day, Philip wore his new uniform of Admiral of the Fleet, complete with cocked hat, gold bullion epaulettes and Garter Star.[19] He and Elizabeth arrived at the Abbey at eleven o'clock, having travelled there in the four-tonne State Coach, drawn by eight greys and attended by scarlet and-gold-coated Beefeaters and postilions. But, although they arrived together, Philip did not walk down the aisle beside Elizabeth, as the Queen Mother had with George VI at his coronation, but instead formed part of the procession that preceded the queen. 'That was very much the advice of Tommy Lascelles,' recalled Lord Charteris. 'It looked *awful*. When they shouted *Vivat! Vivat Regina!* she was on her own … It was not calculated to make him feel cheerful.'[20]

The same might have been said of the overall significance of the coronation as far as Philip was concerned. Formally dedicating his life to playing the supporting role to his wife went against the grain of his overtly masculine character, yet he was the first of the senior peers to pay homage to her after her crowning. 'I Philip, Duke of Edinburgh, do become your liege man of life and limb and of earthly worship,' he vowed, kneeling before her and placing his hands between hers; 'and faith and truth I will bear unto you, to live and die against all manner of folks. So help me God.' On rising to his feet, he then touched her crown and kissed her on the cheek.[21]

* * *

All this was watched subsequently by a worldwide cinema audience of 350 million. In Britain, the live radio broadcast of the coronation reached eleven million licensed British wirelesses and the live television pictures appeared on two and a half million television sets in the country, a fifth of which had been bought in the last few weeks before the coronation. The queen had initially been reluctant to have the service televised, fearful of the additional strain on her and that it might detract from the dignity of the occasion. Philip backed her at first, his concern for her welfare overriding his instinctive modernizer's urge to bring the monarchy closer to the lives of ordinary people.[22] But the force of public protest soon changed everyone's mind and a compromise was agreed whereby cameras were allowed to film virtually everything apart from the most sacred parts of the ceremony – the queen's anointing and her taking of communion.[23] They were supposedly also excluded from taking close-ups of her, although that rule was broken as she walked back down the aisle after having been crowned.

The BBC television commentator, Richard Dimbleby, had done his final preparations aboard his Dutch sailing barge, which he had sailed up the Thames from Chichester and slept on for the duration of the coronation celebrations. Moored close to Westminster Pier, it afforded him far better access to the Abbey than any alternative lodging place, he reasoned.[24] In his commentary, Dimbleby perfectly caught the euphoria and expectancy of the new reign, his descriptions adding colour to the black and white images on television screens. In his diary he recorded that he would 'never forget those hours in the Abbey, when the whole nation was swept by the same sense of love and pride that filled those of us standing so near the Queen'. However, he was also dismayed by the seedy detritus left behind by the peers on their benches in the Abbey: 'sandwich wrappings, sandwiches, morning newspapers, fruit peel, sweets and even empty miniature bottles'.[25]

For Elizabeth, meanwhile, probably the most disappointing feature of the day was that, on emerging from Westminster Abbey, her sister, Princess Margaret, had been observed by journalists to affectionately flick a piece of fluff from the uniform of Group Captain Peter Townsend, the divorced Battle of Britain ace who was by then Comptroller of the Queen Mother's household. Elizabeth had known about their romance since the beginning of the year, and had discussed with them their predicament over dinner at Buckingham Palace with Philip – whose attempts to lighten the atmosphere with some light-hearted banter had not gone down especially well. Elizabeth had expressed her sympathy for the couple's plight, yet in view of the forthcoming coronation she had pleaded for them to wait a year. Margaret's careless gesture 'disastrously sabotaged the agreement that the romance should remain secret', according to Elizabeth's biographer Robert Lacey, and hence the new reign was 'instantly shadowed by the spectres of divorce and scandal that had marked the abdication'.[26]

On the day itself, Elizabeth and Philip had been oblivious to the furore, and had themselves returned after the service in the State Coach to Buckingham Palace, where they posed for photographs taken by Cecil Beaton – who was relieved to have been chosen by Elizabeth as the official photographer in view of Philip's obvious preference for Baron, the prince's 'most unexpected friend', as Beaton sniffily described him in his diary.[27] As they gathered for the photo shoot in the Green Drawing Room, Beaton recorded that Philip

stood by making wry jokes, his lips pursed in a smile that put the fear of God into me. This is a pity because, although I am not one for 'Navy type' jokes, and obviously have nothing in common with him, I admire him enormously, and think he is absolutely first-rate at his job of making things comparatively lively and putting people at their ease. Perhaps he was disappointed that his friend, Baron, was not doing this job today; whatever the reason he definitely adopted a rather ragging attitude towards proceedings.[28]

The photographer also complained that Philip's grin ruined several shots taken with the queen, although when he photographed the consort alone 'in spite of his preconceived notions he was flattered by my attentions'.[29]

Philip would continue to exhibit a ragging attitude throughout his time as consort. It was intrinsic to his character. It also served as a means of release from his straitjacketed existence, Elizabeth's coronation having put the final seal on the sacrifice he had made of his freedom. Having also relinquished his cherished naval career, he was obliged to channel his energies into his new responsibilities, only driven now by his strong sense of duty rather than by his passion.

He had already done much to help Elizabeth in her public duties, enabling her to overcome her shyness in the same way that the Queen Mother had with the stammering George VI.[30] If he occasionally outshone her – as on the Canadian tour – for the most part during these early years he had stayed deliberately in her shadow, playing the supportive role, bolstering her confidence in private and acting as backup in public.[31] In 1957, *Time* magazine credited him 'for the fact that his mousy, slightly frumpy and occasionally frosty bride has blossomed into a self-confidently stylish and often radiantly warm young matron'.[32]

Her transformation owed much to the strength and sense of stability that she derived from their marriage. Those who did not know them better were sometimes taken aback by the cross words that passed between them. 'How bloody stupid!' or 'Don't talk such rubbish!' Philip might say if he disagreed with something his wife had said. The break-up of his family when he was ten had helped to make him a strikingly self-reliant character, but his toughness and refusal to kowtow was a big part of why she loved him.

Elizabeth would sometimes give as good as she got, but at others she deemed it more sensible to keep her head down until the storm had passed. 'I'm not going to come out of my cabin until he is in a better temper,' she told one courtier after a row on the royal yacht *Britannia*. 'I'm going to sit here on my bed until he's better.'[33] But as well as the quarrels there always seemed to be plenty of laughter, and, although some thought Philip something of a 'cold fish', others witnessed a great deal of sensitivity and tenderness. The overriding impression seems to have been of a distinctly happy union.

In the evening, he often attended dinners alone and gave speeches while she remained behind to work on her boxes or watch television or do the crossword. During the day, however, they were in almost constant touch, often breakfasting together, working in adjoining offices on an upper floor at the Palace, lunching together and carrying out many of their engagements as a couple.

Here, too, he was an invaluable foil. Elizabeth was not good at putting people at their ease. Her conversational gambits tended to be too stiff and her smile too controlled to be encouraging. Frequently, there would loom the awkward possibility of utter silence in her presence, at which point Philip was adept at sauntering up and saying something that somehow diffused all the tension and allowed conversation to flow. His breezy irreverence was evident even at formal dinners at Buckingham Palace, when he was apt to examine a menu written in elaborate French and remark cheerily to the guests: 'Ah, good. Fish and chips again.'

Yet alongside this informality and self-confidence there was a surprising touchiness, again presumed by those who knew him to stem from his unsettled youth. 'He has never had the love,' said one friend. 'There was no one really close – that day-to-day parental contact you need to smooth off the rough edges. That's where his rudeness comes from – not enough slap-down when it mattered.'[34]

One of the reasons that biographers keep returning to Prince Philip is that, quite apart from his unique position in the life of the nation, his character is so full of paradoxes. He is intelligent and enquiring, interested in psychology, philosophy and religion, as well as in science, technology and the natural world. Nevertheless, his ideas are not always well thought through. While he goes to great lengths to keep himself well informed he has been known to hold forth on a subject in which he is not well versed in front of an audience who are. Dynamic, driven, outspoken and prone to explosions of both ardour and anger, he was never cut out by temperament for a secondary role; however, that is what he ultimately chose for himself. 'Still he puzzles me,' wrote one of his authorized biographers, Tim Heald. 'Real humility sits uneasily alongside apparent arrogance, energy and optimism with sudden cold douches of cold water; real kindnesses are mingled with inexplicable snubs; certainty and uncertainty, sensitivity and insensitivity, walk hand in hand. He is gregarious, he is a loner; he loves argument, he hates to lose one … These apparent inconsistencies certainly make him intriguing but they also make him exasperating. He is energetic, mercurial, quixotic, and ultimately impossible to pin down – partly on purpose.'[35]

Philip never liked sycophancy, yet neither did he take well to criticism. Throughout his public life, he exhibited a contempt for journalists, and yet he also collected cartoons that were aimed at himself. If he was sometimes contemptuous of those who reported his diplomatic faux pas, he was nevertheless also happy to declare himself a specialist in 'dontopedalogy', as he called it, 'the science of opening your mouth and putting your foot in it'. He could be a martinet and a bully – especially towards his eldest son – however, at other times he was disarmingly sensitive towards the plight of others, and he demonstrated a soft spot for the underdog. The contradictions seem to be endless. Yet nobody can dispute that he has performed his principal role of supporting the queen with utter devotion.

'I've no doubt that he had a very wholesome effect on her,' says one diplomat. 'He helped to make her what she's become. She is very shrewd but she had a protective shell around her, and he brought her out of it. We are extremely fortunate that he married her.'[36]

NOTES

The following abbreviations are used in the source notes:

ADM – Admiralty Office Papers, National Archives
BA – Broadlands Archives
BL – British Library
BP – Buckingham Palace Archives
CAB – Cabinet Office Papers, National Archives
FO – Foreign Office Papers, National Archives
GMH – George, Marquess of Milford Haven
GV – King George V
HSA – Hesse State Archives, Darmstadt
MP – Mountbatten Papers, University of Southampton
NK – Nona Kerr
RA – Royal Archives
UT – Binswanger Papers, University of Tübingen
VMH – Victoria, Marchioness of Milford Haven
WORK – Ministry of Works and Pensions Papers, National Archives

Prologue

1. *The Times*, 17 November 1937, p. 16.
2. 6 December 1935, BP, cited in Hough, *Louis and Victoria*, p. 363.
3. *The Times*, 17 November 1937.

4. Ibid.
5. *Time* magazine, 29 November 1937.
6. *New York Times*, 29 November 1937.
7. Hugo Vickers, *Alice: Princess Andrew of Greece*, p. 273.
8. *Gordonstoun Record*, 1947.
9. Jonathan Petropoulos, *Royals and the Reich*, p. 94.
10. Ibid., pp. 94–5.

One: Kings of Greece

1. Basil Boothroyd, *Philip: An Informal Biography*, p. 54.
2. Georgina Battiscombe, *Queen Alexandra*, pp. 4–5.
3. Miranda Carter, *The Three Emperors*, p. 39.
4. Ibid.
5. Battiscombe, pp. 8–9.
6. British, Russian, Greek, Norwegian, Belgian, Romanian, Yugoslav, Spanish and Danish.
7. Prince Christopher of Greece, *Memoirs*, p. 29.
8. Sir Horace Rumbold, *Recollections of a Diplomatist*, vol. II, pp. 125–6.
9. E. F. Benson, *As We Were*, p. 158.
10. Lloyd C. Griscom, *Diplomatically Speaking*, p.138.
11. Rumbold, p. 137.
12. Roger Fulford, ed., *Your Dear Letter*, p. 147.
13. Grand Duchess George of Russia, *A Romanov Diary*, p. 2.
14. Ibid.
15. Tim Heald, *The Duke*, p. 76.
16. Prince Nicholas of Greece, *My Fifty Years*, p. 22.
17. Cited in Celia Bertin, *Marie Bonaparte*, p. 92.
18. Sarah Bradford, *Elizabeth*, p. 82.
19. Christopher, p.16.
20. James Pope-Hennessy, *Queen Mary*, pp. 256–7.
21. Christopher, p. 29.
22. Nicholas, p. 33.
23. Boothroyd, p. 68.
24. Christopher, p. 44.
25. Benson, pp. 154–7.
26. Nicholas, p. 91.
27. Heald, p. 17.
28. Christopher, p. 43.

29. Boothroyd, pp. 67–8.
30. Ibid., p. 69.

Two: House of Battenberg

1. See Maurice Paleologue, *The Tragic Romance of Alexander II*, and Prince Von Bülow, *Memoirs*, vol. 4, pp. 384–5.
2. Prince Louis of Battenberg *Recollections*, pp. 93 and 75, MP.
3. Laura Beatty, *Lillie Langtry*, p. 179.
4. Ibid.
5. VMH *Recollections*, p.49, unpublished, MP.
6. Richard Hough, *Mountbatten: Hero of Our Time*, p.15.
7. Ibid.
8. Vickers, *Alice*, p. 8.
9. Philip Ziegler, *Mountbatten*, p. 24.
10. VMH, p.122.
11. Meriel Buchanan, *Queen Victoria's Relations*, p. 173.
12. Ibid.
13. VMH, p. 149.
14. Hough, *Louis and Victoria*, p. 176.
15. Queen Alexandra of Yugoslavia, *Prince Philip: A Family Portrait*, p. 27.
16. Vickers, *Alice*, p. 52.
17. VMH, p. 216.
18. Buchanan, p. 175.
19. Grand Duchess of Mecklenburg-Strelitz to QM (Princess of Wales), 20 May 1903, RA GV/CC/30/36, cited in Vickers, *Alice*, pp. 58–60.
20. Mark Kerr, *Land, Sea and Air*, pp. 129–30.
21. *New York Times*, 27 September 1903.
22. Alexandra, p. 27.
23. Prince Andrew of Greece, *Towards Disaster*, preface, p. v.
24. *Acropolis*, 14 February 1907, *Chronos*, 15 February 1907, cited in Sir F. Elliot to Sir E. Grey, 4 March 1907, FO 286/507.
25. Sir F. Elliot to Sir E. Grey, 4 March 1907, FO 286/507.
26. Andrew, pp. vi–vii.
27. Christopher Warwick, *Ella*, p. 219.
28. Vickers, *Alice*, p. 94.
29. 26 October 1912, MP, MB1/A2.
30. Ibid.
31. 2 November 1912, copy in HSA.

32. Nona Kerr to VMH, 13 November and 1 December 1912, BP, cited in Vickers, *Alice*, pp. 101–2.

33. Sir F. Elliot to Sir E. Grey, 1 April 1913, FO 285/558.

34. Ibid.

35. Ibid.

36. Boothroyd, p. 15.

37. Hough, *Louis and Victoria*, p. 335.

38. Kenneth Rose, *George V*, p. 171.

39. Ibid.

40. Martin Gilbert, *Winston Churchill*, vol. III, pp. 147–9.

41. Rose, *George V*, p. 172.

42. Ziegler, *Mountbatten*, p. 36.

43. Obituary of Princess George of Hanover, *Daily Telegraph*, 30 November 2001.

44. Buchanan, p. 183.

45. Rose, *George V*, p. 174.

46. Hough, *Louis and Victoria*, p. 320.

47. Ziegler, *Mountbatten*, p. 44; Mark Kerr, *Prince Louis of Battenberg*, p. 289.

48. Rose, *George V*, pp. 212–17.

49. Andrew, p. ix.

50. Giles Milton, *Paradise Lost*, p. 207.

Three: Boy's Own Story

1. Alexandra, p. 32.

2. VMH to Nona Kerr, 28 February 1921, BA, cited in Vickers, *Alice*, p. 151.

3. HRH Grand Duchess of Hesse, the wife of Victoria's brother, Ernie.

4. Alice to Grand Duchess Eleonore of Hesse, 3 July 1921, HSA.

5. Douglas Liversidge, *Prince Philip*, p. 14.

6. Andrew, p. 23.

7. Michael Llewellyn-Smith, *Ionian Vision*, p. 224.

8. Andrew, pp. 26–9.

9. Alice to Grand Duchess Eleonore of Hesse, 3 July 1921, HSA.

10. Lord Kinross, *Atatürk*, pp. 268–9.

11. Ibid., p. 227.

12. Hough, *Louis and Victoria*, p. 333.

13. Andrew, p. 26.

14. Ibid., p. 118.
15. Ibid., p. 221.
16. Ibid., pp. 189–90.
17. Ibid., p. 236.
18. Ibid., p. 239.
19. Ibid., p. 293; Llewellyn-Smith, pp. 244–6.
20. VMH to GMH, 24 April 1922, MP, MB1/Y27.
21. VMH to NK, 20 March 1922, BA, cited in Vickers, *Alice*, p. 158.
22. VMH to GMH, 7 May 1922, MP, MB1/Y27.
23. Louise to NK, 21 March 1922, BA, cited in Vickers, *Alice*, p. 159.
24. VMH to GMH, 27 March 1922, MP, MB1/Y27.
25. Ziegler, *Mountbatten*, p. 69.
26. Andrew, p. 289.
27. C. H. Bentinck to Lord Curzon, 6 September 1922, FO 371/7585, p.104.
28. Francis Lindley to FO, 29 September 1922, FO 371/7585, p. 195.
29. Lindley to FO, 1 October 1922, FO 371/7585, p. 205.
30. VMH to Mountbatten, 25 October 1922, and VMH to NK, 28 October 1922, BA, cited in Vickers, *Alice*, pp. 163–4.
31. Lindley to FO, 3 November 1922, FO 371/5786 and Col. Hoare Nairn to Bentinck, 2 December 1922, FO 421/303, p. 181.
32. Alice to VMH, circa 9 September 1922, passed to KGV; RA PS/GV/M 1823/2.
33. *Daily Express*, 29 December 1922.
34. Christopher, pp. 174–5.
35. Curzon to Crowe, 29 November 1922, RA GV/M 1823/17, cited in Vickers, *Alice*, p. 169.
36. Stamfordham to VMH, 8 December 1922, RA PS/GV/M 1823/56, cited in Vickers, *Alice*, p. 174.
37. Vickers, *Alice*, p. 168.
38. Hough, *Louis and Victoria*, p. 348.
39. Curzon to Athens No. 5, 28 November 1922, RA PS/PSO/ GV/C/M/1823/17.
40. Sir R. Graham to Curzon, 7 December 1922, FO 421/303, p. 185.
41. Llewellyn-Smith, p. 329, Bentinck to Curzon, 8 December 1922, FO 421/303 no. 108.
42. Llewellyn-Smith, pp. 565–6.
43. Lindley, telegram, 8.30 p.m., 28 November 1922, RA PS/GV/ M1823/15.
44. Ibid.

45. Bentinck to Crowe, 29 November 1922, RA PS/GV/M 1823/23.

46. *New York Times*, 3 December 1922.

47. Boothroyd, p. 75.

48. Bentinck to Curzon, 3 December 1922, FO 421/303, pp. 174–5.

49. Ibid.

50. Bentinck to Curzon, 4 December 1922, FO 421/303, p. 183.

51. Graham to Curzon, 7 December 1922, FO 421/303, p. 185.

52. Heald, pp. 11–13.

53. Gyles Brandreth, *Philip & Elizabeth*, p. 70.

Four: Family in Flight

1. Captain H. A. Buchanan-Wollaston, RN, to his aunt, 6 December 1922; cited in Boothroyd, pp. 80–81.

2. *New York Times*, 7 December 1922.

3. Sir R. Graham to Curzon, 7 December 1922, FO 412/303, pp. 185–6.

4. *New York Times*, 8 December 1922.

5. Col. Waterhouse to Lord Stamfordham, record of telephone message from Downing Street, 4 December 1922, RA PS/GV/M 1823/45, cited in Vickers, *Alice*, p. 172.

6. Ibid.

7. Stamfordham to VMH, 8 December 1922, RA PS/GV/M 1823/56, cited in Vickers, *Alice*, p. 174.

8. RA GV/PRIV/GVD, 19 December 1922.

9. Louise to NK, 20 January 1923, BA, cited in Vickers, *Alice*, p. 176.

10. *New York Times*, 27 December 1922.

11. Prince Andrew of Greece to Sir Gerald Talbot, 29 May 1923, FO 286/862.

12. *New York Times*, 27 December 1922.

13. Ibid., 24 June 1908.

14. Ibid., 18 January 1923.

15. Bentinck to Curzon, 13 January 1923, FO 286/862.

16. *New York Times*, 18 January 1923.

17. *New York Times*, 27 January 1923.

18. Ibid., 21 March 1923.

19. Stelio Hourmouzios, *No Ordinary Crown*, p. 57.

20. Celia Bertin, *Marie Bonaparte*, p. 94.

21. Ibid., pp. 85–6.

22. Ibid., p. 94.

23. Vickers, *Alice*, p. 178.
24. *New York Times*, 27 December 1922.
25. Heald, p. 32.
26. Prince Andrew to Sir Gerald Talbot, 29 May 1923, FO 286/862.
27. Prince Andrew to Bentinck, 29 May 1923, FO 286/862.
28. Patrick Ramsay to Col. Sir Clive Wigram, 23 May 1931, FO 371/15240, p. 87.
29. Hourmouzios, p. 284.
30. Boothroyd, p. 112.
31. Janet Morgan, *Edwina Mountbatten*, p. 98.
32. Heald, p. 33.
33. Alexandra, p. 43.
34. Ibid., p. 42.
35. Hough, *Louis and Victoria*, p. 351.
36. Heald, p. 33.
37. *The Times*, 19 December 1923.
38. Ibid., 20 February 1924.
39. Ibid., 26 March 1924.
40. Boothroyd, p. 109.
41. Louise to NK, 28 July 1923, BA, cited in Vickers, *Alice*, p. 191.
42. Hough, *Louis and Victoria*, p. 351; Alice to NK, 30 October 1924, BA.
43. Hélène Cordet, *Born Bewildered*, p. 18.
44. *Look* magazine, June 1954, cited in John Parker, *Prince Philip*, p. 36.
45. Cordet, p. 20.
46. Ibid., p. 27.
47. Alexandra, p. 38.
48. Heald, p. 35; Alexandra, p. 39.
49. Boothroyd, p. 109.
50. Ibid.
51. Ivor Porter, *Michael of Romania*, pp. 24–7.
52. Ibid., p. 27.
53. Alexandra, p. 40.
54. Hough, *Louis and Victoria*, p. 351.
55. VMH to NK, 20 June 1926, BA, cited in Hough, *Louis and Victoria*, p. 352.
56. Ibid., 21 August 1926, BA, cited in Hough, *Louis and Victoria*, p. 352.
57. Vickers, *Alice*, pp. 193–5.
58. Herbert Jacobs, *Schoolmaster of Kings*, p.48.
59. Boothroyd, p. 112.

60. *Christian Science Monitor*, 27 November 1947.
61. Jacobs, p. 61.
62. Liversidge, pp. 39–40, original source *Christian Science Monitor*, 27 November 1947, article by Catherine Levitsky.
63. Alexandra, p. 42.
64. Ibid.
65. Jacobs, p. 61.
66. Ibid.
67. Ibid.
68. Ibid., p. 59.

Five: Orphan Child

1. Jacobs, p. 59.
2. Heald, p. 35.
3. VMH statement, 8 May 1930, UT, cited in Vickers, *Alice*, p. 142.
4. Vickers, *Alice*, p. 195.
5. Brandreth, p. 65.
6. RA PS/PSO/GV/PS/C/M/2537/5, 19 October 1927; cited in Vickers, *Alice*, pp. 181–4.
7. Binswanger note, 27 June 1930, UT, cited in Vickers, *Alice*, p. 200.
8. Vickers, *Alice*, pp. 200–201.
9. Ibid., p. 201.
10. VMH to NK, 2 January 1930, cited in Vickers, *Alice*, p. 202.
11. Vickers, *Alice*, pp. 205–7.
12. Alice to Cecile, 3 April 1930, HSA.
13. VMH to NK, 11 April 1930, BA, cited in Vickers, *Alice*, p. 207.
14. Ibid.
15. Vickers, *Alice*, pp. 208–10.
16. Ibid., p. 210.
17. Hough, *Louis and Victoria*, pp. 352–3.
18. Alice to Miss M. Edwards, 8 September 1928, RA Geo V AA68-211, cited in Vickers, *Alice*, p. 197.
19. Hough, *Louis and Victoria*, p. 350.
20. Barbara Goldsmith, *Little Gloria … Happy at Last*, p. 130.
21. C. Hankinson, *A History of the Battenberg Family*, unpublished, MP.
22. *Dictionary of National Biography*.
23. Ibid.
24. Goldsmith, p. 151.

25. Ibid., p. 127.
26. Interview with Lady Butter.
27. Raleigh Trevelyan, *Grand Dukes and Diamonds*, p. 413.
28. Goldsmith, pp.150–53.
29. Ibid., pp. 153–4.
30. Robin Dalton, *An Incidental Memoir*, p. 31.
31. Trevelyan, pp. 341, 413.
32. 22 May 1930, D24 No 74/2, HSA.
33. Hough, *Mountbatten*, p. 84.
34. Petropoulos, pp. 13 and 82–93.
35. Ibid., pp. 92–3.
36. March 2004, Petropoulos, pp. 13–14.
37. Vickers, *Alice*, p. 206.
38. 15 June 1930, HSA.
39. 23 June 1930, HSA.
40. 21 June 1930, HSA.
41. Alice to Philip, 28 July 1930, BP, cited in Vickers, *Alice*, p. 216 n.
42. Nana Bell to Philip, 24 July 1930, BP, cited in Vickers, *Alice*, p. 216 n.
43. Brandreth, pp. 67–8.
44. Fiammetta Rocco, 'A Strange Life: Profile of Prince Philip', *Independent on Sunday*, 13 December 1992.
45. Interview with Oliver James.

Six: Prep School Days

1. Anthony Holden, *Charles Prince of Wales*, p. 99.
2. Edward Peel, *Cheam School from 1645*, p. 181.
3. Ibid., p. 218.
4. Ibid., pp. xi and 224.
5. Ibid., p. 222.
6. Ibid.
7. Ibid., p. 221.
8. *Time* magazine, 21 October 1957.
9. Peel, p. xi.
10. Interview with Jimmy Taylor.
11. Interview with John Wynne.
12. Wynne, cited in Graham Turner, *Elizabeth: The Woman and the Queen*, pp. 26–7.
13. Turner, p. 27.

14. Louise to NK, 26 December 1930, BA, cited in Vickers, *Alice*, p. 223.
15. Petropoulos, pp. 1–4 and p. 103.
16. Ibid., p. 91.
17. Ibid., p. 116.
18. Vickers, *Alice*, p. 224.
19. VMH to GMH, 8 February 1931, MP, MB1/Y27.
20. John Parker, *Prince Philip*, p. 38.
21. Goldsmith, pp. 275–6.
22. Gloria Vanderbilt, *Without Prejudice*, p. 145.
23. Goldsmith, p. 295.
24. Interview with Michael Bloch.
25. Memo, 1 December 1969, S395 BA, cited in Philip Ziegler, *King Edward VIII*, p. 227.
26. Louise to NK, 19 August 1931, BA, cited in Vickers, *Alice*, p. 231.
27. Vickers, *Alice*, p. 232.
28. Ibid., p. 242.
29. Ibid., p. 245.
30. Ziegler, *King Edward VIII*, p. 24.
31. Hough, *Louis and Victoria*, pp. 353–4.
32. Trevelyan, p. 338.
33. Ibid., p. 339.
34. Trevelyan, p. 328; interview with Lady Butter.
35. Interview with Lady Butter.
36. Ibid.
37. MP, MB1/Y16.
38. Peel, p. 231.
39. Boothroyd, p. 127.
40. MP, MB1/H260 Folder 2.
41. VMH to NK, 14 March 1933, BA, cited in Hough, *Louis and Victoria*, p. 362.

Seven: *Dodging the Hitler Youth*

1. Holden, *Charles A Biography*, p. 55.
2. H. Röhrs and H. Tunstall-Behrens, eds, *Kurt Hahn*, Preface, p. x.
3. D. A. Byatt, *Kurt Hahn*, Foreword by HRH Duke of Edinburgh, p. 5.
4. Entry on Kurt Hahn, *Dictionary of National Biography*.
5. Heald, p. 41.
6. Rose, *Kings, Queens & Courtiers*, p. 139.

7. Röhrs and Tunstall-Behrens, eds, pp. 146–7.
8. Robert Skidelsky, *English Progressive Schools*, pp. 191–2.
9. *Listener*, 28 November 1934, pp. 910–11.
10. Heald, p. 41.
11. Kurt Hahn, 'The Seven Laws of Salem', Copy of Illustrated Lecture, p. 40, BL.
12. Ibid., p. 30, BL.
13. *Listener*, 28 November 1934.
14. Ibid.
15. Skidelsky, p. 192.
16. Röhrs and Tunstall-Behrens, eds, p. 24.
17. Ibid., p. 25.
18. Ibid., p. 29.
19. Röhrs and Tunstall-Behrens, eds, p. 29.
20. Ibid., pp. 167–9.
21. Henry L. Brereton, *Gordonstoun*, pp. 143–4; Röhrs and Tunstall-Behrens, eds, p. 145.
22. Martin Flavin, *Kurt Hahn's Schools & Legacy*, p. 86.
23. Brereton, p. 145.
24. Flavin, p. 85.
25. Ibid., p. 110.
26. Ibid., p. 94.
27. Ibid., p. 88.
28. Ibid., p. 113.
29. Ibid., p. 107.
30. Ibid., p. 109.
31. Boothroyd, p. 127.
32. Fiammetta Rocco, 'A Strange Life: Profile of Prince Philip', *Independent on Sunday*, 13 December 1992.
33. Brandreth, p. 72.
34. *Gordonstoun Record*, Easter 1947, p.4.
35. VMH to GMH, 3 July 1934, MP, MB1/Y27.
36. Ibid., 18 July 1934, MP, MB1/Y27.

Eight: Off to Gordonstoun

1. Skidelsky, p. 205.
2. Ibid.; Martin Gilbert, *The Roots of Appeasement*, pp. 145–6.
3. Skidelsky, p. 206.

4. T. C. Worsley, *Flannelled Fool*, pp. 182–3.
5. Arthur Marwick, *Clifford Allen*, p. 143.
6. Ibid., p. 144.
7. Adam Arnold-Brown, *Unfolding Character*, p. 3.
8. Elma Napier, *Youth Is a Blunder*, p. 29.
9. Arnold-Brown, p. 15.
10. Heald, p. 47.
11. Jonathan Dimbleby, *The Prince of Wales*, p. 71.
12. William Boyd, *School Ties*, p. 11.
13. Ross Benson, *Charles, The Untold Story*, p. 53.
14. Peter Lane, *Prince Philip*, p. 101.
15. Heald, pp. 46–7.
16. Ibid., p. 47.
17. *Gordonstoun Record*, Easter 1947, pp. 4–5.
18. *Listener*, 28 November 1934.
19. Worsley, p. 186.
20. Ibid.
21. Arnold-Brown, p. 29.
22. *Gordonstoun Record*, Easter 1947.
23. Alexandra, p. 58; Hugh Heckstall-Smith, *Doubtful Schoolmaster*, p. 135.
24. Lane, p. 101.
25. Report headed 'Prince of Greece and Denmark', 14 December 1938, Gordonstoun School Archives.
26. Arnold-Brown, p. 14.
27. Skidelsky, p. 204.
28. *Daily News*, 2 October 1934, cited in Goldsmith, p. 286.
29. *Sun*, 4 October 1934, cited in Goldsmith, p. 298.
30. *New York Mirror*, 5 October 1934, cited in Goldsmith, p. 298.
31. Cited in Goldsmith, p. 339.
32. Ibid., pp. 338–42.
33. Goldsmith, pp. 479–80.
34. Ziegler, *King Edward VIII*, p. 200.
35. Goldsmith, p. 259.
36. *Time* magazine, 10 September 1934.
37. Ziegler, *King Edward VIII*, p. 202.
38. Boothroyd, pp. 134–5.
39. Bertin, pp. 190–91.
40. David Irving, *Göring*, p. 127.
41. Petropoulos, pp. 115–17.

42. Princess Sophie to Landgravine Margarethe, 27 February 1933; Petropoulos, p. 117.
43. Petropoulos, p. 115.
44. Hough, *Louis and Victoria*, p. 355.
45. 6 February 1935, BA, cited in Hough, *Louis and Victoria*, p. 355.
46. VMH to Mountbatten, 5 November 1935, BA, cited in Hough, *Louis and Victoria*, p. 357.
47. Vickers, *Alice*, pp. 259–60.
48. *Daily Mirror*, 2 October 1962.
49. Waterlow to Sir John Simon, 2 January 1935, FO 371/19504, p. 124.
50. 23 November 1935, FO 371/19509, p. 325.
51. VMH to Mountbatten, 5 November 1935, BA, cited in Hough, *Louis and Victoria*, p. 357 and Vickers, *Alice*, pp. 263–4.
52. Waterlow to Anthony Eden, 8 January 1936, FO 371/20389, p. 276.
53. Waterlow to Eden, 27 May 1936, FO 371/20389, p. 114.
54. Waterlow to Eden, 23 November 1936, FO 371/20393, pp. 278–85.
55. Alexandra, pp. 52–3.
56. Ibid., p. 53.
57. Ibid., p. 54.
58. Cited in Hough, *Louis and Victoria*, p. 357.
59. *Gordonstoun Record*, Easter 1947, p. 6.

Nine: Blow after Blow

1. *Gordonstoun Record*, December 1936.
2. Ibid., 1947.
3. Arnold-Brown, pp. 28–9.
4. *Gordonstoun Record*, December 1937, pp. 50–51; also *Gordonstoun Record*, Easter 1947.
5. Vickers, *Alice*, p. 255.
6. Alice to Cecile, 28 December 1936, HSA.
7. Ivor Porter, *Michael of Romania*, p. 48.
8. VMH to NK, 13 April 1937, BA, cited in Vickers, *Alice*, p. 257.
9. Alice to Philip, undated, BP, cited in Vickers, *Alice*, p. 268.
10. Cecile to VMH, 16 July 1937, BA, cited in Vickers, *Alice*, pp. 268–9.
11. VMH to NK, 5 August 1937, cited in Vickers, *Alice*, p. 270.
12. *Gordonstoun Record*, December 1937.
13. VMH to NK, 12 September 1937, cited in Hough, *Louis and Victoria*, p. 363.

14. Vickers, *Alice*, p. 271.
15. Petropoulos, p. 94.
16. Michael Bloch, *Ribbentrop*, p. 121; Petropoulos, p. 93.
17. VMH to Philip, 29 October 1937, BP, cited in Hough, *Louis and Victoria*, p. 364.
18. VMH to Philip, 29 October 1937, BP, cited in Vickers, *Alice*, pp. 271–2.
19. *The Times*, 21 December 1937.
20. Interview with Lady Mountbatten.
21. Richard Hough, *Mountbatten, Hero of Our Time*, p. 88.
22. Ibid., p. 364.
23. Bloch, pp. 125–7.
24. Ibid., p. 144.
25. *The Times*, 17 November 1937, p. 16.
26. Andrea to VMH, 11 December 1937, BA, cited in Vickers, *Alice*, p. 274.
27. Binswanger note, 10 March 1947, UT, cited in Vickers, *Alice*, p. 275.
28. Interview with Oliver James, 2010.
29. *Gordonstoun Record*, 1947, see also Prologue.
30. VMH to GMH re Naval Review, undated, MP, MB1/Y27.
31. Trevelyan, p. 344.
32. Brandreth, p. 71.
33. Ziegler, *Mountbatten*, pp. 100–101; Hough, *Louis and Victoria*, p. 365.
34. 12 February 1938, BA, cited in Ziegler, *Mountbatten*, p. 101.
35. VMH to Prince Philip, 3 February 1938, BP, cited in Hough, *Louis and Victoria*, p. 365.
36. Ziegler, *Mountbatten*, p. 101.
37. Ibid.
38. Ziegler, *Mountbatten*, p. 101.
39. Fiammetta Rocco, 'A Strange Life: Profile of Prince Philip', *Independent on Sunday*, 13 December 1992.
40. Pimlott, p. 90.

Ten: The Man with the Plan

1. Heald, p. 50.
2. Ziegler, *Mountbatten*, p. 101.
3. Ibid., p. 77.
4. Ibid., p. 110.

5. Ibid., pp. 111–12; Alex von Tunzelmann, *Indian Summer*, p. 73; *San Francisco Chronicle*, 3 October 1926.

6. 16 March 1938, Lady Mountbatten Papers, cited in Ziegler, *Mountbatten*, p. 102.

7. Quoted in Hough, *Mountbatten*, p. 86.

8. Interview with Lady Mountbatten.

9. Robert Rhodes James, ed., *Chips*, 30 April 1942, p. 328.

10. Ziegler, *Mountbatten*, p. 102.

11. MP, MBI/H260, Folder 2, record of interview with Markgrafin of Baden.

12. Alexandra, p. 64.

13. Ibid.

14. Ibid., pp. 60–63.

15. Bradford, *Elizabeth*, pp. 110–11.

16. Alexandra, p. 60.

17. *New York Times*, 9 May 1937.

18. Ibid., 13 April 1939.

19. Interview with Cobina Wright Junior, *Town and Country* magazine, June 1973.

20. Kitty Kelley, *The Royals*, pp. 48–51.

21. 'Cobina', by Stephen Birmingham, *Town and Country* magazine, June 1973.

22. Confidential interview.

23. *Gordonstoun Record*, December 1938; ibid., Easter term 1947, p. 5.

24. Ibid., December 1938.

25. Final Report to Parents, 12 December 1938, Gordonstoun Archives.

26. Ibid.

27. See various references to their friendship in P. J. Vatikiotis, *Popular Autocracy in Greece 1936–41*.

28. Alice to Philip, 5 December 1938, BP, cited in Vickers, *Alice*, p. 281.

29. Interview with Lord Gainford.

30. Alice to MtB, 12 March 1939, BA, cited in Vickers, *Alice*, p. 283.

31. Vickers, *Alice*, p. 283.

32. 15 June 1939, BP, cited in Vickers, *Alice*, p. 284.

33. 24 June 1939, BP, cited in Vickers, *Alice*, p. 284.

34. Jennifer Ellis, ed., *Thatched With Gold*, p. 227.

35. Cited in Ziegler, *Mountbatten*, p. 102.

36. Ziegler, *Mountbatten*, p. 102.

37. Interview with Captain North Dalrymple-Hamilton.

38. Marion Crawford, *The Little Princesses*, p. 59.

Eleven: A Good War

1. Alice to NK, 6 August 1939, BA, cited in Vickers, *Alice*, p. 284.
2. 14 September 1939, BA, cited in Vickers, *Alice*, p. 285.
3. 1 December 1939, BP, cited in Vickers, *Alice*, p. 286.
4. See VMH to NK, 26 September 1939, BA, cited in Vickers, *Alice*, p. 285; Ziegler, *Mountbatten*, p. 308.
5. 26 September 1939, BA, cited in Vickers, *Alice*, p. 285.
6. 27 November 1939, MP, MB1/A11.
7. Alden Hatch, *The Mountbattens*, p. 402.
8. Ziegler, *Mountbatten*, p. 308.
9. Midshipman's Journal, 28 February 1940, BP.
10. Ibid., 1 April 1940.
11. Ibid.
12. Ibid., 12 May 1940.
13. Boothroyd, p. 92.
14. Midshipman's Journal, 22 July 1940, BP.
15. Ibid.
16. Ibid., 27 July 1940.
17. Ibid., 15 December 1940.
18. Ibid.
19. Ibid., 5 January 1941.
20. Ibid., 12 January 1941.
21. Richard Hill, *Lewin of Greenwich*, p. 74.
22. George II of Greece to VMH, 20 January 1941, BA, cited in Vickers, *Alice*, p. 290.
23. Rhodes James, ed., 21 January 1941.
24. Ibid., 8 and 9 January 1941.
25. Vickers, *Alice*, p. 289.
26. Alexandra, p. 68.
27. Ibid., p. 69.
28. Midshipman's Journal, 27 March 1941, BP.
29. See Ronald Seth, *Two Fleets Surprised*; A. B. C. Cunningham, *A Sailor's Odyssey*; and *Dictionary of National Biography*, entry on Cunningham.
30. Midshipman's Journal, 28 March 1941, BP.
31. 15 April 1941, ADM 1/11516; copy also in Midshipman's Journal, BP.
32. Quoted in Wheeler-Bennett, *King George VI*, p. 749.

33. Alexandra, p. 70.
34. Ibid.
35. Midshipman's Journal, 29 March 1941, BP.
36. Ibid., 22 May 1941, BP.
37. Ibid.
38. Antony Beevor, *Crete*, p. 44.
39. Ibid., pp. 168–70.
40. Ziegler, *Mountbatten*, p. 146.
41. 10 June 1941, Lady Mountbatten Papers, cited in Ziegler, *Mountbatten*, p. 144.
42. Mountbatten to Crown Princess of Sweden, undated, BA, B11e, Ziegler, *Mountbatten*, p. 145; Hough, *Bless Our Ship*, p. 169.
43. John Terraine, *The Life and Times of Lord Mountbatten*, p. 79; Von Tunzelmann, p. 112 and n.
44. Alexandra, pp. 70–71.
45. Boothroyd, p. 88.

Twelve: Osla and Lilibet

1. Wheeler-Bennett, p. 749.
2. King George VI's diary, 18/20 October 1941, cited in Wheeler-Bennett, p. 749.
3. 31 October 1941, BA, cited in Vickers, *Alice*, p. 318.
4. Sarah Baring, *The Road to Station X*, p. 35.
5. Interview with the Hon. Mrs Sarah Baring.
6. Interview with the Hon. Janie Spring.
7. Interview with the Dowager Countess of Cromer.
8. Richard Henry Brinsley Norton Grantley, *Silver Spoon*, p. 7.
9. Ibid., pp. 199–200.
10. Interview with the Dowager Countess of Cromer.
11. Interview with the Hon. Mrs Sarah Baring.
12. Anne de Courcy, *Debs at War*, p. 105.
13. James Lees-Milne, *A Mingled Measure, Diaries 1953–1972*, 30 December 1971, p. 183.
14. Interview with Lady Margaret Stirling-Aird.
15. Interview with the Hon. Mrs Janie Spring.
16. To Patricia Mountbatten, 29 March 1942, Lady Mountbatten Papers, cited in Ziegler, *Mountbatten*, pp. 307–8.
17. Heald, p. 66.

18. Boothroyd, p. 103.
19. Ibid.
20. Obituary in the *Independent*, by Tim Heald.
21. Ibid.
22. Robert Lacey, *Royal*, p. 125.
23. Eileen Parker, *Step Aside for Royalty*.
24. Trevelyan, pp. 335–6, and p. 345.
25. Cited in Trevelyan, pp. 371–4.
26. Vickers, *Alice*, p. 314.
27. Lane, p. 121.
28. Harry Hargreaves cited in the *Observer*, 28 December 2003.
29. 7 September 1943, BA S176, cited in Ziegler, *Mountbatten*, p. 224.
30. Crawford, p. 85.
31. *The Times*, 20 December 1943.
32. Crawford, p. 85.
33. Lisa Sheridan, *Cabbages to Kings*, p. 115.
34. Crawford, p. 86.
35. Princess Elizabeth to Marion Crawford, 1 January 1944, RA QEII/OUT/BUTHLAY, cited in Shawcross, p. 578.
36. Duff Hart-Davies, ed., *King's Counsellor: Abdication and War*, 26 December 1943, p. 189.
37. John Gordon to Beaverbrook, 23 March 1954, Beaverbrook Papers, BBK H/165, quoted in Bradford, *Elizabeth*, p.103.
38. Prince Philip to Queen Elizabeth, 31 December 1943, RA QEQM/PRIV/RF, cited in Shawcross, p. 578.
39. Prince Philip to Queen Elizabeth, 23 July [1944], RA QEQM/PRIV/RF, cited in Shawcross, p. 578.
40. Rhodes James, ed., 16 February 1944, p. 386.
41. Lascelles unpublished diary, vol. II, p. 41, LASC 1/2/2, cited in Pimlott, p. 95.
42. Shawcross, p. 578.
43. Ellis, ed., *Thatched With Gold*, p. 227.
44. Nicolson unpublished diary, Balliol College, Oxford, 12 June 1955, quoted in Bradford, *George VI*, p. 420.
45. Bradford, *George VI*, p. 420.
46. Wheeler-Bennett, p. 751.
47. King George VI to Queen Mary, 17 March 1944, Royal Archives, Queen Mary Collection, quoted in Wheeler-Bennett, p. 749.
48. Bradford, *George VI*, p. 102.

49. Turner, *Elizabeth*, p. 22.
50. Ibid., p. 21.

Thirteen: Steady on, Dickie

1. Boothroyd, p. 13.
2. 2 April 1944, BA, cited in Vickers, *Alice*, p. 318.
3. 10 June 1944, Buckingham Palace, cited in Vickers, *Alice*, pp. 318–19.
4. Bradford, *Elizabeth*, pp. 104–5.
5. Sir Michael Duff to Lady Desborough, 12 July 1944, D/ERV C711/12, cited in Richard Davenport-Hines, *Ettie: The Intimate Life and Dauntless Spirit of Lady Desborough*, p. 355.
6. Interview with the Hon. Mrs Janie Spring.
7. Trevelyan, p. 346.
8. Turner, p. 32; Brandreth, p. 166.
9. 10 August 1944, cited in Ziegler, *Mountbatten*, p. 308.
10. 10 August 1944, S96, BA, cited in Ziegler, *Mountbatten*, p. 308.
11. 19 August 1944, Miles Lampson, *The Killearn Diaries, 1934–1946*, p. 311.
12. Pimlott, pp. 96–7.
13. 28 August 1944, BA, vol. XIII, cited in Ziegler, *Mountbatten*, p. 308.
14. 9 February 1945, BA, vol. XIII, cited in Ziegler, *Mountbatten*, p. 308.
15. 8 February 1945, BA, cited in Vickers, *Alice*, pp. 319–20.
16. Mary Henderson, *Xenia: A Memoir. Greece 1919–1945*, p. 47.
17. Ibid.
18. *Daily Express*, 29 October 1994; Vickers, *Alice*, pp. 297–300.
19. 11 December 1941, BP, cited in Vickers, *Alice*, pp. 293–4.
20. 25 May 1942, BP, cited in Vickers, *Alice*, p. 295.
21. 31 May 1942, BP, cited in Vickers, *Alice*, p. 296.
22. Petropoulous, pp. 305–312.
23. Martin Allen, *Hidden Agenda: How the Duke of Windsor Betrayed the Allies*, p. 296; Bradford, *George VI*, p. 324; Petropoulos, pp. 11–12 and p. 226.
24. Petropoulos, pp. 308–9.
25. VMH to Nona Kerr, 16 October 1943, BA, cited in Vickers, *Alice*, p. 301.
26. Petropoulos, p. 311.
27. 23 April 1944, BP, cited in Vickers, *Alice*, p. 302.

28. Harold Macmillan, *The Blast of War 1939–1945*, pp. 588–90.
29. 20 January 1945, BP, cited in Vickers, *Alice*, p. 308.
30. VMH to Mountbatten, 20 January 1945, BA, cited in Vickers, *Alice*, p. 308.
31. Liane de Pougy, *My Blue Notebooks*, p. 43.
32. Ibid., p. 104.
33. Internet movie database.
34. Alexandra, p. 81.
35. Vickers, *Alice*, p. 309, citing letter from Alice to Philip, 10 May 1945, BP.
36. Mountbatten to Philip, immediate naval message, BP, cited in Vickers, *Alice*, p. 307.
37. Pimlott, p. 89.
38. Alice to Philip, 2 January 1945, BP, cited in Vickers, *Alice*, p. 312.
39. Ziegler, *Mountbatten*, p. 307.
40. *A Right Royal Rescue*, BBC Radio 4, January 2006; *Daily Mail*, 21 January 2006, HMS *Whelp*, service history.
41. Eric Bailey interviewed in Lane, p. 123.
42. Alexandra, pp. 78–9.
43. Brandreth, p. 164.
44. Robin Dalton, *An Incidental Memoir*, p. 14.
45. Brandreth, pp. 164–5.
46. Interview with Leading Signalman Ted Longshaw.
47. Crawford, p. 92.
48. Wheeler-Bennett, p. 626.

Fourteen: Nothing Ventured ...

1. 14 September 1946, RA QEQM/PRIV/RF, cited in Shawcross, p. 625.
2. Crawford, p. 99.
3. Correspondence from Professor Max Boisot, November 2010.
4. Interview with Lady Mountbatten.
5. John Dean, *HRH Prince Philip, Duke of Edinburgh*, pp. 35–6.
6. Crawford, p. 99.
7. *Daily Telegraph*, 2 April 1946.
8. Petropoulos, p. 303.
9. John Costello, *Mask of Treachery*, pp. 445–6.
10. Vickers, *Alice*, p. 314.
11. *New York Times*, 10 June 1946.

12. Boothroyd, p. 114.
13. Pimlott, p. 98.
14. Brandreth, p. 177.
15. Vickers, *Alice*, p. 324; Dean, p. 51.
16. VMH to Mountbatten, 19 February 1946, BA, cited in Vickers, *Alice*, p. 308; also Vickers, *Alice*, p. 316.
17. Andrew Barrow, *Gossip: A History of High Society, 1920–1970*, p. 137.
18. 12 June 1946, RA QEQM/PRIV/RF, cited in Shawcross, p. 624.
19. Boothroyd, p. 24.
20. Shawcross, p. 624; Wheeler-Bennett, p. 752; Bradford, *Elizabeth*, p. 116; Bradford, *George VI*, p. 422; Lacey, *Majesty*, pp. 125–6.
21. 14 September 1946, RA QEQM/PRIV/RF, cited in Shawcross, p. 625.
22. Wheeler-Bennett, p. 752.
23. Ellis, ed., p. 225.
24. Brandreth, pp. 181–2.
25. Vickers, *Elizabeth, The Queen Mother*, pp. 233–5 and 268.
26. George VI's gamebook records a grouse shooting party on 19 August 1946, consisting of 'Philip, Eldon, Cranborne, David L, Althorp and myself (King G VI)'; Aubrey Buxton, *The King in His Country*, p. 73.
27. Pimlott, p. 103.
28. Ralphe M. White, *The Royal Family, A Personal Portrait*, p. 119.
29. F. J. Corbitt, *Fit for a King*, p. 187.
30. Buxton, p. 132.
31. Unpublished Colville diary, end of August 1947, cited in Pimlott, p. 104.
32. *DNB*, 2004, vol. 32, p. 589.
33. Ellis, ed., pp. 229–30.
34. Turner, p. 22.
35. Ibid.
36. Ibid., p. 23.
37. Ibid.
38. Turner.
39. Pimlott, p. 104.
40. Ibid.
41. Lord Thorneycroft to Philip Ziegler; Ziegler, *Mountbatten*, p. 341.
42. Ziegler, *Mountbatten*, p. 341.
43. Ibid., p. 457.
44. Cited in Bradford, *George VI*, p. 422.

45. Fiammetta Rocco, 'A Strange Life: Profile of Prince Philip', *Independent on Sunday*, 13 December 1992.
46. Wheeler-Bennett, p. 750.
47. Ibid.
48. Francis Wheen, *Tom Driberg*, p. 211.
49. Ibid.
50. 14 August 1946, Lord Bradwell Papers, cited in Wheen, *Tom Driberg*, p. 212; Tom Driberg, *Ruling Passions*, p. 227.
51. 14 August 1946, Lord Bradwell Papers, cited in Pimlott, p. 100.
52. Mountbatten to Driberg, 4 December 1946, Lord Bradwell Papers.
53. Admiralty to Prime Minister, 5 November 1946, ADM 178/389.
54. Pimlott, p. 100, citing Mountbatten to Lascelles, RA GVI 270/25, 15 November 1946, and Mountbatten to Philip, 15 November 1946, RA GVI 270/26.
55. *Daily Telegraph*, 6 December 1946.
56. Cited in *News Chronicle*, 10 December 1946.
57. Ibid.
58. David Kynaston, *Austerity Britain 1945–51*, p. 243.
59. Interview with the Hon. Mrs Sarah Baring.
60. Anne Chisholm, *Beaverbrook*, p. 493.
61. Arthur Christiansen, *Headlines All My Life*, pp. 256–7.
62. Lacey, p. 130.

Fifteen: True Brit

1. Janet Morgan, *Edwina Mountbatten*, p. 385.
2. Ziegler, *Mountbatten*, p. 308.
3. *Daily Telegraph*, 19 March 1947.
4. *Daily Mail*, 19 March 1947.
5. 22 November 1972, MP, MBI/K200, cited in Pimlott, p. 101.
6. Boothroyd, p. 39.
7. Wheeler-Bennett, p. 751.
8. Boothroyd, p. 39.
9. Ibid.
10. *The Times*, 10 July 1947, p. 4.
11. Dean, pp. 37–8.
12. 28 January 1947, RA QEQM/PRIV/RF, cited in Shawcross, p. 626.
13. 29 January 1947, BA S176, cited in Ziegler, *Mountbatten*, p. 457.
14. 11 June [1947], RA QEQM/PRIV/RF, cited in Shawcross, p. 626.

15. Crawford, p. 106.
16. 7 July 1947, RA QEQM/OUT/ELPHINSTONE, cited in Shawcross, p. 626.
17. *Daily Mail*, 10 July 1947; *Daily Telegraph*, 10 July 1947.
18. Vickers, *Alice*, p. 326.
19. *The Times*, 11 July 1947, p. 4.
20. Harold Nicolson, *Diaries and Letters, 1945–1962*, 10 July 1947.
21. Ellis, ed., pp. 228–9.
22. Cited in Davenport-Hines, *Ettie*, p. 363.
23. *Daily Telegraph*, 10 July 1947.
24. *Daily Express*, 10 July 1947.
25. Geoffrey Bocca, *Elizabeth and Philip*, p. 71.
26. Cited in Boothroyd, p. 28.
27. Ziegler, *Elizabeth's Britain*, p. 120.
28. Florence Speed, cited in Kynaston, p. 243.
29. *Time* magazine, 21 July 1947.
30. Ziegler, *Crown and People*, p. 81.
31. Colville unpublished diary, 10 July 1947, cited in Pimlott, p. 123.
32. Louis Wulff, *Queen of Tomorrow*, p. 184, cited in Pimlott, p. 123.
33. *News Chronicle*, 21 March 1947.
34. Wheen, *Tom Driberg*, p. 212.
35. 6 September 1945, BA S176, cited in Ziegler, *Mountbatten*, p. 308.
36. 3 December 1946, RA QEQM/PRIV/RF, cited in Shawcross, p. 625.
37. Cited in Bradford, *Elizabeth*, p. 123.
38. 28 July 1947, cited in Wheen, *Tom Driberg*, pp. 212–14.
39. Mountbatten to Tom Driberg, cited in Wheen, *Tom Driberg*, pp. 212–14.
40. 25 July 1947, MP, MB1/E5, and 27 July 1947, MP, MB1/Q61, cited in Van Tunzelmann, p. 211.

Sixteen: Royal Wedding

1. *The Times*, 23 October 1947.
2. Dean, pp. 45–6.
3. Ibid., p. 48.
4. Colville unpublished diary, end of August 1947, cited in Pimlott, p. 125.
5. Ibid., end of November 1947, cited in Pimlott, p. 138.
6. Turner, p. 31.

7. Interview with Lady Mountbatten.
8. Pimlott, p. 125.
9. *The Times*, 4 October 1947.
10. RA Queen Mary's Collection, 6 November 1947, cited in Wheeler-Bennett, p. 753.
11. Von Tunzelmann, p. 297.
12. Lacey, *Majesty*, p. 132.
13. Marriage of HRH Princess Elizabeth and Lieutenant Philip Mountbatten, RN, List of Wedding Gifts, St James's Palace, 1947, no. 1211, p. 114, cited in Pimlott, p. 133.
14. Ellis, ed., p. 230; Lacey, *Majesty*, p. 132.
15. *The Times*, 6 October 1947.
16. Norman Hartnell, *Silver and Gold*, p. 113, cited in Pimlott, p. 135.
17. Ibid., p. 113.
18. Boothroyd, p. 32.
19. *Daily Telegraph*, 31 October 1947.
20. Colville unpublished diary, 30 October 1947, cited in Pimlott, p. 13.
21. Queen Alexandra, *For a King's Love*, pp. 157–8.
22. Rhodes James, ed., 26 November 1947, pp. 419–20.
23. Bradford, *Elizabeth*, p. 125.
24. *Daily Telegraph*, 17 July 1947.
25. 10 November 1947, BA, cited in Vickers, *Alice*, p. 328.
26. Vickers, *Alice*, p. 328.
27. Brandreth, p. 196; John Parker, *Prince Philip*, p. 122; Turner, p. 33.
28. Bocca, p. 77.
29. Dean, p. 56.
30. Interview with Lady Mountbatten.
31. Bradford, *Elizabeth*, p. 129.
32. John Colville, *Footprints in Time: Memories*, pp. 219–20.
33. 2 December 1947, BP, cited in Vickers, *Alice*, p. 328.
34. *The Times*, 21 November 1947.
35. Rhodes James, ed., 20 November 1947, p. 418.
36. Corbitt, *Fit for a King*, p. 42.
37. James Lansdale Hodson, *Thunder in the Heavens*, pp. 61–2.
38. Colville, p. 218.
39. Heald, p. 86.
40. Wheeler-Bennett, pp. 754–5.
41. Fisher papers, vol. 276, ff 1–11, Lambeth Palace Library, cited in Bradford, *Elizabeth*.

42. Alexandra, *For a King's Love*, p. 162.
43. Ziegler, *Crown and People*, p. 84.

Seventeen: Duke of Hazards

1. *The Queen*, vol. 195, no. 9582, 23 July 1947, p. 8, cited in Von Tunzelmann, p. 297.
2. Dean, p. 61.
3. 22 November 1947, RA QEQM/PRIV/RF, cited in Shawcross, p. 630.
4. 24 November 1947, RA QEII/PRIV/RF, cited in Shawcross, p. 631.
5. 30 November 1947, RA QEQM/PRIV/RF, cited in Shawcross, p. 631.
6. 3 December [1947], RA QEQM/RF, cited in Shawcross, p. 631.
7. 15 December 1947, Colville unpublished diary, cited in Pimlott, p. 144.
8. Rhodes James, ed., 17 November 1947, p. 418.
9. Turner, p. 34.
10. Boothroyd, p. 142.
11. Brandreth, p. 209.
12. Eileen Parker, p. 35.
13. *DNB*.
14. 15 September 1947, BA E23, cited in Ziegler, *Mountbatten*, p. 458.
15. Richard Mead, *General 'Boy'*, p. 199.
16. 15 March 1965, cited in Mead, pp. 199–200.
17. Mead, p. 197.
18. Ibid., p. vii, Foreword by HRH The Duke of Edinburgh.
19. Ibid., p. 201.
20. Dean, p. 99.
21. Colville unpublished diaries, 14 January 1948, cited in Pimlott, p. 149.
22. Pimlott, p. 151.
23. *The Times*, 14 May 1948.
24. John Colville, *Fringes of Power*, p. 588.
25. Selina Hastings, *Nancy Mitford*, p. 182.
26. Colville, *Fringes of Power*, p. 588.
27. Elizabeth Longford, *Elizabeth R*, p. 123.
28. Anthony Holden, *Charles: A Biography*, pp. 15–16.
29. Rhodes James, ed., 30 May 1948, p. 425.
30. Harold Nicolson to Vita Sackville West, 8 June 1948, Nicolson Papers, Balliol College, Oxford, cited in Bradford, *Elizabeth*, p. 133.
31. 'The Happy Prince', *Evening Standard*, 2 July 1948.
32. *Sunday Pictorial*, 6 March 1949.

33. Dalton, p. 64.
34. *Time* magazine, 18 February 1957.
35. Pimlott, p. 271.
36. Anthony Summers and Stephen Dorril, p. 25; John Parker, *Honeytrap*, p. 140.
37. *Daily Mirror*, 24 June 1963, cited in David Profumo, *Bringing the House Down*, pp. 196–7.
38. John Parker, pp. 206–7.
39. Profumo, p. 285.
40. Dalton, p. 65.
41. Bradford, *Elizabeth*, p. 266.
42. Pimlott, p. 271.
43. *Time* magazine, 18 February 1957.
44. Pat Kirkwood, *The Time of My Life*, pp. 139–44.
45. *Daily Mirror*, 15 January 1996.
46. Turner, p. 37.
47. Bradford, *Elizabeth*, p. 400.
48. Confidential interview.
49. Bradford, *Elizabeth*, p. 141; Pimlott, p. 2 and pp. 153–4; Holden, *Charles, Prince of Wales*, p. 46.
50. Dermot Morrah, *To Be a King*, pp. 6–7.
51. Bradford, *Elizabeth*, p. 141; Pimlott, p. 155.
52. Holden, *Charles: A Biography*, p. 17; Dean, p. 107.
53. Holden, *Charles, Prince of Wales*, p. 49.
54. Jonathan Dimbleby, *The Prince of Wales*, p. 3.
55. 25 June 1948, BP, cited in Vickers, *Alice*, p. 334.
56. 24 November 1948, BP, cited in Vickers, *Alice*, p. 332.
57. 14 December 1948, BA, cited in Vickers, *Alice*, p. 332.
58. Holden, *Charles: A Biography*, p. 18.
59. Dean, p. 109.
60. Ibid., p. 108.
61. Pimlott, p. 157.

Eighteen: Their Happiest Time

1. Various reports dated November 1947, WORK 19/1175, cited in Bradford, *Elizabeth*, p. 134.
2. Browning to Sir Eric de Normann, 13 July 1950, WORK 19/1175.
3. Cited in D. G. Brock to Normann, 1 August 1951, WORK 19/1175.

4. Memo 18/3/48, WORK 19/1175.

5. *Evening Standard*, 26 January 1949.

6. Bocca, p. 112.

7. Charles Smith, *Fifty Years with Mountbatten*, p. 46.

8. Lacey, *Royal*, pp. 161–2; Bradford, *Elizabeth*, pp. 138–9.

9. Dean, p. 112.

10. Ibid., p. 112.

11. Bradford, *Elizabeth*, p. 135, citing WORK 19/1175.

12. John Gibson, *From Belfast's Sandy Row to Buckingham Palace*, p. 119.

13. Ibid. pp. 119–21.

14. Dean, p. 114.

15. Gibson, p. 109.

16. Ibid., p. 115.

17. Ibid., p. 123.

18. Dean, p. 113.

19. Gibson, cited in Turner, p. 35.

20. Flavia Leng, *Daphne du Maurier*, pp. 187–90.

21. Trevelyan, pp. 414–15.

22. Cited in Turner, p. 36.

23. Ziegler, *Mountbatten*, p. 487; Morgan, p. 438.

24. 3 November 1949, Lady Mountbatten Papers, cited in Ziegler, *Mountbatten*, p. 491.

25. 21 November 1949, Lady Mountbatten Papers, cited in Ziegler, *Mountbatten*, p. 492.

26. Dean, p. 119.

27. 8 and 14 December 1949, Lady Mountbatten Papers, cited in Ziegler, *Mountbatten*, p. 492.

28. Dean, p. 121.

29. Ibid., p. 117.

30. *Daily Mail*, 15 October 1949.

31. Ziegler, *Mountbatten*, p. 513.

32. Interview with Lady Pamela Hicks.

33. Morgan, p. 444.

34. Pimlott, p. 162.

35. Holden, *Charles: A Biography*, p. 25.

36. Bradford, *Elizabeth*, p. 276; Pimlott, p. 262.

37. Bradford, *Elizabeth*, p. 276.

38. *News Chronicle*, 12 November 1949, cited in Dimbleby, p. 21.

39. Confidential interview.

40. *Daily Mail*, 11 and 14 January 1949, cited in Vickers, *Alice*, p. 333.
41. Boothroyd, p. 144.
42. *Daily Telegraph*, 15 August 1950.
43. 29 September 1950, BP, cited in Vickers, *Alice*, p. 339.
44. Hill, p. 74.
45. Alexandra, p. 121.
46. Ibid.
47. Boothroyd, p. 147.
48. Turner, p. 37.
49. Fiammetta Rocco, 'A Strange Life: Profile of Prince Philip', *Independent on Sunday*, 13 December 1992.
50. Bradford, *Elizabeth*, pp. 266–7.
51. Rocco.

Nineteen: Second Fiddle

1. *The Times*, 21 July 1951.
2. Dean, pp. 117–18.
3. *The Times*, 24 February 1951.
4. Buxton, p. 132.
5. Shawcross, p. 647.
6. See letter to Hardy Amies, 24 September 1951, cited in Pimlott, p. 170.
7. Richard Weight, *Patriots*, p. 236.
8. Bod/BAAS, 3 January 1951, cited in Weight, p. 236.
9. Weight, p. 236.
10. Cited in ibid., p. 236.
11. 9 August 1951, Peter Catterall, ed., *The Macmillan Diaries*, pp. 93–4.
12. 2 June 1952, cited in Weight, p. 236.
13. Weight, pp. 236–7.
14. Ibid.
15. Prince Philip to Martin Gilbert, 23 June 1987, cited in Gilbert, *Winston Churchill*, vol. VIII, p. 638.
16. Harold Nicolson, *Alex*, p. 294.
17. *The Royal Canadian Tour*, published by Pitkins Pictorials in association with the *Daily Graphic*.
18. Bradford, *Elizabeth*, pp. 162–3.
19. Princess Elizabeth to Queen Elizabeth, 15 October 1951, cited in Shawcross, p. 649.
20. Ibid., 4 November 1951, cited in Shawcross, pp. 649–50.

21. *Sunday Dispatch*, 27 January 1952.
22. *News Chronicle*, 26 January 1952.
23. Alexandra, p. 131.
24. Ibid., p. 130.
25. Dean, p. 134.
26. Ibid., pp. 132–3.
27. Brandreth, p. 242.
28. Dermot Morrah, *The Work of the Queen*, p. 31.
29. 2 November 1951, Harry S. Truman Papers, cited in Pimlott, p. 172.
30. Cited in *The Times*, 3 November 1951.
31. Morrah, *The Work of the Queen*, p. 32.
32. Boothroyd, p. 148.
33. *The Times*, 15 November 1951.
34. Ibid., 18 November 1951.
35. British Pathé video newsreel entitled 'Prince Philip', reel 3.
36. Cited in Gilbert, *Winston Churchill*, vol. VIII, pp. 662–3.
37. 28 November 195, cited in Wheeler-Bennett, p. 801.
38. Alexandra, pp. 134–5.
39. Wheeler-Bennett.
40. *The Times*, 28 December 1951; Shawcross, p. 651.
41. Ibid., 31 January 1952.
42. Interview with Lady Pamela Hicks.
43. Buxton, p. 137; interview with Lord Buxton.
44. Macdonald to Wheeler-Bennett, cited in Shawcross, p. 652.
45. Shawcross, p. 653.
46. Gilbert, *Winston Churchill*, vol. VIII, p. 697.
47. Pimlott, p. 175.
48. Interview with Lady Pamela Hicks.
49. Pimlott, p. 175.
50. Turner, p. 41; Heald, p. 99.
51. Heald, p. 99.

Twenty: Oh, the Future!

1. *Daily Telegraph*, 14 January 1952, Vickers, *Alice*, p. 343.
2. 6 February 1952, BP, cited in Vickers, *Alice*, p. 344.
3. Trevelyan, p. 413.
4. Boothroyd, p. 49.
5. Ibid., p. 49.

6. Cited in Brandreth, p. 251.

7. 20 June 1952, Colville unpublished diary, cited in Pimlott, p. 186.

8. Rose, *Kings, Queens & Courtiers*, p. 87.

9. Brandreth, p. 258.

10. Turner.

11. Pathé newsreel: Death of George VI, 7 February 1952.

12. Brandreth, p. 250.

13. Harold Macmillan, cited in Lacey, *Majesty*, p. 152.

14. Brandreth, p. 249.

15. Heald, p. 104; Boothroyd, p. 49.

16. Pimlott, p. 204.

17. Queen Elizabeth to Sir Alan Lascelles, 25 February 1952, RA PS/PSO/ AL/Box B; Lascelles to Queen Elizabeth, 26 February 1952, RA QEQM/ PRIV/MISCOFF; cited in Shawcross, p. 663.

18. Shawcross, p. 677.

19. Pimlott, pp. 182–3.

20. Longford, p. 155.

21. 4 April and 9 April 1952, Colville unpublished diary, cited in Pimlott, p. 185.

22. Longford, p. 155.

23. 18 February 1952, CAB 128/24 CC(52), cited in Bradford, *Elizabeth*, p. 170.

24. Bradford, *Elizabeth*, p. 170.

25. Declaration in Council, 9 April 1952, cited in Ziegler, *Mountbatten*, pp. 681–2.

26. 7 April 1952, CAB 129/51 C(52) 114, cited in Bradford, *Elizabeth*, p. 171.

27. 3 April 1952, Catterall, ed., p. 155.

28. Pimlott, p. 185.

29. Lacey, *Royal*, p. 173.

30. Confidential interview.

31. Earl Mountbatten, *The Mountbatten Lineage*, p. 362.

32. Mountbatten to Lady Longford, 21 February 1973, BA K17, cited in Ziegler, *Mountbatten*, p. 682.

33. Interview with Countess Mountbatten.

34. John Gordon to Beaverbrook, Beaverbrook Papers, BBK H/121, cited in Bradford, *Elizabeth*, p. 171.

35. Michael Bloch, *The Secret File of the Duke of Windsor*, pp. 257, 265.

36. Cited in Bradford, *Elizabeth*, p. 172.

37. Confidential interview.
38. Lacey, *Royal*, pp. 173–4.
39. Clark, *Palace Diary*, p. 23, cited in Lacey, *Royal*, p. 174.
40. Longford, p. 155.
41. Hugo Vickers, *Cecil Beaton: The Authorized Biography*, p. 359.
42. Rose, *Kings, Queens & Courtiers*, p. 237.
43. Undated (1952) RA QEII/PRIV/RF, cited in Shawcross, p. 662.
44. Morrah, *To Be a King*, p. 21.
45. Dean, p. 116.
46. Bloch, *The Secret File of the Duke of Windsor*.
47. Corbitt, p. pp. 184–94.
48. Pimlott, p. 267.
49. J. Bryan III, 'The Duke of Edinburgh', *Holiday* magazine, May 1956, cited in Longford, p. 154.
50. Basil Boothroyd, 'Prince Philip', *The Times*, 10 June 1981.
51. Pimlott, p. 267.
52. Mead, p. 207.
53. Bradford, *Elizabeth*, p. 179.
54. Turner, p. 105.
55. Ziegler, *Mountbatten*, pp. 493–4.
56. Prince Philip to Timothy Good, undated, cited in Wheen, *How Mumbo Jumbo Conquered the World*, p. 137; www.timothygood.co.uk
57. Wheen, *Mumbo Jumbo*, pp. 137–8.
58. Ibid.
59. Boothroyd, p. 152.
60. Ibid., p. 156.
61. Ibid., p. 161.
62. Elspeth Huxley, *Peter Scott, Painter and Naturalist*, pp. 166–7.
63. Interview with Lady Pamela Hicks.

Twenty-One: Her Liege Man

1. Duchess of Kent to Mountbatten, 2 December 1952, cited in Vickers, *Alice*, p. 345.
2. Mark Pottle, ed., *Daring to Hope: The Diaries of Violet Bonham Carter*, 6 May 1953, p. 122.
3. *Daily Mirror*, 28 February 1953.
4. *Sunday Dispatch*, 26 April 1953.
5. Bradford, *Elizabeth*, p. 181.

6. Rose, *Kings, Queens & Courtiers*, pp. 227–8.
7. Eileen Parker, p. 131.
8. Longford, p. 159.
9. Lacey, *Royal*, p. 175.
10. Cited in Pimlott, p. 208.
11. L. A. Nickolls, *The Crowning of Elizabeth II*, pp. 67–8.
12. Pimlott, p. 209.
13. Philip Hoare, *Noël Coward*, p. 401.
14. Vickers, *Alice*, p. 348.
15. Margarita to Mountbatten, 5 March 1952, BA, cited in Vickers, *Alice*, p. 347.
16. Mountbatten Papers, cited in Pimlott, p. 208.
17. James A. Frere, *The British Monarchy at Home*, p. 165, cited in Longford, p. 159.
18. Owen Chadwick, *Michael Ramsey: A Life*, p. 81.
19. Bradford, *Elizabeth*, p. 187.
20. Turner, p. 43.
21. Bradford, *Elizabeth*, p.185.
22. Lacey, *Royal*, p. 178.
23. Bradford, *Elizabeth*, p. 176.
24. Jonathan Dimbleby, *Richard Dimbleby*, pp. 234–5.
25. Ibid., p. 24.
26. Lacey, *Royal*, pp. 183–7.
27. Cecil Beaton, *The Strenuous Years, Diaries 1948–55*, p. 136.
28. Ibid., p. 148.
29. Vickers, *Cecil Beaton*, p. 368.
30. Bradford, *Elizabeth*, p.156.
31. Lacey, *Majesty*, p. 251.
32. *Time* magazine, 21 October 1957.
33. Pimlott, p. 270.
34. Lacey, *Royal*, p. 123.
35. Heald, p. 251.
36. Cited in Turner, p. 37.

BIBLIOGRAPHY

Alexandra, Queen of Yugoslavia, *For a King's Love*, Doubleday, 1956
— *Prince Philip: A Family Portrait*, Hodder & Stoughton, 1960
Allen, Martin, *Hidden Agenda: How the Duke of Windsor Betrayed the Allies*,
    M. Evans & Co., 2002
Andrew, Prince of Greece, *Towards Disaster: The Greek Army in Asia Minor*
    in 1921, John Murray, 1930
Arnold-Brown, Adam, *Unfolding Character: The Impact of Gordonstoun*,
    Routledge & Kegan Paul, 1962
Aronson, Theo, *A Family of Kings: The Descendants of Christian IX of*
    Denmark, Cassell, 1976
Baring, Sarah, *The Road to Station X*, Wilton 65, 2000
Barker, Brian, *When the Queen Was Crowned*, Routledge & Kegan Paul,
    1976
Battiscombe, Georgina, *Queen Alexandra*, Constable, 1969
Beaton, Cecil, *The Strenuous Years, Diaries, 1948–55*, Weidenfeld &
    Nicolson, 1973
Beatty, Laura, *Lillie Langtry*, Chatto & Windus, 1999
Beevor, Antony, *Crete*, John Murray, 1991
Benson, E. F., *As We Were: A Victorian Peep-Show*, Longmans Green, 1930
Bertin, Celia, *Marie Bonaparte*, Harcourt Brace Jovanovich, 1930
Bloch, Michael, *The Secret File of the Duke of Windsor*, HarperCollins, 1989
— *Ribbentrop*, Bantam, 1992
Bocca, Geoffrey, *Elizabeth and Philip*, Henry Holt, New York, 1953
Bodley, J. E. C., *The Coronation of Edward the Seventh*, Methuen, 1903
Boothroyd, Basil, *Philip: An Informal Biography*, Longman, 1971
Boyd, William, *School Ties*, Hamish Hamilton, 1985
Bradford, Sarah, *George VI*, Weidenfeld & Nicolson, 1989

— *Elizabeth*, Heinemann, 1996

Brandreth, Gyles, *Philip & Elizabeth: Portrait of a Marriage*, Century, 2004

Brereton, Henry L., *Gordonstoun, Ancient Estate and Modern School*, Gordonstoun School, 1982

Buchanan, Meriel, *Queen Victoria's Relations*, Cassell & Co., 1954

Buxton, Aubrey, *The King in His Country*, Longmans, 1955

Byatt, D. A., *Kurt Hahn: An Appreciation of His Life and Work*, published privately by Gordonstoun School, 1976

Carter, Miranda, *The Three Emperors*, Fig Tree, 2009

Catterall, Peter, ed., *The Macmillan Diaries: The Cabinet Years, 1950–1957*, Macmillan, 2003

Chadwick, Owen, *Michael Ramsey: A Life*, Clarendon Press, 1990

Chisholm, Anne, *Beaverbrook: A Life*, Pimlico, 2003

Christiansen, Arthur, *Headlines All My Life*, Heinemann, 1961

Christmas, Walter, *The Life of King George of Greece*, Eveleigh Nash, 1914

Christopher, Prince of Greece, *Memoirs of HRH Prince Christopher of Greece*, Hurst & Blackett, 1939

Clarke, David, and Roberts, Andy, *Flying Saucerers: A Social History of UFOlogy*, Alternative Albion, 2007

Clogg, Richard, *A Concise History of Modern Greece*, Cambridge University Press, 2002

Colville, John, *Footprints in Time: Memories*, Collins, 1976

— *The Fringes of Power: The Downing Street Diaries, 1939–55*, Weidenfeld & Nicolson, 2004

Cookridge, E. H., *From Battenberg to Mountbatten*, Arthur Barker, 1966

Corbitt, F. J., *Fit for a King*, Odhams, 1956

Cordet, Hélène, *Born Bewildered*, Peter Davies, 1961

Costello, John, *Mask of Treachery*, Collins, 1988

Crawford, Marion, *The Little Princesses*, Cassell & Co., 3rd edn, 1952

Cunningham, A. B. C., *A Sailor's Odyssey*, Hutchinson, 1951

Dalton, Robin, *An Incidental Memoir*, Viking, 1998

Dean, John, *HRH Prince Philip, Duke of Edinburgh. A Portrait by His Valet*, Robert Hale, 1954

Dimbleby, Jonathan, *Richard Dimbleby*, Hodder & Stoughton, 1975

— *The Prince of Wales*, Time Warner, 1995

Elliot, H. G., *Some Revolutions and other Diplomatic Experiences*, John Murray, 1922

Ellis, Jennifer, ed., *Thatched With Gold: The Memoir of Mabell Countess of Airlie*, Hutchinson, 1962

Flavin, Martin, *Kurt Hahn's Schools & Legacy*, Middle Atlantic Press, 1996

Forster, Margaret, *Daphne du Maurier*, Chatto & Windus, 1993

Frischauer, Willi, *Margaret, Princess Without a Cause*, Michael Joseph, 1977

Fulford, Roger, ed., *Your Dear Letter, Private Correspondence of Queen Victoria and the Crown Princess of Russia, 1865–71*, Evans Bros, 1971

George, Grand Duchess of Russia, *A Romanov Diary*, Atlantic International, 1988

Gibson, John, *From Belfast's Sandy Row to Buckingham Palace*, Mercier Press, 1994

Gilbert, Martin, *Winston S. Churchill*, vol. VIII, *Never Despair, 1945–65*, Heinemann, 1988

Goldsmith, Barbara, *Little Gloria … Happy at Last*, Macmillan, 1980

Griscom, Lloyd C., *Diplomatically Speaking*, John Murray, 1941

Hall, Unity, *Philip: The Man Behind the Monarchy*, Michael O'Mara Books, 1987

Hart-Davies, Duff, ed., *King's Counsellor: Abdication and War. The Diaries of 'Tommy' Lascelles*, Weidenfeld & Nicolson, 2006

Hargreaves, Harry, *It Wasn't All Mayhem: The Musings of a Matelot*, Compaid Graphics, 2005

Hastings, Selina, *Nancy Mitford*, Vintage, 2010

Hatch, Alden, *The Mountbattens*, W. H. Allen, 1966

Heald, Tim, *The Duke: A Portrait of Prince Philip*, Hodder & Stoughton, 1991

Heckstall-Smith, Hugh, *Doubtful Schoolmaster*, Peter Davies, 1962

Henderson, Mary, *Xenia: A Memoir. Greece 1919–1945*, Ulverscroft, 1991

Higham, Charles, and Moseley, Roy, *Elizabeth & Philip: The Untold Story*, Sidgwick & Jackson, 1991

Hill, Richard, *Lewin of Greenwich*, Cassell, 2001

Hoare, Philip, *Noël Coward*, Mandarin, 1996

Hodson, James Lansdale, *Thunder in the Heavens*, Alan Wingate, 1949

Hoey, Brian, *Mountbatten*, Sidgwick & Jackson, 1994

Holden, Anthony, *Charles, Prince of Wales*, Weidenfeld & Nicolson, 1979

— *Charles: A Biography*, Weidenfeld & Nicolson, 1988

— *A Tarnished Crown*, Bantam Press, 1993

Hollis, Leslie, *The Captain General*, Herbert Jenkins, 1961

Hough, Richard, *Louis and Victoria*, Hutchinson, 1974

— *Advice to a Grand-Daughter*, Heinemann, 1975

— *Mountbatten, Hero of Our Time*, Weidenfeld & Nicolson, 1980

— *Bless Our Ship: Mountbatten and the Kelly*, Hodder & Stoughton, 1991

Hourmouzios, Stelio, *No Ordinary Crown: A Biography of King Paul of the Hellenes*, Weidenfeld & Nicolson, 1972

Huxley, Elspeth, *Peter Scott, Painter and Naturalist*, Faber & Faber, 1993

Irving, David, *Göring*, Macmillan, 1989

Jacobs, Herbert, *Schoolmaster of Kings*, Berkeley, 1982

Judd, Denis, *Prince Philip*, Michael Joseph, 1980

Kelley, Kitty, *The Royals*, Warner Books, 1997

Kerr, Mark, *Land, Sea and Air*, Longman, 1927

— *Prince Louis of Battenberg*, Longman, Green & Co., 1934

King, Stella, *Princess Marina*, Cassell, 1969

Kinross, Lord, *Atatürk*, Weidenfeld & Nicolson, 1964

Kirkwood, Pat, *The Time of My Life*, Robert Hale, 1999

Knightley, Philip, and Kennedy, Caroline, *An Affair of State: The Profumo Case and the Framing of Stephen Ward*, Jonathan Cape, 1987

Kynaston, David, *Austerity Britain 1945–51*, Bloomsbury, 2007

Lacey, Robert, *Majesty: Elizabeth II and the House of Windsor*, Harcourt Brace Jovanovich, 1977

— *Royal, Her Majesty Queen Elizabeth II*, Little, Brown, 2002

Lampson, Miles, 1st Baron Killearn, *The Killearn Diaries, 1934–1946*, Sidgwick & Jackson, 1972

Lane, Peter, *Prince Philip*, Robert Hale, 1980

Lees-Milne, James, *A Mingled Measure, Diaries 1953–1972*, John Murray, 1974

Leng, Flavia, *Daphne du Maurier: A Daughter's Memoir*, Mainstream, 1994

Liversidge, Douglas, *Prince Philip: First Gentleman of the Realm*, Arthur Barker, 1976

Llewellyn-Smith, Michael, *Ionian Vision*, Allen Lane, 1973

Longford, Elizabeth, *Elizabeth R*, Weidenfeld & Nicolson, 1983

Macmillan, Harold, *The Blast of War 1939–1945*, Macmillan, 1967

Marwick, Arthur, *Clifford Allen, The Open Conspirator*, Oliver & Boyd, 1964

Masters, Brian, *Dreams About HIM The Queen and Other Members of the Royal Family*, Blond and Masters, 1972

Mead, Richard, *General 'Boy': The Life of Lieutenant General Sir Frederick Browning*, Pen & Sword, 2010

Milton, Giles, *Paradise Lost*, Sceptre, 2008

Morgan, Janet, *Edwina Mountbatten*, HarperCollins, 1991

Morrah, Dermot, *The Work of the Queen*, William Kimber, 1958

— *To Be a King*, Hutchinson, 1968

Mountbatten, Louis, Earl, *The Mountbatten Lineage*, privately published, 1958

Nahum, Baron Henry Stirling, *Baron by Baron*, Frederick Muller, 1957

Nicholas, Prince of Greece, *My Fifty Years*, 2nd edn, Hutchinson, 1927

Nickolls, L. A., *The Crowning of Elizabeth II*, Macdonald & Co., 1953

Nicolson, Harold, *Alex: The Life of Field Marshal Earl Alexander of Tunis*, Weidenfeld & Nicolson, 1973

— *Diaries and Letters, 1945–1962*, Collins, 1968

Napier, Elma, *Youth Is a Blunder*, Jonathan Cape, 1948

Paleologue, Maurice, *The Tragic Romance of Alexander II of Russia*, Hutchinson, 1926

Parker, Eileen, *Step Aside for Royalty*, Bachman & Turner, 1982

Parker, John, *Prince Philip: His Secret Life*, Sidgwick & Jackson, 1990

Paxman, Jeremy, *On Royalty*, Viking, 2006

Pearson, J., *The Ultimate Family. The Making of the Royal House of Windsor*, Michael Joseph, 1986

Peel, Edward, *Cheam School from 1645*, Thornhill Press, 1974

Petropoulos, Jonathan, *Royals and the Reich*, Oxford University Press, 2006

Pimlott, Ben, *The Queen: A Biography of Elizabeth II*, HarperCollins, 1996

Pope-Hennessy, James, *Queen Mary*, Allen & Unwin, 1959

Pottle, Mark, ed., *Daring to Hope: The Diaries of Violet Bonham Carter, 1946–1969*, Weidenfeld & Nicolson, 2000

Profumo, David, *Bringing the House Down: A Family Memoir*, John Murray, 2006

Rhodes James, Robert, ed., *Chips, The Diaries of Sir Henry Channon*, Weidenfeld & Nicolson, 1967

Rocco, Fiammetta, 'A Strange Life: Profile of Prince Philip', *Independent on Sunday*, 13 December 1992

Röhrs, H., and Tunstall-Behrens, H., eds, *Kurt Hahn*, Routledge & Kegan Paul, London, 1970

Rose, Kenneth, *George V*, Weidenfeld & Nicolson, 1983

— *Kings, Queens & Courtiers*, Spring Books, 1989

Rumbold, Sir Horace, *Recollections of a Diplomatist*, 2 vols, Edward Arnold, 1902

Seth, Ronald, *Two Fleets Surprised: The Story of the Battle of Cape Matapan*, Godfrey Bles, 1960

Shawcross, William, *Queen Elizabeth The Queen Mother*, Macmillan, 2010

Sheridan, Lisa, *From Cabbages to Kings*, Odhams, 1955

Skidelsky, Robert, *English Progressive Schools*, Penguin, 1969

Smith, Charles, *Fifty Years with Mountbatten*, Hamlyn, 1951

Stewart, W. A. C., *Progressives and Radicals in English Education, 1750–1970*, Macmillan, 1972

Summers, Anthony, and Dorril, Stephen, *Honeytrap: The Secret Worlds of Stephen Ward*, Weidenfeld & Nicolson, 1987

Terraine, John, *The Life and Times of Lord Mountbatten*, Hutchinson, 1968

Trevelyan, Raleigh, *Grand Dukes and Diamonds: The Wernhers of Luton Hoo*, Secker & Warburg, 1991

Turner, Graham, *Elizabeth: The Woman and the Queen*, Macmillan, 2002

Vanderbilt, Gloria Morgan, *Without Prejudice*, Robert Hale, 1937

Van Der Kiste, John, *Kings of the Hellenes*, Sutton, 1994

Vickers, Hugo, *Alice, Princess Andrew of Greece*, Viking, 2000

— *Cecil Beaton: The Authorized Biography*, Weidenfeld & Nicolson, 2002

— *Elizabeth, The Queen Mother*, Hutchinson, 2005

Von Bülow, Prince, *Memoirs 1849–1897*, Putnam, 1932

Von Tunzelmann, Alex, *Indian Summer*, Simon & Schuster, 2007

Warwick, Christopher, *Ella: Princess, Saint and Martyr*, Wiley, 2006

Weight, Richard, *Patriots: National Identity in Britain 1940–2000*, Macmillan, 2002

Wheeler-Bennett, John, *King George VI*, Macmillan, 1958

Wheen, Francis, *Tom Driberg: His Life and Indiscretions*, Chatto & Windus, 1990

— *How Mumbo Jumbo Conquered the World*, Harper Perennial, 2004

White, Ralphe M., *The Royal Family, A Personal Portrait*, David Mackay Company, New York, 1969

Ziegler, Philip, *Crown and People*, Collins, 1978

— *Mountbatten*, Collins, 1985

— *Elizabeth's Britain*, Country Life Books, 1986

— *King Edward VIII*, Collins, 1990

— *King Edward VIII*, Sutton, 2001

INDEX

BRITISH OLYMPIC HEROES

The Best of British Gold Medallists

Kitty Carruthers

STACEY
INTERNATIONAL

CONTENTS

ACKNOWLEDGEMENTS

It was my good friend and fellow croquet player Alec Thomas' idea to do this book. Although its shape has evolved from what we first envisaged, he has been the driving force. Without his hard work and constant encouragement it would never have seen the light of day.

My husband, Jonathan Edwards – not the triple jumper but, yes, a distant cousin of Eddie 'the Eagle' – has been my mainstay throughout and without his practical and moral support I would have thrown in the towel long ago. My brother, Alan Kittermaster, another keen sportsman, was also a source of help and encouragement.

I am enormously grateful to Bill Mallon and Jeroen Heijmans of the International Society of Olympic Historians who provided invaluable information and patiently answered my questions. Tony Bijkerk, Secretary-General of the ISOH and a walking encyclopaedia of the Olympic Games, took the time to read the manuscript and correct my errors. I cannot sufficiently thank him for his efforts to ensure the accuracy of this work; his contribution has improved it immeasurably. If any errors remain, they are no fault of his.

I am, as ever, deeply indebted to Tom Stacey, who believed in the book, and all at Stacey International who made it a reality.

KC

FOREWORD by Sir Chris Hoy, MBE

It is a huge honour to represent one's country at the Olympics, and an incredible opportunity for an athlete to take part in one of the greatest sporting events in the world.

As many British athletes start their journey towards the London 2012 Olympics and prepare for the unique experience of competing in a home Games, this book celebrates a wealth and diversity of British sporting talent and achievement.

British Olympic Heroes features many contemporary and deservedly well-known names. It also includes figures from the past like Launceston Elliot, the first British Olympian, who combined Olympic success in one-handed weightlifting with rope-climbing, the discus and the 100 metres. And John Boland, who arrived at the 1896 Games as a spectator and ended up winning the singles and doubles tennis events.

The biographies document the important details and highlights of each athlete's career, but the book is also full of amusing anecdotes and little-known facts: did you know that the great all-rounder Max Woosnam beat Charlie Chaplin at table tennis playing with a butter knife, or that Kitty Godfree swapped her prizes to buy a sports car, or that Allan Wells was the first Olympic athlete to wear lycra shorts?

My own sporting heroes – Gavin Hastings, Graeme Obree and Chris Boardman – are an important source of inspiration and help spur me on to achieve my goals. I hope that today's aspiring athletes will read and enjoy this book and draw from it the inspiration to add to Britain's fantastic Olympic medal-winning achievements.

Chris Hoy

INTRODUCTION

Great Britain is one of only five countries to have competed in every Summer Olympic Games of the modern era, and one of only three to attend every Winter Games. In all, more than five hundred Britons have been awarded one or more gold medals. The exact figure depends on whether one includes the early curiosities such as Art and Alpinism (as we do) and the Second International Olympic Games (also known as the Intercalated Games). These Games were held in Athens in 1906, the Greeks having unilaterally decreed that the Olympics were their birthright and should be held permanently in Athens. The Greek Olympic Committe declared that the 1904 Games had been so badly run that they would show the world how things should be done. Thus three Games were held in the space of eight years. The IOC at first recognised the 1906 Games, but later expunged the results from the record books. A second interim Games was scheduled for 1914, but Baron de Coubertin, founder of the modern Olympics, won the battle to ensure that they were hosted by a different country each time.

It was not until 1906 that the now familiar sequence of gold, silver and bronze medals were awarded, so the athletes from the early Games included here as 'gold medallists' received either a silver medal, a small sum of money or a piece of art, and a laurel wreath. But they won, and that is what counts.

Those featured here are not necessarily the most famous. They are, rather, the most arresting, whose sporting and private lives have been inspiring and impressive or sometimes downright incredible. Our coverage in fact includes a larger number of Olympians in that the medal is sometimes shared between pairs or teams, as in swimming, rowing, sailing, skating or bobsledding.

Many of Britain's gold medallists have left a lasting legacy. Some made barely a ripple. Some single-mindedly devoted their lives to sport with the one goal of winning for their country, others found themselves on the podium quite by chance. In this book you will find those like Seb Coe, Chris Hoy and Kelly Holmes – household names today – inspiring countless others. There are those like Tommy Green and the

Doherty brothers who overcame adversity and emerged victorious, and others like Max Woosnam whose truly amazing prowess is all but forgotten today. A few particularly unlikely participants appear, such as John Boland who went to Athens as a spectator and ended up the victor in two tennis events. And, in spite of its title, this book would be the poorer without at least a passing mention of our spectacular failures and unlucky losers, like Eddie 'the Eagle' Edwards and Philip Plater.

Since the first modern Olympics Games of 1896, various sports have disappeared from the Olympic programme, and with every new Games other sports are added. In many of the early events the British did extremely well. It was not difficult to foresee a British victory in the 1908 rackets competition, since no other nation took part. Nor in the cricket in 1900, which though ostensibly between Britain and France featured only a couple of players on either side who were not British. At those early Games, Britain managed to pick up a couple of gold medals in the water motor sports, two silvers in the rugby, and two of each in the tug-of-war. Polo, real tennis, golf and lacrosse accounted for a further 30 medals. Britain won three gold medals in Art, a 'sport' for many years included. One of these was for Town Planning in 1932. And the Everest expedition of 1922 earned the team, which included Mallory, an Alpine gold medal in 1924. A full list of all British gold medallists can be found at the end of the book.

An international group of dedicated Olympic researchers, led by American Bill Mallon, has compiled an Olympic database (the product of 60 man-years' work, they reckon) of great thoroughness and authority and their statistics are noted when they differ from the IOC's official lists. The leaders of this group went on to found the International Society of Olympic Historians in 1991

The 2012 London Olympics are the third time Britain will have hosted the Games. There will emerge new heroes, including, we trust, for Britain.

Kitty Carruthers, April 2011

OLYMPIC TIMELINE

Venue (Summer) (Winter)	Year	Notable Events
	1892	Baron Pierre de Coubertin puts plans for International Olympic Committee to delegates from 12 countries.
	1894	First session of IOC awards first Olympic Games to Athens.
Athens	1896	Games open with approximately 245 male competitors from 14 nations. Olympic hymn played during opening ceremony. Winners awarded silver medals and laurel wreaths.
Paris	1900	First women compete. Most winners do not receive medals and some receive cash prizes. Many never know they competed in Olympics.
St Louis	1904	Originally awarded to Chicago then moved to St Louis to be part of the Louisiana Purchase Exposition. Games take four and a half months to complete.
Athens	1906	The 2nd International Olympic Games. Unhappy with the organisation of the previous Games and claiming the Olympics as their birthright, the Greeks hold 'interim' Games. Winners receive gold, silver and bronze medals, IOC publishes the results, but in 1949 rule that the Games should not count.
London	1908	Games scheduled to be held in Rome, but Mt Vesuvius erupts. Within ten months the English build Shepherd's Bush stadium. Games launched with the support of the Franco-British Exhibition. First official opening ceremony to have parade of nations. Ray Ewry of USA wins eight gold medals. Dorando Pietri collapses in marathon and is carried across the line, forfeiting his medal but becoming a celebrity.
Stockholm	1912	First use of electronic timing and public address system. Jim Thorpe breaks records in first pentathlon and in decathlon, but is later stripped of medals for taking part in professional baseball. His medals posthumously reawarded.

	1914	De Coubertin designs Olympic flag.
Antwerp	1920	War prevents 1916 Games and Germany and other aggressor nations banned. Olympic flag flown for first time. Olympic Oath taken for the first time by Victor Boin. De Coubertin outlines Olympic Charter. Ice hockey and figure skating included for only time in Summer Games.
	1921	De Coubertin introduces Olympic motto, 'citius, altius, fortius' (faster, higher, stronger).
Chamonix	1924	'International Winter Sports Weeks' held prior to Summer Games, and later designated the first Winter Olympics. Britain wins 4 medals – a record.
Paris		Summer Games have first radio broadcast and closing ceremony. Johnny Weissmuller (Tarzan) and Dr Spock win medals.
St Moritz	1928	Winter Games begin in blizzard and end in 25°C. Several events cancelled for lack of ice and snow. Sonja Henie wins skating gold aged 15.
Amsterdam		Generally harmonious Games, women allowed to compete in track and field for first time, until some girls collapse after finishing the 800m. Calls are made to remove the event from Olympic programme and as a result it does not re-appear on programme until 1960. Olympic flame burns for duration of Games. Opening ceremony sees Greece enter first and hosts last, setting precedent for all future Games.
Lake Placid	1932	Warm weather again adversely affects Games. Eddie Eagan, boxing medallist in 1920, wins bobsleigh to become only man to win Winter and Summer medals. Ski instructors banned as professionals so Swiss and Austrians refuse to compete.
Los Angeles		Fewer athletes but record crowds attend. First Games to make a profit. Male athletes housed in dedicated Village for first time, and women stay in luxury hotel. Podium, award ceremony and flag raising introduced. Prohibition lifted allowing athletes to imbibe alcohol. Photo-finish cameras introduced. Swedish equestrian loses dressage silver medal for 'clicking' to his horse.

Garmisch-Partenkirchen	1936	Last year in which Winter and Summer Games held in same country. Alpine skiing makes its first appearance. 28 nations take part.
Berlin		Jewish groups call for boycott, but fail. Black athlete Jesse Owens wins four gold medals – one in the eye for Hitler. Torch relay introduced. First television coverage and wire service for results. Leni Riefenstahl's film *Olympia* released. German equestrian von Wangeheim breaks collarbone in steeplechase, falls again under horse, but remounts, goes clear, and Germany win team gold.
	1938	Japan returns Olympic Games to IOC because of war in China. IOC awards 1940 Games to Garmisch-Partenkirchen and Helsinki.
	1940	WWII causes cancellation of Winter and Summer Games.
	1944	War again prevents Games taking place.
St Moritz	1948	Twenty-eight countries compete. Two American hockey teams turn up claiming to be official representatives. Olympic flag stolen twice.
London		Germany and Japan banned, but record 59 nations take part. First political defections occur. Fanny Blankers-Koen wins four gold medals on track. First Stoke Mandeville Games held, blueprint for Paralympics.
Oslo	1952	Olympic flame lit in home fireplace of skiing pioneer Sondre Nordheim. Flame also lit atop Pallastunturi in Finland by rays of midnight sun and later combined with flame from Olympia. Torch relay conducted by 94 participants on skis.
Helsinki		Highly successful Games lead to calls for them to be held permanently in Scandinavia. Emil Zàtopek becomes only person to win 5,000m, 10,000m and marathon at same Olympics. Women allowed to enter open dressage event and Lis Hartel wins silver despite being paralysed below the knees.
Cortina d'Ampezzo	1956	First Winter Games to be televised. Torchbearer enters stadium on skates, falls and almost extinguishes flame. Soviet Union attends for first time and wins the most medals.

Melbourne & Stockholm	1956	First Games to be held in southern hemisphere. Many nations boycott: Egypt, Iraq and Lebanon at Israeli-led invasion of Suez Canal, and Netherlands, Spain and Switzerland at Soviet invasion of Hungary (45 Hungarians refuse to return home). West and East Germany enter combined team. Following idea submitted by young Chinese boy, closing ceremony is forever changed by mingling all competitors into one Olympic Family. Due to obstacles of quarantine and difficulties in transporting horses, equestrian events held in Stockholm and designated Equestrian Olympic Games.
Squaw Valley, USA	1960	Opening and closing ceremonies produced by Walt Disney. First Winter Games to have dedicated athlete's Village and to have computerised results. Women take part in speed skating for first time.
Rome		Rome finally gets its chance and holds many events at ancient sites. Pope watches the canoeing from his summer residence. Yugoslavia wins football tournament after qualifying on a coin toss. First official Paralympic Games take place.
Innsbruck	1964	Warm weather causes lack of snow and Austrian army imports snow and ice. Luge competitor killed in pre-race run.
Tokyo		First Games held in Asia. Torchbearer born in Hiroshima on day atomic bomb dropped. Politics cause South Africa to be banned and Indonesia and North Korea to withdraw. Computerised scoring introduced to Summer Games. Ukrainian Larysa Latynina brings medal tally to18, nine of them gold. Two cyclists set record for standing still (21:57 minutes), while waiting for the right moment to sprint home.
	1967	IOC draws up list of banned substances.
Grenoble	1968	First Games to be broadcast in colour. Organising Committee sell TV rights for US$2m. Claude Killy sweeps all men's alpine skiing events.
Mexico City		Student riots and Black Power activist athletes cause disruption. Altitude causes problems for athletes in endurance events. First drug testing introduced, as well as sex testing. Swedish entrant tests positive for alcohol. First woman lights Olympic cauldron. First truly synthetic track used. Dick Fosbury revolutionises high jump and Bob Beamon sets astonishing 8.9m long jump record.

Sapporo	1972	Issue of amateurism vs professionalism clouds Games. First and only Spanish slalom winner. Ard Schenk of Netherlands wins three gold medals in speedskating.
Munich		Largest Games yet, intended to celebrate peace, but eleven Israeli athletes murdered by Palestinian terrorists. Mark Spitz wins seven gold medals. Lasse Viren falls in 10,000m final but wins. Teenage gymnast Olga Korbut becomes a star.
Innsbruck	1976	Citizens of Denver refuse to host Games, so Innsbruck takes them for the second time, and two Olympic flames are lit. First Winter Paralympics held.
Montreal		Poor budgeting causes long-lasting debt to Canadians, but Games run smoothly. Games boycotted by 22 African nations in protest at All Blacks tour of South Africa. Nadia Comaneci of Romania awarded seven perfect scores in gymnastics. Japan's Shun Fujimoto breaks leg in floor exercise but competes in the rings, dislocating knee on dismount.
Lake Placid	1980	The Summer Games boycott overshadows the event. Liechtenstein becomes smallest country to produce a gold medallist. American Eric Heiden wins all men's speedskating events, taking five gold medals.
Moscow		US President Carter leads mass boycott over Soviet invasion of Afghanistan. Drug-enhanced Soviets win 11 of 13 swimming events and all 54 rowers win a medal. Coe and Ovett face off in the 800m and 1,500m. Both gold- and silver-medal winning coxless pairs are identical twins.
Sarajevo	1984	Games go without hitch despite impending civil war. Torvill and Dean awarded perfect score in ice dancing.
Los Angeles		First Games to be staged without government finance make US$223m profit. 140 nations take part. China sends first team for 52 years. Soviet Union stages revenge boycott. John Williams composes 'Olympic Fanfare and Theme'. Carl Lewis wins 100m, 200m, long jump and 4x100m relay. Professionals allowed to play football if they have not taken part in World Cup.
Calgary	1988	First Winter Games to last 16 days. Eddie 'the Eagle' Edwards makes the headlines. The Jamaican bobsleigh team surprisingly qualify and are later made heroes by the film Cool Runnings. Yvonne van Gennip of Netherlands beats drug-enhanced DDR competitors and wins three gold medals.

Seoul	1988	South Korea adopts democracy to host Games. North Korea, Cuba, Ethiopia and Nicaragua boycott. Canadian Ben Johnson tests positive for drugs and is disqualified.

Albertville 1992 Last Winter Games held the same year as Summer Games. Events spread out over the Savoie region. Germany competes as a single nation for the first time since 1964.

Barcelona South Africa re-enters after 32 years in the wilderness. After fall of Communism, Yugoslavia banned because of military aggression, but individuals allowed to enter. Estonia and Latvia make first appearance since 1936, and Lithuania since 1928. Other ex-Soviet countries compete as the 'Unified Team'. The 10,000m race sees first black African female gold medallist. Men's basketball allows professionals and the American 'dream team' average 117 points per game and never call a timeout.

Lillehammer 1994 Czechoslovakia divides and Slovakia makes first Olympic appearance. Games said to be 'Best Olympic Winter Games' ever. Women's figure skating in uproar after Nancy Kerrigan is assaulted by Tonya Harding's ex-husband.

Atlanta 1996 Over 10,000 athletes from 197 nations take part. Major organisational problems occur, particularly in transport. Terrorist bomb kills two and injures 111 at Atlanta concert. Football teams are allowed three professionals regardless and Nigeria beat Argentina in the final. Hubert Raudashl of Austria becomes the first person to compete in nine Olympics.

Nagano 1998 Record 2,180 athletes and 72 nations take part. New world records set in speed-skating due to the innovative clap skate. Norway's Björn Daehlie wins three golds and one silver, bringing his Olympic medal tally to twelve, of which eight are gold.

Sydney 2000 More than 10,600 athletes take part, and the authorities crack down on doping. East Timor takes part despite not being recognised by the IOC, bringing the number of nations participating to 199. The Bahamas becomes the smallest country to win a team event, in the 4x100m women's relay. Haile Gebreselassie of Ethiopia wins photo-finish 10,000m race. Steve Redgrave wins fifth gold medal in rowing.

Salt Lake City 2002 Games marred by scandal over claims that IOC officials received bribes in 1999 to award them to Salt Lake City. Controversy between Canada and Russia over the pairs figure skating after French judge pressurised to mark up the Russians. Both pairs eventually awarded gold at a second ceremony.

	2003	Vancouver awarded the 2010 Winter Games.
Athens	2004	Organisers silence critics by being ready on time. Kelly Holmes becomes first British woman to win two gold medals.
Turin	2006	Italy awarded second Winter Games and adops the motto 'Passion lives here'. A record 80 nations take part. Official mascots are a female snowball and a male ice cube. Ethiopia and Madagascar send one athlete each.
	2005	London awarded the 2012 Games, to become the first city officially to host them three times. IOC calls for Games to be limited to a maximum of 10,500 athletes.
Beijing	2008	China hosts $40b Olympics in spite of human rights record as IOC warns against politicising the Games. Almost 11,000 athletes attend and receive the largest television audience in Olympic history. 'Bird's Nest' stadium takes five years to build. Longest torch relay, lasting 130 days and covering 85,000 miles (taking in Mt Everest), encounters difficulties from protesters along the way. IOC reverses ban on Iraq's attendance. South African swimmer Natalie du Toit becomes first amputee to compete in Olympics. American Michael Phelps wins eight swimming gold medals. Usain Bolt of Jamaica breaks three world records to become the world's fastest man. Britain's Chris Hoy wins three gold medals in cycling. China pull out the stops with spectacular pyrotechnic closing ceremony with 90,000 audience and 1.5 billion viewers. Mayor of Beijing hands Olympic flag to Mayor of London and David Beckham kicks football into crowd.
Vancouver	2010	2,600 athletes participate from 82 nations. Canada beats the Soviet Union's 1976 record of Winter Olympic gold medals by one - taking 14 in all. Amy Williams wins skeleton gold medal, the first British individual Winter gold since 1980, and is awarded the MBE.

SIXTY OF
THE BEST

Launceston Elliot

1896 Athens

Weightlifting, one-handed lift

Launceston Elliot was the first British Olympic Champion. Not content with winning Britain's first ever Olympic medal in the one-handed lift, he entered the 100m sprint, where he came third, the heavyweight wrestling, coming fourth and the rope climbing competition. Then, at the 1900 Games, when no weightlifting events were held, he entered for the discus.

A member of the aristocratic Scottish family headed by Lord Minto, Elliot's strange family history warrants a mention. His father's first wife fell to her death from a hotel balcony in Australia in unexplained circumstances, whereupon his father married the hotel receptionist. He then married again (though what happened to the receptionist is not recorded), and Launceston was the fruit of this third marriage, conceived in Launceston, Tasmania, and born in India.

A man of superb physique, Elliot took to weightlifting early and at the age of only 16 entered the first British Championships in London's Piccadilly. By the time he was 19 he had succeeded in winning the event.

When he went to Athens in 1896, Elliot's handsome features and muscular build attracted much attention, even offers of marriage. The official Olympic report described him as being of 'uncommon beauty . . . impressive stature, tall, well-proportioned'. The weightlifting contest boiled down to a contest between Elliot and Vigo Jensen, a Dane. The rules were somewhat hazy, and after the two-handed event both men had lifted 111.5 kgs. The judges, however, preferred Jensen's style and placed him first. But in the one-handed lift, Elliot completed a lift of 71 kgs, 13 kgs more than Jensen could manage.

Before turning professional in 1905 Elliot had set four new world records at the 1899 Amateur Championships. His professional career became somewhat more colourful when he turned to the music hall stage. He and a partner would perform as gladiators, and at the end of the show Elliot's *pièce de résistance* was to support a bicycle and rider at each end of a pole across his mighty shoulders, turning in ever-faster circles until the riders were swinging horizontally. He was fond of including pretty girls in his act, and at one stage had 12 stunners to assist him. His wife would accompany him everywhere on tour, largely, one suspects, to repel the advances of his entourage and audience.

He retired in 1920 and farmed in Essex for several years before settling in Australia with his wife, where he died of spine cancer in 1930.

John Boland

1896 Athens

Lawn tennis, doubles & singles

The reluctant sportsman, John Boland, hand on hip, in 1896. His German partner, Fritz Traun, leans forward to talk to their Greek opponents.

John Boland was a most unlikely Olympian. He turned up to watch and ended by winning both the singles and the doubles tennis tournaments.

The son of a Dublin baker and a man of broad erudition, he studied at the Catholic University School in Dublin, Edgbaston Oratory, and the Universities of Oxford, London and Bonn. He was a fine cricketer and very good at tennis as well as being a keen rugby player, but had little top-class competitive experience.

While at Oxford, he had become friendly with Thrasyvoalos Manaos, Secretary of the 1896 Organising Committee, who invited him to the Games in Athens. Expecting only to spectate, he was reluctantly persuaded by Manaos to enter the tennis tournament. In spite of having no international experience, and wearing leather-soled shoes with heels, he borrowed a racket and won not only the singles title, but the doubles as well, with a German whose partner had suddenly withdrawn.

Boland was called to the Bar in 1897, became Member of Parliament for South Kerry from 1900 to 1918, and was General Secretary of the Catholic Truth Society for 21 years. He was an ardent proponent of Irish independence and the Irish language, and helped found the National University of Ireland, which promoted the Irish language as an essential examination subject.

The first Irish-born Olympic medallist, he died in London on St Patrick's Day 1958, at the age of 88.

Laurie and Reggie Doherty
1900 Paris and 1908 London

Laurie   *Lawn tennis, singles & doubles (1900)*
Reggie   *Lawn tennis, doubles & mixed doubles (1900)*
          Lawn tennis, doubles (1908)

The Doherty brothers were possibly the greatest doubles partnership in the history of tennis and dominated the game at the turn of the century. Between them they won eight Wimbledon doubles and nine singles titles, three US titles, six Olympic medals and were unbeaten in their five Davis Cup rubbers. Their record is all the more remarkable since both were plagued by ill health from boyhood and frequently competed in the teeth of medical advice. Spectators at the 1898 Wimbledon final, however, would hardly have known that they suffered from respiratory difficulties, for the brothers played 45 games in 55 minutes. Known as Big Do and Little Do, the handsome pair drew large crowds to their matches and were said to cause women to swoon by the courtside.

Laurie, three years younger than 'Big Do', is generally reckoned to be the better of the two, and the finest British player of all time after Fred Perry. In 1903 he became the first foreign male player to win the US singles title, taking the Wimbledon singles and doubles titles and the Davis Cup in the same year, making him the first true 'Grand Slam' champion.

The dashing Doherty brothers, Reggie reclining and Laurie on the right.

The two men entered the singles, doubles and mixed doubles tournaments of the 1900 Olympic Games. After winning the doubles in three straight sets, Laurie was scheduled to meet his brother in the semi-finals of the singles, but Reggie conceded a walkover and Laurie went on to beat the Irishman, Harold Mahoney, in the final. The two met again in the mixed doubles semi-final, Laurie partnered by the American Marion Jones and Reggie by Chattie Cooper. Reggie and Chattie went on to win the competition without dropping a set.

By 1906, the health of both players had deteriorated and they were so exhausted in chasing their ninth successive Wimbledon doubles title that their tearful mother begged them to give it up. Laurie dutifully took heed, and turned to golf instead, but Reggie entered the Olympics again in 1908, where he won his second doubles gold medal, this time with George Hillyard. He continued to play, taking two titles at the South African Championships in 1909, but the effort was to prove too great a strain, and he died the following year.

In spite of his frailty, Laurie joined the Royal Naval Reserve in 1914 but the rigours of life in the Anti-Aircraft branch took their inevitable toll. He was invalided out and after a long illness died in 1919.

The Dohertys found time during their brief and busy lives to co-author a book on tennis instruction, *RF & HL Doherty on Lawn Tennis*, a rare and much sought-after title. Their good looks and popularity at the turn of the century did much to revive the fortunes of the All England Lawn Tennis and Croquet Club, which at the time was barely making a profit on the annual Championships. In 1931 their brother, the Rev. William, donated the Doherty Memorial Gates to Wimbledon, a fitting tribute to such a talented and influential pair.

Charlotte (Chattie) Cooper
1900 Paris

Lawn Tennis, single and mixed doubles

Born in London in 1870, Chattie Cooper has entered the record books for more than her two wins in Paris in 1900: she was the first woman to become an Olympic champion, the oldest winner of the Wimbledon singles title, and the longest-lived Olympian. In 1900 she beat the French champion, Hélène Prévost, in straight sets to win

the singles and then took the doubles gold medal with Reggie Doherty as her partner. She also won a silver medal in the mixed doubles with Max Woosnam.

Chattie Cooper in her prime in 1900.

Slender but strong, Cooper cut an impressive figure on the courts in her ankle-length skirts and high collars, but the restrictive Edwardian-style attire failed to stop her successfully competing until well into her 50s. In all, she won five Wimbledon singles titles, the last at the age of almost 38, having returned to the game after an absence to raise her family. She was married at the late (for her era) age of 30 to fellow tennis player, Alfred Sterry, who became President of the Lawn Tennis Association. Their daughter, Gwen, was also a talented player and was part of the British Wightman Cup team.

It is possible that Cooper might have won more medals had she been allowed to compete in the first Games, but in 1896 only men were allowed to enter.

Henry Taylor

1906 Athens and 1908 London
Swimming, 1-mile freestyle (1906)
Swimming, 400m freestyle, 1,500m freestyle & 4x200m freestyle (1908)

Born into poverty and orphaned at an early age, Henry Taylor went on to become one of Britain's most successful swimmers, winning a record eight Olympic medals in four successive Games. His tally of three gold medals at one Olympics is a British achievement matched only by Chris Hoy in 2008. Semi-literate and only 5'5" tall, Taylor's prodigious talent earned him 35 trophies and more than 300 medals during his career, yet he died in obscurity.

Brought up and trained by his elder brother Bill, Taylor learned to swim in the canal in his home town of Oldham. At the age of seven he entered his first race at the local baths, beating rivals much older than himself. He trained hard and was soon noticed and selected for the Games in 1906 where he won the 1-mile freestyle gold medal. Later the same year he set a world record for the 880 yards and was an obvious choice for the 1908 Games. There he lost only one race, the second 400m semi-final, but powered home in the final ten seconds ahead of the field, going on to finish first in the 1,500m final and winning his third gold medal in the 4x200m relay.

Henry Taylor with his impressive display of trophies.

Four years later in Stockholm, Taylor anchored the 4x200m bronze-winning freestyle relay team. The 1916 Games were cancelled because of the war and Taylor joined the Navy, but he returned for his fourth Games in 1920 and again won a bronze medal with the relay team. During the war Taylor achieved the status of 'Champion Swimmer' by swimming round the entire fleet, then anchored at Scapa Flow – quite an achievement given the size of the British fleet at the time and the choppy conditions. He also represented England at water polo.

In spite of his small stature, Taylor cut a fine figure in his handmade silk swimming costume, complete with 'modesty slip' – a sort of knotted handkerchief worn like a thong. At the age of 41 he retired from competitive swimming. Never adept at managing his finances, he pawned most of his numerous trophies to buy an inn, but failed to make a success of it and the silverware was lost to him forever. He took a job as an attendant at Oldham's Chadderton Baths and at the age of 65 died impoverished and forgotten, a sad end for a man once hailed as 'Britain's Greatest Amateur Swimmer'. A measure of belated recognition was accorded in 2002 when a blue plaque to him was unveiled at Chadderton Baths, where some of his trophies have been gathered together and displayed.

John Jacob Astor, 1st Baron Astor of Hever

1908 London
Rackets, doubles

When John Jacob Astor won his rackets gold medal in the London Olympics in 1908 he still had both legs. In later life, he was still winning squash tournaments with one leg!*

Born in New York in 1886 into the Astor banking family, John Jacob came as a child to England, where he and his family were naturalised in 1899. After Eton and a short period at Oxford, he took a commission in the Life Guards, serving as ADC to Lord Hardinge, then Viceroy of India. At the outbreak of war he returned to active duty, distinguishing himself by his bravery. In September 1918, he was wounded in 14 places and his right leg was amputated. To take his mind off his injuries, his father gave him Hever Castle.

Inheriting a fortune on the death of his father in 1919, he sought a more meaningful role in life. He was elected to Parliament as Unionist member for Dover in 1922, a seat he held until 1945, but is perhaps best known for his stewardship of *The Times* newspaper, of which he was chief proprietor from 1922 to 1966. He famously sponsored Colonel John Hunt's expedition by which Hillary and Tensing conquered Everest in 1952.

At Eton, as well as opening the batting for the cricket team in 1904 and 1905, he won the public schools rackets championship with M. W. Bovill in 1905. In 1908, he won the Army singles rackets championship, and the doubles with Lord Somers.

The two 1908 Olympics rackets events were contested only by British players. Astor won gold in the doubles, with Vane Pennell, and bronze in the singles. After the war and in spite of his tin leg, as he called it, he continued to play, winning the parliamentary squash rackets competition in 1926 and 1927. He also played cricket, tennis and golf, and became President of the MCC in 1937.

Lord Astor, notwithstanding his wealth, power and achievements, lived frugally and unassumingly. In later life he took up painting, and died in 1971.

Lord Astor in Life Guards' uniform as ADC to Lord Hardinge.

---

* There *was* a one-legged Olympian. American George Eyser won three gold medals, two silvers and a bronze in the 1904 gymnastics wearing a wooden leg.

Wyndham Halswelle

1908 London
Athletics, 400m

The lonely figure of Wyndham Halswelle as he wins the 400m in a walkover. His victory prompted one newspaper to offer the headline 'Halswelle That Ends Well'.

Wyndham Halswelle was a first-class sprinter and the winner of Scotland's first Olympic gold medal. It was unfortunate that his victory should have been achieved in such controversial circumstances, and that he should be remembered largely for being the only man in Olympic history to win in a walkover.

Although London-born, Halswelle took the nationality of his Scottish grandfather, General Nathaniel Gordon. He excelled in athletics at Charterhouse School and Sandhurst, then took a commission in the Highland Light Infantry, who were sent in 1902 to fight the Boer War. His athletic ability was recognised while in South Africa, and when the regiment returned the following year Halswelle took up running seriously. Having won races in the Army and the AAA, he became part of the squad for the 1906 Games, taking a silver medal in the 400m and bronze in the 800m. That year, too, he achieved the impressive feat of winning the 100, 220, 440 and 880 yards races in a single day.

In the run-up to the 1908 Games, Halswelle succeeded in setting world and British records in the 300 and 440 yds. In qualifying for the finals of the 400m at the Games themselves, he set an Olympic record of 48.4. But the final itself was to prove a messy affair. Alongside Halswelle were three Americans, and the race was to be run without lanes. Coming off the final bend, Halswelle was in third place, poised to pass in the last straight, as was his habit. As he did so, Carpenter, the American in second place, ran wide, elbowing Halswelle almost off the track. The umpire cried 'Foul!' and the race was declared void. Blocking at the time was allowed in American races, but not in the Olympics, and Carpenter was disqualified. The race was to be re-run in lanes. Siding with the disgruntled Carpenter, the two remaining American athletes refused to take part, and Halswelle won in a walkover, with a sedate time of 50.2.

The only positive outcomes of this debacle were that from then on all 400m races were run in lanes, and the Amateur Athletics Federation was founded to standardise rules and prevent similar mishaps.

Halswelle, however, was disenchanted and ran only one more race before retiring. He was killed by a sniper bullet at the Battle of Neuve Chapelle in March 1915.

Paulo Radmilovic

1908 London, 1912 Stockholm, 1920 Antwerp
Water polo (1908, 1912 & 1920), Swimming 4x200m freestyle relay (1908)

Born in 1886, Paulo Radmilovic (known as Paul or Raddy) was one of Britain's greatest Olympians, and has often been dubbed 'Wales's greatest ever sportsman'. In an Olympic career which spanned 22 years he competed in six consecutive Games – the first Briton to do so, and the last until Tessa Sanderson in 1996 – and his record of four gold medals in three successive Olympic Games was only broken when Sir Steve Redgrave won his historic fifth gold at Sydney in 2000. He is also one of only a handful of Olympians to have won medals in two different disciplines.

Born in Cardiff of Croatian-Irish descent, Radmilovic's family relocated to Weston-Super-Mare when he was a child, and there he began swimming in the waters of the Bristol Channel. From an early age he showed great promise as an all-round sportsman, his talents reaching beyond swimming and water polo to football, athletics, boxing and (as a scratch player) golf. When he was only 15 years old began his international career as a member of the Welsh national water polo team.

Radmilovic made his Olympic debut at the 1906 Intercalated Games, but he failed to make the medal table in the three swimming events he entered. In 1908, he attended the London Olympics as part of the British men's water polo team, as well being recruited at the last minute for the 4x200m freestyle relay team. Within the space of two days he won gold medals in both events, scoring twice in the final of the water polo and becoming the first Welshman to win an Olympic gold.

Returning for the 1912 Games in Stockholm, Radmilovic won his third gold medal, captaining the British water polo team which beat the Austrians by a resounding 8-0 in the final.

On his next appearance, at the Antwerp Olympics in 1920, he won his fourth gold medal with the British water polo squad. In a tight final against the home side, Radmilovic, again the captain, scored three minutes from time to put the British 3-2 ahead. As the final whistle went,

Paolo Radmilovic (middle row, right) with Great Britain's gold medal-winning water polo team in 1920.

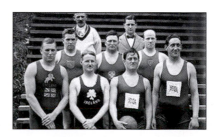

the highly-incensed Belgian crowd started a riot and the victorious team had to be escorted from the pool under armed guard.

Paris 1924, and there was Radmilovic again, now aged 38, but the water polo team failed to make the medals. The same disappointment faced them in 1928 in Amsterdam, Radmilovic's last Olympic appearance.

Although his four gold medals gained him recognition for water polo, Radmilovic's swimming career was also a long and illustrious one: he won nine ASA freestyle titles at various distances from 100 yards to 5 miles, the English Long Distance Championships in 1907 and 1925 and, in 1926, the English One Mile Championship. His last victory came at the age of 43 in a 440 yards event, but even in his late seventies he continued to swim a quarter of a mile every day. When he retired from swimming, Radmilovic became the licensee of the Imperial Hotel in Weston-Super-Mare.

In 1967 he was inducted into the Swimming Hall of Fame, and 1993 into the Welsh Sports Hall of Fame. His achievements were further recognised in Wales with a plaque at the Cardiff International Pool, paid for by the 2012 London Olympics Committee and the Welsh Assembly and unveiled in 2008 on the 100th anniversary of his double-gold Olympic success. As part of this belated recognition, attempts were made to track down Radmilovic's Olympic medals, which went missing after his death in 1968 and subsequent family squabbles. Sadly, there is still no sign of them.

Curiously, in 1992 Guyana issued a set of postage stamps featuring Olympic gold medalists from the past. A $25 stamp shows Radmilovic in the water, his arms outstretched, with the caption '*Paul Radmilovic. GDR. 1920 Waterpolo (team)*'. Does anyone have an explanation?

Madge Syers
1908 London
Figure skating, ladies

Florence 'Madge' Syers was the first female World and Olympic figure skating champion and, to date, the oldest.

Already known as the world's finest woman skater, she really caught the public's attention in 1902 when she came second in the World Championships. The fact that she had entered at all was a nasty shock to the organisers, the International Skating Union, who had not dreamed that a woman would dare do so and had omitted in their rules to ban them. It was just as much of a shock that she came second. Many thought she should have won, even the winner Ulrich Salchow, who reportedly handed her his gold medal as soon as it was presented to him. The ISU immediately prohibited women from competing against men on the grounds that their long skirts made it hard for the judges to see their feet. Syers responded by shortening her skirts to mid-calf, thereby setting a trend.

One of 15 children born into a wealthy family in London, Madge Cave learned to skate, like many young society girls, at the Prince's Skating Rink in Knightsbridge. But unlike most of her contemporaries, she was a gifted athlete and took it seriously. At the same time as developing as a first-class skater, she was winning prizes for swimming and riding.

When she met Edgar Syers her life and her skating style changed dramatically. Edgar became her coach, encouraging her to adopt the free-flowing 'International' style of skating. In 1900 they married, and with the 1899 British pairs championship gold medal under their belts, they came second in the first international pairs competition in Berlin. Though theirs was a formidable pairing, Madge's forte was individual figure skating.

In 1903 Madge won the first British singles championship, and the following year beat her husband to retain the title. In 1905 the ISU rescinded the ban on women competitors, and the next year introduced a separate event for ladies at the World Championships. Madge won in both 1906 and 1907, although it was not until 1920 that these two events were retroactively recognised as official.

Reigning supreme in the sport, she was the clear favourite for the 1908 Olympic women's singles title. The judges unanimously gave her firsts in the two elements of compulsory figures and free skating: she duly returned home with the gold medal. She and Edgar also won a bronze in the pairs event.

Soon after the Games, Madge's health began to fail and in 1917 at the age of 35 she died of influenza.

Madge and Edgar Syers at the Olympics in 1908.

Vivian Woodward

1908 London and 1912 Stockholm
Football

Viv Woodward, winner of 66 international caps and England's most prolific scorer during half a century, was almost certainly the greatest centre forward the country has ever produced. Known to his friends as Jack, and to his peers and the press as 'football's gentleman', Woodward was in his prime in an era when England led the world in football and he still appears in the list of top ten goal scorers and in the Football Association's top 100 players of all time. In 1908 he put eight of England's 15 goals past the French, a match tally never bettered by an England player, and the following year he scored four goals against Holland.

Woodward captained the England team to victory in two Olympic Games, scoring in every match. He was 33 when he led the English team in Stockholm. His leadership and sportsmanship endeared him to his team mates and earned him admiration within and beyond the world of football. One colleague, Bobby Steel of Clacton Town, described him as 'the finest centre forward I have ever seen. He was a gentleman and in all my association with him I never saw him commit a foul or retaliate – and he did get some pastings.'

Born into a wealthy family and an architect by profession, he remained an amateur all his life. He started his career with Clacton Town FC, but his most prolific years were spent first with Tottenham Hotspur, and then with Chelsea. Although almost certain of selection for club and international matches, he often put work commitments first. As a first-class tennis player he sometimes preferred to be on the court rather than the pitch, and warned Spurs when he signed for them that he might be unavailable unless it was 'convenient'. He also excelled at cricket, captaining Essex when in his 40s, and seems to have been something of a whiz on rollerskates.

At the start of the First World War, Woodward joined the Middlesex Regiment, enlisting in the 17th 'Footballer's' Battalion. In 1915 his club, Chelsea, reached the final of the FA Cup, and he was given leave to take the place of the injured (and one-eyed) Bob Thompson. But when he heard that Thompson had recovered, with typical generosity and sportsmanship he refused to play, since Thompson had played in all previous cup matches and he had not. He was wounded in 1916, which put an end to his career. But he retained his links with the game, becoming a director of Chelsea from 1922 to 1930.

A superstar in his day, well before the days of celebrity sportsmen, Woodward died lonely and forgotten in 1954 in a London nursing home, a tragic end to one of England's finest.

Emil Voigt
1908 London
Athletics, 5 miles

Winner of the 5 mile race in 1908, Emil Voigt – who died in 1974 – still holds the title more than twenty-five years after his death since the event was never held again. Voigt's further unique claim to fame is that he was the only vegetarian among the 2,023 Olympic entrants.

Born in Manchester of German parents, and described by the press as 'one of the most stylish runners ever seen on the path', Voigt was a well-travelled polyglot and a man of great energy and good cheer. Only 5'5" tall and weighing eight stone, he eschewed meat, tobacco and alcohol, and was a lifelong proponent of a planned (vegetarian) diet, deep breathing and the benefits of massage in building up athletic prowess.

Although keen on cycling and football in his youth, running became Voigt's passion, and a versatile runner he was, winning races at anything between 800 metres and 10 miles. He had been thinking about retiring from athletics, but since the Olympics were to be held in his home country, he asked the officials if he could enter the trials at two weeks' notice. On a whim he asked to be entered in the 5-mile race (a distance he had never raced before) and at the last minute they agreed. He won the trial but had little time to prepare for the Games. He used the AAA 4-mile race in London as a warm-up and won it in style. But the training and racing had left him with painful feet, so he and his coach, keeping close counsel, decided he should take things easy until just before the Olympics.

In the heats in Manchester, Emil and six others lined up and set off. Tucked in the pack, he was jostled, tugged and rapped on the heels. So with a mile left to run, he decided to get out of harm's way. He turned on the turbos, went clear and won by 150 yards. But immediately he broke down, his foot muscles torn and an arch collapsed. It was assumed that he would take no further part.

That night Voigt took the train to London to see a specialist who strapped the foot and built a special plaster of Paris arch support to go inside his shoe. On the day of the final, Voigt was unsure whether he could compete at all, let alone

Emil Voigt, winner of the last 5-mile Olympic event, poses for the cameras in 1908.

finish. Keeping his doubts to himself, he told the press he was 'in good trim', and lined up with the other nine finalists. Blanking out the pain, Voigt ran the race of his life. With his trademark spurt, in the last 700 yards he flashed past the field to win by 70 yards and break the world record – to the astonishment of the crowd, most of whom had never heard of him. Back home in Manchester, a huge crowd greeted him and carried him shoulder-high through the streets.

Putting thoughts of retirement behind him, Voigt continued to run at various distances, winning the 1-mile, 4-mile and 5-mile British championships. In 1911 he moved to Australia. He designed the cinder circuit in Melbourne, the first of its kind in the Southern Hemisphere. He soon became the Australian 6-mile champion and in 1913 the 2-mile record holder.

He also became a pioneer in broadcasting and founded his own radio station. Having long been interested in politics, he used his station to promote social justice and champion the underdog. This brought him under the scrutiny of the secret services in the UK and Australia as a suspected Communist, but, although he had leanings that direction, he was never a member of the Party.

In his 80s Voigt was still running several miles a day (up a volcano!), gliding, fishing and generally keeping happy and active. He ended his days in New Zealand, where he died at the age of 90.

Arnold Jackson
1912 Stockholm
Athletics, 1,500m

In 1912, the 21-year-old undergraduate Arnold Jackson came from behind to win what has been described as 'the greatest race ever run', breaking the world record and becoming the youngest ever Olympic 1,500m gold medallist.

Jackson, one of the dying breed of Edwardian gentlemen-amateurs, was not one to over-exert himself in practice, relying instead on his natural talent: his idea of training during the Olympics was to sit in the shade and ogle the good-looking lady tennis players, and after the 1,500m heats he decided his best preparation for the final would be to have a nap. An outsider, Jackson was not expected to beat the Americans, who at the time dominated the event. Coming off the final turn, three of the Americans, two of them mile and 1,500m world record holders, ran abreast, forcing Jackson to go wide. For 50 yards they ran together, but with a final burst Jackson pipped them at the post by a tenth of a second in a time of 3:56.8. So close was the finish that, for the only time in the 1912 Olympics, a photo finish was needed to decide the outcome. It was the pinnacle of Jackson's short athletics career.

Arnold Jackson leads the field in the final of the 1,500m in 1912.

In all Jackson won only six major races, but he described his Olympic triumph as, 'a perfect day [against] capital fellow competitors'.

After studying law at Oxford (where he also rowed, played hockey and football) 'Jackers'

joined up during the First World War and served with great distinction. He became the British Army's youngest Brigadier General. He was awarded the DSO and three bars, the last for 'conspicuous gallantry and brilliant leadership'. He was mentioned in despatches nine times, but wounds received in action left him permanently lame and put an end to his sporting career.

Having changed his name to Arnold Nugent Strode Strode-Jackson, in 1921 he became a delegate at the Paris Peace Conference and was awarded the CBE.

Jackson practised as a barrister and was a member of the British Olympic Council in 1920. The following year he emigrated to America, becoming a US citizen in 1945. When his wife died in 1963, he returned to England where he died in 1972.

Kitty Godfree
1920 Antwerp
Lawn Tennis, Ladies' Doubles

The good-natured and gregarious Kitty Godfree (née Kathleen McKane) was the golden girl of British tennis in its heyday in 1920s and '30s. Considered the finest woman tennis player the country has produced, she is one of its most successful Olympians, winning one gold, two silvers and two bronze medals in successive Games in Antwerp and Paris. Her gold medal in Antwerp was won with Margaret McNair, and the mixed doubles silver medal with the legendary

Max Woosnam. She had a terrific all-round game, was a particularly good volleyer (a rarity in those days), but her main strength lay in her mental toughness and gritty determination. The final of the Wimbledon Ladies' Singles match against Helen Wills in 1924 well demonstrated this: having lost the first set 4-6, and two breaks of serve and 40-15 down in the second, Kitty fought back to take the title 4-6, 6-4, 6-4, inflicting 'Little Miss Poker Face's' only defeat in nine

Wimbledon appearances. 'This is the point where the English girl is so wonderful, where the grit of her country shows in her,' wrote the French tennis star Suzanne Lenglen at the time.

In 1926 she won the title again, and with it the prize of a £10 voucher and a bracelet worth five guineas from the jewellers Mappin & Webb. She later added this to other prize vouchers, and traded in her gems for a two-seater sports car.

Godfree was a remarkable all-round athlete, excelling not only at tennis but at lacrosse, badminton, skating, cycling, croquet and cricket. At the age of nine, she cycled from London to Berlin – a 600-mile journey which was to her a mere 'outing'. She played lacrosse at International level and was four times the All England Badminton Champion. Such was her stamina that she was still playing competitive tennis in her nineties. At 92, as an honoured guest she attended the Seoul Olympics in 1988, the first time since 1924 that tennis had been included as a medal sport.

Godfree and her husband, Leslie, are the only married couple ever to win the Wimbledon Mixed Doubles title and, until Venus and Serena Williams, she and her sister were the only siblings to contest a Wimbledon Ladies' Doubles final. In her impressive Wimbledon career, Godfree won 111 of her 146 matches, and in 1925 became the first person to reach the singles finals of the French Championships and the US Championships in the same year.

Kitty Godfree is undoubtedly one of the best-remembered and popular tennis players of any era. Self-taught, modest about her manifold talents and amiable to all, she was an inspiration to many. As the BBC commentator Dan Maskell said in the introduction to her biography, 'Her victories sowed the seeds of Wimbledon wins. I feel she showed Britain the way in the world of tennis.'

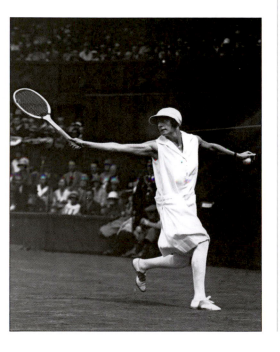

The stylish Kitty Godfree at the Wimbledon Championships in 1926, where she beat Miss Lili de Alvarez of Spain in the final.

Material Victory – The Evolution of Equipment

Since the early 1800s human beings have become significantly taller, stronger and longer-lived, and in the field of sport and competition parallel developments and adaptations of equipment and apparel have taken place. The invention of new materials and devices and the harnessing of sophisticated technology have in one way or another enhanced virtually every sporting endeavour. Whether it be a £30,000 state-of-the-art dinghy or a video replay of races, infrared beams on the finishing line or a stopwatch on the wrist, all provide an edge.

Take the pole vault. Originally, poles were made of solid wood, but by the early 1900s more flexible bamboo poles had been introduced – these being lighter, athletes were able to use longer poles and take a faster run-up, naturally resulting in higher clearances. A scarcity of bamboo during the Second World War led to the use of hollow aluminium and steel poles, but a far more significant development was the introduction of carbon-fibre poles. So flexible are they that in 1994, the Russian Sergey Bubka, using the 'catapult' technique, was able to clear an astonishing 6.14 metres (the Olympic record is 5.96 metres, set in 2008).

In sprinting, where the difference between winning and losing can be measured in milliseconds, technology has likewise made a huge difference – starting blocks, spikes and wafer-thin shoes, clothing which cuts down wind resistance and improved tracks have all led to faster times. In the ancient Games, runners would line up, their toes resting in grooves in a stone starting sill – hence the expression 'to toe the line'. In the early modern Games, they would set off from a standing start, which in time developed into the crouching start, fingers on the ground. The first man to try this stance was an American, Thomas Burke. When he crouched, with his knee on the ground, it

Harry Babcock of the USA vaulting to victory with a bamboo pole in 1912. He cleared 3.95m, which was 2.01m less than the Olympic winning vault in 2008.

threw the officials into confusion. Eventually he was permitted to start from this 'uncomfortable position' and won both the 100m and 400m races. In 1936, Jesse Owens was given a small shovel to dig his own starting groove in the cinder track, as was Fanny Blankers-Koen. But, come the starting blocks, records began to tumble as athletes were able to push off and get into their stride more quickly. Technology aside, one might question how much more the human body can be 'improved'; humans today may be 'swifter, higher, stronger', but little over half a century since Roger Bannister achieved the 'impossible' by running a mile in under four minutes, only 1.9 seconds have been shaved from his record of 3:59.4.

Cycling has seen even more eye-opening developments. Evolving from the early bone-shakers, through the introduction of gears and tubular tyres, the appearance of Chris Boardman's revolutionary Lotus 'superbike' at the 1992 Games caused a sensation. The bike comprised a 'composite monocoque with minimum-drag aerodynamic cross-sections and . . . monoblade with aerofoil cross-section': whether or not the public grasped these technicalities, they certainly understood that the space-age machine, ridden by 'the fastest man on two wheels', was breaking records and winning medals.

In these and so many other Olympic disciplines have the rules and equipment evolved. In shooting and archery where weapons have developed ever-greater range, lightness and accuracy; in sailing where craft are lighter and more stable, use radar to detect wind and riblets to reduce drag; in skating, where the blades are honed and polished using NASA technology; in table tennis where cigar-box lids and champagne corks have been replaced by carbon-fibre rackets and hollow balls which can travel at 160km an hour; in fencing, skiing, rowing, skating and sledding – all these have seen huge advances through new technology and changes in technique.

When one-thousandth of a second can make the difference between a gold medal and a silver, when the difference between gold and bronze can mean full sponsorship or no financial backing at all, and when the rewards to sponsors and manufacturers can be measured in millions of pounds, the quest for perfection in performance is intense. In 2008 Loughborough University launched a £15m sports technology institute to work on developing equipment and training aids to ensure that British athletes have the best possible chance in 2012.

But losers are ever wont to complain. In 1908, the Americans objected to the standard-issue hobnailed boots worn by the Liverpool Police tug-of-war team which

The City of Liverpool Police tug-of-war team, wearing their 'illegal' boots.

knocked them out in the first pull. The bobbies volunteered to take them on in their socks, but the offer was declined and the Americans left in a huff.

A hundred years on and the war over 'unfair advantage' is still being waged; in Beijing the furore centred on Speedo's racer swimsuits. With ultrasonically bonded seams, the LZR suit was the common denominator in 37 world-record performances, but at around £500 each and with many teams tied to other sponsors, there were calls for it to be banned. In the spring of 2009, a succession of even more advanced suits were launched onto the market. One, the Jaked 101, made of 100 per cent polyurethane, compresses muscle and traps air, adding to buoyancy – all of

which sparked another outcry and cries of 'cheating'. Rebecca Adlington, the double gold medallist from Beijing, refused to wear it, calling it 'technological doping', but swimming's governing body, FINA, was forced to drop its ban of the suits after threats of legal action from the manufacturers. Adidas, too, brought out a new hydrofoil suit, fully laminated to reduce drag. All these suits take half an hour and the help of several others to don!

But in July 2009, FINA resolved to ban all high-tech swimsuits, allowing only suits reaching to the knees, or 'jammers' as they are known. The ban did not come into force until January 2010, by which time numerous records had been broken. Since they were first introduced, more than 130 world records have been broken by swimmers wearing the high-tech suits. It is widely acknowledged that it will be some time before the records are broken again in the pool – or even matched.

The authorities have the difficult duty of ensuring that sports should be even contests between competitors, not a test of who has the best equipment. It is a duty the International Olympic Committee and the individual governing bodies largely fulfil, keeping pace with technology, revising the rules in the light of advances, and maintaining fair play and sportsmanship.

Henry Mallin

1920 Antwerp and 1924 Paris
Boxing, middleweight

Harry Mallin, a London policeman, achieved the unique record of never having been beaten in 300 amateur fights.

His victory in the middleweight division at the Antwerp Games was relatively straightforward, but when he came to defend his title in Paris in 1924 extraordinary scenes ensued. Having cruised through the early rounds, he met local hero Roger Brousse in the quarter-finals. During the second round, with Mallin busy punishing the Frenchman with his powerful left, Brousse tried to bite him on the arm.

In the third and final round, Brousse succeeded in sinking his teeth into Mallin's chest, clean through his vest. At the end of the fight, which he figured he had won comfortably, Mallin protested to the referee and showed the teeth marks on his chest. A doctor examined him but declared that since Mallin's opponent had been wearing a gumshield on his lower set, it was impossible for him to have inflicted the wound. For the first time in his life, Mallin was declared the loser.

The British officials did nothing – neither the Earl of Cadogan, President of the British Olympic Association, nor the President of the International Amateur Boxing Federation. However, a Swedish official lodged a formal complaint on Mallin's behalf. Late that night and well into the following evening's scheduled events, the appeal jury examined the evidence. Eventually it was announced that Brousse had been disqualified. The French went berserk and fights broke out around the hall. Throughout the semi-final and final the disruptions and eruptions in the audience continued, and little was seen of Mallin's victory as he became the first man ever successfully to defend an Olympic boxing title.

During his astonishing career, Mallin not only won two Olympic gold medals, but five ABA titles as well, and when he retired after the Paris debacle no one had ever beaten him.

In 1936 he managed the British Olympic boxing team, and in 1937 gave the first ever television sports commentary in Britain on a fight at Alexandra Palace. He managed the British team again in 1952. His brother, Frederick, was also five-times British middleweight champion.

Henry Mallin retired undefeated after 300 amateur middleweight fights.

Max Woosnam

1920 Antwerp
Lawn Tennis, doubles

Max Woosnam was an outstandingly versatile sportsman, the like of whom the world will probably never see again. Here was a man, an amateur all his life, who acquired a degree and five Blues from Cambridge University, won Olympic gold and silver medals on the same day, a Wimbledon title, was captain of the English football team and Manchester City FC as well as of the British Davis Cup squad, made a perfect 147 break in a snooker match, was a scratch golfer, scored a century at Lords – oh, and he fought in the trenches and rose to sit on the Board of one of the biggest chemical companies in the world.

At Winchester, Woosnam played football and squash and captained the school's golf and cricket teams. In a school match against the MCC at Lords, he scored 144 not out in his first innings. When he went up to Trinity College, Cambridge, he got his Blues in football, cricket, tennis, real tennis and golf.

In 1914, he was playing first division football for Chelsea when war broke out. He volunteered, and saw action at Gallipoli, in the Middle East and on the Western Front. After the war he took a job in an engineering firm, but sport remained his passion. In 1919 he joined Manchester City and became widely regarded as the best midfielder and captain the club had ever known. Such was his talent that he was invited to join the British Olympic football squad for the 1920 Games, but he had already committed himself to play tennis. Although knocked out early in the singles, he went on to win the men's doubles (with Noel Turnbull) and later in the day won silver in the mixed doubles with his partner Kitty Godfree.

The year 1921 was a busy one for Woosnam: he played the full season with Manchester City, becoming its captain midway through, captained

Max Woosnam (top left) and partner Oswald Turnbull in action against Ichiya Kumagae and Seiichiro Kashio of Japan. Great Britain won the match to claim the gold medal.

the England amateur football team to a win over Wales, entered Wimbledon and was runner-up in the mixed doubles title, and headed for America as captain of the Davis Cup team.

It was during this visit to the States that Charlie Chaplin invited the team to stay at his Hollywood mansion. Chaplin first challenged Woosnam to a tennis match, and was soundly beaten. Next Chaplin challenged Woosnam to a game of table tennis. He was beaten again and, adding insult to injury, by a man using a butter knife instead of a bat! To crown it all, Woosnam playfully tossed him into his own swimming pool in the middle of his pre-dinner speech.

The following year Woosnam broke his leg in a match against Newcastle, which effectively put an end to his football career. Less mobile now, he nonetheless continued for the rest of his life to enjoy the other sports at which he once excelled. In 1940, he joined the chemical giant, ICI, eventually becoming a member of the Board.

Blond-haired, blue-eyed and with thighs like 'telegraph poles', Woosnam was described by the press as 'Captain Courageous', and 'The Admirable Crichton of sport'. Modest and self-effacing, he never gave an interview in his life, but he was immensely popular in his time. Resolutely refusing to turn professional, Woosnam played sport because he loved it, not for fame or fortune.

Many have asked: Was he the greatest all-round sportsman ever? The answer is almost certainly, Yes.

Harold Abrahams

1924 Paris
Athletics, 100m

Abrahams' 100 metres victory at the 1924 Paris Olympics has become one of the best-known athletics performances of all time, after being immortalised in the Oscar-winning film *Chariots of Fire*. The film allowed itself more than a little artistic licence, since his great rival at the time, Eric Liddell, did not actually compete in the 100m final, his Presbyterian principles preventing him from competing on the Sabbath.

Abrahams had set his sights on winning a gold medal in the 100m, and Liddell's withdrawal must have been a great relief to him, since Liddell had set a record time of 9:7.10 shortly before the Games. They did, however, meet in the 200m final, Liddell winning bronze and Abrahams finishing sixth. It was the only time they met on the track.

Harold Abrahams for many years dominated British long jump and sprint events and winning the Olympic 100m had become an obsession with him. Having competed unsuccessfully in the 1920 Olympics, he caused uproar in the establishment in 1924 by hiring a coach, Sam

Mussabini. The relationship between them was one of the themes of *Chariots of Fire,* and the fierce reaction to this amateur being coached was put down to anti-Semitism. Mussabini gave this advice to Abrahams before the memorable race, 'Only think of two things, the report of the pistol and the tape. When you hear the one, just run like hell until you break the other.' Run like hell he did, setting an Olympic record of 10.6 seconds. He also won a silver medal in the 4x100m relay. A month before the Paris Games, he had set a new English long jump record of 7.36 metres, which stood for 32 years. There were no presentation ceremonies at the 1924 Games, and Abrahams received his medal in the post – after he had paid the excess postage on the package the French had failed to frank sufficiently.

A leg injury in 1925 cut short Abrahams' athletics career and he returned to the law, but he continued to distinguish himself as a writer, broadcaster and prominent figure in English amateur sports, as well as championing the development of Jewish representation in sport. His father had emigrated to England from Lithuania, and Abrahams admitted that his drive to succeed was spurred on by the growing anti-Semitism in England at the time.

Abrahams represented England and Northern Ireland on the International Amateur Athletic Federation, was inducted into the International Jewish Sports Hall of Fame in 1981 and the Veterans of the IAAF in 1948. He was awarded the CBE in 1957, as secretary of the National Parks Commission. He was the author of a number of books on Olympic history.

Harold Abrahams at the 1924 Games in Paris, where he broke the Olympic 100 metres record.

Jack Beresford

1924 Paris, 1932 Los Angeles and 1936 Berlin
Rowing, single sculls (1924), coxless fours (1932) & double sculls (1936)

Jack Jr is acknowledged to be one of the greatest ever British oarsmen. Apart from his three Olympic gold medals, he won silver in the single sculls in 1920 in Antwerp and in the men's eights in 1928 in Amsterdam. His five medals in Olympic rowing is a record beaten only by Steve Redgrave's five gold medals in five separate games from 1984 to 2000, although Beresford might also have won a medal in the 1940 Games, had they not been cancelled because of the war.

Beresford was the son of a Polish furniture maker, Julius Wisniewski (he dropped his father's surname in early 1900), himself a notable oarsman and winner of an Olympic silver medal in 1912. At Bedford School, Beresford excelled at rowing and rugby. A leg wound received in the First World War precluded a career in rugby, but the rowing he did during recuperation set him on the path to a long and distinguished career as an oarsman.

At Henley Royal Regatta Beresford won the Diamond Challenge Sculls four times, the Grand Challenge Cup (eights) twice, the Silver Goblets & Nickall's Challenge Cup (pair) twice, the Stewards Challenge Cup (coxless fours) and Centenary Double Sculls. In the first Empire Games – now the Commonwealth Games – Beresford was runner-up in the men's single sculls.

In all, Beresford won the Amateur Sculling Championship a record eight times from 1920 to 1927.

Beresford said that 'the sweetest race I ever rowed in' was at the Berlin Games when he and Dick Southwood beat the Germans. The British had been warned by the German coach, Englishman Eric Phelps, that their boat was too light to stand a chance of winning. They duly had a heavier boat built, which went missing in transit to Berlin. At the last minute, it was located in a railway siding, and the pair won easily.

Beresford was a member of Thames Rowing Club at Putney in London, as captain in 1928-9 and as president from 1970 until his death in 1977. He became a steward of Henley Royal Regatta in 1946 and a member of the organising committee for the 1948 Olympic Games in London.

He was awarded the gold medal by the International Rowing Federation in 1947, the Olympic Diploma of Merit in 1949, and made a CBE in 1960. In 2005, in recognition of his achievements, English Heritage fixed a blue plaque on his former home in Chiswick, London.

Jack Beresford takes a breather during training in 1921. He went on to win the Olympic single sculls in 1924.

Eric Liddell
1924 Paris
Athletics, 400m

If not the greatest, Eric Liddell is certainly one of the best-known of Britain's sprinters. Universally popular, deeply devout and fast, very fast, Liddell's unique style of running has become familiar to millions after being portrayed in the famous feature film *Chariots of Fire*. Head thrown back, arms flailing and mouth agape, in his early days he ran 'more like a prancing circus pony than a world-class runner', as his Edinburgh University trainer, Tom McKerchar, said. This distinctive style was historically accurate (unlike various other scenes portrayed in the film).

Born in China to missionary parents, Liddell came to England with his elder brother when he was almost six years old, and both were enrolled in Eltham College in London.

In spite of being somewhat undernourished from his years in the inhospitable Great Plain of China, Liddell soon filled out and became an outstanding all-round sportsman. By the age of 15 he was captain of the cricket and rugby teams, as well as being one of the fastest runners. In his senior year he ran 100 yards in 10.2 seconds, a school record not to be broken for 80 years.

In 1921 he went up to Edinburgh University, and continued to excel. He played rugby for his university and was selected for the Scottish national team, playing in seven Five Nations matches. Already dominant in athletics over

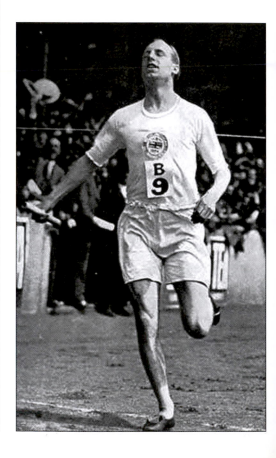

Eric Liddell, in characteristic style with head thrown back and arms flailing, breaks the tape to win the 400m final in 1924.

100m and 400m, he raced for the university and in 1923 won the AAA Championship 100m race in a British record time of 9.7 seconds (a record which stood for 35 years) and the 220 yards.

When the programme was announced for the 1924 Paris Games, and the 100m preliminary scheduled for a Sunday, Liddell declined to enter on religious grounds, opting instead to enter the AAA Championships again, in the 220 and 440 yards as a build-up to entering the Olympics in these distances. He came second in the 220 yards, and won the 440 yards, and headed for Paris.

The 400m final was a classic. Liddell, spurred on by the pipes and drums of the Cameron Highlanders, set off at a blistering pace and won in a World, Olympic and European record time of 47.6 seconds. His time remained a world record for four years and a European record for 12 years. A few days earlier he had won a bronze medal in the 200m.

Liddell returned to university after the Olympics and graduated, but he continued to race. In 1925 at the Scottish AAA meeting he equalled his own Scottish championship record of 10 seconds in the 100 yards, won the 220 yards in 22.2 seconds and the 440 yards in 47.7 seconds, as well as being on the winning 4x400m relay team.

One scene portrayed in *Chariots of Fire* involved a race where Liddell was knocked down at the start of a 440m race. By the time he got to his feet, the field was 20 metres ahead, but with characteristic determination, he went after them, caught them seconds before the finishing line, and collapsed as he crossed in first place. The story was true, although it took place in 1923 at a Triangular Contest and not, as the film depicted, in a Scotland–France meet.

In spite of his passion for sport, it was his deep-rooted faith that was Liddell's driving force. At university and all through his gruelling athletics training, he continued to serve God, studying the Bible, evangelising and doing good works.

After a year of theological study, he was on his way back to China as a missionary to teach in the Anglo-Chinese College. Teaching science, religion and sports, he nonetheless found time to enter the Far Eastern Games, winning the 220 and 400m races.

By 1941, with the Chinese and Japanese long at war, life in China had become dangerous. But Liddell, now ordained and married, accepted a new position at a rural mission station in Shaochang where his brother was already serving. In 1943 he was captured by the Japanese and interned. Under the brutal regime, Liddell retained his humour, his humility and humanity, and his faith, unstintingly giving succour to other unfortunate inmates.

In 1945, overworked and malnourished, he died of a brain tumour. A fellow internee, Langdon Gilkey, later wrote, 'The entire camp, especially its youth, was stunned for days, so great was the vacuum that Eric's death had left.'

Liddell's last words were allegedly 'It's complete surrender.'

David George Burghley (Marquess of Exeter)
1928 Amsterdam
Athletics, 400m hurdles

'Leaping Lord' Burghley, Conservative politician, sports official and one of the world's greatest hurdlers, appeared in three Olympics, the first in 1924, where he was eliminated in the first round of the 100m hurdles, then in 1928 where he won a gold medal, the third in 1932, where he won silver in the 4x400m relay.

A popular and dashing character, he caused a sensation in 1927 during his last year at Cambridge when he ran around the Great Court at Trinity College in the time it took the Trinity Clock to toll 12 o'clock. The event was portrayed in the film *Chariots of Fire,* but credited to Harold Abrahams, which not surprisingly incensed Burghley, who refused to see the film. His time of 43.10 was beaten in 2007 by 19-year-old student Sam Dobin, who shaved 0.33 of a second off it.

At one time Burghley was British record holder in all three hurdles events and the 1,500m relay. In the 400m hurdles, not only did he win a gold medal, but set one world and seven British records, won five AAA titles and a gold medal at the 1930 Commonwealth Games, as well as a gold in the relay. His world record came in the 1927 AAA Championships, when he ran the 440 yards hurdles in 54.2 seconds.

Burghley set a somewhat more unusual record by racing round the promenade deck of the Queen Mary in 57 seconds, dressed in civvies. It was reported that he would place matchboxes on top of the hurdles and practice knocking them off with his lead foot without touching the hurdles. Once, at a race meet in Antwerp, Burghley turned up at the wrong gate and was refused entry. He took a few paces backwards and with bowler hat pulled down and attaché case in hand, leaped the four-foot gate and disappeared into the crowd.

Having entered Parliament in 1931, Burghley took leave of absence to compete in the Los Angeles Olympics. He was Member of Parliament for Peterborough from 1931 until 1943. He later served as President of the AAA for 40 years, President of the International Amateur Athletic Federation for 30 years and as a member of the International Olympic Committee for 48 years. He was also Chairman of the Organising Committee of the 1948 Olympics.

'Leaping Lord' Burghley on his way to winning the 400m hurdles in Amsterdam. For the race, his mother had provided him with silk shorts to prevent chafing of the legs.

Hugh (Jumbo) Edwards

1932 Los Angeles
Rowing, coxless pairs and coxless fours

In 1932 at the Los Angeles Olympics, Edwards became only the second man in history to win two rowing gold medals on the same day. He was scheduled to compete in the coxless pairs with Lewis Clive, a race they duly won in style in the morning. At the last minute one of the crew of the coxless fours was forced through illness to withdraw, and Edwards stepped in to replace him. A reshuffle in the boat saw John Badcock as stroke, Jack Beresford at two, Edwards at three and Roland George as bow. It proved a winning combination, and they stroked to a two-and-a-half length victory in the final that afternoon.

The start of Jumbo Edwards' rowing career was not auspicious. As a freshman at Christ Church, Oxford, he was selected for the 1926 Blue Boat, but collapsed during the race with what was later diagnosed as a hypertrophied heart. The following year his academic career took a nosedive as well, after he was rusticated for failing his exams. In spite of these setbacks, he got a job teaching and continued to row with the London Rowing Club. He returned to university in 1930 to complete his degree, hoping for a commission in the RAF. His winning streak in previous years led to a place in the Blue Boat. Not one to hide his light under a bushel, Edwards declared that he was 'incomparably the best oarsman in either crew'. They lost. His heart condition notwithstanding, he went on to win the English eights and coxed fours at the Empire Games in Canada the same year.

While at Oxford he devoted much of his time to flying and kept his own light plane at university. In 1931 he obtained his commission in the RAF. During the war he served with Coastal Command, won the AFC in 1943 and the DFC in 1944, and his rowing experience stood him in good stead when his plane came down off Land's End in 1943. The only member of the crew to survive the crash, Edwards rowed his dinghy four miles to safety, dodging the mines.

In 1949 Edwards retired from the RAF as Group Captain and was invited back to Oxford to coach. Forthright and uncompromising, Edwards' relations with his colleagues were strained and he left in 1957, only to be brought back in 1959. His return sparked a rebellion and resignations in the squad, but Oxford won the Boat Race that year, and Edwards remains a legend at Oxford. One of Christ Church's coxless fours is named in his honour.

The winning crew of the coxless fours in 1932, Jumbo Edwards at number 3.

Tommy Green
1932 Los Angeles
50km road walk

The 50km walk is a challenging enough event, but to win an Olympic gold medal walking it at the age of 38, having suffered rickets, been gassed and wounded numerous times, is a truly outstanding feat. In his day, Tommy Green was acknowledged to be the finest long-distance walker in the world, and he holds the distinction of being the first Olympic road-walking champion.

Green was born in 1894 and suffered from rickets as a child, and was unable to walk until he was five years old. He left school at 12, and in his late teens joined the 20th Hussars. He was invalided out after an accident, but joined up with the 3rd Hussars at the outbreak of the First World War. He served on the Western Front with the British Expeditionary Force, was wounded several times, gassed and invalided out again, with medals for bravery. Although the gas attack had damaged his lungs, Green remained a keen runner and boxer. In 1925 he was helping a blind friend train for the St Dunstan's London to Brighton walk, and was encouraged to take up the sport himself. The following year he won the first race he entered, from Worthing to Brighton, and there was no looking back. He went on to win the London to Brighton race four times, and the Manchester to Blackpool and Nottingham to Birmingham races six times. In 1930 he won the Milan 100km race, as well as the inaugural British 50km title.

Track walking had waned in popularity and been ruled out of the 1928 Amsterdam Games, but road walking had become fashionable and the British officials mounted efforts to have the sport introduced into the Olympics. They succeeded, and, with his impressive record, Green was an obvious choice for the first Olympic 50km road walk. He duly obliged by taking the gold medal in 4:50:10 – a slow time, but the conditions were said to be 'tropical'.

Having contested every major race every year since 1930 and now in his forties, Green set his sights on retaining his title at the 1936 Berlin Games. It was not to be, and he could only manage fourth place in the 50km Olympic selection race. In a fitting end to a glorious career, Green won his final competitive race at the age of 54, beating competitors half his age in the Poole to Wareham walk. He became a publican, but devoted much of his time to encouraging others to take up sport.

The indomitable Tommy Green, wearing number 12, in a road race in the UK.

Dickie Burnell and Bertie Bushnell

1948 London
Rowing, double sculls

Dickie Burnell and Bertie Bushnell only joined forces six weeks before the 1948 Olympics, but succeeded in winning the double sculls gold medal to a rousing ovation from the 30-deep crowd at Henley.

Like his father and fellow Olympic gold medallist, Burnell was educated at Eton and Magdalen College, Oxford. He rowed in the Oxford boat in 1939, went to war and was decorated for bravery.

In 1948, with Burnell as stroke and Bushnell at bow, they lost the first round of the double sculls at Henley to France, but won the repêchage and went on to win the gold medal. The first-round loss was apparently a deliberate ploy to avoid meeting their chief rivals, Denmark, until the final. The strategy certainly worked.

In later life he commented on the celebrations of his day compared to those of more recent times, saying, 'After the racing, the oarsmen had a dinner, threw bread rolls at each other and then went home.' According to Bushnell, however, the dinner degenerated into a brawl with the Americans, who took exception to the poor standard of food.

Burnell took a bronze medal in the eights at the Commonwealth Games of 1950, and won the Double Sculls Challenge Cup in 1951.

He was *The Times* rowing correspondent from 1946 to 1967, and became a leading historian of the sport, one of his best-known works being *The Complete Sculler*.

Burnell and Bushnell stand proudly to attention for the National Anthem after winning their gold medal in the double sculls in 1948.

Bushnell and Burnell made an unlikely pair in the double sculls, coming as they did from different backgrounds and being of dramatically different stature. Bushnell's family owned a boatyard at Wargrave, with a branch at Henley. When young Bertie showed great promise as an oarsman, his father apprenticed him as a marine engineer rather than taking him into the family firm, thus enabling him to keep his amateur status. The Eton and

Oxford blue, Burnell, topped six foot four, Bushnell a mere five foot nine and several stone lighter. But, having been thrown together only weeks before the event and despite some initial friction, they won the gold medal to the delight of the crowd.

Bushnell had toured South Africa the winter before the Olympics, maintaining an unbeaten record. During the Games, he made friends with Jack Kelly, whose family had come over from Philadelphia. Jack rowed in the single sculls, winning a bronze medal, but it was his sister, Grace, who was the main attraction – particularly for Bushnell, who succeeded where others had failed in taking 'Little Gracie' out on a date. Eighteen months later, he received a postcard from her saying she had enrolled in dance school, her springboard to Hollywood.

Bushnell, born in 1909, retired from rowing in 1951 to join the family firm. He later set up a successful river-cruise hire company on the Thames and retired to Portugal. He has since returned to England, and looks forward to the 2012 London Olympics.

Harry Llewellyn
1952 Helsinki
Equestrian, team jumping

Queen Elizabeth II had just been crowned when the debonair aristocrat Sir Harry Llewellyn and his gelding, Foxhunter, went clear in the final round of the show jumping at Helsinki to give Britain its only gold medal of the Games. The team had had indifferent scores in the preliminary rounds and were lying sixth. On the final morning, Llewellyn himself had three fences down, a refusal and time penalties, and at midday was dejectedly blaming himself for the team's poor performance overall. He refused lunch and lay down for an hour's sleep (while the horse also snoozed). When he returned to the ring, refreshed and focused, he rode a flawless clear round and the gold medal was theirs. Llewellyn and Foxhunter were hailed as heroes. The new Queen and her Prime Minister, Churchill, sent congratulatory telegrams. Llewellyn was embarrassed by the adulation and media attention, and throughout his life sought to play it down, modestly emphasising that, though the captain, he had clocked up the most faults and was undeserving of all the praise.

The son of the Welsh colliery owner and first Baronet, Sir David Llewellyn, Harry went to Oundle and then up to Cambridge. Though a keen sportsman, as a youth his riding was limited to a little hunting and the odd point-to-point. His enthusiasm for the latter was somewhat dampened by the fact that his father, an inveterate gambler, would wager huge sums on his winning. He did, however, go on to become a successful amateur steeplechase jockey, winning 60 races under National Hunt rules and coming second and fourth in the Grand National in 1936 and 1937 respectively. He and Foxhunter took part in the 1948 Olympics, winning the bronze medal.

At the outbreak of war in 1939, Llewellyn took a commission in the Warwickshire Yeomanry, eventually rising to Lieutenant-Colonel, He was senior liaison officer to General Montgomery, was mentioned in despatches, awarded the American Legion of Merit and, in 1944, the OBE.

Although his partnership with Foxhunter lasted a mere five years, between them they succeeded in winning 78 international competitions, including three King George V Gold Cups, show jumping's most prestigious trophy. Llewellyn was known for his easy-going manner, charm and diplomacy, and Foxhunter too appears to have had a sense of humour: at the 1949 Nations Cup, as the prizes were awarded by a Swiss general's wife, the horse caused hilarity in the crowd by calmly munching the floral decoration of her hat.

Llewellyn was married to the daughter of the 5th Baron de Saumarez, and their sons, Dai and Roddy, were much in the public eye during the 1960s and '70s owing to their romantic entanglements – Dai with Tessa Dahl and Beatrice Welles and Roddy with Princess Margaret, who was said to have been much in love with him.

On retirement from competition, Llewellyn continued his involvement in show jumping, becoming chef d'équipe of the British team, notably during the Mexico Games of 1968, and as Chairman and then Honorary Vice-President of the British Show Jumping Association.

Llewellyn and Foxhunter remain one of the best-loved and best-remembered partnerships. When Llewellyn died in 1999, the Chief Executive of the BSJA said of him, 'His was an era of show jumping that to this day we aspire to emulate. His knowledge and experience were second to none.' His ashes were scattered over the grave of his beloved mount.

A caricature of Sir Harry Llewellyn by Dorrien.

Chris Brasher

1956 Melbourne

Athletics, 3,000m steeplechase

Chris Brasher will be remembered for many things other than his gold medal and his part in breaking the four-minute mile. In addition to these notable achievements, he was a journalist, broadcaster, mountaineer, orienteer, businessman and founder of the London Marathon.

Born in Guyana and educated at Rugby and Cambridge, Brasher's athletics career began with middle-distance running, but in 1951 he turned to steeplechasing. In spite of finishing eleventh in the Olympic qualifier final, Brasher made the British team. In 1954, at Iffley Road, Oxford, he secured his place in athletics annals as a contributor in Roger Bannister becoming the first man to run the mile in under four minutes. Brasher acted as a pacemaker for Bannister early in the race, making way for Christopher Chataway in a similar role. Roger Bannister broke the tape in 3 minutes 59.4.

At Melbourne in 1956, Brasher was not expected to win, and, even after finishing with a personal best, Olympic and British record time of 8:41.2, he was still not sure that he had won. Although he was way ahead of the field, an objection was lodged and it was three agonising hours before the result was confirmed. In great relief, he and his friends celebrated until late into the evening, and when he came to receive his medal the next day he was, as he said, 'totally blotto, with an asinine grin on my face'.

Leaving his job with Mobil Oil after Melbourne, Brasher joined the *Observer* as Sports Editor. In 1961, he joined the BBC, starting as a reporter and rising to become Head of General Features.

In 1979 he went to New York to run the marathon, and was so impressed by the egalitarianism of the event he determined London should have its own marathon. By 1981 he had organised it. His highest hopes were fulfilled when more than 7,000 runners assembled in Greenwich Park, most of them making it to the finish at Buckingham Palace, and Brasher himself completing in under three hours. Within a few years, it had become the biggest annual marathon in the world, a testament to his popularity and ability.

He is known also as the father of orienteering. With John Disley he founded the Southern Navigators club, sowing the seeds of enthusiasm in many generations. With the increased interest in running in the 1970s and 1980s, Brasher set up his own sportswear shop (eventually known as the Sweatshop), where he sold, among other things, a lightweight shoe of his own design. He was awarded the CBE in 1996 and died in 2003.

Chris Brasher, followed by Roger Bannister, during the race which saw Bannister break the 4-minute mile.

Use and Abuse – Drugs and the Olympics

The motto of the Olympic Games, *citius, altius, fortius,* (swifter, higher, stronger) encapsulates our instinctive urge to achieve greatness, to strive to be the best, and is no less true of the human spirit today than it was of the ancient Greeks. Although the ethos of the Olympics is, among other things, to encourage fair competition, winning is as important today as it was in 776 BC when the Games began.

Cheating is nothing new. Since humans first stood upright, they have stooped to cheating and skulduggery, either because they cannot bear to lose, are greedy for riches or just because they can. Neither is the use of stimulants a new thing in sport. In the ancient Games, athletes commonly took 'drugs' such as ground horses' hooves and plant extracts to help achieve their goals – which even then was considered cheating, and ultimately led to the Games being discontinued. Today, drugs pose one of the greatest threats to the integrity of the Olympics.

The first record of drug use in the modern Olympics centred on Thomas Hicks, an American track and field athlete. In the 1908 marathon, the first man home, Fred Lorz, was discovered to have covered most of the course by car and was promptly disqualified. Hicks, crossing the finishing line in second place,

immediately collapsed. He had fortified himself with large amounts of strychnine and several large tots of brandy. He was lucky to be awarded the gold medal, and luckier still to survive.

Throughout the first half of the twentieth century, with biotechnological advances and easier access to pharmaceuticals, the use of performance-enhancing drugs in sport became widespread. Anabolic steroids, human growth hormones and erythropoietin (EPO) in particular became the drugs of choice, since they target those hormones already present in the body which control the build-up and breakdown of muscles. At the Rome Olympics in 1960 the Danish cyclist Knud Jensen collapsed during a race and died shortly after. The autopsy revealed a cocktail of drugs in his system. The IOC began to acknowledge that drug-taking was escalating out of control. In 1967 after Tim Simpson, the leader of the British team, died in the saddle during the Tour de France, so full of amphetamines and alcohol he could not tell that his body had passed its limit of endurance, the IOC finally decided to introduce drug testing.

But doping, and the scandals surrounding it, persisted. Communist countries in particular took to steroids with enthusiasm and drug-taking became State-endorsed – many athletes being doped without their knowledge. Between 1968 and 1974 the East German gold medal tally rose from four to 40, largely attributable to drug-taking. Despite calls for disqualifications and redistribution of medals the IOC refused to intervene.

The list of athletes stripped of medals for taking banned substances is a long one, some punished for flagrantly flouting the rules, some for innocently taking cold remedies. The first official Olympic drug disqualification occurred in 1968, when Hans-Gunnar Lijenwall, a Swedish pentathlete, was found guilty of imbibing alcohol and stripped of his bronze medal. And who can forget Ben Johnson, who in 1988 was found to have taken a banned substance and stripped of his gold medal in the 100 metre dash (which he completed in an astonishing 9.79 seconds), only to have his medal awarded to Carl Lewis, who had also tested positive before the Games yet had not been banned. In 1999 the World Anti-Doping Agency was founded. While this silenced some critics, it invited further controversy as to the impartiality and accountability of the Agency.

The Sisyphean task of eradicating drugs from the Olympics is likely to be further complicated by the latest development, 'gene doping', which involves modifying an athlete's DNA, or even injecting them with foreign DNA, and is harder to detect than other drugs. Most people agree that the use of drugs is fundamentally wrong and a blight on sport, and that athletes have a moral duty to obey the rules and provide good role models for the youth of their countries. But the debate extends beyond legislating on banned substances and detecting the culprits: at what point do dietary supplements, psychological training, surgery and implants confer 'unfair' advantage? Should drugs be legalised altogether? Are athletes' human rights violated by the obligation to provide blood and urine samples? It is a debate that will run and run.

The finish of the 1988 100m dash, 'the dirtiest race in history'. Ben Johnson (left) was stripped of the gold medal after testing positive, Carl Lewis (right) tested positive before the Games but was not banned; Linford Christie (2nd right) was banned in 1999 for drug use. Calvin Smith (2nd left) was the only one who never failed a drug test.

Anita Lonsbrough

1960 Rome
Swimming, 200m breaststroke

At the age of 19, Huddersfield's 'Princess of the Pool' achieved the first of Britain's only two gold medals in Rome in a gripping 200m breaststroke final, when she beat the German favourite by half a second in an Olympic and world record time of 2:49.5. Bouts of gastroenteritis, flu and shingles in the run-up to the Games had made her participation doubtful, but by August she had struggled back to fitness. As she lined up for the final race, a bug in the water below her was only a slight distraction for the girl who had had to fish the cockroaches out of the pool in Huddersfield before training. It turned out to be one of swimming's most closely fought races, bringing the crowd and the commentators to the edge of their seats as Lonsbrough and the German, Wiltrud Urselmann, exchanged the lead twice in the closing few metres. It was Britain's last women's swimming gold medal for 48 years, until Rebecca Adlington's achievements at the 2008 Games.

Anita Lonsbrough learned to swim in India, where her Coldstream Guards father was stationed. Settling in Yorkshire in her teens, she began to train in earnest. In 1958 she broke through to the top ranks by winning her first gold medal in the Empire Games in Cardiff. The following year she was voted Amateur Swimming Association's swimmer of the year.

In the years between 1958 and 1962 Lonsborough broke five world records and won seven international gold medals. At one time she held the Olympic, Empire and European titles simultaneously. She became the first female BBC Sports Personality of the Year in 1962 and in 1963 was awarded the MBE.

In 1964 she was again part of the British Olympic team, and was given the honour of bearing the Olympic Flag in the opening ceremony, marking yet another record by being the first woman to do so at a Summer Games. Once more afflicted with illness she nonetheless competed, and although she won no medals, she did meet her future husband, Hugh Porter, an outstanding cyclist, Olympic gold medallist, and World Professional 5,000m Cycling Champion. In November 1964 Lonsborough announced her retirement and in 1965 she and Hugh were married.

The couple moved to Wolverhampton and embarked on long and successful careers in broadcasting, she becoming first the *Sunday* then the *Daily Telegraph*'s swimming correspondent, and he a BBC sports commentator.

'The Princess of the Pool' won the first of Britain's two gold medals in Rome.

Robin Dixon and Tony Nash
1964 Innsbruck
2-man bobsleigh

The story of the Nash-Dixon route to Olympic gold sounds like a tall one, featuring as it does Lord Lucan, tons of imported snow, a broken sled, a selfless Italian and a victorious nation with no bobsleigh run of its own.

The names of Nash and Dixon are inextricably linked – like horse and carriage they go together. And just as firmly wedded to their historic, one-and-only British bobsleigh gold medal is the name of Eugenio Monti, without whom there would have been no British victory.

The Hon. Robin Dixon came to the sport after a chance meeting with his cousin, Lord Lucan, in St Moritz in 1957. Lucan, aware of Dixon's all-round sporting ability and particularly his sprinting, persuaded Dixon to have a go in the

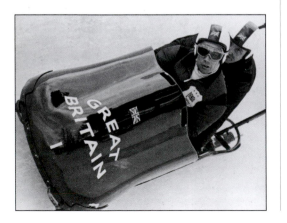

four-man bob. He 'quite enjoyed' it and before long had become part of the British team. Meanwhile, Tony Nash was approaching international sledding from an equally unlikely direction. Although a director in his family's engineering firm which was instrumental in the development of the British bobsleigh, Nash was entirely self-taught, extremely short-sighted and had no driving experience.

By 1958 the pair had met on the four-man team, and in 1960 decided to form a two-man partnership with Nash as pilot and Dixon as brakesman. They entered the 1961 World Championship and came sixth. With no funding forthcoming, an Olympic medal seemed unlikely. Then, thanks to the gregarious Nash's friendship with the Italian team, the duo were invited to join them in training at Cervinio.

By 1964 they were reckoned to be in with a chance of a medal in Innsbruck – if there was enough ice. In the nick of time, 30,000 soldiers managed to shovel in sufficient snow and British confidence rose. Their first run was fast and they were in second place when disaster struck. The bolt attaching the runners to the shell had

Tony Nash (pilot) and Robin Dixon on their way to the gold medal in Innsbruck – Britain's first gold medal at the Winter Olympics in 12 years.

snapped. When Monti, the Italian sledding star, heard of this he said, 'Get an Englishman and a spanner … and they can have my bolt.' The bolt from the Italian sled was fitted, and the British won by 12/100ths of a second.

Monti's generosity had also extended to repairing Canada's damaged sled (enabling them to win the four-man bob), while he himself had to settle for bronze in both events. His selflessness earned him the first Pierre de Coubertin award for fair play. Though criticised by many a disappointed Italian, Monti said, 'Nash didn't win because I gave him the bolt. He won because he had the fastest run.' To the rest of the world he was a hero and the embodiment of Olympic sportsmanship, and deservedly won gold medals in the two- and four-man events at the next Olympics. Nash and Dixon were each awarded the MBE and went on to win the world title in 1964 and 1965. There is a turn at the St Moritz course named after the pair.

Since 1987 Dixon has been the President of the British Bobsleigh Association. He was awarded the CBE in 1993 for services to Northern Ireland and to industry. He succeeded his father as Lord Glentoran in 1998. He has also been Shadow Minister for Northern Ireland for Sport and for Environment, Food and Rural Affairs, and was the Conservative Shadow Minister in the House of Lords for the Olympics.

Mary Rand

1964 Toyko
Athletics, long jump

Mary Rand in action at the Tokyo Games in 1964, as she smashes the world long jump record.

'Mary was the most gifted athlete I ever saw. She was as good as athletes get, there has never been anything like her since. And I don't believe there ever will be.' So said Ann Packer, friend, teammate and roommate at the 1964 Games. It was an opinion shared by a great many people, for Mary Rand became the first British woman to win a gold medal in a track and field event. Blonde, beautiful and charismatic, the 'Golden Girl' of athletics spent her career smashing records and turning men's heads. In Tokyo she beat the Olympic record with all of her seven jumps and took the gold medal with a massive distance of 6.76m.

Born in Somerset in 1940, the schoolgirl Mary Bignal could outrun, outjump and outswim her contemporaries of either sex. When she was 16 she was offered an athletics scholarship at Millfield College, where her immense talent was nurtured. She won the All-England schools title, and once when she joined the British Olympic squad in training, she outjumped the nation's best jumpers.

At 19 she was already an international long jumper, high jumper and hurdler. She was never beaten in the long jump between 1958 and 1960. She had begun an affair with a fellow-student, Jimmy Burakamkovit, and when she defied the headmaster's edict to end it, was expelled from Millfield. She and Jimmy became engaged, but it lasted only until she met the Dutch athlete Eef Kamerbeek. And that romance lasted only until she was introduced to the rower Sidney Rand in 1961. Three days after meeting him they became engaged, and were married within five weeks.

Selected for the British squad at the 1960 Rome Olympics, hopes were high that she would return with at least one medal. But although she led after the qualifying round with a British record jump of 6.33m, nerves got the better of her and she finished only ninth. She also finished fourth in the 80m hurdles.

It was all very different when she went to Tokyo. In the qualifying rounds of the long jump she set an Olympic record of 6.52m, a British record with her first jump of the final, and in the fifth round on a soggy track and with a strong headwind broke the world record. She also won a silver medal in the women's pentathlon (which might have been another gold medal had the real sex of the winner, Irina Press, been discovered sooner) and a bronze in the 4x100m relay. Returning home triumphant, she was voted BBC Sports Personality of the Year and awarded the MBE. She was invited to lunch at Buckingham Palace and the Queen asked her to show the young Prince Andrew just how far the winning leap was. As she paced it out on the floor, the Prince exclaimed, 'Nobody could jump *that* far!' In 1966 she won a gold medal at the Commonwealth Games and in 1968 retired.

Her marriage to Sid Rand ended after five years and there was no shortage of suitors for Mary; Mick Jagger once described her as his dream date. But in 1968 she married another athlete, Bill Toomey, the Olympic decathlon gold medallist. That marriage lasted 22 years, after which she married an American, John Reese, with whom she now lives in California.

Back home in Wells, her winning long jump is marked out on the pavement of the market square. She remains the only British woman to hold a long jump world record.

Mary Rand's world record distance of 6.76m is marked out in her home town of Wells, Somerset.

Lynn Davies

1964 Tokyo

Athletics, long jump

'Lynn the Leap', as Davies was affectionately known to his Welsh compatriots, was a talented athlete. In 1964, in howling wind and driving rain, competing against two men who had regularly jumped a great deal further than him, Davies made the jump of his life and with a distance of 8.07m took the gold medal.

Davies began his sporting career as a footballer, was a fine sprinter and triple-jumper, but truly made his name as an outstanding long jumper, thanks in large part to the encouragement of Ron Pickering, coach and BBC commentator. He made his international debut in 1961 at the European Championships, and the following year at the Commonwealth Games broke the British record. In 1964 he created two new Commonwealth records, and made yet another with his gold-medal winning Olympic leap. At Tokyo he also competed in the 100m and 4x100m relay, reaching the final.

In 1966 Davies became the first athlete to hold the European, Commonwealth and Olympic titles. He continued to improve on the Commonwealth record in 1968, setting a record of 8.23m, which stood for 34 years. Returning to the Olympics that year he was denied the gold medal by Bob Beamon's legendary leap of 8.9 metres – a jump which was not bettered for 40 years and so huge that it was beyond the equipment's range and had to be measured by hand. Davies attended his third Olympics in 1972, but missed out on the medals again.

Ranked as one of Britain's greatest athletes, in 1967 Davies was made an MBE, and in 2006 a CBE. Following his retirement as an athlete in 1973 he was appointed technical director of Canadian Track and Field Association, and on returning to the UK became team manager of the British athletics team.

He was Senior Lecturer in physical education at the University of Wales Institute Cardiff (Uwic), and is currently President of UK Athletics, a position he will hold until 2011. Davies played a key role in London's successful 2012 Olympic bid and continues to be involved in the organisation of the event. He is a consultant and broadcaster for the BBC and a member of the Sports Council for Wales.

Lynn Davies makes the leap of his life in the pouring rain in Tokyo.

Chris Finnegan
1968 Mexico City
Boxing, middleweight

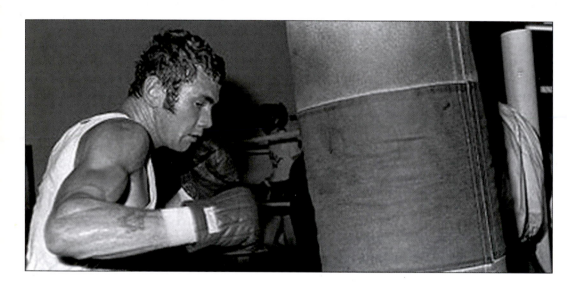

Chris Finnegan works out in preparation for the 1968 Games.

Hard drinking, straight talking and immensely brave, Chris Finnegan was one of Britain's most popular and colourful boxers. His win at the 1968 Games gave Britain its only Olympic boxing gold medal between 1956 and 2000, and its first middleweight gold since 1924.

In his early days, the frequently out-of-work Anglo-Irish brickie Finnegan was a bruiser in and out of the ring, often in trouble with the law and fond of his Guinness. He and his younger brother Kevin, who became European and British middleweight champion, sparred with each other mercilessly, and their training sessions were legendary battles. In 1965, with his long reach and southpaw stance, the elder Finnegan became ABA middleweight champion, and looked to be in line for inclusion in the British squad for Mexico City. But an eye injury prevented him from winning the 1967 ABA championships, making his place uncertain.

Finnegan in his disappointment embarked on a two-week drinking binge. Hauled back on the straight and narrow and offered a place in the Olympic team, he faced another setback when he was summoned to appear in court for non-payment of his National Insurance Stamp. The presiding magistrate, however, gave him a reprieve and wished him luck. When Finnegan returned victorious, his £70 debt to the government was paid by boxing promoter Harry Levene.

In Mexico City, Finnegan survived two standing counts in the semi-final and went on to win the final against the Russian, Aleksei Kisselyov, by a 3-2 verdict. His wife Cheryl was not present for his finest hour, having elected to stay in England in the (delusive) expectation of winning a 'trip of a lifetime' competition staged by Golden Wonder crisps.

When Finnegan stepped out of the ring to be interviewed, he was connected by satellite to Cheryl, knee-deep in crisp packets, who said, 'You 'aven't fucking gone and done it, 'ave you?' To which he replied, 'Yes, old lady, I fucking, fucking 'ave!'

Finnegan returned to England a hero, was awarded the MBE and immediately turned professional. Of his 37 professional contests, he won 29, lost seven and drew one.

In 1971, he moved up to the light-heavyweight division and a meeting with American legend Bob Foster was scheduled for the following year. Finnegan was knocked out in the 14th round of a gruelling fight, but the bout was regarded as a classic and named Fight of the Year by *Ring Magazine*. Finnegan likened Foster's punch to 'being hit with a scaffolding pole with a boxing glove on the end of it'. He lost again that year when defending his European title, but retained his British and Commonwealth titles. Then he met the up-and-coming young Liverpudlian, John Conteh. In 1973 he lost the British, European and Commonwealth title fight to Conteh after 15 rounds, and failed to regain it in the rematch the next year.

In 1975, Conteh relinquished the title to move to world honours, and Finnegan met 'Gypsy' Johnny Frankham for the vacant British title. Although he lost on points after 15 rounds, he won the rematch later the same year and fittingly retired as the title-holder. He always wore a Union Flag and a Shamrock on his boxing trunks to show his joint heritage.

Shortly before the 2008 Olympics, he commented with typically wry humour on the British team's preparations for coping with Beijing's altitude: 'I was up and down a 30-rung ladder all day with piles of bricks on both my flippin' shoulders. That was the only bloody altitude training I did, mate.'

On retirement, the ebullient Finnegan became a publican – alas, an unsuccessful one. He described his life after boxing as being spent 'ducking and diving'. He found time, however, to write his autobiography, *Finnegan: Self-Portrait of a Fighting Man*.

He died in 2008 of pneumonia, only months after the death of his brother Kevin.

David Hemery
1968 Mexico City
Athletics, 400m hurdles

David Hemery's dream of being Olympic champion came true in Mexico City with a blistering, record-breaking run which was watched in the small hours by millions of jubilant Britons. As he crossed the line in a world record time of 48.12, it was a moment when, as he put it, his body and soul were in alignment. His victory gave Britain its only track and field gold medal of the Games.

As Hemery stormed ahead of the field to take the tape, the BBC commentator, David Coleman, hysterically screamed, 'And it's David Hemery in the lead for Great Britain. It's Hemery . . . it's Hemery . . . it's HEMERY! Hemery takes the gold, Hennige, of West Germany, the silver, and who cares who's third? It doesn't matter.' A typical 'Colemanball', since the bronze medal was taken by another Briton, John Sherwood. Hemery's performance earned him the accolade of BBC's Sports Personality of the Year.

Having won the European Championship in 1969, injury kept Hemery off the track for some time, but in 1972 he went to Munich to defend his title. He could only manage third place, but won a silver medal in the 4x400m relay.

On retirement in 1973, Hemery returned to America, where he had been brought up, to coach, though he returned frequently to England on coaching assignments and for a time taught at Millfield School. He received the CBE in 1969 and was elected the first president of UK Athletics in 1998. He is currently the Vice Chairman of the British Olympic Association and is heavily involved with the preparation for the 2012 Games.

To add to his clutch of Olympic and European medals, Hemery won the first *British Superstars* competition in 1973, and again in 1976.

David Hemery hurdling to victory in Mexico City in 1968.

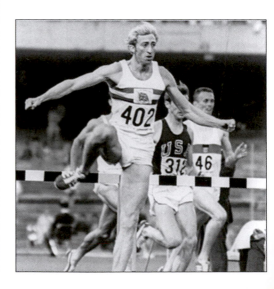

Rodney Pattisson
1968 Mexico City and 1972 Munich
Sailing, Flying Dutchman class

Rodney Pattisson was the first Scot to win an Olympic gold medal in sailing, and until Ben Ainslie's three gold medals in successive Games, he was Britain's most successful Olympic yachtsman with two golds and a silver. He is still considered by many to be one of the greatest Scottish sportsmen, up there with Eric Liddell, Chris Hoy and David Wilkie.

The Flying Dutchman is a two-man racing dinghy, and the significance of Pattisson's three medals is that he won each of them with a different crew. With Iain MacDonald Smith, he won the 1968 World and European Championships, before setting off for Mexico. After meticulous preparation, hard training, and three months practice in the waters off Mexico they won five of their seven races in the fancifully-named *Superdocious* – a shortening of its original *Supercalifragilistic-expialidocious,* which was rather too long to fit on the 20-foot vessel – and beat the opposition by one of the biggest winning margins ever recorded.

In the years following, Pattisson dominated the class, winning the World Championships in 1969, '70 and '71, and was well prepared for his second Games. In 1972, with Christopher Davies, he was on the podium again in the Port of Kiel to receive his medal, the first Scot to win two golds.

For his achievements Pattisson was selected as flag-bearer at the opening ceremony of the 1976 Montreal Olympics. As crew, he had Justin Brooke Houghton, with whom he had won his third World Championship, but they were beaten into second place by the Germans.

Pattisson attended Pangbourne College, the public school largely geared to preparing boys to be naval officers. At 17, he won the world cadet title, with his brother crewing, and on leaving school followed the College's tradition by joining the Royal Navy. When he resigned his commission in 1968 to concentrate full-time on sailing, he was a submarine lieutenant, and in 1969 was awarded the MBE. Although he took no further part in the Olympics after Montreal, in spite of coming close to making the team in 1984, Pattisson co-skippered Peter de Savary's *Victory 83* in the 1983 America's Cup. His passion for the sport extended beyond the Flying Dutchman class in which he was pre-eminent, and included the quarter-ton (in which he was world champion), and 12-metre classes.

Through rigorous attention to detail, supreme fitness and outstanding ability, his success has made Pattisson a yachtsman of whom Scotland and Britain are justifiably proud.

Rodney Pattisson at the helm during the 1972 Munich Games.

Mary Peters

1972 Munich

Athletics, pentathlon

In 1972 Mary Peters was 33 years old when she went to Munich filled with determination to win a gold medal at her third Olympic attempt in the Pentathlon. For two gruelling days she battled it out with the favourite, Germany's Heide Rosendahl. By the end of the first day, Peters had set personal bests in the hurdles, shot putt and high jump and was in the lead. The following day her long jump distance fell short of Rosendahl's 6.83m and success rested on the 200m, which was Rosendahl's strongest event. Peters gave it everything she had, but saw her rival drawing ahead as the line approached. The screams of the sell-out crowd as she crossed the line ten metres behind Rosendahl subsided to an expectant hush. Agonising minutes passed as the scores were calculated. Then a roar went up as it was announced that Peters had won by a mere ten points, with a world and Olympic record score of 4,801 points.

Peters' path to glory had not been easy. Though a world-class athlete and a tireless worker, she admitted to having an attitude problem and to being 'a bit afraid of success'. Born in Merseyside, she was brought up in Northern Ireland and always declared herself an Ulsterwoman. The Troubles in her adopted country formed a backdrop to her entire career. Bullied at school and devastated when her mother died and her father married their housekeeper, she channelled her energies into athletics. She represented Northern Ireland at every Commonwealth Games from 1958 to 1974 and Great Britain internationally from 1961 to 1974. At the Commonwealth Games in 1970 she won gold medals in the shot putt and pentathlon, and in the pentathlon in 1974.

But in 1972 the Troubles were at their height, her father had moved to Australia and she faced huge difficulties with training – commuting through the bombed streets of Belfast to a heavily fortified gym and an inferior track. A gold medal looked improbable, but six weeks before the Games she was offered a scholarship to train in America. Her mental attitude hardened from a desire to do well and be admired into a steely

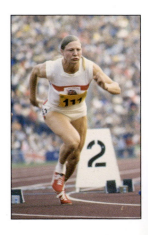

Mary Peters flies off the starting blocks in the 200m sprint, the last discipline of the pentathlon, in 1972.

determination to win. And what a success, what an overwhelmingly popular success! As she was being interviewed by Chris Brasher after receiving the gold medal, from behind a screen stepped her father, whom she had not seen for two years. It was the icing on the cake for Peters.

Two days later came the terrorist attack on the Israelis' Olympic village. Six months later her coach, Buster McShane, was killed in a car crash. Plunged from the heights to the depths, Mary's spirit and goodness nonetheless survived. Now in her 70s, she remains committed to sport and to Northern Ireland, and to helping others. Since retiring from athletics she has dedicated herself to charitable and community causes.

She was awarded the MBE in 1973, the CBE in 1990, was made a Dame Commander of the British Empire in 2000 and in 2009 was elected Lord Lieutenant of Belfast. The Mary Peters Trust, which helps young sportsmen and women of Northern Ireland to achieve their dreams, has set its sights firmly on the 2012 Games and nurturing native talent.

A woman of humility and humour, guts and graciousness, Mary Peters is a true sporting hero and an inspiration to millions.

John Curry
1976 Innsbruck
Figure skating

Known as 'the Nureyev of the ice', John Curry was Britain's first Olympic skating gold medallist, giving one of the most memorable performances in skating history at the Winter Games in 1976.

As a child, he had wanted to be a ballet dancer, but his father disapproved so at the age of seven he took up skating. Such was his talent and dedication that it was only a year before he won his first competition. In 1967 he won the British Junior Championship, and went on to win the British Seniors four times from 1972 to 1975, as well as winning both the World and European Championships in 1976.

After his father died when he was 16, having seen his son skate only twice, Curry moved to London to start the previously forbidden ballet lessons. In 1972 he attended the Olympics in Munich, and although he came nowhere near the medals, succeeded in securing the sponsorship he badly needed to finance his career. With the backing of American millionaire Ed Moseler, Curry went to the United States and trained under the renowned Carlo Fassi in Colorado.

At the peak of his career in 1976, as European, World and Olympic Champion, he turned professional, founded a successful ice dance company, was voted Sports Personality of the Year and was awarded the OBE.

Curry had come out publicly as gay just prior to the Olympics, a brave move given the prevailing attitude to homosexuality. His sexuality, and possibly his troubled relationship with his father, had made him notoriously difficult to work with and highly critical of himself and others. At the post-Sports Personality of the Year award dinner, he was mocked for being a 'fairy', leading to a worsening of his already poor relationship with the press.

In 1987 Curry was diagnosed as HIV positive. When he developed full-blown Aids in 1990 he returned to England to live with his mother. One of his earlier lovers, the actor Alan Bates, returned to look after him in his final days. According to Bates, Curry died in his arms. He was only 44 years old.

Curry's influence on the sport was profound. With his balletic style he transformed skating, turning it into an art form with a combination of athleticism, technique and creative imagination.

John Curry in characteristically artistic pose in 1976.

Sebastian Coe (Baron Coe of Ranmore)
1980 Moscow and 1984 Los Angeles
Athletics, 1,500m

Sebastian Coe is the only man to have successfully defended the Olympic 1,500m title and is possibly the greatest middle-distance runner ever. He dominated international athletics for more than a decade, along with his long-time rival Steve Ovett. In all, he set 12 world records during his career (more than any other Briton), and won two Olympic gold medals and two silvers.

Coe showed early signs of his extraordinary ability, winning the British Youth and Junior 1,500m titles at the age of 16 in 1973. He followed this by setting a new British 800m indoor record of 1:47.6 in 1977, breaking that record twice within a month, and a third time shortly after. In an astonishing show of brilliance, over six weeks in July and August of 1979, he set new world records for the 800m, 1,500m, and 1 mile. In 1980, he became the world record holder at 1,000m, in 1981 broke his own records again at 800m and 1000m, and twice improved the mile time. This extraordinary success continued in 1982, when he contributed a world record time of 1:44.01 to the 4x800m relay, as well as setting new indoor records at 800 and 1,000m. His 800m record of 1:41.73 has only been beaten once, by Wilson Kipketer of Denmark in 1997; it still stands as a British record.

The duel between Coe and Ovett, with their contrasting backgrounds and personalities – Coe the suave, media-conscious runner from London and Ovett the 'bad boy' of athletics who antagonised the press – caught the public imagination and became one of the most famous rivalries in athletics.

The first notable meeting between Coe and Ovett came in the 800m final of the Moscow Olympics in 1980. Coe, the record-holder, was naturally favourite, but he was unaccountably out of sorts on the day of the race. 'I've never known pressure like it,' he said at the time, and afterwards admitted that he could barely remember the race.

Seb Coe raises a hand to salute the crowd as he wins the 1,500m in 1984, and with it his second Olympic gold medal.

Ovett took his time entering the arena, but once on the starting blocks ran the race of his life, beating Coe easily. Coe was devastated. On the rostrum, Ovett offered his hand, which Coe took 'as if he'd just been handed a turd', as Clive James (then television critic for the *Observer*) famously commented. But Coe had his revenge in the 1,500m six days later.

Both athletes had their ardent supporters, and a meeting between them was of intense national interest – more than 20 million people watched the race in Moscow, the broadcast interrupting the *Nine o'Clock News*. Advised by his coach (his

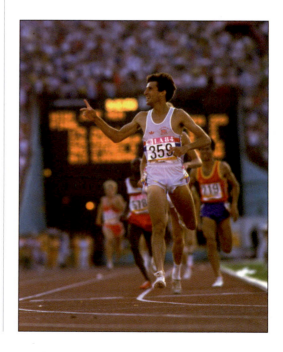

father, Peter) to stick to Ovett come what may, Coe came off the final bend with Ovett at his shoulder and kicked for the tape, taking the German, Jurgen Straub, in the final few metres and claiming the gold medal.

Although they met only seven times (one of those a schools cross-country race), each encounter was a milestone in athletics history. In 1981 the two men trumped each other's world records for the 1,500m three times.

In 1983, Coe contracted toxoplasmosis, a relatively rare blood disease, and his appearance in the 1984 Games looked in doubt after he had lost almost a year of training. But he recovered in time for the trials. Losing to Peter Elliot in the 1,500m trials, he was nonetheless (and somewhat controversially) selected.

At Los Angeles, Ovett had collapsed in the heats, and Coe met another old rival in the form of Steve Cram, but succeeded in taking the 1,500m gold medal, as well as silver in the 800m. Illness again forced him to miss the 1986 Commonwealth Games, but at the European Championships he took the 800m title, and finished second to Cram in the 1,500m.

Throughout his athletics career Coe had taken an active interest in politics, to which he turned on his retirement in 1990. In 1992, he became Conservative MP for Falmouth and Camborne. He became William Hague's chief of staff in his first period of office as Conservative leader, but New Labour's sweeping electoral victory in 1997 persuaded Coe that it was time to leave front-line politics.

Coe was Vice Chairman of the Sports Council from 1986 to 1989, led London's bid to stage the 2000 Games, and in 2003 became an ambassador for the 2012 Games effort and a member of the organising board. In 2004 he became the Chairman of the London Organising Committee. His presentation at the critical IOC meeting in 2005 was said to be instrumental in the success of the bid.

As 'an outstanding personality in the world of sport, a great personality in the Olympic movement,' in the words of FIFA President Sepp Blatter, in September 2006 Coe was appointed the first chairman of FIFA's ethics commission.

In recognition of his talent and services to sport, Coe was awarded the MBE in 1982, the OBE in 1990 and created a life peer in 2000 as Baron Coe of Ranmore in the County of Surrey. He was further recognised by a Special Award at the BBC Sports Personality of the Year ceremony in 2005, and made a KBE in 2006.

In 2008, while Coe was at the Beijing Olympics, his father, who had been a huge influence on his career, died.

Coe was married to former eventer Nicky McIrvine, with whom he has four children. The couple divorced in 2002. He is a worldwide ambassador for Nike, owns a string of health clubs and, as a multimillionaire, is a member of the exclusive East India Club.

An outstanding athlete, successful politician and businessman, and a powerful influence in the Olympic movement, Seb Coe is known throughout the world of sport.

Robin Cousins
1980 Lake Placid
Figure skating

Robin Cousins has had a highly successful and diverse career, not only as a top British skater, but as a choreographer, producer, director, costume designer, author, actor and artist. His superb free skating routine at Lake Placid, which included five triple jumps (more than any other competitor) earned him Olympic gold.

Cousins won his first title at the age of 12, made his international debut aged 14 and joined the British international team at 15. He won the National Senior Championships four years running and the World Free Skating Championships gold medal three times. He was British champion four times.

He has performed in numerous shows, tours and television ice specials as well as having his own successful touring ice shows, *Electric Ice* and *Ice Majesty*. His choreographic credits include *Starlight Express on Ice* and *The Wizard of Oz on Ice*, to name but two. All this as well as appearing in pantomime and presenting and commentating for BBC TV and NBC in America.

Knee and back problems forced Cousins to retire from skating in 2000, but he remains involved in the sport, continuing to produce, direct and choreograph, and appearing in musical theatre. That year he formed his own company, Cousins Entertainment Ltd, an event production company which also supplies and manages ice rinks.

Cousins was awarded the MBE in 1980. He is a judge of ITV's *Dancing on Ice*. He has been voted BBC Sports Personality of the Year and was inducted into the World Figure Skating Hall of Fame in 2005.

Robin Cousins smiles as he displays his gold medal won in the men's figure skating competition on 21 February 1980 in Lake Placid.

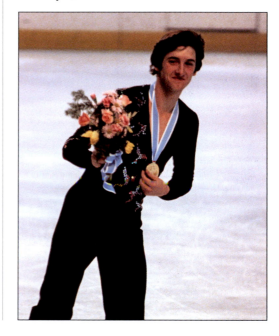

Duncan Goodhew
1980 Moscow
Swimming, 100m breaststroke

Ranked by Channel 4 as one of the 100 Greatest Sporting Moments, Duncan Goodhew's victory in the final of the 100m breaststroke in Moscow made him a national hero. With his bald head and muscular body, Goodhew was instantly recognisable, and with an individual gold and a bronze medal from the 4x100m medley relay he became a household name. His hero status was cemented in 2000 when he saved the life of Labour MP Robert Sheldon with a textbook resuscitation from a heart attack. He was chosen as one of the torchbearers when the Olympic flame reached London on its journey to Beijing in 2008.

Goodhew's path to Olympic fame was not without its difficulties. His school days were made miserable by the fact that he was dyslexic and bald. A fall from a tree when he was eleven caused the rare and permanent condition alopecia universalis, and his dyslexia was not diagnosed until he was 13, by which time he had been dubbed 'Duncan the Dunce' by his peers. Swimming was a way out of the stress of academic life, and his complete lack of hair gave him a fractional advantage in the water. But it was not until he went to Millfield School in Somerset that his potential was recognised. He was spotted by Britain's swimming coach at the time, Paddy Garrett, who remarked prophetically, 'He'll swim for the school, he'll swim for the district, he'll swim for the county and he'll go beyond that.' While still at school, Goodhew was selected for the 1976 Olympics, finishing seventh in the 100m breaststroke.

Leaving Millfield on the premature death of his father, Goodhew won a scholarship to North Carolina State University and went to America to train and race. He went on to win three silver medals in the 1978 Commonwealth Games and bronze in the World and European Championships. As the 1980 Olympics approached, his chance of Olympic gold looked in doubt after the boycott of the Games by many countries in protest at the Soviet invasion of Afghanistan. The American Government imposed a total boycott, and UK Prime Minister Margaret Thatcher asked the British athletes to follow suit. The British Olympic Association opted to attend, and Goodhew had his chance.

The unmistakeable pate of Duncan Goodhew as he goes for gold in 1980.

Goodhew, like his hero Mark Spitz, retired at the peak of his career. He was awarded the MBE, became involved in the highly successful BT Swimathon which has raised over £10m for charity, and took up motivational speaking. His book *Sink or Swim* draws on his own life and describes the dedication and hard work required to succeed in any field. He continues to raise money for charity through swimming events and to inspire youngsters to take up the sport, which he calls the best strategy for all-round health and fitness. 'Whether you're in chlorine or salt water, you can see it, hear it, smell it and taste it – and every square inch of your skin feels it.'

Steve Ovett

1980 Moscow
Athletics, 800m

In the 1970s and '80s, a golden era of British middle-distance running, Steve Ovett's rivalry with Seb Coe was meat and drink to the media. Their contrasting characters – Ovett rough and streetwise, Coe suave and gentlemanly – and their determination to outdo each other was hyped by the press and caught the public interest, and each had a massive partisan following.

Ovett, the original 'bad boy' of athletics, showed precocious talent as a teenager. A promising footballer, he decided instead to concentrate on athletics since he preferred individual sport to those in which he was reliant on teammates. Between the ages of 15 and 19 he set records for his age every year at 800m, his favourite distance. At the age of 18 he won the European Junior title with a record time, and came second in the event at senior level the following year in Rome. Already known for his burst of speed in the final straight, he got a place in the British team for the 1976 Games in Montreal, and came fifth. This turbojet kick in the last 200 metres of the inaugural IAAF World Cup gave him a famous win over the Olympic champion, John Walker, and really brought him to the public's attention.

The 1978 European Championships saw the first senior meeting between the two great rivals. An unexpected burst from the East German, Olaf Beyer, relegated Ovett to second place, with Coe third. But Ovett recovered to win the 1,500m, so far ahead of the field that he eased off before the tape to wave to the crowd. In the following seasons Ovett achieved record times in the 800m and 2-mile races.

With Ovett and Coe both in the squad for the 1980 Olympics, the media spotlight was on them for the showdown. Though not fancied to win the 1,500m, Ovett surprised everyone, particularly Coe, by taking him on the inside and beating him. When Ovett offered his hand at the medal presentation, Coe took it 'as if he'd just been handed a turd', as Clive James famously commented. Coe got his own back in the 800m, taking the gold medal, with Ovett only managing the bronze.

During the season following the Olympics the two were at their peak, although they never met in a race. In the space of ten days they exchanged the world mile record three times.

For most of 1982 and early 1983, Ovett was out of competition through injury, but when fitness returned he broke the 1,500m world record with a time of 3:30.77.

In the run-up to the 1984 Games, in spite of intensive winter training in Australia, Ovett was still dogged by minor injuries and went into the competition with bronchitis. In trying to defend his 800m Olympic title he only narrowly qualified for the final, and when he finished in fourth place he collapsed and was taken to hospital. Unwisely, but with characteristic grit, he returned to compete in the 1,500m. In the last lap he dropped out, collapsed again and was stretchered off.

Although he won the 5,000m at the Commonwealth Games in 1986, Ovett's days at the top of his sport were over. He retired in 1991 and emigrated to Australia, where he is a sports adviser and television commentator. A statue of him, erected in Brighton in 1987, was stolen in 2007 and has yet to be replaced.

Steve Ovett storms ahead to win the 800 metres final at the Moscow Olympics, Sebastian Coe (254) in his wake. Nikolai Kirov (707) takes the bronze.

Daley Thompson
1980 Moscow and 1984 Los Angeles
Athletics, decathlon

'Competition is my life,' said Daley Thompson, one of the world's greatest decathletes. 'Winning is my only goal. Everything I do is directed towards that end.' His dedication to sport has made him the most successful decathlete in history and earned him five gold medals in World, European and Olympic events as well as three Commonwealth Games titles. When he refused to carry the Union Jack at the opening ceremony of 1984 Games for fear that the effort would reduce his chances of winning a medal, he was criticised in some quarters. In sporting circles he was known to be brusque to the point of rudeness, but his talent, success and good looks ensured his popularity throughout his career. These attributes also hugely increased the appeal of the decathlon itself.

Thompson competed in the first of his four Olympics as an 18-year-old in 1976 in Montreal. He returned in 1980 to take his first gold medal, and won again in 1984 to become only the second person in Olympic history to claim two decathlon gold medals. (The first to do so was American Bob Mathias, in 1948 and 1952.) By this time he had been unbeaten in decathlons for six years.

At the end of 1983, Thompson was at his peak. He was European, World, Commonwealth and Olympic champion, the first athlete to hold the titles simultaneously. Going into the Los Angeles Games he had lost his world title to his long-time rival, Jürgen Hingsen of West Germany, but from the start of the competition, Thompson was ahead. In the 1,500m final, he eased off at the finish and

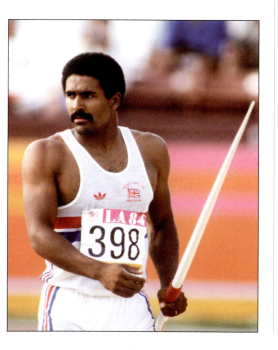

Daley Thompson composes himself for the javelin during the 1984 decathlon.

looked like missing out on regaining the world record. When the photo-finish pictures were studied, however, it was found that he had been awarded a point too few in the 100m hurdles, and was thus equal record holder with Hingsen. When new scoring tables were subsequently introduced, Thompson's score totalled 8,847 points, a world record that stood until 1992.

Thompson has won every major title open to him and broken the world decathlon record four times. 'The most competitive sporting animal I have ever come across,' is how Frank Dick, the British athletics coach, described him.

He was awarded the MBE in 1982, the OBE in 1986, then the CBE in 2000. He was voted BBC Sports Personality of the Year in 1982. In 1992 a recurring hamstring injury forced Thompson to retire from athletics, but he played professional football for Mansfield Town and Stevenage Borough FC, and worked as fitness coach for Wimbledon and Luton Town.

He is an ambassador for the London 2012 Olympics Games – one of many appointed in 2008 to inspire people to become volunteers, coaches and mentors for young athletes around the UK.

Allan Wells
1980 Moscow
Athletics, 100m

Scotsman Allan Wells went into the Moscow Olympics at the relatively late age of 28 with high hopes. With two successful seasons behind him, and in spite of being obliged to use the novelty of starting blocks under the new Olympic regulations, he triumphed in the 100m sprint in a thrilling photo-finish race. Having qualified with a new British record time of 10.11 seconds, he was drawn on the outside with the favourite, Silvio Leonard

Allan Wells gives a clenched-fist salute after winning the 100 metres gold medal in 1980.

of Cuba on the inside. Twenty metres from the line, with the rest of the field beaten, Wells and Leonard were neck and neck – first Wells edging ahead, then Leonard. With seven metres to go Wells leaned hard. Both finished with a time of 10.25, but Wells' lean was just enough to get his head and shoulders past the tape ahead of Leonard's chest. In winning the gold medal, Wells became the oldest Olympic 100m champion, the first Briton to win it for 56 years, and – to date – the last white man to win the event.

In the 200m Wells came close to taking another gold medal. Though setting a British record of 20.21, he lost by 0.02 seconds to the Italian Pietro Mennea. He then participated in breaking a third British record with the sprint relay team, which finished fourth.

As a result of the Soviet invasion of Afghanistan in 1979, and various countries move to boycotting the Moscow Games, it was felt by some that the medals were devalued. The fact that Wells went on to beat all the top athletes of the world in subsequent years, as well as the number of records broken in Moscow – 73 Olympic, 36 world and 29 European – tends to disprove such a contention.

Wells started his athletics career as a jumper. He was Scottish junior triple jump champion in 1970, and Scottish indoor long jump champion in 1974. In 1976 he decided to concentrate on the sprint, and by the following year he had won the AAA 60m indoor title and the Scottish outdoor title – the first of seven such wins. Success after success followed: two gold medals and a silver at the 1978 Commonwealth Games and gold and bronze at the 1979 European Cup.

With his two medals from Moscow, Wells was firmly established as one of the world's greatest sprinters. He returned for his second Olympics in 1984, but failed to win a medal, and injury prevented him competing through most of 1985.

But although in his thirties, Wells was not done, and came back to beat the 100m and 200m Commonwealth champions at Gateshead, as well as coming a respectable fifth at the Commonwealth Games. By the time he retired, Wells had won ten gold medals, six silver and two bronze.

Allan Wells was a trendsetter. He was the first athlete to adopt the now ubiquitous lycra running shorts, which led to him being dubbed 'Wilson of the Wizard', after a 1940s comic book character who wore a tight-fitting costume.

More significantly for the sport, he was the first to concentrate his training on upper-body strength. His strenuous workouts included bench presses, speedball and press-ups and his success in sustaining speed and rhythm throughout a race and the strength that allowed his trademark dip and lean, was to lead others, particularly Linford Christie, to emulate his impressive upper-body development.

After retiring from sprinting Wells became coach for the British bobsleigh team, and now coaches the Bank of Scotland specialist sprint team. His medal-winning times in the 100m and 200m at Moscow remain Scottish records.

Pros and Cons – Amateurism vs Professionalism in Sport

The prevailing attitude in the nineteenth century was that in sport the upper and lower classes should keep their distance, and thus the concept of amateurism developed. Amateurs (the aristocrats) took part for the love of it and sought no reward. They were chaps who espoused fair play and *esprit de corps*. Professionals, on the other hand, were like mercenaries, with neither loyalties nor convictions, so the thinking went.

An aristocrat himself, Baron de Coubertin, founder of the modern Games, was influenced by this English public school ethos. It was said that he had his 'vision' of the Games during a visit to Rugby School. But he was aware at the same time of the inequities of the system and encouraged his fellow aristocrats to become 'patrons' of working-class athletes. However, it was a century before the IOC voted to declare all professionals eligible for the Olympics.

In theory, the early Games were open to all amateurs, regardless of origin or status. But in practice few but the wealthy could afford the time and expense of seriously (or even frivolously) pursuing sporting activities, and most events were closed to women. The rules of the early Olympics were vaguely defined, and the result was a muddle, one for which poor Jim Thorpe paid the price.

In 1912 Thorpe, part native American Indian and one of greatest all-round sportsmen ever, won gold medals in both the pentathlon and decathlon, beating his rivals in all disciplines by massive margins. Presenting Thorpe with his medals, King Gustav V of Sweden told him, 'You, sir, are the greatest athlete in the world.' 'Thanks, King,' said Thorpe, and went home to a ticker-tape reception. A year later an American newspaper revealed that Thorpe received a (trifling) reward for playing semi-professional baseball in 1910. Despite the fact that the 1912 Olympic rulebook stated that protests had to be made within 30 days of the closing ceremony, the IOC stripped him of his medals, only to reaward them posthumously in 1982. A muddle indeed.

The cover of Michael Sheaffer's An Exercise in Frustration, *a fictionalised account of a sports reporter covering a hearing to determine if Jim Thorpe should be allowed to retain his gold medals.*

A similar fate befell Italian gymnast, Alberto Braglia, who won gold in 1908. After the Games, penury pushed him into the circus, working as a human cannonball, and bang went his medal. But he at least was reinstated as an amateur in time to compete in the next Games, where he won two more gold medals.

The IOC's inconsistency extended to many sports. A swordsman himself, de Coubertin declared that professional fencing 'masters' were eligible to compete in the first two Games, no doubt considering them his social equals. And right up until 1952 only military officers were eligible for equestrian events.

The complex rules did not prevent many nations from sponsoring athletes by paying them indirectly into trust funds or – in the case of the Communist bloc – declaring them to be students or enrolling them in the Army to preserve their amateur status. The advantage this gave to the state-sponsored full-time athletes is reflected in their domination of the medal tables of the mid-twentieth century.

When Avery Brundage, a fierce campaigner for retaining the amateur status, retired as IOC President in 1972, the rules were relaxed to allow professional participation to be left up to the international federation of each sport.

Although the word 'amateur' was deleted from the Olympic Charter, it nonetheless failed to iron out completely the anomalies and inequities of the Olympic regulations. Some bodies upheld the old rules, some made up their own: until 1978 all American athletes had to be amateurs, and in 1992 ice hockey players were deemed to be amateurs only if they were under 23.

In 1988 the IOC ruled to allow professionals, 'all the world's great male and female athletes', to participate in all sports, although there are still a few exceptions. Only amateurs are allowed in boxing (in the interests of safety), and in baseball (which in any case saw its last appearance at the 2008 Games). The number of football players over 23 is limited to three per team. The only time football was not included in the Games was in 1932 when the IOC and FIFA were unable to agree about whether or not it should be strictly an amateur competition.

Although the belief still lingers that professionalism compromises an athlete's love of sport and favours the richer nations, the increasing commercialism in all sports makes it unthinkable that competitors should not be rewarded. The Olympics is one of the greatest events in the world, and a chance to participate is open to all who aspire to athletic excellence.

Steve Redgrave

1984 Los Angeles, 1988 Seoul, 1992 Barcelona, 1996 Atlanta and 2000 Sydney
Rowing, coxed fours (1984), coxless pairs (1988, 1992 & 1996), coxless fours (2000)

When describing Sir Steven Redgrave one quickly runs out of superlatives. The most titled rower in history, the man is a towering figure, in stature and in his standing in the world of sport. Nine times winner of the World Championship in pairs or fours, three times winner of the World Cup, three times Commonwealth Champion, and our only athlete ever to win gold medals at five consecutive Games he is justly hailed as Britain's greatest Olympian ever.

Voted the greatest moment in British sporting history in a Channel 4 poll, more than 6.5m viewers tuned in to watch the final of the coxless fours in Sydney. No one would regret staying up until the early hours as the British team scraped home in a nail-biting photo-finish win over the battling Italians. Having made history at the age of 38, the exhausted Redgrave was ecstatic. When the crew, Redgrave, Pinsent, Foster and Cracknell, received their gold medals from the Princess Royal, Redgrave was also given a gold Olympic pin by the IOC President, to mark his outstanding achievement. He later said, 'Sure, it was desperate and fraught at the end, but we never doubted we would win. It was close, but that doesn't matter. Second best is not good enough, it's who crosses the line first.'

Redgrave has won so many events that there is no room here to list them all, but they include a

Sir Steven Redgrave celebrates gold with his son Zac after victory in the coxless fours final at the Sydney Games.

record 23 titles at Henley, an Olympic bronze medal in 1988 to add to the five Olympic golds, as well as two silvers and a bronze to add to his nine World Championships between 1986 and 1999. Of course, he did not achieve all this unaided, but he certainly knew how to choose his coaches and his teammates. One of the latter, Matthew Pinsent, has since equalled his tally of world and Olympic medals. The others who contributed to his Olympic success were Andy Holmes, Adrian Ellison, Richard Budgett, Martin Cross, Patrick Sweeney, Tim Foster and James Cracknell.

The story of Redgrave's accomplishments does not end there: in 1989 he was a member of the British bobsleigh team, as well as national champion; he has run three Marathons; in 1996 he won the UK Celebrity Gladiators competition. He was awarded first the MBE, then the CBE and in 2001 was knighted. All this from a man who is dyslexic, diabetic, has ulcerative colitis and who famously said in 1996 that if anyone found him close to a rowing boat again, they could shoot him.

Redgrave retired from rowing in 2000 and was voted BBC Sports Personality of the Year. He took part in a three-part BBC documentary entitled *Gold Fever,* which had followed the coxless fours in the build-up to the Sydney Games.

A keen and competitive golfer, in 2009 he broke his leg falling down a grass bank after a pro-am European Masters game. He then drove 90 minutes home to watch the Champions League final before finally setting off for hospital.

Although he still enjoys rowing, his life now is filled with public speaking, PR and charity work. The Steve Redgrave Trust was launched in 2001, and his Steve Redgrave Fund has teamed up with Sport Relief and Comic Relief to raise money for young sportsmen and women. He has been widely tipped as the flag-bearer for the 2012 Games.

'I'm just an ordinary guy who went quite quick in a boat, really,' he said. But to us mere mortals there is nothing ordinary about Sir Steve, the consummate competitor and true sporting hero.

Redgrave's impressive tally of five gold medals from five separate Olympic Games.

Tessa Sanderson

1984 Los Angeles

Athletics, javelin

Tessa Sanderson, the first female British black Olympian, competed in six consecutive Olympic Games starting in 1976. She remains the only female British athlete to win an Olympic throwing gold medal. In a career spanning 26 years, she won ten WAAA titles, a World Cup and three Commonwealth gold medals.

Born in Jamaica of Ghanaian parents, Sanderson was brought up by her grandmother and came to England at the age of nine. Settling in the Midlands, she showed considerable ability in junior pentathlon events. It became apparent early on that her particular strength lay in throwing the javelin. She hit her peak in the 1970, but her position as Britain's foremost javelin thrower was usurped in the 1980s by Fatima Whitbread, with whom she shared a close rivalry for many years. Having failed to make the final at the 1980 Moscow Games, she then lost 21 of her first 22 contests against Whitbread. With such poor form she was not expected to shine at the Los Angeles Games, but with her first throw she set a new Olympic record of 69.56m and eventually took the gold medal, beating Whitbread into third place.

In 1991, after a disappointing performance in the European championships, Sanderson took a break from athletics, but returned for the 1992 Games in Barcelona, where she finished fourth. In the same year she won a gold medal at the World Cup, and again turned her back on athletics in favour of a media career. Over the years, she has been a presenter for BBC, ITV, GMTV, Sky and many other television and radio stations.

Then in 1996, at the age of 40, she returned for her sixth Olympic appearance in Atlanta, but was eliminated in the qualifying round.

For her sporting achievements and Vice Chairmanship of Sport England, as well as her tireless work for charities, Sanderson was awarded the CBE in 2004.

Tessa Sanderson in Atlanta in 1996 – her sixth Olympic appearance.

Malcolm Cooper
1984 Los Angeles and 1988 Seoul
Shooting, 50m 3 positions

Malcolm Cooper is widely acknowledged as the finest marksman of all time. In all, he won a total of 149 medals – 61 at Olympic, European or World Championships – and broke or equalled 13 world records.

Cooper took up shooting when his father, a lieutenant in the Royal Navy, was posted to New Zealand. Following the family's return to England, Malcolm became a shipwright's apprentice in Portsmouth and joined the HMS Naval Rifle Club. In 1970 he made it into the British team, going on to win the national three-positions (prone, standing and kneeling) title 12 times.

Utterly single-minded and dedicated to his sport, Cooper trained hard, swimming 30 lengths a day and running miles. He and his wife, Sarah Robinson (at one time British women's shooting champion and a team member in Seoul), shunned all distractions in the pursuit of excellence. They had no children, pets or television. His finest year was possibly 1985, when he won all five events at the European Championships.

The British Government's decision to boycott the 1980 Moscow Olympics in protest at the Soviet invasion of Afghanistan did not prevent individual sports bodies entering if they wished. The National Small Bore Rifle Association upheld the boycott and Cooper was thus denied an almost certain gold medal. But in 1984, he achieved his aim when he scored a record 1,173 points out of 1,200, shooting for five hours in searing temperatures. He returned to the Olympics in 1988 in Seoul and became the only person successfully to defend the title, in spite of having his rifle damaged by a BBC cameraman just before the competition. Ironically, the weapon was repaired by a Russian armourer.

He retired from the sport in 1991, concentrating on developing Accuracy International, an engineering company manufacturing precision rifles which he had established in 1978. The company had helped fund his Olympic ambitions, and in 1998 won the Queen's Award for Export. By 1990, he was supplying the British army with their standard sniper rifles.

Cooper was awarded the MBE in 1984. He was President of the Havant Rifle and Pistol Club from 1988 until his death from cancer in 2001. In recognition of his status as Britain's greatest shooter, a range at the National Shooting Centre in Bisley is named after him.

Malcolm Cooper, double gold medallist and the world's finest marksman in his day.

Christopher Dean and Jayne Torvill
1984 Sarajevo
Figure skating

The partnership of Torvill and Dean is one of the world's best-known sporting pairings and their faultless routine in the 1984 Olympic ice dance final will go down in history as the most brilliant skating performance ever, and one of the most popular in British sport. Watched by a television audience of over 24 million, the pair received a record perfect score for artistic impression from all nine judges, who gave them the highest overall score of all time for their interpretation of Ravel's *Bolero*.

The two skaters teamed up in 1975, when Dean was in the police force and Torvill was already a British junior champion, winning their first trophy in their second year together. They attended the Olympics and World Championships in 1980, finishing fifth and fourth respectively, and thereafter won medals in every World and British Championships until 1996, usually coming first. Coached by Betty Callaway from 1978, and mentored by the singer-actor Michael Crawford from 1981, the two turned professional in 1984. In 1994, thanks to a relaxation of the rules, they were able to revert temporarily to amateur status to enter the 1994 Games in Lillehammer, where they took the bronze medal.

Much as the media would have liked it, the two had no romantic entanglement. In 1998 Torvill and Dean retired from competition, though they continued to perform together in ice dance extravaganzas, notably ITV's *Dancing on Ice*, for some years afterwards, by which time both were married.

In 1982 and 1983 the pair won the Sports Team of the Year award, and in 1984 were named Sports Personalities of the Year. In 1981 they were each awarded the MBE and then OBE in 2000. Between them, Torvill and Dean took ice dancing to a new level, proving an almost unbeatable combination and becoming the darlings of the media. Their remarkable achievements have been acknowledged in their home town of Nottingham, where a number of roads are named after them. They were inducted into the World Figure Skating Hall of Fame in 1989.

Torvill and Dean, ecstatic at the end of their world-famous Olympic routine in 1984.

Sean Kerly

1988 Seoul

Field hockey

Sean Kerly is one of Britain's best-known sportsmen and surely its best-known hockey player, described by the press as 'the Gary Lineker of hockey'. As top scorer at Seoul he rocketed to fame in a sport that had hitherto received little attention but in 1988 captivated millions of British television viewers. When the team beat the West Germans 3-1, with a goal from Kerly and two from Imran Sherwani, to take Britain's third hockey gold medal, the nation rejoiced. And where *were* the Germans?

Kerly, Sherwani and Steve Batchelor formed the backbone of the British team at their three Olympic appearances. For their efforts in 1984 and 1988 the team were awarded the BBC Sports Personality of the Year award, and Kerly was nominated for an individual award in 1988. Having quit his job as a marketing manager to train for the 1988 Games, he found it hard to adjust to the media attention and champagne receptions, the visits to Buckingham Palace and 10 Downing Street, the awards and accolades. He did some public speaking, some television appearances, even had a walk-on part in a pantomime, and eventually settled down and returned to full-time work. He now runs a graphic art and marketing agency.

In an outstanding career, Kerly has made 74 appearances for Great Britain, scored 57 goals, and played in 58 outdoor and nine indoor internationals for England. In Los Angeles he scored seven goals for the bronze medal-winning team, and eight at the Seoul Games. He won silver medals at the 1986 World Cup, the 1987 European Cup and was a member of the Southgate team which won the English Club Championships in 1987 and 1988.

Kerly puts his success down to 'hard work, enthusiasm, bloody-mindedness and a very good team around me'. He retired in 1992 and was awarded the MBE. He has appeared frequently on *Grandstand*, and was part of the BBC's commentary team for the Atlanta and Beijing Olympics.

Sean Kerly leaps in the air as Great Britain beat the Germans in the 1988 hockey final. The clinching third goal prompted the famous comment by the commentator Barry Davies: 'And where were the Germans? And quite frankly, who cares?'

Linford Christie

1992 Barcelona
Athletics, 100m

There can be few more controversial British Olympians than Linford Christie, a man of immense talent and deep grievances. A world-class sprinter and winner of more medals than any other British male athlete, Christie is the only man in history to hold the Olympic, World, European and Commonwealth titles for the 100m, but mention his name and the immediate associations are 'lunchbox', 'drugs cheat', and running feuds with the establishment.

Born in Jamaica, Christie followed his parents to London when he was seven. At school he was a good all-rounder, but did not take up athletics seriously until he was 19, by which time he had sown a good number of wild oats and fathered three children. Failure to make the sprint relay team for the 1984 Games goaded him to train in earnest and in 1986 he won the European Championship 100m and came second at the Commonwealth Games.

At the Olympics in 1988 he earned his first Olympic medal, a silver, and his first positive drugs test. By a margin of eleven to ten, the IOC voted to clear him (although two of the judges were said to be asleep during the vote). In 1991 at the World Championships in Tokyo he took part in one of the greatest 100m races in memory when, for the first and only time, six men broke the mystical ten-second barrier in the same race. It was won by Carl Lewis, and Christie, in spite of breaking his European record by 0.05 seconds, came only fourth.

In 1992, Christie achieved his ambition of Olympic gold, winning the 100m final in a time of 9.96 seconds. At the comparatively late age of 32 he became the oldest Olympic 100m champion. After a bumper year in 1993, taking the four major titles and becoming BBC Sports Personality of the

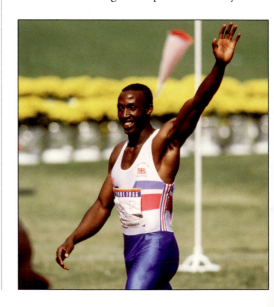

Linford Christie celebrates after running the anchor leg to take the silver medal in the 4x100m relay.

Year, he returned to the Games in 1996, but was disqualified in the final after two false starts.

It was Christie's late flowering that led to the court case against John McVicar, the journalist and ex-con. McVicar had accused Christie in print of being a drugs cheat, questioning how he could have risen from 156th to fourth in one year of sprinting without taking drugs. Christie sued for libel and won. During the trial Christie let loose a tirade about the media's treatment of him, particularly their comments about his manhood and the running joke about his 'lunchbox'. To everyone's amusement, Mr Justice Popplewell had to have the term explained.

Having won his libel action, Christie was to be convicted of doping in 1999 in Germany when he was semi-retired and in the twilight of his career. Found guilty of taking the performance-enhancing drug nandrolone, Christie strenuously denied and continues to deny the charge. Although the verdict of the UK Athletics body was that there was reasonable doubt, the IAAF handed Christie a two-year ban, and the BOA announced he would not be accredited for any future Olympics. At the time, Christie was publicly slated by Sebastian Coe, which led to a long and bitter feud. In 2008, he was snubbed by the London Olympic Organising Committee – first invited by Mayor Boris Johnson to be a torchbearer only to have the offer withdrawn – and the feud reached new heights. Christie blamed Coe for the rejection, launching a furious attack: 'I have nothing good to say about Sebastian Coe at all, absolutely nothing.' He went on to blame institutional racism within the BOA for the fact that he had not received a knighthood.

In spite of all, Christie must remain one of the most talented and successful British athletes. And while he 'swears on his children's lives' that he never took drugs, he has found a measure of peace. He cooks, he gardens (and once did a series for the BBC), cares for his five children and has made a name for himself coaching the likes of Darren Campbell and Katharine Merry. And if he didn't receive the knighthood he thought he deserved, at least he has a stadium in west London named after him.

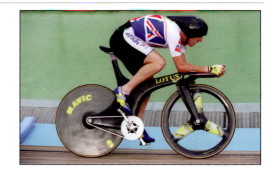

Chris Boardman (see overleaf) on his revolutionary Lotus Superbike as he heads for victory in the 4,000m individual pursuit final in 1992.

Chris Boardman

1992 Barcelona

Cycling, 4,000m individual track pursuit

In spite of winning only one Olympic gold medal, Chris Boardman is one of the most famous of all cyclists. At the Barcelona Olympics, Boardman's revolutionary cycle, designed by Mike Burrows and built by Lotus, caused a sensation. The new 'superbike' overturned bicycle design – the frames and forks were dramatically different, and it had a lenticular wheel at the back made largely of carbon-fibre. It also sported a tri-bar, a handlebar used in the triathlon and designed to reduce the cyclist's wind profile. The bike weighed less than 20lbs and took Boardman to two world records in the preliminary rounds. In the final, he did what no man has ever done before or since in an Olympic 4,000m pursuit final – he lapped his rival. It was Britain's first cycling gold medal since 1920.

A specialist in the individual time trial, Boardman won his first title in the 1984 GHS schoolboy 10-mile championship (an event named for George Herbert Stancer, the renowned cyclist of the mid-1900s). That year he also broke the junior 25-mile national record, going on to win the 1986 junior 25-mile championship. As a senior, he won the hill climb championships four years in succession (1988-1991), five consecutive 25-mile championships (1989-1993), the 50-mile championship in 1991 and 1992, and the men's British time trial championship in 2000. He broke the 25-mile record again in 1992 and 1993, and, as a member of the North Wirral Velo team, broke the 100km team time trial record in 1993 with a time of 2:00:07. In all, he won over 30 national titles. He turned professional in 1993 and joined the French team Gan, winning the Grand Prix Eddy Merckx in Brussels.

He first came to the public attention in 1994 when he won the prologue of the Tour de France in the fastest time ever recorded, but he may be better remembered for breaking the world one-hour record, a blue riband event in cycling, three times.

Altogether Boardman has been engaged in six Olympic Games, as a competitor from 1988 to 2000 (one gold, and a bronze medal in Atlanta in the road race) and most recently in Beijing as part of the 2008 cycling management team.

In 1998, Boardman was diagnosed with a form of osteoporosis. The treatment involved the use of testosterone, a banned substance in sport. Boardman chose to postpone treatment and to continue cycling. In 2000 he decided to retire, ending his phenomenal career with an attempt at a new one-hour record. He reportedly shaved his entire body to increase his chances. In front of a huge crowd, he set a record of 30.723 miles in an hour, beating Eddy Merckx's 1972 distance of 30.716.

Boardman lives with his wife and six children in his native Wirral. He has covered cycling for ITV, and has his name on a quality brand of bicycles.

Sally Gunnell

1992 Barcelona
Athletics, 400m hurdles

Sally Gunnell, the archetypal 'girl next door', is a hugely popular and successful British sportswoman. The first British woman to win a hurdles gold medal at the Olympics, she is also the only woman to hold Olympic, World, European and Commonwealth titles concurrently. In all, she has won 13 gold medals in major championships. In Barcelona, as the team captain, she ran the race of her life to take the 400m hurdles gold medal in a nail-biting finish with the American Sandra Farmer-Patrick. She also won bronze in the 4x400m relay.

Gunnell began her athletics career in the long jump and pentathlon, but with her strength and stamina soon turned to hurdling. In 1986 she won the 100m hurdles at the Commonwealth Games, two years later setting a British record of 12.82. She moved up to the 400m hurdles and earned a place

Sally Gunnell proudly wears the flag after winning the 400m hurdles in Barcelona.

in the squad for the Seoul Olympics in 1988, where she finished fifth. By the Barcelona Games, Gunnell was in peak condition and her personal best was down to a time of 53.16. The electrifying final saw her triumph with a time of 53.23. In a rematch with Farmer-Patrick at the World Championships the following year, she won again in a time of 52.74 – the eighth time she had broken the British record. In 1994 she added the European and Commonwealth to her list of titles, before injury struck in 1995. Though she missed most of the season, she still made it on to the team for the Atlanta Games in 1996, but was forced to withdraw in the semi-finals. It was her 30th birthday; her Achilles tendon failed to see her through.

Gunnell retired in 1997, having served a year as a Red Cross ambassador in Angola. She was awarded the OBE in 1998 and went on to join the BBC as a trackside interviewer and pundit. After a certain amount of adverse comment in the press for her interviewing technique, she complained that the BBC had failed to support her and quit the £60,000 a year job in 2006.

Married to fellow-athlete Jonathan Bigg, she has three children and pursues a successful career as a motivational speaker. As well as being a keen horsewoman, she spearheads many charities and works with the British Heart Foundation and Sport England in improving the nation's fitness.

Matthew Pinsent

1992 Barcelona, 1996 Atlanta, 2000 Sydney and 2004 Athens
Rowing, coxless pairs (1992 & 1996), coxless fours (2000 & 2004)

Between 1991 and 2002 there was not a year in which Matthew Pinsent did not win a gold medal. But it was perhaps the final of the coxless four in Athens that marked his most memorable victory, and was voted Britain's Greatest Sporting Moment that year. Pinsent, Redgrave, Cracknell and Foster battled the Canadians, swapping the lead with almost every stroke as they powered to the finish. In a nail-biting photo finish, the British crew won by 8/100th of a second with a last minute spurt. There were tears in Pinsent's eyes as he stood on the podium, and in those of most of the millions of British spectators.

One of only five athletes to win four consecutive Olympic gold medals, Pinsent's partnerships first with Steve Redgrave and then James Cracknell have netted him an astonishing ten World Championship gold medals, an all-time record.

Pinsent began rowing at Eton, winning the

Junior World Championship in 1987 at the age of 17, and the junior coxless pair with Tim Foster in 1988. On going up to Oxford to study Geography, he teamed up with Steve

Pinsent wipes away a tear as the National Anthem is played in 2004.

Redgrave and they won the coxless pairs at the 1990 World Championships. It was the beginning of a phenomenally successful partnership, which saw them win the World Championships five times and Olympic gold three times, twice in the coxless pairs and once in the fours.

When Redgrave retired in 2000, Pinsent teamed up with James Cracknell and the medals kept coming. Undefeated in 2001, they completed the unique feat of winning the coxed pairs and, two hours later, the coxless pairs. Another year on and they successfully defended their title, breaking the world record by four seconds. In 2003 Pinsent's winning run was broken, and he and Cracknell switched to the men's coxless four, whereupon he won his fourth gold medal.

Another curious claim to fame is that, until he was recently outdone by fellow rower Peter Reed, Pinsent had the largest lung capacity ever recorded in Britain – 8.5 litres of air with every breath.

At the end of 2004 Pinsent retired from rowing, and was awarded the CBE, following the MBE he received in 1993. In retirement he turned to broadcasting, as a sports bulletin presenter for BBC News, as well as working on the BBC series *Inside Sport,* and writing for *The Times* and *Racing News.* His autobiography, *A Lifetime in Race* was published in 2004.

In 2010 Pinsent was chosen as a torch bearer for the Vancouver Winter Olympics.

Ben Ainslie

2000 Sydney, 2004 Athens and 2008 Beijing
Sailing, Laser class (2000), Finn class (2004 & 2008)

Having sailed from the age of four, Ainslie has become the most successful Finn class sailor ever, and together with Rodney Pattisson, one of the most successful sailors in Olympic history winning gold in three consecutive Games. Encouraged by his father Roddy, who had sailed in the first Whitbread Round the World Race of 1973-4, the young Ben began competing at the age of eight, and won a gold medal at the World Youth Championships in 1995 when he was 18 years old.

Having suffered most of his life with a skin photosensitivity which causes blisters and rashes on his face, Ainslie was picked on at school. The bullying, he says, made him 'ferociously determined to be good at something'. And at sailing he became ferociously good. He made his Olympic debut in 1996 in Atlanta, the youngest British sailor to be selected for the Games, winning the silver in the Laser class. In 1998 and 1999 he won the World Championships in this class, and took his first gold at the 2000 Sydney Games, where his unorthodox blocking tactics (a retaliation against the Brazilian Robert Scheidt's dirty tricks in 1996) in the final race resulted in death threats. In 2002, having deliberately gained 18 kilos of weight, he moved to the larger Finn class and won five World Championships, and gold medals in the 2004 and (in spite of contracting mumps days before) the 2008 Games. In 2009 he skippered the British team to victory in the King Edward VII Gold Cup, and in 2010, with Teamorigin, won the World Championship and the Monsoon Cup.

In total, Ainslie has won ten World and eight European Championships, been crowned International Sailing Federation World Sailor of the Year in 1998 and 2002, and voted British Yachtsman of the Year four times. He was inducted into the Finn Hall of Fame in 2004 and in 2008 a CBE was added to his earlier MBE and OBE. He was chosen as skipper for the 33rd America's Cup British challenge in 2010. The revised timing of the 2013 Cup forced Ainslie to make a difficult choice – America's Cup or Olympics. He opted for the Olympics, where a gold medal in 2012 would make him the most successful sailor in Olympic history.

Ben Ainslie holds the Union Flag aloft after winning his third gold medal in Beijing.

Stephanie Cook

2000 Sydney

Athletics, pentathlon

Described by the press as 'the thinking man's sporting pin-up', Steph Cook surprised the world by retiring from sport at the age of 29 at the height of her career to pursue her medical profession.

A committed Christian, she attended both Cambridge and Oxford, where she read medicine. Having rowed at Cambridge, and being already a competent rider, runner and swimmer, on going up to Oxford Cook quickly mastered the other disciplines in the pentathlon. While still an undergraduate, she won a silver medal at the World Championships in 1998 and a team bronze.

The demands of training for five events with the Olympics in sight obliged Cook to put her medical career on hold. The decision paid dividends in the form of a gold medal in Sydney. In the final event, the 3km run, Cook made up a 49-second deficit and took the lead with only 250m to go, to clinch the victory. 'I remember running up towards the line and thinking my life is never going to be the same again,' she later said.

Cook's good looks and engaging personality, not to mention the gold medal, brought her instant fame and offers of radio and television appearances. She was unaffected by her celebrity status and the following year, 2001, she took three gold medals in the World Championships and was awarded the MBE for services to the modern pentathlon.

Cook cites Eric Liddell as a hero and inspiration, and, following his example, she retired in 2001. After relief work in Gujarat, India, helping the earthquake victims, she took up a position as senior house officer in a hospital A&E department.

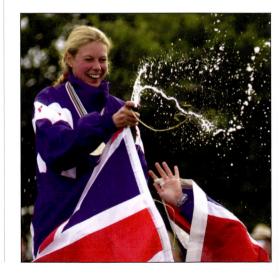

A champagne moment for Steph Cook after her win in the pentathlon in Sydney in 2000.

Three Blondes in a Boat and the Yngling Girls

2000 Sydney, 2004 Athens and 2008 Beijing

Shirley Robertson, (2000 Europe Class & 2004 Yngling Class)
Sarah Ayton, (2004 & 2008 Yngling Class); Sarah Webb (2004 & 2008 Yngling Class)
Pippa Wilson (2008 Yngling Class)

The Yngling is a three-person boat with keel and three sails which replaced the Soling class in Olympic sailing after the 2000 Sydney Games and was competed for in 2004 and 2008. Shirley Robertson was the senior member of the winning Yngling crew of 2004, both in age and experience. She had started sailing at the age of six in her native Scotland and at the age of 32 succeeded in winning her first gold medal at the 2000 Sydney Games in the single-handed Europe Class. She then teamed up with Sarah Ayton and Sarah Webb and the threesome won the first Olympic gold medal for the Yngling class in Athens with a race to spare.

Known as the 'three blondes in a boat', the good-looking trio became overnight stars, featured on the front and back pages of the newspapers, but their beaming faces masked the strains in their relationship. Robertson's strong leadership style from the helm was causing tension and dissension. The two Sarahs felt that they were merely the crew serving the master rather than a team of equals – Sarah Ayton, equally strong-minded, felt the subordination particularly keenly since she had been at the top of her profession since the age of 18. In spite of their triumph in Athens they decided to part company from Robertson.

It took some searching for Ayton and Webb to find a compatible third. Eventually Pippa Wilson, a successful 470 class yachtswoman, was chosen and the team instantly bonded, with teamwork as their watchword. Ayton took over the helm and the trio ('three blondes in a boat: the sequel') knuckled down to training with the aim of beating Shirley Robertson and her new crew to the

The 'three blondes in a boat' share a joke after winning the Yngling Class race in Athens in 2004. From left to right Sarah Webb, Shirley Robertson and Sarah Ayton.

Yngling selection for the Beijing Games in 2008.

Robertson meanwhile was seeking new challenges in different types of craft, had embarked on a successful media career, and started a family. When her focus returned to the Olympics and the Yngling gold medal, she teamed up with Annie Lush and Lucy Macgregor. With only one boat per nation allowed to enter for the Olympics, the competition was intense and heightened by the rivalry and resentments between Robertson and Ayton. The showdown came at the World Championships in 2007 in Portugal. Ayton's crew dominated the event. In the final they still led, but with Robertson a close second. Approaching the mark at the top of the course Wilson fell overboard. She was quickly hauled back into the boat by Sarah Webb but valuable seconds had been lost. With Robertson breathing down their necks, Ayton, unperturbed, steered round the mark and they sailed on to victory and selection for the Games. An unhappy Robertson complained she had been given too little time to prepare, and promptly sold her boat to the Americans. She attended the Beijing Games – as the BBC's sailing commentator and not, as she had hoped, on the water.

The conditions at the sailing venue 500 miles south of Beijing were to begin with so calm as to make sailing unexciting, and sometimes impossible. But on the day of the final, strong winds blew and the sea churned. Electing not to fight a tactical battle in such rough conditions, the 'Yngling girls' (as they were by now known) went out on their own and raced home to take the gold medal just seven seconds ahead of the Germans. It was the first gold for Pippa Wilson and the second for the Sarahs. On the dockside they were joined by Shirley Robertson, their differences temporarily forgotten in patriotic joy. Ayton's fiancé, Nick Dempsey, meanwhile was competing in the windsurfing event, where he came fourth. With the Yngling class dropped from the 2012 Olympics, Sarah Ayton, now teamed with Saskia Clark has set her sights on the double-handed 470 class instead and is expected to do well. As she says, 'I'll be going to win or there is no point'.

The blonde yachtswomen were all rewarded with honours, Robertson, Ayton and Webb with the MBE and OBE, and Wilson with the MBE.

Pippa Wilson, Sarah Webb and Sarah Ayton on their way to overall victory in the Yngling class event on day 9 of the Beijing Games in 2008.

Boycotts and Bombs – Politics and the Olympics

'Keep politics out of the Olympics' you hear the press, pundits and participants exclaim. But how *can* politics and the Olympics be detached?

When Pierre de Coubertin set out to revive the ancient Olympics he had high ideals and a vision of a world united by sport and culture. 'May joy and good fellowship reign, and in this manner, may the Olympic torch pursue its way through ages, increasing friendly understanding among nations, for the good of a humanity always more enthusiastic, more courageous and more pure.' His worthy aims were codified in the Fundamental Principles of Olympism, in force today, which state *inter alia*: 'The goal of Olympism is to place sport at the service of the harmonious development of man, with a view to promoting a peaceful society concerned with the preservation of human dignity.'

You might argue that this in itself is a political statement. But even before the modern Games began, there was a political agenda. Baron de Coubertin – sportsman, philosopher and educationalist – was preoccupied in early life with the moral and spiritual decline of the French nation in the aftermath of their defeat in the Franco-Prussian War. On visits to England he was deeply impressed by the British public school ethos – particularly the 'muscular Christianity' of Rugby School under Dr Thomas Arnold, whom he met several times. De Coubertin perceived that the encouragement of school, club, national and international sport could lead to the reinvigoration of the French character and, more importantly, a stiffening of the Army's backbone. It consumed almost ten years and much of his fortune, and required the backing of European dignitaries and the support of the Greek government for his dream to be realised in 1896.

Since those first Games, politics have to a greater or lesser degree always played a part in the Olympics. Throughout the decades, the Games have been threatened by incompetence, wars, political manipulation, boycotts, corruption, commercialism, terrorism and drugs. They flourish nonetheless. Today, with their ever-increasing global significance, the Games constitute the biggest sporting event in the world, bringing together more than two hundred nations of differing ideologies, politics, religions, languages and customs; they confer prestige and sometimes wealth on the host nation; they directly or indirectly affect the governments and societies of the nations taking part; they provide a focus for national unity. They can scarcely be immune from 'politics' in the round.

Yet at best, the Olympics are an over-riding force for good, a tool for diplomacy, reaching (as Nelson Mandela said) 'areas far beyond any sphere of political influence, doing more to unify nations than any politician has ever done'. As a platform for global fraternity they bring together the world's communities. In 1981, the Games scheduled for 1988 were awarded to South Korea. As political demonstrations broke out in June 1987, the possibility that riots and unrest might jeopardise the country's right to host the Games contributed to the June 29 declaration which ushered President Chun from power and led to direct elections in December that year and served as an impetus for South Korea's transition to democracy. Roh Tae-woo served as the transitional president, directly elected by South Koreans in December 1987, during the Seoul Games.

In 2000, when Cathy Freeman, an Australian Aborigine (and winner of the 400m race), was chosen to light the Olympic Flame it was seen as a symbol of reconciliation with Australia's native peoples. Even in China, some change for the better has been noticeable since the 2008 Games – an improvement in the environment and atmosphere in Beijing, modernisation of public transport links, and an (albeit slight) opening up of its governance to the world's scrutiny (one cannot nevertheless ignore the forcible eviction of thousands of citizens to make way for Olympic venues and the country's continuing human rights abuses).

At worst, the Games have been tainted by attempts at bribery and corruption in the bidding process and the judging of events, an inconsistent political stance on the part of the IOC, burdensome debt to the hosts, terrorist outrage, and violence both in and out of the sporting arena.

The Berlin Games of 1936 and the political double-dealing that led up to them mark a low point in the history of the Olympics. Although the venue was decided in 1931, two years before the Nazis came to power, the threat was evident. As the Games grew nearer, it became apparent that Hitler would take full advantage of the opportunity to promote his belief in Aryan supremacy and use the occasion for Fascist propaganda. While Berlin was assuring the IOC that it would 'not oppose the participation of coloureds', Nazi spokesman Bruno Malitz was simultaneously voicing their view that the Games should be confined to whites only and complaining that sport was infested with 'Frenchmen, Belgians, Polacks and Jew-Niggers'. The IOC, particularly Avery Brundage (later to be IOC President) were determined to go ahead with the Games, although the Americans lobbied strongly for a boycott. In the end, the pro-boycotters were outvoted and America sent a team, which included the black athlete Jesse Owens (who famously won four gold medals), and two Jewish sprinters who were pulled out on the day of the competition (on Brundage's orders, it was suspected). Only the left-wing Spanish government boycotted the Games.

Between 1948 and 1984 boycotts and exclusions continued to affect the Games. In 1940, Germany and Japan (as aggressors in WWII) were not invited to attend. In 1952 West Germany participated for the first time and the USSR returned after 40 years, to fill the vacancy left by (formerly Tsarist) Russia. Meanwhile, the Eastern bloc countries were housed separately. In 1956 China withdrew when the IOC recognised Formosa (Taiwan); Egypt, Iraq and Lebanon stayed away in protest at Israel's invasion of Egypt; and Spain, Switzerland and the Netherlands boycotted over the Soviet invasion of Hungary. (The water polo final between Hungary and the USSR became known as the 'Blood in the Water' match after the two teams set about kicking and punching each

other.) In 1960, South Africa was excluded because of its apartheid policies (and remained excluded until 1992). In 1968 East Germany competed separately for the first time, and the two American athletes who gave the 'Black Power' salute from the podium were expelled.

The Munich Games of 1972 were grievously scarred when Palestinian terrorists killed eleven Israeli athletes and a policeman in the Olympic Village. In 1976, 30 African nations staged a last-minute boycott at New Zealand's inclusion, after the All Blacks rugby team had toured South Africa. Taiwan withdrew when the Canadians gave in to Chinese pressure to deny their right to march under their own flag. In 1980 in Moscow, in the biggest boycott until then, 60 nations refused to attend in protest at the Soviet invasion of Afghanistan. At the next Games in 1984 in Los Angeles, the Soviet bloc retaliated by leading a 14-nation boycott, and in 1988 North Korea and six other nations boycotted the Seoul Games.

Are the Olympics political? – you bet!

At the 1968 Mexico City Games, Americans Tommie Smith (centre) and John Carlos give the 'Black Power' salute as an anti-racist protest as they stand on the podium with Australian silver medallist Peter Norman.

James Cracknell
2000 Sydney and 2004 Athens
Rowing, coxless fours

Double Olympic Champion and World Record holder, along with Matthew Pinsent, Cracknell is an inspirational sporting icon.

He began his rowing career while at Kingston Grammar School and won his first gold medal in the Junior World Championships in 1990 as stroke of the British four. A hatful of medals followed: a total of six in the World Championships in coxless and coxed pairs and coxless fours. In 2001 Cracknell and Pinsent won the coxed and coxless pairs on the same day, and in 2002 smashed the world record in the coxless pairs by four seconds.

Cracknell's Olympic record is equally impressive. Although he qualified in the double scull for the 1996 Games, last minute tonsillitis prevented him racing. In 1977 he teamed up with Redgrave, Pinsent and Foster. The final of the coxless four in Sydney was an event watched by millions around the world, a thrilling race which saw Redgrave win an historic fifth successive gold medal as the British held off the Italian challenge to win by 0.38 seconds. That race, with the lead up to it, was made into a three-part BBC documentary entitled *Gold Fever*.

Thrilling as the Sydney race was, the final in 2004 at Athens was one of the most exciting rowing contests ever seen. In a nail-biting contest with the Canadians, and the lead changing repeatedly in the final 500 metres, the British team edged home to win by a mere seven inches. After the race Cracknell said, 'When you put four years of emotion into six minutes, you end up in a scrambled heap.'

James Cracknell, with determined expression, gives it his all during the British national team trials in 2004.

After retiring from rowing in 2006, Cracknell turned to journalism. As a presenter for ITV and Channel 4 he has covered such diverse sports as the Boat Race, superbike, rugby sevens, the Red Bull Air Race World Series and of course the Boat Race. He is a sports feature writer for the *Daily Telegraph*.

The indefatigable Cracknell has done much to raise money for charity. In 2006 he and Ben Fogle entered the gruelling 3,000-mile Atlantic Rowing race in aid of BBC Children in Need. Having rowed naked much of the way, and capsized once, the pair came third. Their achievement is recorded in the BBC documentary *Through Hell and High Water.*

In 2008, to raise funds for Sport Relief, he set out to reach Africa in ten days by human power alone. He rowed the Channel, cycled more than 1,395 miles and swam the Strait of Gibraltar. In January 2009 he teamed up again with Ben Fogle and Ed Coates to take part in the Amundsen Omega 3 South Pole Race, coming an impressive second, only 20 hours behind the Norwegian long-distance ski experts. The event has been made into a six-part BBC TV series, *On Thin Ice.*

Having followed a punishing training schedule throughout his competitive career, Cracknell has been equally tireless since quitting rowing. As well as his journalistic and charitable works, and being a keen advocate of health and fitness, he is director of Threshold Sports, a consultancy service aimed at sustaining participation in sport.

Cracknell is married to TV and radio presenter Beverley Turner. He was honoured with the MBE in 2001 and the OBE in 2004.

In July 2010 Cracknell suffered serious head injuries when he was hit by a truck while cycling in the US. It is hoped that his fitness, strength and determination will see him make a full recovery.

Jonathan Edwards

2000 Sydney
Athletics, triple jump

Jonathan Edwards, evangelical Christian turned atheist, is the undoubted king of the triple jump, widely regarded as the event's greatest champion. There are few titles he has not won, and his world record of 18.29m at the World Championships in 1995 has yet to be bettered – a huge jump which came immediately after a record-breaking first jump of over 18m. During that year he also set three world and seven British records, and his wind-assisted jump of 18.43m at the European Cup in Lille is the longest triple jump in history.

This sportsman of charm and intelligence reached the climax of his career by winning the gold medal at Sydney, his third Olympic appearance. He entered the arena carrying a tin of sardines – a symbol, he said, of the parable of the loaves and fishes with which Jesus fed the 5,000. Throughout his distinguished athletics career, Edwards attested 'God comes first in my life'. Until 1993 he refused to compete on a Sunday, thus missing out on an almost certain gold medal at the 1991 World Championships.

Edwards was voted British Sportsman of the Year, BBC Sports Personality of the Year and the IAAF Athlete of the Year in 1995, British Male Athlete of the Year in 1995, 2000 and 2001, received the MBE in 1995 and the CBE in 2001. In 2003, having become one of only a handful of athletes to hold all four major titles at the same time – Olympic, World, European and Commonwealth – Edwards retired. The media career which followed has been equally distinguished. For many years he hosted the BBC's *Songs of Praise*, has presented a documentary on St Paul, and is a regular pundit and commentator for radio and television. In addition, he holds honorary doctorates from the Universities of Exeter and Ulster, and is himself a graduate in Physics from Durham.

With his high profile and evangelising, it was inevitable that the media should make much of Edwards' sudden and public loss of faith in 2007,

Jonathan Edwards looks to the heavens after winning the triple jump in Sydney in 2000. The world record distance he jumped in 1995 has yet to be bettered.

when he gave up presenting *Songs of Praise*. He told *The Times* that 'when you think about it rationally, it does seem incredibly improbable that there is a God', but has professed to be 'internally happier than at any time of my life'.

Edwards was an ambassador for the London 2012 bid and has been appointed the athlete member on the London Organising Committee for the Olympic Games, the unanimous choice of the British Athletes Commission.

Darren Campbell

2004 Athens

Athletics, 4x100m relay

Darren Campbell was one of the world's finest sprinters in his day, having won more than 21 medals, including Olympic gold and silver, Commonwealth and World Championship bronze and seven national titles. Twice denied medals by his teammate's drug-taking, he finally achieved his ambition of Olympic gold in the 4x100m relay in 2004.

As a youth in Manchester, Campbell was equally talented at athletics and football. As an athlete, he competed in 100m, 200m and 4x100m relays, winning medals at the English Schools, European Junior and World Junior Championships. He spent much of 1993 in Australia training with Linford Christie and made his senior international debut in the 4x100m race at the Stuttgart World Championships in 1993, but shortly afterwards injury (and possibly peer pressure to use drugs) forced him to return to his other love, soccer. He played for a number of teams, including Plymouth Argyle, Weymouth and Newport County.

In 1995 Campbell returned to sprinting, and by 1996 had his time for the 100m down to 10.17 seconds. His first appearance at the Olympic Games in 1996 proved a disaster when the baton was dropped in the relay and the British team

eliminated. In 2000, he was back for the Sydney Olympics, where he came sixth in the 100m final, and took a surprise silver medal in the 200m, his first senior medal at that distance.

A hamstring injury kept Campbell off the track for much of 2001, but in 2002 he returned to fitness to run in the 100m and 4x100m relay at the

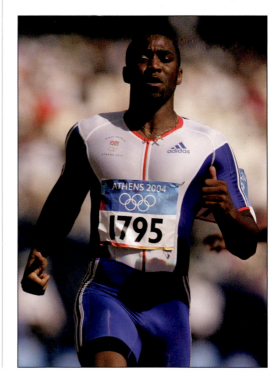

Darren Campbell, looking relaxed as he runs in the heats of the 200m race in Beijing.

European Championships. The event was marred by Dwaine Chambers' doping conviction; Campbell's bronze in the 100m sprint was thus upgraded to a silver, but he and the rest of the team were stripped of the gold medal in the relay. In 2003, he was to lose another medal because of Chambers' drug-taking, again in the 4x100m relay, although he won bronze in the 100m. In Athens Campbell finally won the 4x100m relay gold medal in Athens he had striven so hard for.

The years between 2004 and his retirement in 2006 netted Campbell one more gold medal, in the relay at the European Championships in Gothenburg. In the British team was Dwaine Chambers, and Campbell caused something of a stir by leaving the track immediately after the event without joining his teammates for the lap of honour. This was apparently in protest at Chambers' drug record, and the resultant loss of two medals, as well as his refusal to name his suppliers. Campbell was criticised at the time, since his coach, Linford Christie, had also served a drugs ban: he defended himself by saying he believed Christie had been unjustly convicted.

A man of principle and passion, Campbell was awarded the MBE in 2005 for his services to sport. He retired in 2006, and the following year was appointed the ambassador for Sky Living for Sport, an initiative to involve young potential dropouts in sport, in which role he has proved an inspiration. He was part of the BBC's Radio 5 Live commentary team for the 2008 Beijing Olympics.

Marlon Devonish
2004 Athens
Athletics, 4x100m relay

Marlon Devonish has become one of the world's most decorated sprinters, with a total of nine gold medals at senior level, as well as one silver and four bronzes – an outstanding record which has earned him the nickname 'the Legend'. At the British Championships in 2006, he became the first man since Linford Christie in 1988 to win both the 100m and 200m races at that event.

The young Devonish excelled at football, tennis and basketball at school in Coventry, and at the age of 16 took up running. This was a late age to start a career in sprinting, but within less than a year he had begun winning races. He became English Schools champion at 200m in 1994, at 100m in 1995, and won double gold at the 1995 European Junior Championships.

Devonish's finest performance to date was at the 2004 Athens Games, where Great Britain defeated the favourites, the USA, in the final of the 4x100m relay by a photo-finish one hundredth of a second – a particularly sweet victory since he had lost his silver medal in the 2003 World Championships when Dwaine Chambers tested positive for drugs after the team finished second to

Marlon Devonish punches the air after winning the 200m final at the 2006 British Championships.

His second appearance at the Olympics was something of a disappointment: he failed to make the final in the 200m individual event and the 4x100m relay team was disqualified in the heats after Craig Pickering failed to pass the baton to Devonish on the final leg.

In 2006 Devonish won a European Championship gold in the 4x200m relay. After a disappointing 2010 season, he finished on a high by winning a gold medal with the English 4x200m relay team.

Devonish intends to finish his athletics career after taking part in the 2012 London Games. When not training and racing, he devotes himself to his other passion, art. Devonish was awarded the MBE in 2004.

Chris Hoy

2004 Athens and 2008 Beijing

Cycling, 1km time trial (2004), sprint (2008), team sprint (2008) & keirin (2008)

Born in Edinburgh in 1976, Chris Hoy is already a legend. Dubbed by the press as 'the flying Scotsman' and 'the real McHoy' he is his country's most successful Olympian, the first Briton for a century to win three gold medals at the same Games, and the most successful Olympic male cyclist in history. Add to this a silver medal in international rowing, a degree in Applied Sports Science, three Honorary Doctorates and a knighthood, then throw in good looks and an engaging personality, and you have a true sporting hero.

The only man to have won a world and Olympic title in four different track disciplines and the holder of ten World Championship titles, Hoy's historic success at the Beijing Games rocketed him to international fame and into the hearts of the British nation. His Olympic career began in Sydney in 2000, when he won a silver medal in the team sprint, and four years later in Athens he took gold in the 1 km time trial. This event was then dropped from the Olympics, to make way for the BMX competition, a sport in which Hoy had excelled as a boy. But he turned his attention to the keirin event which replaced the 'Kilo'. The keirin involves riders following a small motorbike or 'derny' around a 250m track. Having built up speed and with 2.5 of the nine laps to go, the derny pulls off and the riders race like fury to the finish. By 2008, Hoy was already the two-time world champion in this discipline, and to no one's surprise took the gold medal at the Beijing Games. Gold medals in the team sprint and individual sprint gave him the historic hat-trick.

A serious hip injury sustained in early 2009 when he crashed out during the Copenhagen World Cup keirin final put Hoy out of action for ten weeks, and prevented him defending his keirin and sprint titles at the World Championships in Poland. He returned to form in August 2009 at the Fenioux Trophy in France – a prestigious competition comprising three sprint events, of which he won two and took the overall title. Hoy's impressive form continued in October, when he won three gold medals in Manchester at the first round of the 2009/10 World Cup series.

A popular and distinguished sportsman even before Beijing, Hoy was named Scottish Sports Personality of the Year in 2003 and was awarded an MBE in 2005. Three years later after returning from Beijing in triumph, he was named Sportsman of the Year by the Sports Journalists' Association of Great Britain, and voted the 2008 BBC Sports Personality of the Year. He was awarded a knighthood in the 2009 New Year Honours List and his mother Carol received an MBE in the same list for services to healthcare.

With 2012 in mind, he opted to attend the European Track Championships in November 2010, rather than the Commonwealth Games in Delhi, but was surprisingly eliminated in the individual sprint. But in December 2010, he left nothing to chance and won the gold medal in the keirin at the Melbourne World Cup.

In the various cycling disciplines he has mastered, Hoy has been ten times World Champion, twice Commonwealth Champion, has won 31 World Cup gold medals, ten silver and four bronze. He holds the records for the Olympic 200m TT and Kilo and the Commonwealth Games Kilo and Team Sprint – and he shows no sign of stopping. Although he will be 36 by 2012, his sights are firmly set on further gold medals.

Chris Hoy celebrates his win in the sprint final at the Laoshan Velodrome in Beijing.

Kelly Holmes

2004 Athens

Athletics, 800m & 1,500m

Kelly Holmes is probably the finest female middle-distance runner Britain has ever produced. At the Athens Olympics of 2004 she overcame injury and depression to race into the record books, becoming the first British woman to win two Olympic track gold medals, the first athlete to do so at the same Games since 1920, and only the third woman in history to achieve the 800m and 1,500m double, setting a new British record in the latter. An outstandingly

Eyes popping with delight, Kelly Holmes celebrates her win in the 800m race in Athens in 2004.

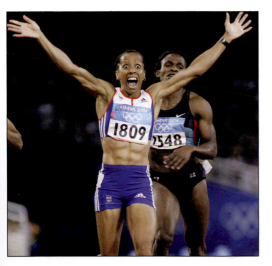

popular winner, she returned home to an ecstatic reception. More than 40,000 people turned out to greet her in her home town of Tonbridge in Kent. She was made an MBE in recognition of her achievement, as well as being awarded the BBC Sports Personality of the Year.

Dogged by injury which affected seven of her 12 years of top class competition, she nonetheless appeared in three Olympic Games, taking the two memorable gold medals as well as a bronze, and won medals in numerous World, Commonwealth and European championships. The guts and determination needed to overcome the repeated setbacks of fractures, ruptured tendons, torn calf muscles and viruses, not to mention the clinical depression which reduced her to self-harm and near suicide, have been a hallmark of her personality and endeared her to millions.

Born in Kent, the daughter of a Jamaican-born car mechanic and an English mother, Holmes had a troubled childhood. She began training for athletics when she was 12 and in only her second season won the English schools 1,500m title. At 18, she joined the British Army, initially as a lorry driver and later as a PT instructor. She became the Army judo champion, won the heptathlon, and even competed in the men's 800m on one occasion, since she was considered too powerful a runner to compete in the women's race without humiliating the others. Watching the 1992

Games inspired her to return to international athletics, and until 1997 she combined her Army and athletics careers.

In 2005 Kelly was created a DBE, and in August she entered her final race in the UK, the 800m at the Norwich Union British Grand Prix, but suffered a recurrence of the Achilles tendon injury and finished only eighth. This final lap of honour of her career had to be completed by buggy, and at the end of that year she announced her retirement. Though no longer competing, she remains a popular figure and one of Britain's most recognisable sportswomen, appearing regularly on television in such diverse programmes as BBC London News (as sports presenter), ITV's *Dancing on Ice* and Five's *Superstars*.

She continues working for charity, as she has done throughout her career, and has set up the DKH Legacy Trust which harnesses the talents of retired athletes to help the less fortunate. In May 2009 she was named as the president of the Commonwealth Games England, succeeding Sir Christopher Chataway.

Bradley Wiggins
2004 Athens and 2008 Beijing
Cycling, individual track pursuit (2004 & 2008), team pursuit (2008)

'It's only bloody sport,' said Bradley Wiggins in Athens, having just become the first Briton for 40 years to win three Olympic medals at a single Games. In 2008 he won the individual pursuit gold medal in Beijing, a second gold in the team pursuit, and with his bronze medal from the 2000 Sydney Games took his Olympic tally to seven medals.

His successes in Athens came in the individual pursuit, the team pursuit and the Madison – a somewhat curious 50km event in which two riders work together to score points in a series of sprints every 20 laps, each sprint kicked off by a 'hand sling' as they take turns to propel each other into action. Halfway through the final, Wiggins' partner, Rob Hayles, crashed out and it looked like their medal chance was gone. But Hayles remounted and they fought back to take the bronze.

At Beijing he became the first ever rider successfully to defend a pursuit title, and with the pursuit team was instrumental in breaking the world record in the heats, and again in the final.

Wiggins' father was a professional cyclist, racing in Belgium where Bradley was born. (He scarpered when his son was just a boy, turned to drink and died in Australis in 2008). Though tall for a cyclist at 6'3", 'Wiggo' proved a natural in the saddle, winning his first race as a 12-year-old. At 18, he won the world junior pursuit title. At 20, Wiggins turned professional and signed for team Linda McCartney, and his career suffered a brief blip as the team disintegrated after internal squabbles. He joined the French team Française des Jeux and resumed his journey to the top of his sport, first with them, then with Crédit Agricole, Cofidis, and the highly successful Garmin-Slipstream.

In July 2009, with close to a million people crowding the slopes of Mont Ventoux to watch the final mountain stage of the Tour de France, Wiggins clung on determinedly to his fourth place to become only the second Briton in a century to finish in the top four. He had shed 7kg before the event as he changed his focus from track to road racing. The 2010 Tour was not such a happy event, however, and as part of the new Team Sky, he could manage only 24th place. The failure was 'a humbling experience'. That, and the death of his beloved grandfather shortly after, have, he says, given him a new perspective on life. Undaunted, he does not intend to give up the Tour, and has also set his sights on the London Olympics and a return to the track.

Wiggins has won medals at every World Championships from 1998 to 2009 (seven of them gold, three of them at the same event in 2008), two silver medals at the Commonwealth Games, the prologue of the Tour de France, and many other stages of international road races.

Wiggins was awarded the OBE in 2005 and became a CBE in 2009. His autobiography, *In Pursuit of Glory,* was published in 2008.

Talented, dedicated and supremely hard-working, Wiggins is laid-back about his status as a cycling superstar and inspirational hero: '. . . it's actually clear and simple. It's just a case of going from point A to B as fast as you can. Why be overawed by the occasion, just because you've got a chance to win the opening stage of the world's biggest race or because three million people are watching on television?'

The changes to the cycling programme for the 2012 Games are not good news for Wiggins, as the men's individual pursuit has been dropped in the interests of giving men and women parity in the events open to them. 'It's a shame,' he said, 'it will probably end up killing off track endurance cycling.'

'Wiggo', draped in the Union Flag, waves to fans after winning the individual track pursuit in 2004.

Rebecca Adlington
2008 Beijing
Swimming, 400m freestyle & 800m freestyle

At the age of 19, Adlington swam into the record books and to international fame by becoming only the second woman to win two gold medals at the same Games for 100 years. In the 800m heats, she set a new British, Commonwealth, European and Olympic record of 8:18.06, and in the final broke the world record with a time of 8:14.10. She also broke the Commonwealth record in the 400m heats with a time of 4:02.24. To add to her two gold medals, Adlington swam the final leg of the 4x 200m relay and won the bronze.

Adlington began swimming at the age of four, and was competing at the age of ten. She trains at the local Sherwood Swimming Baths in Mansfield, Nottinghamshire, which has been renamed in her honour. Defeat in the 2007 World Championships saw her leave the pool in tears after failing to make the final. Spurred on by this setback, she began a punishing training schedule, rising at 5 a.m., swimming 8,000m a day and running and circuit training. 'It's all sleeping, training, driving and occasionally finding time to eat. That's what my life is about,' she says. The hard work paid off when she qualified for the Olympic 200, 400 and 800 freestyle events.

Adlington returned from Beijing to a heroine's welcome in her home town of Mansfield. An overnight star, she has become known not only for her prodigious talent, but for her love of shoes.

Her mother's reward to her for qualifying for the British Olympic team was a £275 pair of Christian Louboutin shoes. She was made an OBE in 2008 as well as being named the Sports Journalists' Association Great Britain's Sportswoman of the Year.

When the new go-faster 100 percent polyurethane swimsuits were launched on the market in 2009, most of her fellow competitors enthusiastically adopted them. The governing body of the sport, FINA, initially banned them, but had to lift the ban after threats of lawsuits. A

Adlington watches the scoreboard and sees that she has broken the 800m freesylte world record in Beijing.

similar storm had greeted the introduction of the Speedo LZR suit (which Adlington wears) two years previously. Since the new suits reduce drag and provide buoyancy some consider they confer unfair advantage and constitute a form of cheating. Adlington called it 'technological doping' and was adamant that she would not switch. 'I would never in a million years take a drug to help me, so why would I wear a suit just to improve my performance?' Though criticised in some quarters at the time, she has been vindicated by FINA's decision in the summer of 2009 to ban all full-body super-suits.

In November 2010 at the Commonwealth Games in Delhi, Adlington added two more gold medals to her tally, in the 400 and 800m freestyle.

Adlington plans to add the 200m to her repertoire for the 2012 London Olympics, where British hopes will be riding on her for the hat-trick.

Victoria Pendleton

2008 Beijing
Cycling, sprint

Victoria Pendleton is not just a pretty face, she is Britain's most successful woman cyclist, the winner of an Olympic gold medal, twelve World Championship medals (eight of them gold) and is the reigning National, Commonwealth, World and Olympic sprint champion. Anyway, to call her pretty would be an understatement. In a sport where short limbs and huge muscles are the norm, Pendleton is lithe and tall, and glamorous. When she returned from Beijing with the gold medal, the media went wild for interviews, photoshoots and public appearances – more than for all the other Olympic victors put together – and sponsors and TV shows courted her. Since then she has appeared on numerous magazine covers, in advertising and marketing campaigns and famously posed naked on her cycle for the *Observer Sports Monthly*.

Pendleton's father was a British national grass track cycling champion and encouraged his three children to take up the sport at a very early age. Victoria and her twin brother began competing at the age of nine on local grass tracks in Bedfordshire. Although spotted as a promising talent at the age of 16 and invited to Manchester for national trials, she decided to concentrate on her education. Nonetheless, the trial gave her a taste for indoor track cycling and she competed when her studies allowed. On graduating from Northumbria University in 2002 she became a full-time cyclist.

Though showing great promise in competing in the European Championships and Commonwealth Games, success in the sprint eluded her, and she became frustrated. Chosen for the squad for the 2004 Athens Games, it looked like her hour had come, but she froze and could only manage sixth place. She was devastated, cried for days and considered giving up the sport for ever.

Working with the British team's psychiatrist, Steve Peters, she gradually succeeded in renewing her self-belief, drive and commitment to cycling. In March 2005 she won her first World Championship sprint title in Los Angeles. She followed this with World Cup and Commonwealth Games wins in 2006, but lost the world title later in Bordeaux.

Teaming up with a new coach, Jan van Eijden, in 2007 seemed to provide a formidable boost to her confidence and she won three gold medals at the World Championships that year, as well as being awarded the Sunday Times Sportswoman of the Year award. In the build-up to the 2008 Games, Pendleton won two more gold medals and a silver at the Track World Championships. And there in Beijing, to no one's surprise, she won the gold medal. Together with the rest of the British Olympians, she was invited to a reception at Buckingham Palace, and later in the year received the MBE.

At the 2009 World Championships, Pendleton again won the World Track sprint title, and in 2010 made it five titles in six years. At the British National Track Championships in both 2009 and 2010 she yet again took the sprint and keirin titles, as well as the 500m time trial in 2010. (For those who have lost count, that makes a total of nine successive national sprint titles.)

In December 2009 the IOC ratified the changes to the 2012 cycling programme, to give men and women parity with five events each – sprint, keirin, team sprint, team pursuit and omnium. This means that Victoria Pendleton has every chance of emulating Sir Chris Hoy's achievement of three gold medals at a single Games.

A delighted Victoria Pendleton wins the sprint title in Beijing in 2008.

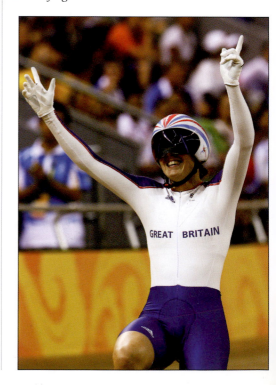

Glorious Failures, Unlucky Losers and Other Oddities

A book on British Olympic greats would not be complete without some mention of those unfortunates who should have won but didn't and those who gloriously, heroically and memorably failed in their endeavours.

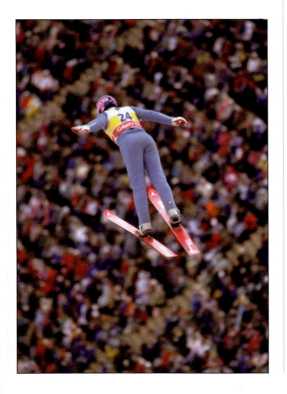

Eddie Edwards, soaring like an eagle, launches himself into last place in the 70m ski jump in Calgary and into the hearts of millions.

Eddie 'the Eagle' Edwards, the buffoonish, bespectacled, bulky plasterer from Cheltenham, is Britain's – if not the world's – favourite failure. Coming last in the 70m and 90m ski jump competitions at the 1988 Winter Games in Calgary, he captured the hearts of millions. The worse he did, the more they loved him. As the world watched, unsure whether it was bravery or idiocy they were witnessing and convinced that he was leaping to his death, Eddie twice launched himself into space, arms flailing and half-blind, and . . . survived on landing.

A mere two years before the Games, Eddie had developed an urge to compete in the Olympics and reckoned that since there were no other British entrants in the ski jumping, here lay his chance. A self-taught skier, he had never jumped, had no kit, no funding, and when he eventually decided to take lessons from the experts most of it went over his head since he didn't speak French or German. He was overweight and needed thick glasses to see where he was going. Arriving in Canada, his luggage burst open on the airport carousel, damaging his ski bindings. He managed only one practice jump, got locked out of his cabin and was refused entry to his own press conference because he didn't have his credentials on him.

The Olympic officials were not amused and thought Eddie was taking the mickey. But his personality, wit and sheer guts won them round in the end. In his closing speech, the President of the Games said, 'At this Olympic Games some competitors have won gold and some have broken records, and one has even flown like an eagle.' It was the only time in Olympic history that an individual has been thus singled out, and the 100,000-strong audience roared, 'Ed*deee!* Ed*deee!*'

But however endearing he was, the IOC determined that there should be no repeat of this clownish performance and instigated the 'Eddie the Eagle rule', by which Olympic hopefuls are required to compete in international events and be in the top 30% of competitors. Thus ended Eddie's further Olympic dreams. He returned to plastering but did, however, make a successful sideline out of media appearances and after-dinner speaking, wrote his autobiography, and went on to study law.

Not many remember who won in 1988, but everyone remembers Eddie.

It was 1908, the Olympic venue was London, and **Philip Plater** of Great Britain became the Olympic small-bore rifle champion that never was. In fading light, wind and drizzle, with only half an hour to go before the time limit, Plater fired 80 rounds, setting a new world record of 391. He was declared the winner. A day later it emerged that he was not officially entered in the 12-man competition, after a disastrous mix up by the British team officials. The entry forms for one of the squad, George Barnes, had been lost and Plater put down as 12th man. Barnes' entry form was then discovered, he was awarded the bronze medal and the unfortunate Plater's superb effort was discounted. Perhaps it was some consolation to him to receive a gold medal and a diploma from the British Olympic Council, but his name will never show up in the official Olympic records as gold medallist.

British fencer **Judy Guinness** (whose full name was Heather Seymour Guinness Penn-Hughes) was another who was denied a gold medal, all because of her sporting nature and sense of fair play. At the 1932 Los Angeles Games the scores showed that she had beaten her opponent, Ellen Preis of Austria, in the final. Guinness pointed out to the officials that they had failed to spot two of Preis' touches. This sportsmanship, embodying the true spirit of the Olympic movement, meant she returned home with only a silver medal.

In 1948, four happy Britons stood on the podium, received their gold medals for the 4x100m relay and heard their national anthem ring out. The Americans had beaten them to the finish, but were disqualified for a baton passing infringement. But hardly had the Brits had time to admire their medals before the verdict was reversed after a review of the race footage, and they reluctantly swapped gold for silver.

And spare a thought for **Lorna Johnstone** who attended three Olympic Games and, six months short of her 70th birthday, came fifth in the mixed dressage team equestrian event in 1972. Fifth place may also have been second-to-last, but she has entered the record books as the oldest British Olympic competitor. The oldest ever Olympian is Oscar Swahn of Sweden, who won three gold medals, two bronze and a silver for shooting deer (well, deer-shaped targets) at the age of almost 73.

While we are straying from the point, here are a few more curiosities: in 1900 the shooting events included live pigeons. It was a messy affair by all accounts. American sports historian Andrew Strunk described it thus in 1988: 'Maimed birds were writhing on the ground, blood and feathers were swirling in the air and women with parasols were weeping in the chairs set up nearby.' That event was the only time medals were awarded for killing a live creature and was won by a Belgian.

Another somewhat absurd event, held only in 1900, was the long jump for horses. It was won by another Belgian, but the horse, Extra Dry, was British through and through. Even so, it failed to clear anything like the distance achieved by human Olympians.

The 1992 Games featured an even more pointless event – solo synchronised swimming.

Whatever happened to the little lad who was in the winning boat of the coxed pairs in 1900? At the last minute, the Dutch jettisoned the 29-year-old doctor who had coxed them in the heat and installed a young French boy half his weight and more than half his age. After his 15 minutes of fame he became no more than a footnote in IOC records and no one even knows his name.

Table of All British Gold Medallists

Abrahams, Harold	1924	Athletics, 100m
Adlington, Rebecca	2008	Swimming, 400m Freestyle
		Swimming, 800m Freestyle
Ahearne, Timothy	1908	Athletics, Triple Jump
Ainslie, Ben	2000	Sailing, Laser Class
	2004	Sailing, Finn Class
	2008	Sailing, Finn Class
Ainsworth-Davis, John	1920	Athletics 4x400m Relay
Allhusen, Derek	1968	Equestrian, 3-Day Team
Altwegg, Jeannette	1952	Figure Skating
Amoore, Edward	1908	Shooting, Small Bore Rifle Team
Applegarth, William	1912	Athletics, 4x100m Relay
Archer, Alex	1936	Ice Hockey
Aspin, John	1908	Sailing, 12m Class
Astor, John Jacob, 1st Baron Astor of Hever	1908	Rackets, Men's Doubles
Atkin, Charles	1920	Field Hockey
Attrill, Louis	2000	Rowing, Coxed Eights
Ayton, Sarah	2004	Sailing, Yngling Class
	2008	Sailing, Yngling Class
Bacon, Stanley	1908	Wrestling, Middleweight Freestyle
Badcock, John	1932	Rowing, Coxless Fours
Bailey, Horace	1908	Football
Baillon, Louis	1908	Field Hockey
Barber, Paul	1988	Field Hockey
Barrett, Edward	1908	Tug-of-War
Barrett, Herbert Roper	1908	Lawn Tennis, Men's Indoor Doubles
Barridge, J.E see Burridge		
Bartlett, Charles	1908	Cycling, 100km
Batchelor, Stephen	1988	Field Hockey
Beachcroft, C.B.K.	1900	Cricket
Beesly, Richard	1928	Rowing, Coxless Fours

Bellville, Miles	1936	Sailing, 6m Class
Bennett, Charles	1900	Athletics, 1,500m
	1900	Athletics, 5,000m Team
Bennett, John	1920	Field Hockey
Bentham, Isaac	1912	Water Polo
Beresford, Jack	1924	Rowing, Single Sculls
	1932	Rowing, Coxless Fours
	1936	Rowing, Double Sculls
Beresford, John	1900	Polo
Berry, Arthur	1908	Football
	1912	Football
Bevan, Edward	1928	Rowing, Coxless Fours
Bhaura, Kulbir Singh	1988	Field Hockey
Bignal-Rand, Mary see Rand, Mary		
Bingley, Norman	1908	Sailing, 7m Class
Birchell, Francis	1900	Cricket
Birkett, Arthur	1900	Cricket
Blackstaffe, Harry	1908	Rowing, Single Sculls
Boardman, Chris	1992	Cycling, Individual Pursuit
Boardman, Christopher	1936	Yachting, 6m Class
Boland, John Pius	1896	Lawn Tennis, Men's Singles
	1896	Lawn Tennis, Men's Doubles
Bond, Richard	1948	Sailing, Swallow Class
Borland, Jimmy	1936	Ice Hockey
Bowerman, Alfred	1900	Cricket
Brabants, Tim	2008	Canoeing, K-1 1000m
Braithwaite, Bob	1968	Shooting, Trap
Brasher, Chris	1956	Athletics, 3,000m Steeplechase
Brebner, Ronald	1912	Football
Brenchley, Edgar	1936	Ice Hockey
Brown, Arthur	1936	Athletics, 4x400m Relay
Bruce, Charles Granville[2]	1924	Alpine & Mixed Alpinism (Reaching summit of Mt Everest 1922)

Bruce, Geoffrey[2]	1924	Alpine & Mixed Alpinism (Reaching summit of Mt Everest 1922)
Buchanan, John	1908	Sailing, 12m Class
Buckenham, Claude	1900	Football
Buckley, George	1900	Cricket
Bucknall, Henry	1908	Rowing, Coxed Eights
Budgett, Richard	1984	Rowing, Coxed Fours
Bugbee, Charles	1912	Water Polo
	1920	Water Polo
Bullen, Jane	1968	Equestrian, 3-Day Team
Bunten, James	1908	Sailing, 12m
Burchell, Francis	1900	Cricket
Burgess, Edgar	1912	Rowing, Coxed Eights
Burghley, Lord David George	1928	Athletics, 400m Hurdles
Burn, Thomas	1912	Football
Burnell, Charles	1908	Rowing, Coxed Eights
Burnell, Richard	1948	Rowing Double Sculls
Burridge T.E. aka Barridge, J.E.	1900	Football
Bushnell, Bertie	1948	Rowing, Double Sculls
Butler, Guy	1920	Athletics, 4x400m Relay
Campbell, Charles (Sir C. R. Campbell, Bt)	1908	Sailing, 8m Class
Campbell, Colin	1920	Field Hockey
Campbell, Darren	2004	Athletics, 4x100m Relay
Canning, George	1920	Tug-of-War
Carnell, Arthur	1908	Shooting, Small Bore Rifle
Cassels, Harold	1920	Field Hockey
Cecil, David (6th Marquess of Exeter) see Burghley, Lord David		
Chalk, Alfred	1900	Football
Chapman, Frederick	1908	Football
Chappell, James	1936	Ice Hockey
Christian, Frederick	1900	Cricket

Christie, Linford	1992	Athletics, 100m
Clancy, Ed	2008	Cycling, Team Pursuit
Clift, Robert	1988	Field Hockey
Clive, Lewis	1932	Rowing, Coxless Pairs
Coales, William	1908	Athletics, 3-Mile Team
Cochrane, Blair	1908	Sailing, 8m Class
Coe, Sebastian (Baron Coe of Ranmore)	1980	Athletics, 1,500m
	1984	Athletics, 1,500m
Coe, Thomas	1900	Water Polo
Coleman, Robert	1920	Sailing, 7m Class
Coode, Ed	2004	Rowing, Coxless Fours
Cook, Steph	2000	Athletics, Modern Pentathlon
Cooke, Harold	1920	Field Hockey
Cooke, Nicole	2008	Cycling, Road Race
Cooper, Charlotte 'Chattie'	1900	Lawn Tennis, Mixed Doubles
	1900	Lawn Tennis, Women's Singles
Cooper, Malcolm	1984	Shooting, Small Bore Rifle
	1988	Shooting, Small Bore Rifle
Corbett, Walter	1908	Football
Corner, Harry	1900	Cricket
Cornet, George	1908	Water Polo
	1912	Water Polo
Cousins, Robin	1980	Figure Skating
Coward, John	1936	Ice Hockey
Cracknell, James	2000	Rowing, Coxless Fours
	2004	Rowing, Coxless Fours
Crawford, Colin	1924	Alpine & Mixed Alpinism (Reaching summit of Mt Everest 1922)
Crawshaw, Robert[2]	1900	Water Polo
Crichton, Charles	1908	Sailing, 6m Class
Crockford, Eric	1920	Field Hockey
Cross, Martin	1984	Rowing, Coxed Fours
Crummack, Reginald	1920	Field Hockey
Cudmore, Collier	1908	Rowing, Coxless Fours

Cuming, Frederick	1900	Cricket
Currie, Lorne	1900	Sailing, ½-1 Ton Class
	1900	Sailing, Open Class
Curry, John	1976	Figure Skating
D'Arcy, Victor	1912	Athletics, 4×100m Relay
Dailley, Gordon	1936	Ice Hockey
Daly, Denis St. George	1900	Polo
Davey, John Gerald	1936	Ice Hockey
Davies, Chris	1972	Sailing, Flying Dutchman Class
Davies, Lynn	1964	Athletics, Long Jump
de Relwyskow, George	1908	Wrestling, Lightweight Freestyle
Deakin, Joseph	1908	Athletics, 3-Mile Team
Dean, Christopher	1984	Ice Dancing
Dean, William	1920	Water Polo
DeGale, James	2008	Boxing, Middleweight
Dennis, Simon	2000	Rowing, Coxed Eights
Derbyshire, John	1908	Swimming, 4 × 200m Freestyle Relay
Devonish, Marlon	2004	Athletics, 4×100m Relay
Dines, Joseph	1912	Football
Dixon, Charles	1912	Lawn Tennis, Indoor Mixed Doubles
Dixon, Richard	1908	Sailing, 7m Class
Dixon, The Hon. T. Robin (Earl of Glentoran)	1964	Bobsleigh, Two-man
Dod, William	1908	Archery, York Round
Dodds, Richard	1988	Field Hockey
Doherty, Lawrence	1900	Lawn Tennis, Men's Singles
	1900	Lawn Tennis, Men's Doubles
Doherty, Reginald	1900	Lawn Tennis, Men's Doubles
	1900	Lawn Tennis, Mixed Doubles
	1908	Lawn Tennis, Men's Doubles
Donne, William	1900	Cricket
Douglas, Johnny	1908	Boxing, Middleweight
Douglas, Rowley	2000	Rowing, Coxed Eights
Downes, Arthur	1908	Sailing, 12m Class
Downes, John Henry	1908	Sailing, 12m Class

Duke, H (John) [1]	1908	Tug-of-War
Dunlop, David	1908	Sailing, 12m Class
Easte, Peter	1908	Shooting, Team Trap
Eastlake-Smith, Gwendoline aka Gladys	1908	Lawn Tennis, Women's Indoor Singles
Edwards, Hugh	1932	Rowing, Coxless Pairs
	1932	Rowing, Coxless Fours
Edwards, Jonathan	2000	Athletics, Triple Jump
Eley, Charles	1924	Rowing, Coxless Fours
Elliot, Launceston	1896	Weightlifting, One-Handed Lift
Ellison, Adrian	1984	Rowing, Coxed Fours
Erhardt, Carl	1936	Ice Hockey
Etherington-Smith, Raymond	1908	Rowing, Coxed Eights
Exshaw, E. William	1900	Sailing, 2-3 Ton Class
Faulds, Richard	2000	Shooting, Double Trap
Faulkner, David	1988	Field Hockey
Fenning, John	1908	Rowing, Coxless Pairs
Field-Richards, John	1908	Motor Boats, Class B
Finnegan, Chris	1968	Boxing, Middleweight
Fleming, John	1908	Shooting, Small Bore Rifle Moving Target
Fleming, Philip	1912	Rowing, Coxed Eights
Fletcher, Jennie	1912	Swimming, 4x100m Freestyle
Forsyth, Charles	1908	Water Polo
Foster, James	1936	Ice Hockey
Foster, Tim	2000	Rowing, Coxless Fours
Foster, William	1908	Swimming, 4 × 200m Freestyle Relay
Fox, Jim	1976	Modern Pentathlon
Freeman, Harry	1908	Field Hockey
Garcia, Russell	1988	Field Hockey
Gardener, Jason	2004	Athletics, 4x100m Relay
Garton, Arthur	1912	Rowing, Coxed Eights

George, Roland	1932	Rowing, Coxless Fours
Gillan, James	1908	Rowing, Coxless Fours
	1912	Rowing, Coxed Eights
Gladstone, Sir Albert, 5th Baronet	1908	Rowing, Coxed Eights
Glen-Coats, Thomas	1908	Sailing, 12m Class
Godfree, Kitty	1920	Lawn Tennis, Ladies' Doubles
Goodfellow, Frederick	1908	Tug-of-War
Goodhew, Duncan	1980	Swimming, 100m Breaststroke
Goodison, Paul	2008	Sailing, Laser Class
Gordon-Watson, Mary	1972	Equestrian, 3-Day Team
Gore, Arthur	1908	Lawn Tennis, Men's Indoor Singles
	1908	Lawn Tennis, Men's Indoor Doubles
Gosling, William	1900	Football
Grace, Frederick	1908	Boxing, Lightweight
Green, Eric	1908	Field Hockey
Green, Thomas	1932	Athletics, 50km Walk
Gretton, John (1st Baron Gretton)	1900	Sailing, ½-1 Ton Class
	1900	Sailing, Open Class
Griffiths, Cecil	1920	Athletics, 4x400m Relay
Grimley, Martin	1988	Field Hockey
Grinham, Judy	1956	Swimming, 100m Backstroke
Gruber, Luka	2000	Rowing, Coxed Eights
Gunn, Richard	1908	Boxing, Featherweight
Gunnell, Sally	1992	Athletics, 100m Hurdles
Halswelle, Wyndham	1908	Athletics, 400m
Hampson, Tommy	1932	Athletics, 800m
Hannam, Edith	1912	Lawn Tennis, Women's Indoor Singles
	1912	Lawn Tennis, Indoor Mixed Doubles
Hanney, Edward	1912	Football
Hardman, Harold	1908	Football
Harmer, Russell	1936	Yachting, 6m Class
Harrison, Audley	2000	Boxing, Super Heavyweight

Haslam, A.	1900	Football
Haslam, Harry	1920	Field Hockey
Hawkes, Robert	1908	Football
Hawtrey, Henry	1906[4]	Athletics, 5 miles
Hemery, David	1968	Athletics, 400m Hurdles
Henry, William	1900	Water Polo
Herbert, Garry	1992	Rowing, Coxed Pairs
Hill, Albert	1920	Athletics, 800m
	1920	Athletics, 1,500m
Hill, Arthur Edwin	1912	Water Polo
Hill, Bertie	1956	Equestrian, 3-Day Team
Hillyard, George	1908	Lawn Tennis, Men's Doubles
Hirons, William	1908	Tug-of-War
Hoare, Gordon	1912	Football
Hodge, Percy	1920	Athletics, 3,000m Steeplechase
Holman, Frederick	1908	Swimming, 200m Breaststroke
Holmes, Frederick	1920	Tug-of-War
Holmes, Dame Kelly	2000	Athletics, 800m
	2000	Athletics, 1,500m
Hope, Linton[1]	1900	Sailing, ½-1 Ton Class
	1900	Sailing, Open Class
Hore, Edward	1900	Sailing, 3-10 Ton Class
Horsfall, Ewart	1912	Rowing, Coxed Eights
Hoy, Sir Christopher	2004	Cycling, 1km Time Trial
	2008	Cycling, Team Sprint
	2008	Cycling, Sprint
	2008	Cycling, Keirin
Hughes, John	1932	Art, Town Planning
Humby, Harold	1908	Shooting, Small Bore Rifle Team
Humphreys, Frederick	1908	Tug-of-War
	1920	Tug-of-War
Hunt, Kenneth	1908	Football
Hunt-Davis, Ben	2000	Rowing, Coxed Eights
Hunter, Mark	2008	Rowing, Lightweight Double Sculls

Ireton, Albert	1908	Tug-of-War
Jackson, Arnold	1912	Athletics, 1,500m
Jackson, Laurence[2]	1924	Curling
Jackson, Willie[2]	1924	Curling
Jacobs, David	1912	Athletics, 4x100m Relay
James, Tom	2008	Rowing, Coxless Fours
Jarvis, John	1900	Swimming, 1,000m Freestyle
	1900	Swimming, 4,000m Freestyle
Jefferson, H. N.	1900	Sailing, 3-10 Ton Class
Johnson, Victor	1900	Cycling, 660 Yards
Johnstone, Banner	1908	Rowing, Coxed Fights
Jones, Ben	1968	Equestrian, 3-Day Team
Jones, Benjamin	1908	Cycling, 500m
	1908	Cycling, Team Pursuit
Jones, Christopher	1920	Water Polo
Jones, J.	1900	Football
Kelly, Frederick	1908	Rowing, Coxed Eights
Kemp, Peter	1900	Water Polo
Kenny, Jason	2008	Cycling, Team Sprint
Kerly, Sean	1988	Field Hockey
Kierly, Tom	1904	Athletics, Decathlon
Kilpatrick, Jack	1936	Ice Hockey
Kingsbury, Clarence	1908	Cycling, 20km
	1908	Cycling, Team Pursuit
Kinnear, William	1912	Rowing, Single Sculls
Kirby, Alister	1912	Rowing, Coxed Eights
Kirkwood, Jimmy	1988	Field Hockey
Knight, Arthur	1912	Football
Knowles, Durward[3]	1964	Sailing, Star Class
Knox, Debbie	2002	Curling

Lambert Chambers, Dorothea	1908	Lawn Tennis, Women's Singles
Lance, Thomas	1920	Cycling, Tandem
Lander, John	1928	Rowing, Coxless Fours
Larner, George	1908	Athletics, 3,500m Walk
	1908	Athletics, 10 Mile Walk
Laurie, Ran	1948	Rowing, Coxless Pairs
Law, Leslie	2004	Equestrian, 3-Day Event
Laws, Gilbert	1908	Sailing, 6m Class
Leaf, Charles	1936	Sailing, 6m Class
Leahy, Cornelius	1906[4]	Athletics, High Jump
Leightson, Arthur	1920	Field Hockey
Leman, Richard	1988	Field Hockey
Lessimore, Edward	1912	Shooting, 50m Small Bore Rifle Team
Lewis, Denise	2000	Athletics, Heptathlon
Lewis-Francis, Mark	2004	Athletics, 4×100m Relay
Liddell, Eric	1924	Athletics, 400m
Lindberg, Viktor	1900	Water Polo
Lindsay, Andrew	2000	Rowing, Coxed Eights
Lindsay, Robert	1920	Athletics, 4×400m Relay
Lister, William	1900	Water Polo
Littlewort, Henry	1912	Football
Llewellyn, Sir Harry	1952	Equestrian, Show Jumping Team
Lockett, Vivian	1920	Polo
Logan, Gerald	1908	Field Hockey
Longstaff, Tom	1924	Alpine & Mixed Alpinism (Reaching summit of Mt Everest 1922)
Lonsbrough, Anita	1960	Swimming, 200m Breaststroke
Lowe, Douglas	1920	Athletics, 800m
	1928	Athletics, 800m
MacBryan, Jack	1920	Field Hockey
MacDonald, Fiona	2002	Curling
MacDonald-Smith, Iain	1968	Sailing, Flying Dutchman Class

Macintosh, Henry	1912	Athletics, 4 ×100m Relay
Mackenzie, John	1908	Sailing, 12m Class
Mackinnon, Duncan	1908	Rowing, Coxless Fours
Mackworth-Praed, Cyril	1924	Shooting, Running Deer Double
Maclagan, Gilchrist	1908	Rowing, Coxed Eights
Maddison, William	1920	Sailing, 7m Class
Mallin, Harry	1924	Boxing, Middleweight
Mallory, George	1924	Alpine & Mixed Alpinism (Reaching summit of Mt Everest 1922)
Manning, Paul	2008	Cycling, Team Pursuit
Marcon, Charles	1920	Field Hockey
Martin, Albert	1908	Sailing, 12m Class
Martin, Leonard	1936	Yachting, 6m Class
Martin, Rhona	2002	Curling
Martin, Sam	1988	Field Hockey
Martin, Stephen	1988	Field Hockey
Matthews, Kenneth	1964	Athletics, 20km Walk
Matthews, Maurice	1908	Shooting, Small Bore Rifle Team
Matthews, Thomas (Johnnie)[2]	1906[4]	Cycling, 2000m Tandem
Maudsley, Algernon[2]	1900	Sailing, ½-1 Ton Class
	1900	Sailing, Open Class
Maunder, Alexander	1908	Shooting, Team Trap
McBryan, John	1920	Field Hockey
McGrath, George	1920	Field Hockey
McIntyre, Michael	1988	Sailing, Star Class
McKane, Kathleen see Kitty Godfree		
McMeekin, Thomas	1908	Sailing, 6m Class
McNabb, James	1924	Rowing, Coxless Fours
McNair, Winifred	1920	Lawn Tennis, Women's Doubles
McTaggart, Dick	1952	Boxing, Lightweight
McWhirter, Douglas	1912	Football
Meade, Richard	1968	Equestrian, 3-Day Team
	1972	Equestrian, 3-Day Individual

Meade, Richard (cont.)	1972	Equestrian, 3-Day Team
Melvill, Teignmouth	1920	Polo
Meredith, Leonard 'Leon'	1908	Cycling, Team Pursuit
Merlin, Gerald	1906[4]	Shooting, Men's Trap, Single Shot 16m
Merlin, Sidney	1906[4]	Shooting, Men's Trap Double Shot 14m
Merriman, Frederick	1908	Tug-of-War
Miller, Charles	1908	Polo
Miller, George	1908	Polo
Millner, Joshua	1908	Shooting, 100yds Free Rifle
Mills, Edwin	1908	Tug-of-War
	1920	Tug-of-War
Mitchell, Harry	1924	Boxing, Light Heavyweight
Moore, Belle	1912	Swimming, 4x100m Freestyle
Moore, Frank	1908	Shooting, Team Trap
Moore, Isabella	1912	Swimming, 4x100m Freestyle
Moorhouse, Adrian	1988	Swimming, 100m Breaststroke
Morris, John	1924	Alpine & Mixed Alpinism (Reaching summit of Mt Everest 1922)
Morris, Stewart	1948	Sailing, Swallow Class
Morrison, Robert	1924	Rowing, Coxless Fours
Morshead, Henry	1924	Alpine & Mixed Alpinism (Reaching summit of Mt Everest 1922)
Morton, Lucy	1924	Swimming, 200m Breaststroke
Morton, Margaret	2002	Curling
Murray, Robert	1912	Shooting, 50m Small Bore Rifle Team
Murray, Tom	1924	Curling
Nash, Tony	1964	Bobsleigh, Two-man
Neame, Philip	1924	Shooting, Running Deer Double
Nevinson, George	1908	Water Polo
Newall, Queenie	1908	Archery
Nicholas, J.	1900	Football
Nicholson, William	1928	Art, Graphic Works

Nickalls, Guy	1908	Rowing, Coxed Eights
Nickalls, Patteson	1908	Polo
Nightingale, Danny	1976	Athletics, Modern Pentathlon
Noble, Alan	1908	Field Hockey
Noel, Evan	1908	Rackets, Men's Singles
Noel, John	1924	Alpine & Mixed Alpinism (Reaching summit of Mt Everest 1922)
Norton, Edward	1924	Alpine & Mixed Alpinism (Reaching summit of Mt Everest 1922)
O'Connor, Peter	1906[4]	Athletics, Hop, Step & Jump
O'Kelly, Con	1908	Wrestling, Heavyweight Freestyle
Ohuruogu, Christine	2008	Athletics, 400m
Oldman, Albert	1908	Boxing, Heavyweight
Osborn, John	1976	Sailing, Tornado Class
Ovett, Steve	1980	Athletics, 800m
Packer, Ann	1964	Athletics, 800m
Page, Edgar	1908	Field Hockey
Palmer, Charles	1908	Shooting, Team Trap
Pappin, Veryan	1988	Field Hockey
Parisi, Angelo[5]	1980	Judo, Heavyweight
Parker, Adrian	1976	Modern Pentathlon
Parker, Bridget	1972	Equestrian, 3-Day Team
Pattisson, Rodney	1968	Sailing, Flying Dutchman Class
	1972	Sailing, Flying Dutchman Class
Payne, Ernest	1908	Cycling, Team Pursuit
Peacock, William	1920	Water Polo
Pendleton, Victoria	2008	Cycling, Sprint
Pennell, Vane	1908	Rackets, Men's Doubles
Pepe, Joseph	1912	Shooting, 50m Small Bore Rifle Team
Percy, Iain	2000	Sailing, Finn Class
	2008	Sailing, Star Class
Perry, Herbert	1924	Shooting, Running Deer Double

Peters, Mary	1972	Athletics, Pentathlon
Pett, Billy	1906[4]	Cycling, 20 km
Phillips, Captain Mark	1972	Equestrian, 3-Day Team
Pike, James	1908	Shooting, Team Trap
Pimm, William	1908	Shooting, 50m Small Bore Rifle Team
Pinsent, Matthew	1992	Rowing, Coxless Pairs
	1996	Rowing, Coxless Pairs
	2000	Rowing, Coxless Fours
	2004	Rowing, Coxless Fours
Postans, John	1908	Shooting, Team Trap
Potter, Jon	1988	Field Hockey
Powlesland, Alfred	1900	Cricket
Pridmore, Reggie	1908	Field Hockey
Purcell, Noel	1920	Water Polo
Purchase, Zac	2008	Rowing, Lightweight Double Sculls
Purnell, Clyde	1908	Football
Quash, William	1900	Football
Queally, Jason	2000	Cycling, 1km Time Trial
Quentin, Cecil	1900	Sailing, 20+Ton Class
Radmilovic, Paulo	1908	Swimming, 4x200m Relay
	1908	Water Polo
	1912	Water Polo
	1920	Water Polo
Rampling, Godfrey	1936	Athletics, 4x400m Relay
Rand, Mary	1964	Athletics, Long Jump
Rankin, Janice	2002	Curling
Rawlinson, Sir Alfred, 3rd Baronet	1900	Polo
Rawson, Ronald	1920	Boxing, Heavyweight
Redgrave, Sir Steven	1984	Rowing, Coxed Fours
	1988	Rowing, Coxless Pairs
	1992	Rowing, Coxless Pairs

Redgrave, Sir Steven (cont.)	1996	Rowing, Coxless Pairs
	2000	Rowing, Coxless Fours
Redwood, Bernard	1908	Motor Boats, Class B
	1908	Motor Boats, Class C
Reed, Peter	2008	Rowing, Coxless Fours
Rees, Percy	1908	Field Hockey
Rhodes, John	1908	Sailing, 8m Class
Rimmer, John	1900	Athletics, 400m Steeplechase
	1900	Athletics, 5,000m Team
Ritchie, Josiah	1908	Lawn Tennis, Men's Singles
Rivett-Carnac, Charles	1908	Sailing, 7m Class
Rivett-Carnac, Frances	1908	Sailing, 7m Class
Roberts, William	1936	Athletics, 4x100m Relay
Robertson, Arthur 'Archie'	1908	Athletics, 3-Mile Team
Robertson, Arthur G	1900	Water Polo
Robertson, Shirley	2000	Sailing, Europe Class
	2004	Sailing, Yngling Class
Robinson, Eric	1900	Water Polo
Robinson, John	1908	Field Hockey
Robinson, Sidney	1900	Athletics, 5,000m Team
Romero, Rebecca	2008	Cycling, Individual Pursuit
Rook, Laurence	1956	Equestrian, 3-Day Team
Rushen, Arthur	1906[4]	Cycling, 2,000m Tandem
Russell, Arthur	1908	Athletics, 3,200m Steeplechase
Ryan, Harry	1920	Cycling, Tandem
Sanders, Terence	1924	Rowing, Coxless Fours
Sanderson, Ronald	1908	Rowing, Coxed Eights
Sanderson, Tessa	1984	Athletics, Javelin
Scarlett, Fred	2000	Rowing, Coxed Eights
Searle, Greg	1992	Rowing, Coxed Pairs
Searle, Jonny	1992	Rowing, Coxed Pairs
Sewell, John	1920	Tug-of-War

Sharpe, Ivan	1912	Football
Sheen, Gillian	1956	Fencing, Foil
Shepherd, John	1908	Tug-of-War
	1920	Tug-of-War
Sherwani, Imran	1988	Field Hockey
Shoveller, Stanley	1908	Field Hockey
	1920	Field Hockey
Simpson, Andrew	2008	Sailing, Star Class
Smith, Charles Sydney	1908	Water Polo
	1912	Water Polo
	1920	Water Polo
Smith, Herbert	1908	Football
Smith, William	1920	Field Hockey
Somers-Smith, John	1908	Rowing, Coxless Fours
Somervell, Howard	1924	Alpine & Mixed Alpinism (Reaching summit of Mt Everest 1922)
Southwood, Dick	1936	Rowing, Double Sculls
Spackman, F.G.	1900	Football
Speirs, Annie	1912	Swimming, 4x100m Freestyle
Spinks, Terry	1956	Boxing, Flyweight
Staff, Jamie	2008	Cycling, Team Sprint
Stamper, Harold	1912	Football
Stapleton, F.	1900	Water Polo
Stapley, Harold	1908	Football
Steer, Irene	1912	Swimming, 4x100m Freestyle
Stewart, Douglas	1952	Equestrian, Show Jumping Team
Stiff, Harry	1920	Tug-of-War
Stinchcombe, Archibald	1936	Ice Hockey
Strutt, Bill	1924	Alpine & Mixed Alpinism (Reaching summit of Mt Everest 1922)
Styles, William	1908	Shooting, Small Bore Rifle Disappearing Target
Sutton, Henry	1908	Sailing, 8m Class
Swann, Sidney	1912	Rowing, Coxed Eights

Syers, Madge	1908	Figure Skating
Symes, John	1900	Cricket
Tait, Gerald	1908	Sailing, 12m Class
Taylor, Henry	1908	Swimming, 400m Freestyle
	1908	Swimming, 1,500m Freestyle
	1908	Swimming, 4x200m Freestyle Relay
Taylor, Ian	1988	Field Hockey
Taylor, J. Howard	1900	Sailing, 3-10 Ton Class
Thomas, Geraint	2008	Cycling, Team Pursuit
Thomas, Henry	1908	Boxing, Bantamweight
Thompson, Alfred	1948	Art, Painting
Thompson, Daley	1980	Athletics, Decathlon
	1984	Athletics, Decathlon
Thompson, Don	1960	Athletics, 50km Walk
Thompson, Gordon	1908	Rowing, Coxless Pairs
Thorne, Ernest	1920	Tug-of-War
Thornycroft, Isaac	1908	Motor Boats, Class B
	1908	Motor Boats, Class C
Thould, Thomas	1908	Water Polo
Toller, Montague	1900	Cricket
Torvill, Jayne	1984	Ice Dancing
Trapmore, Steve	2000	Rowing, Coxed Eights
Triggs-Hodge, Andrew	2008	Rowing, Coxless Fours
Turnbull, Oswald	1920	Lawn Tennis, Men's Doubles
Turner, R.R.	1900	Football
Tysoe, Alfred	1900	Athletics, 800m
	1900	Athletics, 500m Team
Vaile, Bryn	1988	Sailing, Star Class
Voigt, Emil	1908	Athletics, 5 Miles
Wakefield, Arthur	1924	Alpine & Mixed Alpinism (Reaching summit of Mt Everest 1922)

Walden, Harold	1912	Football
Warriner, Michael	1928	Rowing, Coxless Fours
Webb, Sarah	2004	Sailing, Yngling Class
	2008	Sailing, Yngling Class
Weldon, Frank	1956	Equestrian, 3-Day Team
Wells, Allan	1980	Athletics ,100m
Wells, Henry	1912	Rowing, Coxed Eights
West, Kieran	2000	Rowing, Coxed Eights
White, Reg	1976	Sailing, Tornado Class
White, Wilf	1952	Equestrian, Show Jumping Team
Whitlock, Harold	1936	Athletics, 50km Walk
Whitty, Allen	1924	Shooting, Running Deer Double
Wiggins, Bradley	2004	Cycling, Individual Pursuit
	2008	Cycling, Individual Pursuit
	2008	Cycling, Team Pursuit
Wilkie, David	1976	Swimming, 200m Breaststroke
Wilkinson, Cyril	1920	Field Hockey
Wilkinson, George	1900	Water Polo
	1912	Water Polo
Williams, Amy	2010	Skeleton
Williams, Steve	2004	Rowing, Coxless Fours
	2008	Rowing, Coxless Fours
Wilson, Herbert Haydon	1908	Polo
Wilson, Jack	1948	Rowing, Coxless Pairs
Wilson, Pippa	2008	Sailing, Yngling Class
Wodehouse, John (3rd Earl of Kimberley)	1920	Polo
Wolff, Frederick	1936	Athletics, 4x400m Relay
Wood, Arthur	1908	Sailing, 8m Class
Wood, Harvey	1908	Field Hockey
Woodward, Vivian	1908	Football
	1912	Football
Woosnam, Max	1920	Lawn Tennis, Men's Doubles
Wormwald, Leslie	1912	Rowing, Coxed Eights
Wright, Cyril	1920	Sailing, 7m Class

Wright, Dorothy	1920	Sailing, 7m Class
Wright, Gordon	1912	Football
Wyman, Robert	1936	Ice Hockey
Zealley, James	1900	Football

[1] Listed by the IOC but not by Mallon

[2] Listed by Mallon but not by the IOC

[3] Competing for the Bahamas

[4] The Second International Olympic Games (or 'Intercalated Games'), first included and subsequently excluded from Olympic records

[5] Won bronze medal in 1972 competing for Great Britain, and, although his gold and two silver medals were won competing for France, IOC still have him as a British gold medallist

Bibliography

ARLOTT, John, ed., *The Oxford Companion to Sports and Games*, OUP, 1975.

BUCHANAN, Ian, 'Britain's First Olympic Champion: Launceston Elliot', in *Citius, Altius, Fortius*, (later *Journal of Olympic History*), Vol. 3, No.1 Winter 1997.

——, *British Olympians*, Guinness Publishing Ltd, London, 1999.

BUTCHER, Pat, *The Perfect Distance: Ovett and Coe The Record-Breaking Rivalry*, Weidenfeld & Nicolson, London, 2004.

COLLINS, Mick, *All-Round Genius*, Aurum Press Ltd, London, 2006.

COUGHEY, Ellen, *Eric Liddell. Olympian and Missionary*, Barbour, Uhrichsville OH, 2000.

FINNEGAN, Chris, *Self-portrait of a Fighting Man*, Macdonald and Jane's, London, 1976.

GILKEY, Langdon, *Shantung Compound*, Harper & Row, London, 1966.

GREEN, Geoffrey, *Kitty Godfree, Lady of a Golden Age*, Kingswood Press, London, 1987.

Huddersfield Daily Examiner, Interview Dec 13, 2003, Tony Pogson.

International Swimming Hall of Fame.

JOHNSON, Michael, *The Olympics Athens to Athens 1896-2004*, Weidenfeld & Nicolson, London, 2004.

KENT, GRAEME, *Olympic Follies*, JR Books, London, 2008.

KITTERMASTER, Charlotte, 'The Beijing Olympic Games: an analysis of the human rights issues', LLM dissertation, Birkbeck, University of London, 2008.

LENNARTZ, KARL, 'The 2nd International Olympic Games in Athens 1906' in *Journal of Olympic History*, Vol 10 ISOH, December 2001/January 2002.

McCANN, Liam, *The Olympics, Facts, Figures and Fun*, Sterling Publishing Co. Inc., 2006

MILLER, David, *The Official History of the Olympic Games and the IOC: Athens to Beijing, 1894-2008*, Mainstream Publishing Co., Edinburgh, 2008.

NELSON, Cordner & QUERCETANI, Robert, *The Milers*, Tafnews Press, California, 1985.

Observer Sport Monthly, Sunday 5 March, 2006.

PINSENT, Matthew, *A Lifetime in a Race*, Ebury Press, London, 2004.

SEARS, Edward, 'The Revival of the Olympic Games' in *Running through the Ages*, McFarland, 2001.

SMITH, P.R., *Great Moments of Sportsmanship*, privately published, London, 2008.

VOIGT, Robin, 'Emil Voigt, the Unique Olympian' in *Journal of Olympic History*, Vol 16, ISOH, December 2008.

WALLECHINSKY, David & LOUKEY, Jaime, *The Complete Book of the Olympics*, Aurum Press, London, 2008.

YAPP, Nick, *Chasing Gold: Centenary of the British Olympic Association*, British Olympic Association (with Getty Images), 2005.

websites:
www.azhockey.com
www.bbc.co.uk/Manchester
www.belfasttelegraph.co.uk
www.british.rowing.org.uk
www.brunel.ack.uk
www.content.ericliddell.org
www.history1900s.about.com
www.independent.co.uk
www.inthewinningzone.com
www.isoh.org
www.la84foundation.org
www.news.bbc.co.uk
www.olympic.org
www.sport.guardian.co.uk
www.sportscorrespondent.info
www.sports-reference.com
www.telegraph.co.uk
www.thenorthernecho.co.uk
www.timesonline.co.uk.
www.trackandfield.about.com/od/polevault
www.wikipedia.com

Index